AF323199

SOFTWARE ENGINEERING ENVIRONMENTS
Volume 3

ELLIS HORWOOD BOOKS IN INFORMATION TECHNOLOGY

General Editor: Professor V. A. J. MALLER, ICL Chair in Computer Systems,
Loughborough University of Technology; formerly of Thorn EMI Information
Technology Ltd
Consulting Editors: Dr JOHN M. M. PINKERTON, Information Technology
Consultant, J & H Pinkerton Associates, Esher, Surrey, and formerly Manager
Strategic Requirements, International Computers Limited; and PATRICK HOLLIGAN,
Department of Computer Studies, Loughborough University of Technology

C. Baber	SPEECH TECHNOLOGY IN CONTROL ROOM SYSTEMS: A Human Factors Perspective
E. Balagurusamy & J. A. M. Howe	EXPERT SYSTEMS FOR MANAGEMENT AND ENGINEERING
M. Barrett & A. C. Beerel	EXPERT SYSTEMS IN BUSINESS: A Practical Approach
M. Becker, R. Haberfellner & G. Liebetrau	ELECTRONIC DATA PROCESSING IN PRACTICE: A Handbook for Users
A. C. Beerel	EXPERT SYSTEMS: Strategic Implications and Applications
A. C. Beerel	EXPERT SYSTEMS: Real World Applications
K. Bennett	SOFTWARE ENGINEERING ENVIRONMENTS: Research and Practice
D. Berkeley, R. de Hoog & P. Humphreys	SOFTWARE DEVELOPMENT PROJECT MANAGEMENT: Process and Support
A. C. Bradley	OPTICAL STORAGE FOR COMPUTERS: Technology and Applications
P. Brereton	SOFTWARE ENGINEERING ENVIRONMENTS
R. Bright	SMART CARDS: Principles, Practice and Applications
D. Clarke & U. Magnusson-Murray	PRACTICAL MACHINE TRANSLATION
V. Claus & A. Schwill	ENCYCLOPAEDIA OF INFORMATION TECHNOLOGY
D. Cleal & N. O. Heaton	KNOWLEDGE-BASED SYSTEMS: Implications for Human–Computer Interfaces
I. Craig	THE CASSANDRA ARCHITECTURE: Distributed Control in a Blackboard System
T. Daler, *et al.*	SECURITY OF INFORMATION AND DATA
D. Diaper	KNOWLEDGE ELICITATION: Principles, Techniques and Applications
D. Diaper	TASK ANALYSIS FOR HUMAN–COMPUTER INTERACTION
G. I. Doukidis, F. Land & G. Miller	KNOWLEDGE-BASED MANAGEMENT SUPPORT SYSTEMS
P. Duffin	KNOWLEDGE-BASED SYSTEMS: Applications in Administrative Government
C. Ellis	EXPERT KNOWLEDGE AND EXPLANATION: The Knowledge–Language Interface
J. Einbu	A PROGRAM ARCHITECTURE FOR IMPROVED MAINTAINABILITY IN SOFTWARE ENGINEERING
A. Fourcin, G. Harland, W. Barry & V. Hazan	SPEECH INPUT AND OUTPUT ASSESSMENT: Multilingual Methods and Standards
M. Greenwell	KNOWLEDGE ENGINEERING FOR EXPERT SYSTEMS
F. R. Hickman *et al.*	ANALYSIS FOR KNOWLEDGE-BASED SYSTEMS: A Practical Guide to the KADS Methodology
P. Hills	INFORMATION MANAGEMENT SYSTEMS: Implications for the Human–Computer Interface
E. Hollnagel	THE RELIABILITY OF EXPERT SYSTEMS
R. Kerry	INTEGRATING KNOWLEDGE-BASED AND DATABASE MANAGEMENT SYSTEMS
K. Koskimies & J. Paakki	AUTOMATING LANGUAGE IMPLEMENTATION
J. Kriz	KNOWLEDGE-BASED EXPERT SYSTEMS IN INDUSTRY
F. Long	SOFTWARE ENGINEERING ENVIRONMENTS: Volume 3
M. McTear & T. Anderson	UNDERSTANDING KNOWLEDGE ENGINEERING
W. Meyer	EXPERT SYSTEMS IN FACTORY MANAGEMENT: Knowledge-based CIM
U. Pankoke-Babatz	COMPUTER-BASED GROUP COMMUNICATION: The AMIGO Activity Model
J. M. M. Pinkerton	UNDERSTANDING INFORMATION TECHNOLOGY: Basic Terminology and Practice
S. Pollitt	INFORMATION STORAGE AND RETRIEVAL SYSTEMS: Origin, Development and Applications
C.J. Price	KNOWLEDGE ENGINEERING TOOLKITS
S. Ravden & G. Johnson	EVALUATING USABILITY OF HUMAN–COMPUTER INTERFACES: A Practical Method
S. Savory	EXPERT SYSTEMS FOR THE PROFESSIONAL
U. J. Schild	EXPERT SYSTEMS AND CASE LAW
P. E. Slatter	BUILDING EXPERT SYSTEMS: Cognitive Emulation
H. T. Smith, J. Onions & S. Benford	DISTRIBUTED GROUP COMMUNICATION: The AMIGO Information Model
H. M. Sneed	SOFTWARE ENGINEERING MANAGEMENT
M. Stein	BUILDING EXPERT SYSTEMS MODEMS FOR DATA TRANSMISSION
R. Stutely	ADVANCED DESKTOP PUBLISHING: A Practical Guide to Ventura Version 2 and the Professional Extension
J. A. Waterworth	MULTIMEDIA: Technology and Applications
J. A. Waterworth & M. Talbot	SPEECH AND LANGUAGE-BASED COMMUNICATION WITH MACHINES: Towards the Conversational Computer
R. J. Whiddett	THE IMPLEMENTATION OF SMALL COMPUTER SYSTEMS

SOFTWARE ENGINEERING ENVIRONMENTS

Volume 3

Editor
FRED LONG
Department of Computer Science
The University College of Wales, Aberystwyth

ELLIS HORWOOD

NEW YORK LONDON TORONTO SYDNEY TOKYO SINGAPORE

First published in 1991 by
ELLIS HORWOOD LIMITED
Market Cross House, Cooper Street,
Chichester, West Sussex, PO19 1EB, England

A division of
Simon & Schuster International Group
A Paramount Communications Company

Printed and bound in Great Britain
by Bookcraft Ltd, Midsomer Norton, Avon

British Library Cataloguing-in-Publication Data

Long, F.
Software Engineering Environments: Volume 3
CIP catalogue record for this book is available from the British Library
ISBN 0–13–832601–0

Library of Congress Cataloging-in-Publication Data available

Table of Contents

Preface

This book contains the proceedings of the Software Engineering Environments 1991 conference, held at the University College of Wales, Aberystwyth, UK on 25–27 March 1991. The conference was sponsored by the Institution of Electrical Engineers, the Commission of the European Communities, under its SPRINT and ESPRIT Programmes, and the Information Technology Division of the Department of Trade and Industry.

This was the fifth in a series of major conferences held to review, discuss, debate and learn about the most recent practice and research results in the field of software engineering environments. The previous four conferences were held at the Universities of York, Lancaster, Keele and Durham.

All twenty-five papers presented at the conference are included here, collected into separate parts of the book as they were presented in the different sessions of the conference. There is also an overall summary of the conference, which appears as the first chapter. All papers were invited, and all but three are reproduced as received from the authors. The remaining three were reformatted by the editor.

I have included at the end of the book a list of addresses of the members of the programme committee and the authors.

The programme committee was:

Professor Keith Bennett (Durham)
David Callahan (Commission of the European Communities)
Dr Fred Long (Aberystwyth)
Gavin Oddy (GEC Marconi)
Professor Dr Wilhelm Schäfer (Dortmund)
Professor Mike Tedd (Aberystwyth, Chairman)
Malcolm Verrall (Sema Group)
Dr Ray Welland (Glasgow)

I would like to thank the programme committee for their time and effort in producing such a worthwhile programme. I would like to thank:

Jim Wallace, the College Conference Officer, for his help and support in organising the conference;

Frank Bott, Head of the Department of Computer Science, who willingly allowed his department, its facilities and staff to be hijacked during the preparations for and running of the conference;

Ruth Scott, **Donna Lansley** and **Margaret Anthony**, our departmental secretaries, who dealt with telephone enquiries, correspondence and the thousand and one things needed to run a conference like ours; and

Rosemary Law, the department's Administrative Assistant, whose smiling, friendly efficiency encouraged us all.

Finally, I would like to thank all the authors who made my life easy by submitting their papers (more or less) on time.

Fred Long
Department of Computer Science
The University College of Wales
Aberystwyth

1

Summary

Mike Falla
35 Benbrook Way, Gawsworth,
Macclesfield, Cheshire, SK11 9RT, UK
Fred Long
The University College of Wales,
Department of Computer Science,
Penglais, Aberystwyth, SY23 3BZ, UK

Introduction

This chapter is intended to give a brief summary of the whole conference. The conference was attended by some 110 people, including about 25 from outside the UK.

The major themes which emerged from the conference, especially in comparison with earlier conferences in the series, were:

- the growing relevance of commercial environment products;

- the growing importance and availability of standards;

- the move away from a PTI-oriented view of Software Engineering Environment architectures;

- greater focus on the needs of the user.

Although primarily concerned with R&D efforts, the conference seemed more aware then in previous years of commercial influences. This was shown, for example, by presentations on DEC's COHESION environment, and on using Atherton's Software BackPlane, and by the talks on developing and tracking standards. Discussion also readily acknowledged the huge investment in commercial tools and the need to accommodate them.

There seemed to be less sense of technology in search of a problem than in 1989 and certainly than in earlier conferences. Even so, one still does not get much sense of systems being developed from an analysis of the user requirements. Several speakers, however, did emphasise the need to satisfy real users with a real interest in getting the job done rather than developing environment technology.

The conference was composed of six sessions:

1. Process Modelling;

2. Invited Speaker;

3. Reference Models;

4. Integration of Methods and Tools;

5. Environment Projects and

6. Standards and Reuse.

1   Process Modelling

Process Modelling is clearly becoming prominent in Software Engineering Environment research. Colin Tully made the point that in order to control the product, one must control the process by which the product is created.

Process Modelling is an important aspect of integration in Software Engineering Environments and four prototype systems were described in this session: MASP in the talk given by Jean-Daniel Zucker, PMMS by Jeremy Smith, MELMAC by Volker Gruhn, and REX by Wolfgang Obst. The aim of all this work is to find formal notations which can be used to define the software development process while still allowing the flexibility needed for dynamic configuration and reconfiguration.

2   Invited Speaker

This session was devoted to a talk by Lee Osterweil who spoke about "Some Key Software Environment Research Projects in the US". His conclusions were:

- environment development requires large amounts of resources;

- there is steadily growing agreement on the key architectural features;

- we are actually building flexible frameworks, rather than environments and

- CASE tool integration is the driving force.

Lee thought that broader attention was needed on: User Interface aspects, measurement and evaluation, and process development support.

3   Reference Models

This was a discussion session, introduced by three short talks: Anthony Earl on the ECMA TGRM Reference Model, Ted Dowling on an alternative, object-oriented view of this model, and Mark Gibbons on standardisation and support environment technology.

The discussion focussed on the "Toaster Diagram" and whether it was meaningful, or even useful, to try to represent something as complicated as the TGRM Reference Model with a fairly simple diagram. No conclusions were reached but a fair amount of light was shed.

4   Integration of Methods and Tools

Three of the talks in this session considered general aspects of integration: Alan Brown discussed integration and reuse and showed that these can place conflicting requirements on a Software Engineering Environment, Matthias Hallmann presented an integration approach based on structured analysis and information modelling, and Antoinette Kieback talked about some evaluation work which could be used in the selection of tools for a particular environment.

The other three talks of the session presented specific examples of integration from the large ESPRIT project ATMOSPHERE: Jeremy Dick on integrating VDM and "Software thru Pictures", Ron Koymans on integrating COLD and SDL, and Markus Lindqvist on integrating SDL and LOTOS. These specific cases illustrate the demand for method and tool integration, but the session as a whole showed that there is still much work to be done before general integration frameworks can be realised.

5   Environment Projects

The presenters in this session gave information about some environments that are currently available: Christer Fernström on an ESF pilot factory for real-time software, Marcel Franckson on another ESF subproject called PEBA (Production Environment for Business Applications), Jørgen Knudsen on the Mjølner BETA system, and Tom Welsh on Digital's COHESION environment.

An interesting point in discussion was how sophisticated an organisation needs to be to install and use various kinds of environment. Is it the case, as someone suggested, that an organisation has to be at the SEI's level three before it can benefit from a full-scale Software Engineering Environment?

6   Standards and Reuse

Five of the talks in this session were concerned with the infrastructure for Software Engineering Environments: John Dawes talked mainly about the PCTE standard ECMA–149 (and he also gave some up-to-date information on the PCIS programme), Michael Aslett spoke about Atherton's Software BackPlane, Malcolm Verrall described the objectives of the ESF Software Bus, John Warne presented the Advanced Networked Systems Architecture (ANSA), and Mike Imber outlined the CASE Data Interchange Format Standards (CDIF) work.

The final talk of the session (and the conference), by Thierry Moineau, described the reuse of Ada code as supported by the ESF ROSE project.

After Dinner Talk

On the first evening, Vic Stenning gave a talk after dinner which, although billed as light-hearted and indeed very funny, contained a good deal of wisdom from a seasoned veteran. Are Software Engineering Environments needed and/or wanted?

"Would you buy a used SEE from this man?"

"If I could find an SEE that was used, I'd buy it from anyone!"

The focus nowadays must be on whether Software Engineering Environments really serve the user. The Software Engineering Environment community must stop reinventing technology that other people are building, probably better, and use existing standards wherever possible.

Conclusions

The conference was full of people talking about real achievements in the field
of software engineering environments. The informal atmosphere encouraged
discussion outside the organised sessions. A great deal of consensus seems to
be emerging about the architecture of a Software Engineering Environment.

In general one got a good sense of the scale of the problem and of the
difficulty of making sound decisions in an area where decisions are expensive
and the technology is changing fast.

SEE '93

The sixth Software Engineering Environments conference will be held at
the University of Glasgow and the programme committee chairman will be
Dr. Ray Welland. The timetable will be as follows:

- Call for papers — September 1992,

- Announcement — January 1993,

- Conference — 5–8 April 1993.

Part 1

Process Modelling

2

Software process issues in software engineering environments

Colin J. Tully
Colin Tully Associates, 2 Myrtle Cottages,
Park Road, Crowborough, East Sussex, TN6 2QW, UK

1 Introduction

The purpose of this paper is to introduce current thinking and work on software process modelling in general, particularly as it relates to software engineering environments, and thus to set the scene for other papers which describe specific software process initiatives.

The term **software process** denotes a subclass of the class **engineering process**. An engineering process, and therefore in particular a software process, may be defined as

> the system of **tasks**, and supporting **methods, practices, standards, tools** and **data**, used to produce a product and its associated deliverables.

It is important to distinguish **actual processes** (which are carried out in the real world) and **process models** (which are representations of actual processes). Process models may themselves be partitioned into **instantiated process models** (which model actual processes, at whatever level of granularity) and **generic process models** (which model common features of classes of instantiated processes).

Process models may also be partitioned into **universal process models** and **organisational process models**.   Universal process models exist in the public domain, for instance as part of accepted professional practice; they are always generic.   Organisational process models exist within individual organisations, resulting from mutual adaptation between universal process models and other organisational practices; they may be generic or instantiated.

Process is not synonymous with **project**.   Projects constitute a class of processes; and project models (such as critical path networks) constitute a class of process models.

Finally, for the record, **generic process models** are not the same as **process metamodels** — a distinction sometimes misunderstood.   Process models are expressed in a variety of formalisms; and a process metamodel is a model of the terms used in such a process modelling formalism.   A generic process model is a model of a class of processes; a process metamodel is a model of a class of models.

2   Some propositions about the software process

2.1   Product attributes are determined by process

To influence the attributes of a product it is not much use waiting until it has been produced: you must operate on the process that produces it.   This is obvious in principle, and is well understood in practice in most branches of manufacturing and engineering.

A good process, that will result in a good product, does not come about by chance.   It must be both well defined and well designed.   In other words it must be represented by an effective process model, the minimum criterion of which is that it should provide a readily usable process definition.   Most definitions of the software process are not usable, and so are not used: they occupy metres of shelf space, gathering dust and leaving the process to be improvised, to good or bad effect.

A process definition, in the form of an effective process model, provides the basis for process improvement, for process adaptation and reuse, for process control and standardisation, for proper exercise of the quality function, for systematic metrication, and for reliable cost and time estimating.

This emphasis on management issues and process improvement is the basis of the work at the Software Engineering Institute, Carnegie Mellon University, on process maturity models and capability assessment, especially associated with the name of Watts Humphrey.

2.2 The concepts of process and system are interchangeable

Any system may be regarded as a process; and any process may be regarded as a system. Each of those twin points leads to an important conclusion.

Any system may be regarded as a process — irrespective of how static or passive we may think it is. All systems undergo processes of change: they have life histories, and their state variables change over time. In particular, all systems built by software engineers are processes, and the systems which they support and within which they function are processes; and software engineers are used to building models of those processes.

The reasons for making this entirely obvious point are that it leads to three observations. The first is that we already have a lot of experience of building processes and process models: we should draw on that experience where it is relevant. The second is that there may however be differences between the processes and process models we are accustomed to building for applications and those that we find we now need for the more effective management of our own activity: we should investigate and account for those differences. The third is that building new kinds of processes and process models to support our own activity may lead to new insights into how we can build application systems, which are often to do precisely with the more effective management of *clients'* processes: in other words, we may find we have a rich new paradigm which we can apply outwardly in developing products, as well as inwardly for managing that development process.

Then, **any process may be regarded as a system.** What we say about something when we call it a system is that its properties cannot be calculated from the properties of its components or subsystems, but are critically determined by the patterns of flow across the set of interfaces which connect them. This is the so-called principle of emergence, which is not about anything mystical like Excalibur emerging from the lake, but simply calls attention to interfaces rather than components.

All systems are founded eventually on simple components, maybe after many levels of decomposition. If a system is complex, its complexity emerges from the variety of interfaces connecting its elementary components and its various levels of subsystems, and from the variety of flows across those interfaces. Systems analysis, systems design and systems engineering are in essence interface analysis, interface design and interface engineering.

Thinking of processes as systems therefore focusses on their decomposition into subprocesses and eventually, maybe via many stages, into simple tasks. The properties and complexity of the whole process arise from the interfaces by which it is built up, and the interfaces.   In the software process, those interfaces carry information — the various intermediate deliverables in the process.

2.3 Mechanisation occurs at lower levels of a process hierarchy

Mechanisation of a process necessarily starts at the bottom of a process hierarchy and works upward, whether we are mechanising existing processes or creating new ones, whether the processes being mechanised are physical or intellectual, and whatever combination of hardware and software is used for mechanisation.   The lower-level processes are simpler, and simpler processes are easier to mechanise.   This is what has happened in terms of software applications, and in terms of tools to mechanise the software process itself.

Above the upper limit of mechanisation in a process hierarchy, activities are undertaken by human beings, making use of the mechanised facilities at lower levels.   Software process modelling addresses these higher levels in the software process hierarchy, in order to understand, manage and support them better.

2.4 Processes must be controlled

Any designed process (system) is designed to meet a set of objectives or requirements. No designed process, however well engineered, has a 100% probability of continually meeting those objectives: even if its internal structure can be guaranteed correct, there is no way of guaranteeing that all eventualities which its operating environment may throw at it have been foreseen in the requirements.   In order to detect when a mechanised process is failing to meet its defined objectives, and to take corrective action, the process must be subjected to control; and process control is itself a process.   The same argument applies, *a fortiori*, to higher-level unmechanised processes.

Process control activities themselves may be either mechanised or not, depending on their complexity.   Thus the set of subprocesses and tasks making up a complete process may be partitioned into two subsets, one which performs what we may call the mainstream process, and a second which controls the first.

The higher levels of process control, those which are unmechanised and performed by human actors, are critically dependent on a clear understanding of the mainstream process being controlled, in order that failures may be quickly and reliably handled.   That clear understanding can best be provided by effective process models.   This amounts to a restatement, in informal systems-theoretic terms, of the argument for process models set out more loosely in 2.1 above.

The software process often displays a very high degree of complexity. Very complex process models, although they are much easier to understand and manage than the processes which they represent, can themselves present their human users with severe problems of understanding and management. For that reason the models themselves should be mechanised, to gain the consequent advantages of maintenance, correctness checking, distribution, navigation, view mechanisms, simulation etc. Those are important aims of software process modelling.

2.5 Process models should be enactable

The term **enactability** has been coined to describe a desirable characteristic of software process models. An enactable model is one which interacts dynamically with the human actors whose activities it models.

What is meant by dynamic interaction in this context is that each influences the other, over the very long execution time of the process. The model influences the human actors, through some blend of teaching, advice, guidance, direction and proscription. The human actors influence the model, in that the model cannot be a fully accurate prediction of what actually happens, since human beings are part of the execution mechanism and are not programmable like machines: the model must therefore be updated as the "time cursor" progresses through it.

The power of the model is critically affected by its ability to handle this dynamic interaction when actuality and model diverge. To the extent that the model is right, there will have to be some backtracking and amended replay of the actual process; a powerful model ing facility will support this. To the extent that the actual process is right, the change must be captured in the model, and the effects of the change must be projected into the model ahead of the time cursor; a powerful modelling facility will support this as well.

3   Some characteristics of process models

3.1 Components

The following is a representative list of object types which are catered for in software process modelling formalisms. There is no formalism which caters for them all; nor is it claimed that the list comprehensively includes all object types from all formalisms.

actions	messages	time
activities	methods	tools
agendas	obligations and permissions	triggers
agents	pre- and post-conditions	types
configurations	resource utilisation	versions
deliverables	roles	views
events	rules	

3.2 Formalisms

In terms of vocabulary and syntax, software process modelling formalisms may be textual, graphic, tabular, or some combination of those.   In terms of semantics, they vary on the spectrum between informality and formality.

In terms of expressive capability, they vary (a) in the range of granularity which they can encompass, (b) in their ability to cover both generic and instantiated processes, (c) in the extent to which they support four key notions: hierarchy and inheritance, multiple forms of presentation, nondeterminism, and parallelism.

4   Implications for environments

4.1 Process services in environments

If process services are to be provided within an environment, storage of a process model is a basic necessity.   A range of services, in the form of a tool or toolset, can then be provided to operate on the model.

A critical distinction is whether the stored process model is used only by the process tools, and is therefore local to them, or whether it is also used by other services in the environment.   In the latter case we may refer to the environment as a **stored-process environment** (by analogy with the concept of a stored-program computer); it is often said to be driven by a **process engine**, in the sense that the process model has a major effect on user communications, tool invocation, and data storage and retrieval.

Stored-process environments fall into three categories: (a) where both the process modelling formalism and the set of process services are fixed; (b) where the formalism is fixed and the services can be varied; (c) where both the formalism and the services can be varied.   Non-stored-process environments also fall into three categories: (a) where a process model is local to a process tool(set), as already described; (b) where the environment is designed to support a given process, but no process model is stored and the process therefore remains implicit; (c) where the environment as designed is completely independent of any process.

4.2 Alternative environment architectures

A software engineering environment integrates three classes of services: (a) **user services**, commonly called tools or toolsets; (b) **baseline services**, commonly called platforms or infrastructure; (c) **environment services**, which achieve the integration of (a) and (b), and which may include things called frameworks, common services etc. Where an environment includes process services, some or all will fall under the heading of user services; whether some fall under the heading of environment services depends on their rôle in achieving integration.

Integration in environments can be achieved in a number of ways. **Process (or method) integration** ensures that the methods supported by the various tools combine together into a coherent process, and that the environment as a whole provides as intelligent a level of support for this process as possible. Process services are clearly essential for any degree of process integration, except in the degenerate case where an environment is designed to support one process and one only, without a stored process model or any explicit process services. **Presentation**, **data** and **control** integration are ways of economising (respectively) on communication between tools and users, on information storage and on communication between tools. Process modelling is sometimes said to be a form of control integration, but this is a mistaken view: a process model, by defining process/method integration (see above) may define certain tool chains and therefore certain control integration *requirements,* but has nothing to do with control integration *mechanisms.* Finally, **networking** integration concerns the integration of baseline services.

There are three main architectural strategies for achieving integration in environments, based on how the environment services provide interfacing among the other services: **monolithic** (with minimal environment services providing *ad hoc* interfaces among a fairly fixed set of user services, often all running on the same platform, without conformance to external standards); **framework-based** (with often extensive environment services packaged into a predefined framework, ported onto a variety of platforms, and providing standard interfaces for user services); and **open** (with again minimal environment services, but this time providing the capability of interconnecting a wide range of diverse user services, running on different platforms, via a standard communications medium such as a bus). Process services can be accommodated in any of those architectures.

A given service in a given environment may be classified in three ways. First, a service may be **specific** to the environment (designed specially for it), **modified** for the environment (not having been initially designed for it), or **encapsulated** for the environment (not having been initially designed for it and not requiring any modification to the service itself). It is possible that fine–grained process models could provide encapsulation capabilities. Second, a service may be **compulsory** (in the sense that the environment cannot function without it) or **optional**. Third, a service may be **wired–in** (in the sense that it can only be replaced by reprogramming) or **plug–in**. This classification gives a twelve-way relationship between a service and an environment. Process services in general can fit anywhere into that classification, although the different variants of stored–program and non–stored–program environments imply certain restrictions.

4.3 Specialist process environments

It should be noted that there are a number of environments which are specialist process environments. In other words, they have been constructed as research prototypes with the purpose of providing an effective context in which to exercise and investigate process modelling and support services. They are not general–purpose software engineering environments, although it is possible that they could evolve into such environments.

5   Process in some current environments

5.1 ESPRIT and EUREKA

Two major ESPRIT projects are currently active in the field of software process. One is **ALF** (started October 1987), which intends to provide a next generation of environments as enhancements of PCTE. The ALF process modelling formalism is called MASP (model for assisted software processes), and allows for both generic and instantiated processes. MASP models have been built of *(inter alia)* VDM, HOOD and COCOMO. The other is **ATMOSPHERE** (started March 1989), which intends to build on current practice in software engineering across a large consortium of participants to achieve a significant advance in the use of enviroments to enhance European *systems* engineering practice. ATMO-SPHERE is developing *(inter alia)* a process modelling interchange format. The ATMO-SPHERE consortium includes interlocking partners with the ESF and EAST projects (see below), and it collaborates with those projects on process and other issues.

DAIDA (1986–1990), based on an AI approach, developed a range of assistants to support different life–cycle phases, and used the knowledge base of those assistants to provide process modelling and services.

TOOL-USE (1984-1989) and **REPLAY** (1987-1990) used the DEVA language for modelling domains, applications and processes. TOOL-USE, like ALF, set out to be an evolution from PCTE to the next generation of environments, which would be parametrised in terms of the methods they supported. REPLAY aimed to support the top-down replay of plans, processes and configurations, and the subsequent bottom-up assembly of components.

RUBEIC (1986-1989) developed rule-based enterprise modelling techniques; **TEMPORA** extended the technique to cope with dynamic and temporal features. It is likely that there is some overlap between process and enterprise modelling.

Finally among this selection of ESPRIT projects, **PIMS** (1985-1989) developed a storyboard approach to project modelling and management. While it has been said above that process models are more general than project models, they must at least be able to accommodate them.

The EUREKA programme has two large environment projects, which both started in 1987, and in both of which process is central. **EAST** is a direct extension of the PCTE architecture, building further on the PACT common services. **ESF** is an attempt to develop an open architecture for environments, based on a software bus and a process engine Both are closely linked to ATMOSPHERE through interlocking partners, and the three projects form a major strategic European thrust, with clearly separate but related missions. ESF has reputedly picked up the PIMS work.

5.2 UK — Alvey and JFIT

There are three projects with some relevance to the software process in the UK Alvey Programme and its successor, the Joint Framework for Information Technology. **IPSE 2.5** (1986-1990) developed the process modelling language PML. The **ISF Study** (1987-1988) made process modelling central to its recommendations for a future generation of systems factories. **IOPT** (started 1990) is a project aimed at the introduction of process technology in practice, with an emphasis on its use to support teamwork and change.

5.3 Other European

EPOS (Norwegian Institute of Technology) is based on the AI concepts of planning, production systems and pre- and post-conditions. It aims to integrate configuration and process management, and to support task hierarchies and parallelism.

OIKOS (University of Pisa) uses ESP (Extended Shared Prolog) as a "logic distributed coordination language". It uses blackboards and agents, and provides a meta–environment to permit the exploration of several approaches to process.

5.4 USA

There is only space to include a small selection of US work. Other projects are covered by Osterweil elsewhere in these proceedings, together with more information on ARCADIA.

ARCADIA is a project of a similar level of ambition (though with far smaller resources) to ESF. It is the most advanced exponent of the *process programming* approach, which seeks to adapt conventional programming formalisms to the wider problem of process modelling; the language used is called APPL–A, an adaptation of Ada.

The PMDB project at TRW is founded on a thorough–going and pragmatic entity modelling approach; and in **PMDB+**, among other things triggers have been introduced to provide an active database as the process model and the foundation for process support.

HP Encapsulator is Hewlett–Packard's companion product to the HP SoftBench environment, providing process support and tool integration facilities.

Marvel is a long–running and well known project at Columbia University under Gail Kaiser, based (like EPOS) on production rules, pre– and post–conditions and opportunistic processing, using the Marvel Strategy Language (MSL) to model both the process itself and process data.

E–L is an extensible (wide–spectrum) language, and an associated support environment, being developed at Harvard University by Tom Cheatham. One application being considered is process modelling. A formalism called transaction graphs is proposed, and the problems of very long execution are being specifically addressed.

5.5 Japan

Again only a small selection is possible. I have the impression that a number of Japanese initiatives, interestingly, are directed at the use of process models as ways of *teaching* the software process.

VELA (Shizuoka University) is founded on a knowledge base and inference engine, and provides a framework for cooperative work support and knowledge sharing.

KyotoDB (Kyoto University) models the relationships between deliverables and plans.

SAGE9X (Tokyo Institute of Technology) offers an object–oriented process modelling formalism, running on the method–independent VERSA platform.

6   Conclusion

In very brief conclusion, five main driving forces may be perceived in current process work. They are (1) the programming paradigm, (2) AI paradigms, (3) the database/entity-relationship paradigm, (4) CASE integration, environments and factories, (5) management concerns and process improvement.

3

ALF: Accueil de logiciel futur

Jean-David Zucker
GIE Emeraude, c/o BULL – 58F32,
68 Route de Versailles,
F–78430 Louveciennes, France

1 Preface

This preface identifies the intended readership. The most important terms used in this report are briefly introduced in appendix A. This document should help everybody interested in questions of software development is helped to understand the main aims of the ALF project [1] and the basic concepts for reaching these aims. Readers who are familiar with the field of software process modeling and who have a rough idea of the software process modeling approach pursued in ALF can skip section 2 without harm. Section 3 discusses the architecture of the software engineering environment developed in the ALF project. Finally, section 4 concludes our work, pointing out what remains to be done.

Much of the contents of this report has been described in more detail in ALF project internal papers. This paper has been made as self-contained as possible.

---

[1] ALF is partially funded by the Commission of the European Communities under the ESPRIT Research Programme.

2   Introduction to ALF and its Main Concepts

ALF develops a software engineering environment based on software process
modeling. By exchanging the software process model of the environment
developed in ALF (the ALF system for short), the ALF system behavior can
be changed. Thus, the ALF system is a configurable open framework for
integrated programming support environments. One of the main focuses of
ALF is to provide assistance and guidance to all people involved in software
development.

The aim of this introductory section is threefold. Firstly, we describe the
basic concepts of ALF and their relation to other software process modeling
approaches. Secondly, we describe how these basic concepts can be used for
configuring software engineering environments (called ALF-based Integrated
Programming Support Environments (IPSEs) hereafter). Thirdly, this introduction points out what the differentiating features of the ALF system are
and how these features contribute to the appearance of ALF. Thereby, we
clarify who is expected to benefit from using ALF-based IPSEs.

2.1   A Configurable Open Framework for IPSEs

The ALF system is a software engineering environment of the third generation. This term has been defined in different ways [SW88, Fed86, Tul87,
Fer88]. In order to clarify what this means we introduce the term *software engineering environment* briefly. We restrict ourselves to two definitions which
represent a kind of consensus.

> *A software engineering environment is a name given to a set
> of tools, structures, rules, and procedures that together provide
> a framework for software development and support* [Fed86].

A software engineering environment is

> *a collection of computer-based facilities to support the activities of
> programmers, software engineers, system designers, project man-
> agers, etc., to achieve higher productivity and higher product qual-
> ity* [Tul87].

Three generations of software engineering environments can be distinguished. Software engineering environments of the first generation are a set
of tools, which support different phases of software processes. The standard

example of first generation environments **are UNIX**[2] **tool** boxes. In contrast to first generation environments, second **generation environments** contain tools which are integrated over a common **object management** system and/or a common user interface system.

For first generation environments **as well as for** second generation environments there is a duality between **software process** models and software engineering environments. That means, **each of these** environments implement one particular software process **model, or at best a** family of closely related software process models. In **general, first or second** generation environments determine the features of **software processes** that can be carried out within these environments. Such an environment implements a software process model by providing tools that have to be applied in a certain order. Thus, there exists a duality between environment of the first and second generation on the one hand and software process models on the other. This duality was a basic motivation for developing environments which can be adapted to particular needs and which can be tailored to the requirements of particular projects and companies. These environments are called third generation environments. They are characterized by being based on software process models which are not hard-wired. That means, it is possible to put a software process model into a third generation environment, such that the environment behaves according to the information given in the software process model. For implementing this flexibility a software process model interpretation mechanism is required to ensure that software processes actually carried out within the environment follow the supplied software process model.

Figure 1 sketches the typical environment of a third generation software engineering environment [SW88].

The top level box called *control component* represents the interpretation mechanism. The box entitled *SPM* represents the software process model which determines the actual behavior of the software engineering environment. Tools are represented by the boxes labeled with $T_1, \ldots, T_n$. The basic components which are already used in second generation software engineering environments are the user interface system (represented by the box entitled *UIS*) and the object management system (represented by the box entitled *OMS*). The arrows represent a *use*-relationship between the components. Some other projects aiming at developing third generation software engineering environments are the ESF project [ESF88], the Arcadia project [TBC⁻88], and the ISTAR project [Dow87b, Dow87a].

---

[2]UNIX is a registered trademark of AT&T Bell Laboratories

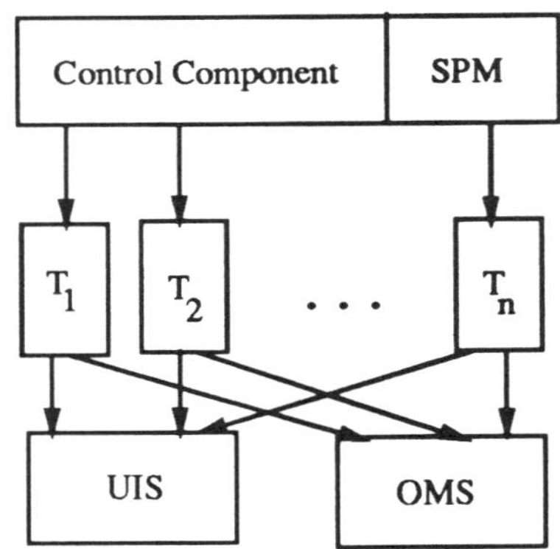

Figure 1: Architecture of third generation software engineering environments

The architecture shown in Figure 1 shows that a third generation's software engineering environment can be parameterized by a software process model. Thereby, a third generation's software engineering environment can be adapted to particular ideas about how a software process is expected to look.

The ALF system is a software engineering environment of the third generation. It provides facilities to define software process models and to build ALF-based IPSEs based on these models. It allows the adaptation of IPSEs to the needs of different projects and companies.

2.2   The ALF basic Models

The main aim of ALF is to support teamwork software development and to provide assistance and guidance to all people involved in software development. Therefore, it aims at making software development as easy as possible, at freeing software developers from menial activities and, thereby, at providing a basis for increasing software development productivity and software quality. Our approach to reach this aim is based on the formal modeling of software processes.

A software process is the set of activities performed during software development. Bearing in mind this idea of a software process, it is obvious that there is one software process for each software system that is developed. Several software processes are driven by the same software process model. A software process model describes general features of a class of processes but not those features which are specific for each process. Well-known examples of software process models are the waterfall model [Roy70], the spiral model [Boe88], and prototyping models [BJG83]. Software process models describe which activities have to be performed by which people, who is allowed to access which documents, which activities have to be performed when, and which tools are used within which activities. Software process models are the basis of software processes.[3] Software processes can be considered as software developments following a particular software process model. A language suited for describing software process models is called a software process modeling language.

The aim to describe software process models is not new. Each company and each project has an idea of its way to carry out a software process. Kellner points out that *'narrative descriptions have long been employed by organizations to record their standard operating procedures'* [Kel88]. Guidelines and advice summed up in manuals belong to this kind of software process models. Other narrative descriptions of software process models are represented by standards, laws, and policies.

But not only natural language is used for describing software process models. Various kinds of graphic languages are used for software process modeling. Several of these languages are used for describing project plans, configuration plans, and interaction diagrams. Well-known examples are PERT diagrams [Was71] and Gantt charts [LH89].

The software process modeling approach pursued in ALF is based on an executable software process modeling language. By executing software process models, it is possible to enforce the prescriptions fixed in a software process model in real software processes. For the design of a software process modeling language, it is at first necessary to identify those entities of software processes that must be modeled.

The whole range of software process model entities is sketched by the following quotation.

> *'Those things which models must be able to represent, either as primitives or as constructs, are generally agreed to include at least some of the following: actions, activities, agendas, agents, configurations, deliverables, events, messages, methods, obligations, permissions, pre- and post-conditions, roles, rules, tools, triggers, types, versions, views.'* [Tul88b]

This quotation shows that set of entities that belong to a software process

---

[3] We say a software process model *governs* a software process.

model are not clearly defined. We identified a subset of these entities that enable a comfortable modeling of software processes. These entities build the skeleton of our software process modeling concept, called **MASP** (Model for **A**ssisted **S**oftware **P**rocesses) and for the software process modeling language related to this concept, called **MASP/DL** (**MASP/D**escription Language).

A MASP comprises the following **components:**

Object Model The object model specifies which object types are dealt with in the specified software process **model. Apart** from defining the object types, the relations between object **types are defined** as well. The object model is the object model of PCTE, based on typed entity-relationship diagrams.

Operator Types The operator types specify the names, the signatures, and the pre- and postcondition of operators that are to be carried out in the modeled software processes.

Expressions Expressions appear as part of operator types' pre- and postconditions, rules, and characteristics. By enumerating and naming them it is possible to refer to expressions without writing them again and again.

Rules Rules describe under which conditions an operator is tried to be executed.

Orderings Orderings describe constraints of the order in which operators are executed. For specifying orderings a path expression like formalism is used.

Characteristics Characteristics describe expressions which have to be true in each state of a software process. Thus, they specify integrity constraints. Whenever a characteristic is violated all efforts are focused on making this characteristic true again.

Before a software process model in general and a MASP in particular can be executed it is necessary to supply some additional information. This is called instantiation or enaction in the literature [Dow86, Tul88a]. An instantiated MASP (called IMASP for short) contains all information needed for its execution.

Our concept for using software process models for governing software processes is based on the concept of **lazy instantiation.**

Generally speaking, the concept of **lazy instantiation** means that an operator type or an object type is instantiated **when this** instantiation is needed and not necessarily before. By postponing **instantiation steps** until they have necessarily to be done we provide the **possibility to know** as much about the already carried out software process as **possible when the** instantiation step is done. Thus, the concept of lazy instantiation **provides a** degree of flexibility that corresponds to the fact that **software processes** cannot be completely defined a priori, i.e. before they are **carried out.** This concept corresponds to the concept of lazy evaluation as **used in functional** languages.

On the other hand we can imagine **situations in which** a customer wants to get a MASP that is completely ready for execution. In that case it does not make sense to bother him with instantiation steps. Therefore, the concept of lazy instantiation should be understood as a chance for a high degree of flexibility, which may or may not be taken. It is also possible to instantiate a MASP completely before it is delivered to a customer.

In principle we distinguish between operator type and object type instantiation.

Object model During the instantiation of the object model it is necessary to identify the objects which must be made known.

One kind of object model instantiation is based on object model importation. If an object that must be made known during an instantiation dialogue exists in another IMASP, let us say IM_1, and if the object model of the MASP from which IM_1 is derived is imported by the MASP which is currently instantiated, then the objects of IM_1 can be made visible in the new IMASP. Thus, the substantial problem of object model instantiation is to identify objects which have to be shared and to give access to these objects. Cooperation between different IMASPs is achieved by means of object sharing. If an object that is shared between two different IMASPs is manipulated by one of them, then that manipulation becomes visible for the other IMASP. Thus, a shared object implements a communication between the IMASPs that share the object.

The information about the objects that are to be shared and the rights to access them are found out in an instantiation dialogue. During this dialogue the context of instantiation is displayed (which MASP is instantiated, how does the object model of that MASP look, which MASPs have an object model that contains some of the object types of the MASP under instantiation). The process modeler / MASP instantiator can in that dialogue identify **those shared objects** which the new IMASP requires by giving their **names, by giving** the IMASPs they are taken from and by identifying the **access rights** of the new IMASP.

But object sharing is not the only **way of instantiating** an object type. Another way of instantiating an **object type** is to insert objects of that type explicitly during the instantiation **dialogue.**

Operator model During the instantiation of the operator model of a MASP it is necessary either to identify **tools (or any other** kind of executable software) that can be linked to **operator types or to** identify MASPs that are of the corresponding types (MASPs are explicitly typed [DBB+90]). Here we have to face the problem that instantiation is based on assumptions about tools and MASPs. Each available tool and each MASP is typed. A tool is typed by the person who brings that tool into the ALF context. Let us assume that we have an operator type *compile* in a certain MASP. All tools that can potentially be used for instantiating that operator type are classified as *compilers*. During instantiation the type information about tools and MASPs are considered to be correct. That means we rely on the specifications given by the typing of tools and MASPs.

We distinguish three possibilities for instantiating operator types. These are to link an operator type to a tool, to share an operator type's instantiation, and to link an operator type to a MASP of the corresponding type. In the latter case the operator type's instantiation is continued by instantiating the linked MASP.

- An operator type is linked to a tool. In general it is necessary to build an envelope around that tool. This notion of envelopes corresponds with envelopes as used in MARVEL [KFP88, Cag90]. This building of envelopes contains the setting of paths, for example.

- An operator type shares the instantiation of an operator type used in a different IMASP. This is analogous to the sharing of objects. Sharing of operator type instantiations is less critical than sharing of objects, since no side-effects are introduced. A prerequisite for sharing the instantiation of an operator type, is that the operator types used in the different MASPs that are instantiated are the same. This is the case if operator type descriptions are exactly the same, or if the operator type is defined in one MASP and imported by the other one. To share an instantiation can either

> mean linking the operator **type to a tool** (if the operator type, whose instantiation is shar**ed, is instantiated** by a tool) or linking the operator type to an **already existing** IMASP (if the operator type, whose instantiation is **shared, is instan**tiated by a MASP).

- This possibility for instantiating **an operator** type is the most sophisticated one, it consists **of linking an operator** type to a MASP of that type. When the linked **MASP is** not instantiated the instantiation is continued by **instantiating the** linked MASP.

2.3   Benefits of ALF: The "ALFness"

Up to now we may have given the impression that ALF is an environment that ntegrates software process modeling facilities similar to other environments (IPSE2.5 [War89], MELMAC [DG90a, DG90b], Marvel [KFP88], Oikos [ACM90], Arcadia [TBC+88]). In this section we stress those features that are specific to ALF. Additionally we point out how these features can be exploited by different persons participating in software development.

When we speak of "ALFness" two main general characteristics must be highlighted: a wide range of of issues under the concept of assistance and a global view of software process activities. We shall study in detail these two topics.

In ALF assistance is understood in a general sense. A user - we shall not qualify the kind of user until the next paragrapgh - working under the ALF framework receives assistance from a system that automatically executes actions when some predefined situations are identified. These predefined situations are defined within MASP rules. When the user encounters some kind of problem that prevents him from progressing with his activity facilit es that will try to solve the problem or, at least, show the way to solve it, will automatically be activated—these facilities work upon assertions that model operators behaviour—. If a user cannot carry on because he does not know how, he will be able to ask the system how to proceed with a given activity —Guidance will provide him with this information. He also will be receive explanations on those decisions taken by the system or the reasons that prevented the correct execution of a command whose exectution was requested by him. Furthermore, the work performed by the user can be monitored in order to enhance its quality. This can be performed through the use of metrics in cooperation with some of the facilities described above so that unsuitable design decisions are identified and the user may be warned. Eventually, alternative design decisions can be suggested to the user or act ons may be performed by the system with the objective of solving the problem of unsuitable design decisions. **Finally, and** according to Lehman's opinion that states that any software **process model** can be changed due to human interaction, feedback is used to **adapt a given** model to the knowledge that is gathered within a software process. **For instance**, thanks to feedback, the process of designing a test can be **deferred** until soem experience on the subject to be tested is acquired.

The framework developed within **the ALF project** supports a global view of the software process in the sense **that it not only** is prepared to support the software developer activities, traditionally **the most** frequent in software environments, but also project manager **and quality** assurance responsible. Even more, we can say that the framework is not limited to these roles thanks to the flexibility of its software process model representation and it might be, eventually, used to support other different ones. Thanks to the monitoring performed the project manager can be made aware of late tasks —the system will warn him— or, much more important, of those parts of the project that are presenting most problems, as a result of the study on the quality issues. Therefore, the efficiency of his management activity can be easily increased.

The real "ALFness" comes from the conjunction of the above described two characteristics: with a given formalism, the MASP, to which, through its use, we are able to provide software process descriptions on most of the software development issues and an instrumentation that handles these concepts providing various kinds of assistance we have a framework able to provide a high and characteristic level of asistance and control.

In the ALF system, the modeling of software processes is supported by providing a set of predefined service MASPs. Each of these should be understood as a repository of mechanisms related to a particular subject of MASP improvement (such as observation, history generation, feedback). These repositories are written down as MASPs. They provide services that can be used by MASP designers for future MASPs. Below we give an idea about the predefined service MASPs.

Observation MASP It is evident that discipline in thought and its expression promotes efficiency and quality in actions taken. This, in fact, has been the primary objective of the work now under way in software process modeling. It is, also, believed that if mechanisms could be automated, first, to "observe" how well one does with the actions taken and, second, to put preventive or corrective changes to the corresponding activities into effect then such mechanisms would contribute to improved quality and productivity, and as a secondary effect, to the personnel training objectives of an organization. It is towards the realization of these objectives that the ALF team has worked in the development of performance description "metrics" and knowledge/data accumulation mechanisms that are suitable for support of ALF-based SEE users. In ALF, the MASP Model has been used to represent performance observation and history accumulation processes where metrics and history generation tools are implemented as operators in the respective MASPs. The observation MASP contains a set of predefined mechanisms related to the observation of project performance attributes (such as project start and end dates, estimated and actual effort, program and module size, structuredness of programs), related to the observation of environment performance attributes (such as storage needs of programs, execution time of programs, development team motivation characteristics, level of integration of tools), and related to user performance attributes (such as development team experience, development team capabilities). If particular processes are to be observed it is possible to use or to adapt some of the predefined observation mechanisms available in the predefined observation MASP. The raw data collected within an observation are used as input for a history generation MASP.

History Generation MASP By history generation we mean the processing of observation data at appropriate time intervals and the storage of those data/knowledge elements in appropriate objects or attributes for subsequent use. In ALF, data of "historical" value is accumulated on projects developed with the system, the development teams and the particular developing environment used and target environment on which the final product will run. As already indicated, such historical data can be used for project planning, project cost estimation, hardware-software procurement and placement, familiarization of development personnel with particular tools or MASPs and so on. Of course, this support can be realized in coordination with the explanation, guidance and feedback mechanisms provided by the ALF environment. Figure 1 describes in an abstract manner the process of observation and history generation in ALF.

History generation filters are simply observation data processing algorithms whose function is to operate on raw data and transform it into a format suitable for use by particular project planning or development tools or by the guidance and feedback mechanisms of ALF. Specific algorithms will be specified in different cases to suit particular organizational requirements. The advantage offered by the ALF system, in this respect, is that a single uniform software process model is used to

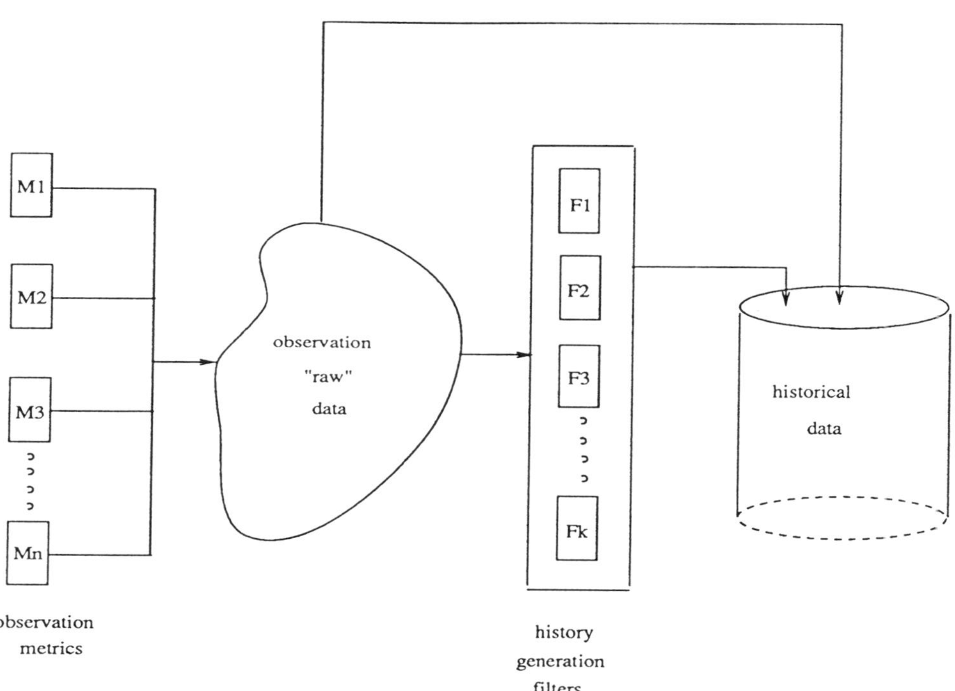

Figure 2: Observation and History Generation in ALF

describe historical data and **knowledge. At the** initiative of the system or the user historical data can **be acted upon by** specific operators to support the ALF user.

Feedback MASP The Feedback MASP **is an additional** measure to react to the widely discussed idea of ***Process Programming***. The *Uncertainty principle* described by Lehman [**Leh89**] **says that** human interaction dominates software development, **and that, therefore,** any software pro-cess model can be changed due **to human interaction.** He objects to the idea of Process Programming **as introduced** by Osterweil [Ost87]. In order to care for this uncertainty we use a feedback MASP. A feedback MASP adapts a MASP to the knowledge that is gathered within a software process. Thereby, it is possible to overcome the problems of modeling software process parts that deal with later phases of software development. An example is that it is known in the initial modeling phase that a test of the produced system will take place, but that it is not known in detail how this test will look. By means of the feedback MASP, the process modeler has the chance to postpone the detailed modeling of the test phase. The Feedback MASP initially developed in ALF should be understood as a repository of feedback mechanisms from which a Feedback MASP adapted to a particular software process model can be derived.

3   ALF Architecture

This section is subdivided into three parts. Section 3.1 describes the architecture of the ALF system (i.e. of the software system developed in ALF), section 3.2 sketches the architecture of an ALF-based IPSE (i.e. of an environment that is adapted to the company or project specific requirements by using the ALF system). Section 3.3 outlines the relationship between the ALF system and PCTE.

3.1   Architecture of the ALF system

Figure 3 sketches the architecture of the software system developed in ALF. It is based on PCTE, on top of which the *Information System* is built. The *Information System* is discussed in more detail in section 3.2.2. On top of the *Information System* some tools and predefined MASPs used in the development of MASPs can be found. First, there are two tools used for deriving instantiated MASPs from MASPs. These tools are represented by the boxes labeled with **MASP Gener. Tool** (MASP Generation Tool) and **MASP Inst. Tool** (MASP Instantiation Tool). Beside these boxes we find two other tool boxes representing the syntax-driven **MASP Editor** and the **ITFM** (Inconsistency Tracker for MASPs). These tools help to produce MASPs which are syntactically correct and that do not contain severe semantic errors (such as the contradiction between two characteristic expressions). The other boxes directly below the **MASP Developer Interface** represent the predefined service MASPs sketched above.

MASP Developer Interface						
MASP General Tool	MASP Inst. Tool	MASP Editor	ITFM	Obs. MASP	HG MASP	Feed- back MASP
Information System						
PCTE OMS						

Figure 3: ALF system architecture

3.2   ALF-based IPSEs

This section is subdivided into various parts. In the first part (section 3.2.1) the overall architecture of an ALF-based IPSE is sketched. In the other parts the main components of an ALF-based IPSE are discussed in little more detail.

3.2.1   Architecture of an ALF-based IPSE

In this section we discuss the architecture of an ALF-based IPSE. This architecture is depicted in Figure 4. The components sketched in Figure 4 are discussed in detail in the subsequent sections. Therefore, we do it without discussing them here. The only thing we want to mentioin explicitly is that the Expalantion and Guidance facilities are services provided by the Piloting System. Due to their prevailing importance in ALF they are explicitly identified in Figure 4.

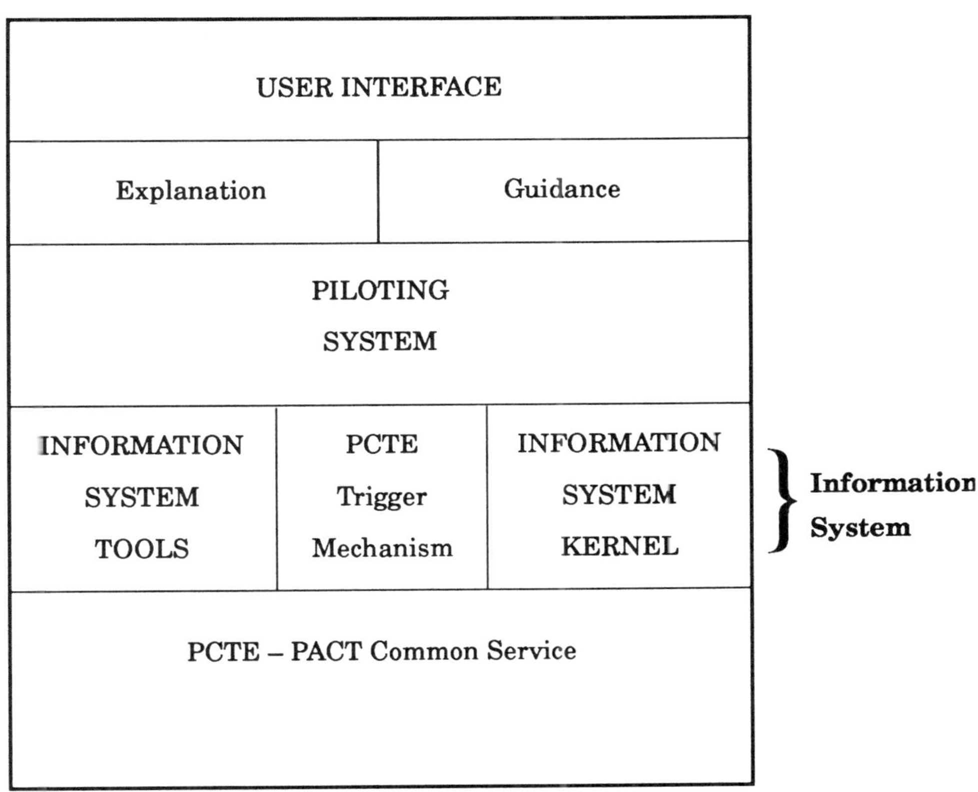

Figure 4: Architecture of an ALF-based IPSE

3.2.2 Information System

In this section the architecture of a component that enables the enaction of software process models in live projects is outlined.

On top of PCTE [Cam88] there is an *Information System*. This information system has the following characteristics:

1. It allows **storing** and retrieving of all the information necessary to represent, generate, instantiate and **interpret a** software process model.

2. It **enforces** semantics integrity of the PCTE object base necessary for the specific knowledge representation defined for ALF.

3. It provides a mechanism that detects **any relevant change** in the state of the object base: trigger mechanism.

Information System Kernel and Information System Tools

A PCTE data structure (schema definition set: sds) has been defined for each of the MASP concepts. All static and dynamic kinds of information are permanently stored in the base as objects or composite entities. All the Information System Tools needed to maintain those composite entities are also provided. They allow the creation, deletion, modification of complex structures such as an IMASP.

As it is explained in the Piloting System subsection, the MASP interpreter in its final version will have for sole data repository the object base. This ensures that there is a **unique** and complete representation of the knowledge of a model and its interpretation, in the object base.

Information System Semantics

The level of semantics needed to represent the MASP, IMASP, ASP structures is higher than the one implicitely offered by PCTE. At the level of IMASP for example, sharing of instances is required. Though PCTE OMS allows type sharing it does offer a mechanism to describe partial instance sharing. The ALF information system provides among others, this mechanism.

A set of semantic constraints have been defined to fully describe the semantics of the ALF concepts. These semantics are enforced by the use of triggers.

Trigger Mechanism

An important actor of the ALF Information System architecture is a *trigger mechanism*. This mechanism allows the description of events, actions and condition of execution for actions. When a predefined "event" is raised, the associated "action" is fired at the proper time and in the proper "condition of execution".

The trigger mechanism event model is **a superset of the** MASP/DL one. This ensures that all the relevant changes of **the object base** are known by the Piloting System. This mechanism also **enforces semantics** integrity necessary to represent the ALF concepts.

This environment as a whole provides **a complete** description of the information needed to describe all the **stages of a** software process model definition instantiation and enaction.

3.2.3 Piloting System

The Piloting System (PS) is the component which provides assistance and control at the various stages of the software development, including management and quality issues. From a behavioral point of view, the PS operates as a system that monitors the work done by the software developer and that takes initiatives whenever necessary. Some other services are also provided upon explicit request by the user, such as how to get a given activity to progress. The Piloting System provides many of the most characteristic functionalities of the ALF system. These functionalities are obtained, among other thinks, through interpretation of software process models described using the MASP formalism, and carried out by the MASP Interpreter, termed *MINT*. The PS can decide whether a user initiative is allowed according to a given MASP and provide system initiatives when predefined situations occur. In order to support the full range of functionalities the PS is enabled to make estimates of the work to be performed. These estimates, based on observed data, are used to improve the quality of the software process either by informing the software developer or the project manager.

We shall present how the PS makes its work. First we shall study the interpretation process and, then, the other facilities used to implement the whole set of functionalities required to conduct the software process activities as defined in ALF [BBC+89].

To understand the kind of work that the MINT does we must look briefly again at the components of the MASP presented in 2. We have already explained that the MASP is formed by a model of objects, operators, expressions, rules, characteristics and orderings and we also presented the semantic associated to each model. We should note these models are semantically dependent [DBB+90].

For the purpose of performing the interpretation process we need a representation of the MASP components that can be properly handled. This representation is directly dependent on the implementation issues. We can assume that each state of the software process development has a corresponding MASP object model state. Each initiative, represented by an operator execution request, shall modify the state of the object model. The MINT, by interpreting the model, will react either when previously defined states occur or when a state cannot be reached because some problem exists. MASP rules indicate situations in which a given action can be accomplished when the precondition of a rule is true. Through the interpretation process these rules are fired according to a policy previously established and with this mechanism we implement the system initiative. Furthermore, the system will actively help the user when he is unable to execute an operator —this occurs when an operator precondition is false— or when the execution of an operator leaves the system inconsistent —for instance when a characteristic has been violated—. What the system does is generating a plan to to solve the situation. This plan consists of a set of operators that should make the expression —precondition or characteristic— true. For this task, the MINT uses operator pre- and postconditions with a backward chaining policy.

While we can work directly with the PCTE OMS to implement the interpretation, using the description of the Object model without any modification we must use some other tools or mechanisms to handle Rules, Expressions — pre-, post-conditions, and Characteristics— and Orderings. Actually, the MINT has been built using ALFRete [Zuc90] together with PCTE mechanisms.

ALFRete is based on XRete [Tho89], a production system based on the Rete matching algorithm. It supports the integration of the knowledge represented by rules with existing applications algorithmicly programmed, providing data sharing between the procedural and the heuristic parts of an application. ALFRete works together with the PCTE OMS [Zuc90] using an integration mechanism that has been designed to fullfil this function and that is based on the PCTE triggers as it has been explained in 3.2.2. Whenever it is necessary to access the Information System from the MINT, this is performed through direct calls to PCTE primitives. Any modification to an object in the IS is communicated to the MINT via triggers, using an event queue as shown in Figure 5. Therefore, we are able to handle OMS objects directly from ALFRete, what help us from having two copies of the OMS object.

ALFrete supports production rules in the form of *IF condition THEN action* with forward chaining. These rules can be grouped into packets. Enhancements such as backward chaining, composite structures, quantifiers, and a mechanism for dynamic activation of rule packets with shared memory have also been introduced in order to support the interpretation features fully . All these features together with the PCTE concurrency synchronization and communication mechanisms have been used extensively.

Though the MINT plays an important role within the task of providing assistance and control some other facilities are needed in order to meet the requirements. These facilities —Guidance, Explanation, Observation, History Generation and Feedback— are closely related among them and to MINT and we can say that the support given to the software process activities is a result of the cooperative operation of all the facilities described within this section.

Guidance and Explanation are two more parts of the Piloting System. They rest, to some extent, on the MINT and their objective is completed by two important issues of the assistance: to support requests of how to further the progress of a software process and explain to the user what is happening inside the system. Guidance is implemented making use of functions provided by the MINT. Explanations are provided either when the system, as a result of the interpretation, considers that an action or situation must be explained to the user or when a user initiative cannot be executed because, for instance, a precondition is false. Explanation is implemented partly using MASP primitives and partly using XRete mechanisms.

One of the sources of information that can be used to support the ALF functionalities is collected —*observed*— data, concerning the software process. This data can be processed afterwards and a *history of the process* can be generated based on the use of metrics. The combination of this history with MASP rules, for instance, allows you to pilot the software process guaranteeing by means of *a posteriori* intervention of the systems that quality conforms to some standards. Both Observation and History Generation are implemented through MASP descriptions, that is, the tasks of observation and history generation are considered as software process activities and dealt with as such. As far as they are implemented as MASPs they are handled by the MINT. In any case, and from a functional point of view, they should be understood as facilities provided by the PS in order to pilot the software process.

The results of the History Generation is used, finally, to obtain a level of *Feedback* according to a model also described by means of a MASP. This feedback intends to influence the software process. Feedback can be considered as the highest level of sophistication in the objective of piloting the software process.

The conjunction of the MINT work together with guidance and explana-

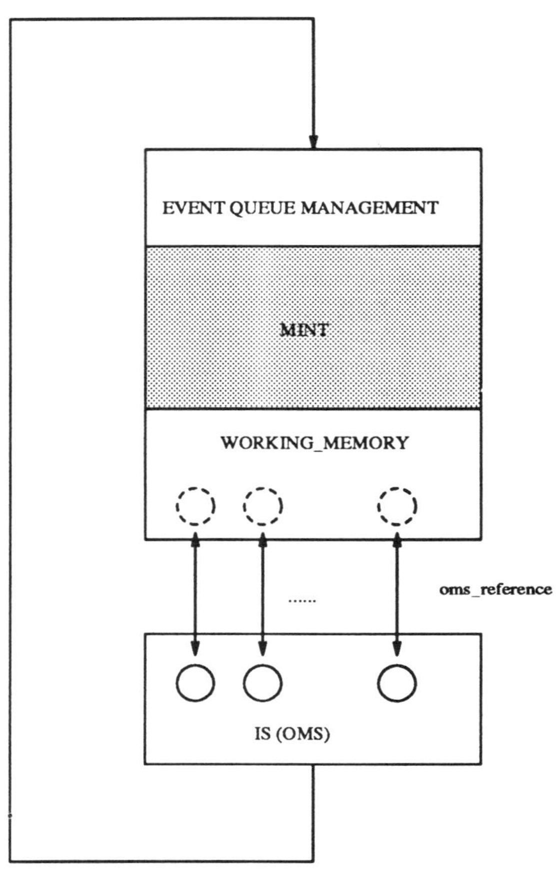

Figure 5: ALFRete/OMS Interface

tion, observation, history generation **and feedback provides** the basis for the piloting of the software process according **to the ALF** concepts.

In Figure 6 we present the PS operational environment. As we can see, the MINT communicates with the UI and **IS. The MINT** receives messages from the UI containing user requests and **sends messages to** the UI with display requests. Both the UI and the MINT **are PCTE** processes and, therefore, the PCTE interprocess communication facilities are used in this case. The MINT invokes OMS primitives in order to request services from the IS. In [DBB$^+$89] we explained that we may have several **IMASPs and ASPs** active at the same time. From an implementation point **of view** this means that we may have several MINT processes running concurrently. Any modification made to an an IS entity is communicated to all the MINT processes via triggers. In this way we are able to have a consistent view of the IS from any MINT process at any time. In Figure 6 we also see *tools*. These tools represent either elementary operators or any other kind of tools needed and are invoked from the MINT and when a tool finishes, the MINT becomes aware of it. We make a distinction between the tools that implement operators corresponding to MASPs that support some PS functionalities such a History Generation or Feedback and those that support any other kind of MASP. The reason is that, though their operation is the same, functionally speaking they are clearly different.

The dotted line that surrounds *LIB* indicates that tools are really stored in libraries facilitating their reuse since, according the the MASPs concepts [DBB$^-$89], operators can be imported from previously defined MASPs.

The system will react in the case where the user initiative cannot be performed or as a result of the the user initiative. It is a responsibility of the MINT to request a system initiative, as we have explained before. Message displays can be produced from a MASP operator tool, a request to Guidance, or as a consequence of the need to provide an explanation.

3.2.4   User Interface

The User Interface is formed of a layered model composed by a Presentation, Dialogue Control and an Application Interface Level. The presentation layer deals with the mechanisms of setting pixels on the screen and receiving inputs from the user and consists of the X-window system, the Window Manager and a component termed the Presentation Manager. The Dialogue Controller understands how user/application dialogues are constructed and handles prescribed parts of those dialogues on behalf of the application. Finally, the Application Layer is an event driven program which interacts with

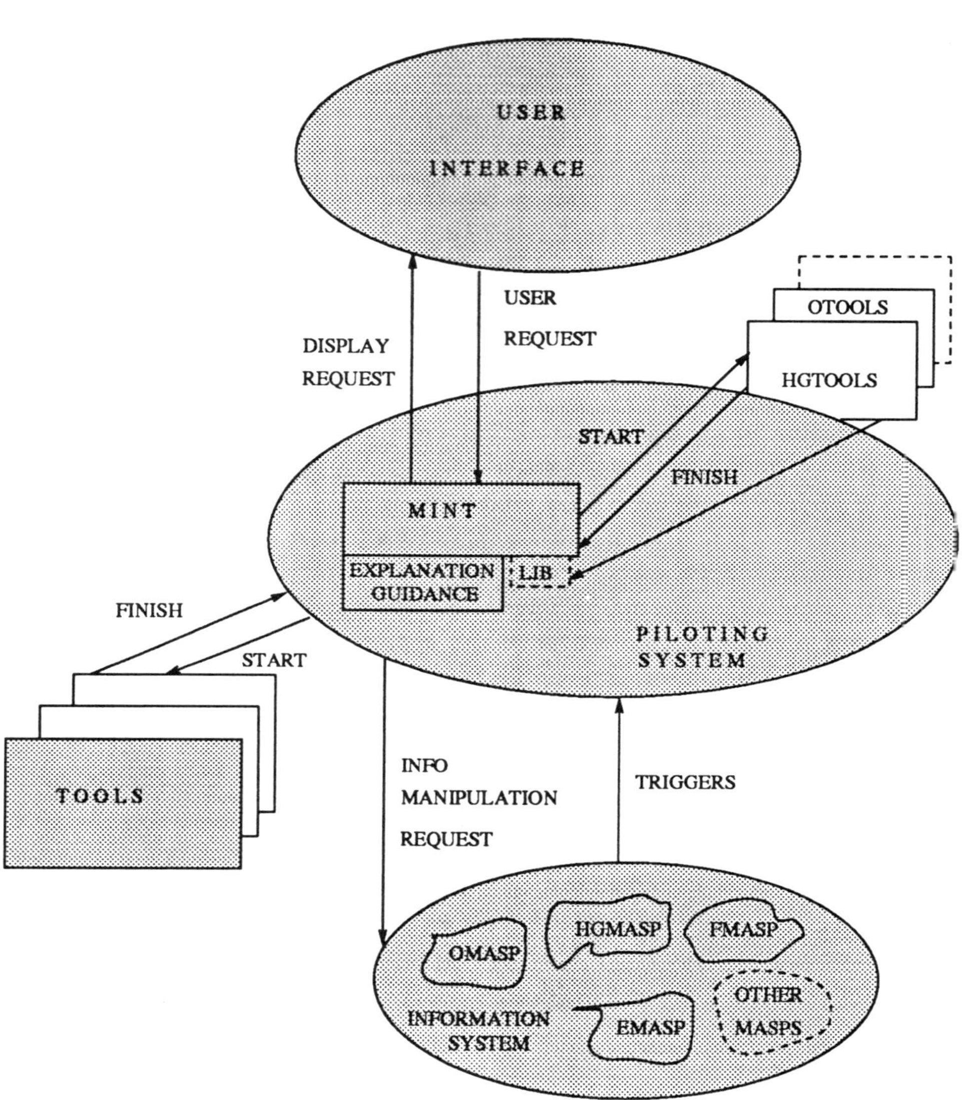

Figure 6: Piloting System Environment

the Dialogue Controller to process user input and make requests for the user to be shown things by the Presentation Manager.

Dialogues are defined by *dialogue objects* which specify what is to shown to the suer and application semantics that tell the application which dialogue object has been involved in an interaction with the user. Examples of low level dialogue objects are buttons, menus and windows.

Figure 7 shows an example of a ALF user interface screen. In the foreground we see the ALF login window, in the background we see the interface of the Instantiation Tool, MASP designer shell. In the MASP designer shell we see a pull-down menu that offers different kinds of help to the MASP designer.

3.3   ALF and PCTE (An open CASE repository)

PCTE has emerged over the last few years as an Open Repository to serve as the basis for project support environments. The reference model developed by ECMA in its technical report 55 describes Computer Aided Systems Engineering Environment Frameworks.
This has been produced in parallel with the Standardisation of PCTE as ECMA 149.

PCTE is now perceived as offering the necessary repository and data integration facilities for the construction of integrated project support environments (IPSE) by the addition to PCTE of accompanying services for presentation (Motif or Open look) and control integration, and by the integration of CASE tools.
The level (or depth) of this latter integration can vary from loose encapsulation through to re-engineering to make best use of PCTE.

In this way several projects and products are using PCTE as their fundamental data integration substrate, or repository.
It is an open repository in the sense that it is an international standard, so in the public domain.
It has also been designed to facilitate tool integration, in particular for tools able to run under Unix; while not requiring that the underlying operating system be Unix, or that there be a particular implementation of PCTE.

The aspects of data management and data integration between cooperating tools in an IPSE are only one dimension of the system engineering environment problem.

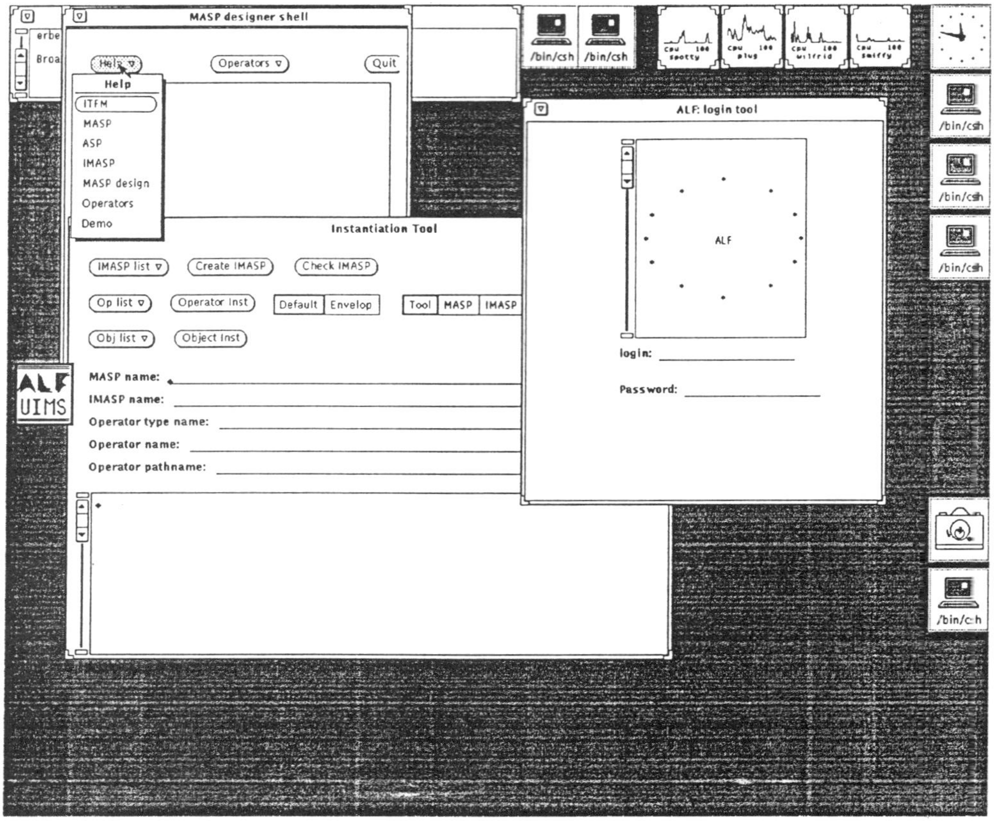

MASP designer shell
erbe
Broa
Help
Operators
Quit
Help
ITFM
MASP
ASP
IMASP
MASP design
Operators
Demo
Instantiation Tool
IMASP list
Create IMASP
Check IMASP
Op list
Operator Inst
Default
Envelop
Tool
MASP
IMASP
Obj list
Object Inst
MASP name:
IMASP name:
Operator type name:
Operator name:
Operator pathname:
ALF
UIMS
/bin/csh
/bin/csh
cpu 100 spotty
cpu 100 plus
cpu 100 wilfrid
cpu 100 smiffy
ALF: login tool
ALF
login:
Password:
/bin/csh
/bin/csh
/bin/csh
/bin/csh

Each realistic IPSE being built on **PCTE is addressing** itself to the question of task management, or work flow, or **dynamic control** integration, etc.
In o her words they are seeking specific **solutions in** the domain the research com nunity calls the Software Process.

ALF offers a complementary approach **to PCTE in** which ALF provides means to support the Software (or System) **Development Process** in an Open way.
Although ALF is not into standardisation **as yet** (!) its underlying approach is to facilitate another dimension of **tool integration**: integration into the development process to be used in the engineering environment by a given organisation. Openness comes from the possibilities of being able to tailor this ntegration in terms of the methods, techniques and procedures to be employed in a given environment.

When integrating a tool into one of the emerging PCTE based IPSEs, one of the main tasks is to insert the data model for the tool's data into the context of the IPSE. This can be done by describing the tool's data in terms of the PCTE data model, taking account of the already existing modelled data in the given IPSE. This is already found to be a very useful approach to getting a better integrated environment.
However, this does not imply the tool will respect the methods and procedures that are being followed in the IPSE.

What ALF provides is a way to model the development process in terms of rules enacting operations (e.g. tools) on information (using the PCTE object model).
What this means is that when integrating a tool into a given environment, as well as modelling its data and integrating the data models with those already existing, the integrator of the environment will develop the rules associated with the use of the method or technique for which the tool respresents a set of operations.

What may often happen, at any rate in the short term, is that a tool will often be seen as a small set (perhaps one) of operations. The integration of a new tool may not even impact the methods already in place, but simply be a means to implement the relevant operators.
However, it is to be anticipated that, in the longer term, large monolithic tools will be decomposed into more elementary operations; this will provide

a finer granularity for the application of the rules to the results of the tool
and will lead to more precise monitoring and control of the development process.

Of course, what ALF brings to the end-user of an environment built using ALF and PCTE is something quite different. What we have seen up
to now is a superficial introduction to the technical interest of ALF for the
environment integrator. This helps the software house or large organisation's
methods group to produce its required environment using an Open CASEE
Framework.
This is in itself an appreciable advance, comparable with the use of PCTE as
Open Repository instead of all the proprietary solutions (e.g. Istar, Maestro,
etc.).

However, what ALF means to the end-user is a much more helpful development environment. Some of this help comes from the application of rules
that constrain the developer to follow the procedures and methods of his
organisation and to use the techniques chosen by that organisation for the
different tasks he has to carry out. Although this may seem to some (anar-
chists, in particular) like too much control, it will ease the developer's work
by helping him to avoid forgetting the right way to do certain things and ig-
noring which technique (tool) to use for a particular stage of his development.

Yet more help comes from being able to get guidance on how best to proceed,
explanation on what has been happening and why, and access to the ever-
increasing historical information that can be used to make improved forecasts
of what is likely to occur in the future.
Just being able to use those tools which are appropriate to his work will be a
great help to the normal software developer who is becoming snowed under
by the variety of tools he can find on his work station.

The ALF System is based on the Emeraude implementation of PCTE 1.5
enhanced with new features such as composite objects, versions and triggers.
Hereafter, this PCTE implementation will be referred simply as PCTE.
    PCTE provides to ALF the basic services for:

- Object Management

- Event Triggering

3.3.1   Object Management

The PCTE component that provides object management facilities, including integrity and concurrency control, is the Object Management System (OMS).

The PCTE's OMS provides services to manage all the objects produced and used in the ALF System while enforcing their integrity. The object base managed by PCTE's OMS is transparently distributed over a set of workstations interconnected by a local area network.

The tools that instantiate MASP operator types are integrated via the OMS object base. This data integration is achieved making the information required by a tool (and produced by another tool) available to that tool in the syntax and semantics it expects. The PCTE's OMS also provides the services for data integration between the components of the ALF System and tools instantiating MASP operator types.

A MASP is instantiated, by instantiating its operator types with tools or instantiated MASPs and its object model with an object set.

A MASP object model defines the organisation of object type definitions into OMS Schema Definition Sets (SDS). Each SDS gathers a set of related type definitions. Examples of SDSs are the set of definitions that are necessary for all users working on a given project, the set of definitions that are specific to a given user role, and the set of definitions that are specific to a given project activity.

An important feature of SDSs is sharing: the sharing of SDSs between MASPs and the sharing of type definitions between SDSs. This is provided by the "importation facilities". The importation of an SDS from a MASP into another makes all the type definitions of this SDS visible in both MASPs. The importation of a type definition from an SDS into another makes this definition visible in both SDSs. In this way, type definitions can be shared among several SDSs and MASPs.

The view of the object base defined in a MASP object model is given by the set of type definitions which is the union of all of the type definitions in the set of SDSs. For instance, objects of a given type that is in one or more SDSs of the set are seen as having as attributes and possible relationships the ones whose types are applied to the object type in these SDSs.

An IMASP's object set is a logical object base having as schema the MASP object model associated with the IMASP. It can be defined in such a way that some objects in the set are shared with some other object sets. Each software process enacting an IMASP accesses these shared objects through its MASP object model view point.

A shared object then becomes the synthesis of several different software process activities, where each one contributes to build the object in function of the software process model view point it enacts.

It is worth noting that PCTE's OMS is also used for describing and managing MASPs, IMASPs and ASPs representations.

3.3.2   Event Triggering

MASP expressions are described in terms of events and logical conditions. The PCTE trigger mechanism provides the basis for describing these events and triggering the appropriate reactions.

Events are defined as "what happens in the environment" in terms of execution of tools and access of the object base. The associated reactions are carried out at defined (relative) moments, in a synchronous or asynchronous way, by the invocation of specified tools or the communication of specified messages.

These events and reactions are defined following an object approach where the types of events raised and reactions executed are attached to the types of objets and tools (which are also represented as objects).

This mechanism is the means to support communication and synchronisation between the MINT software process interpreters, tools, and the PCTE's OMS.

4   Conclusion

In this paper we introduced the main aims and the main concepts of the ESPRIT I project ALF. We related the work carried out in ALF to the field of software process modeling. Moreover, we sketched the architecture of the ALF environment, and the benefits potential users can gain from using ALF. By pointing out how existing software development experience and knowledge can be moved to ALF based software development we provide the basis for the innovating step of using ALF environments. We outlined that multi-paradigm software process modeling language we have developed enables several software developers to cooperate in software development, and that this language builds the basis of an incremental and modular software development. Our contribution to extend the notion of views onto a databse by the notion of views onto a software process model together with implementing the PCTE object managment system as repository that can store persistant objects reaches a new quality of software modeling environments.

Acknowledgements: The authors acknowledge the contribution to this paper from all the members of the ALF consortium, who are: GIE Emeraude (France), CSC (Belgium), Computer Technologies Co. (Greece), Grupo de Mecanica del Vuelo, S.A. (Spain), International Computers Limited (United Kingdom), University of Nancy-CRIN (France), University of Dortmund-Informatik X (Germany), Cerilor (France), Université de Catholique de Louvain (Belgium) and University of Dijon-CRID (France).

A Glossary

ALF	Accueil de Logiciel Futur: Esprit Project 1520
ISK	Information System Kernel
MASP	Model of an Assisted Software Process
IMASP	Instantiated MASP
ITFM	Inconsistency Tracker For MASPs
MASP/DL	MASP Description Language.
PS	Piloting System
MINT	MASP Interpreter
ASP	Assisted Software Process
PCTE	Portable Common Tool Environment
PCTE+	Secure version of PCTE
OMS	Object Management System
ERA	Entity-Relationship-Attribute model
CM	Configuration Management

B Cross-references

References

[ACM90] V. Ambriola, P. Ciancarini, and C. Montangero. *Software Process Enactment in Oikos.* In *Proceedings of the Fourth ACM SIGSOFT*

Symposium on Software Development Environments, Irvine, California, USA, December 1990. appeared as Software Engineering Notes, 15(6), December 1990.

[BBC+89]   K. Benali, N. Boudjlida, F. Charoy, J.C. Derniame, C. Godart, P. Griffiths, V. Gruhn, P. Jamart, A. Legait, D.E. Oldfield, and F. Oquendo. *The Presentation of the ALF project.* In N. Madhavji, W. Schäfer, and H. Weber, editors, *Proceedings of the First International Conference on System Development Environments and Factories*, London, 1989. Pitman Publishing.

[BJG83]   R. Balzer, T.E. Cheatham Jr., and C. Green. *Software Technology in the 1990's: Using a New Paradigm. IEEE Computer*, 16(11), November 1983.

[Boe88]   B.W. Boehm. *A Spiral Model of Software Development and Enhancement. Computer*, May 1988.

[Cag90]   M.R. Cagan. *The HP SoftBench Environment: An Architetcure for a New Generation of Software Tools. Hewlett-Packard Journal*, June 1990.

[Cam88]   I. Campbell. *Portable Common Tool Environment. Computer Standards and Interfaces*, (8), 1988.

[DBB+89]   J.C. Derniame, K. Benali, N. Boudjlida, R. Champagne, F. Charoy, J. Garbarjosa, C. Godart, P. Griffiths, V. Gruhn, and P. Jamart. *The MASP Concepts and their rationales in the ALF Project.* ALF/NCY-JCD/WP-2/1/2.D3, October 1989.

[DBB+90]   J-C. Derniame, K. Benali, N. Boudjlida, P. Boveroux, P. Griffiths, V. Gruhn, P. Jamart, and D.E. Oldfield. *Reference Manual for the MASP Definition Language.* Technical Report ALF/NCY-JCD/WP-3/5/2.D2, The ALF Consortium, 11 1990.

[DG90a]   W. Deiters and V. Gruhn. *Managing Software Processes in MEL-MAC.* In *Proceedings of the Fourth ACM SIGSOFT Symposium on Software Development Environments*, Irvine, California, USA, December 1990. appeared as Software Engineering Notes, 15(6), December 1990.

[DG90b]   W. Deiters and V. Gruhn. *Software Process Model Analysis Based on FUNSOFT Nets. Mathematical Modeling and Simulation*, 1990.

[Dow86]   M. Dowson, editor. *"Iteration in the Software Process"* Proceedings of the 3rd *International Software Process Workshop*, Beckenridge, Colorado, USA, November 1986.

[Dow87a] M. Dowson. *ISTAR and the Contractual Approach.* In *Proceedings of the 9th International Conference on Software Engineering*, Monterey, CA, USA, 1987.

[Dow87b] M. Dowson. *ISTAR - An Integrated Project Support Environment.* In *Proceedings of the ACM SIGSOFT/SIGPLAN Software Engineering Symposium on Practical Software Development Environments*, January 1987. appeared also as SIGPLAN Notices, Vol.22, No.1.

[ESF88]   The ESF Consortium. *ESF Technical Reference Guide*, 1988.

[Fed86]   E. Fedchak. *An Introduction to Software Engineering Environments.* In *Proceedings of the Computer Software and Aplications Conference (COMPSAC) 1986*, Chicago, Illinois, USA, October 1986.

[Fer88]   C. Fernstrom. *Design Considerations for Process Driven Software Environments.* In *Proceedings of the 4th Int. Software Process Workshop Moretonhamstead UK*, May 1988.

[Kel88]   M.I. Kellner. *Representation Formalisms for Software Process Modelling.* In *Proceedings of the 4th International Software Process Workshop*, Moretonhampstead, Devon, UK, May 1988.

[KFP88]   G.E. Kaiser, P.H. Feiler, and S.S. Popovich. *Intelligent Assistance for Software Development and Maintenance. IEEE Software*, May 1988.

[Leh89]   M. Lehman. *Uncertainty in Computer Application and its Control Through the Engineering of Software. Journal of Software Maintenance*, 1(1), July 1989.

[LH89]   L. Liu and E. Horowitz. *A Formal Model for Software Project Management. IEEE Transactions on Software Engineering*, 15, October 1989.

[Ost87]   L. Osterweil. *Software Processes are Software Too.* In *Proceedings of the 9th International Conference on Software Engineering*, Monterey, California, April 1987.

[Roy70]   W.W. Royce. *Managing the development of large software systems: Concepts and techniques*. In *Proc. WESCON*, 1970.

[SW88]   W. Schäfer and H. Weber. *The ESF-Profile. Handbook of Computer Aided Software Engineering*, 1988.

[TBC⁺88]   R.N. Taylor, F.C. Belz, L.A. Clarke, L. Osterweil, R.W. Selby, J.C. Wileden, A.L. Wolf, and M. Young. *Foundations in the ARCADIA Environment Architecture*. In *Proceedings of the ACM SIGSOFT/SIGPLAN Software Engineering Symposium on Practical Software Development Environments*, Boston, 1988. appeared as Software Engineering Notes, 13(5), February 1989.

[Tho89]   Thomson. Specification du language xrete (in french). Technical report, Thomson Csf LCR, 1989.

[Tul87]   C.J. Tully. *Prospects for Future Environments: Introduction to Panel Session*. In *Proceedings of the 9th International Conference on Software Engineering*, Monterey, California, April 1987.

[Tul88a]   C.J. Tully, editor. *Proceedings of the 4th International Software Process Workshop*, Moretonhampstead, Devon, UK, May 1988. Appeared as ACM SIGSOFT Software Engineering Notes, Volume 14, Number 4, June 1989.

[Tul88b]   C.J. Tully. *Software Process Models and programs: Observations on their nature and context*. In *Proceedings of the 4th International Software Process Workshop*, Moretonhampstead, Devon, UK, May 1988.

[War89]   B. Warboys. *The IPSE 2.5 Project: Process Modelling as the basis for a Support Environment*. In N. Madhavji, W. Schäfer, and H. Weber, editors, *Proceedings of the First International Conference on System Development Environments and Factories*, London, 1989. Pitman Publishing.

[Was71]   E. Wasielewski. *Einfache Netzplantechnik (in German)*. Carl Hanser Verlag, Munich, FRG, 1971.

[Zuc90]   J.D. Zucker. *Xrete development for ALF*. ALF/EMR-JDZ/CT-3, 2 1990.

4

The arise process modelling system

R. H. Pierce and J. Smith
IPSYS Software plc, Marlborough Court,
Pickforc Street, Macclesfield, Cheshire, SK11 6JD, UK

1. THE PROBLEM DOMAIN

The discipline of software engineering demands that many detailed standards and procedures be followed at all stages in the development of a sofware system. Such procedures include those concerned with the formal review of ccmponents, approval and release, and change control. All of which are integral to the adopted quality assurance system used for a given development. Other procedures concerned with project management and control will also be required. Such procedures must be followed regardless of the degree to which Computer Aided Software Engineering (CASE) tools are usec in the development environment, and it is perhaps more important to establish the quaity assurance and other procedures to be used on a new project than to select the methods and CASE tools to be employed.

The traditional vehicle for describing the quality assurance aspects of a project's procedures is the written quality plan. This will be supplemented by additional documents which cover project control procedures. Following standards and procedures can be tedious and unpopular. There is a temptation for junior staff to ignore the standards and procedures laid down in the quality manual because they are boring and for intermediate management to ignore them because they cost time and money to apply. The result is often inadequately inspected and tested software which costs a disproportionate amount to rectify during system integration and maintenance.

2. THE APPLICATION OF PROCESS MODELLING

The typical quality assurance manual provides a number of activities that must be undertaken and guidelines to which procedures must adhere. More often than not this can be abstracted into a series of concurrent interacting tasks with identifiable inputs and outputs. Expressing an activity in a machine processable form would hopefully engender greater precision and internal consistency. It might also highlight parts of activities that are excessively time consuming.

Accepting these premises the question then becomes one of application. Many process modelling environments have attempted a high level of prescriptive control; projects such as IPSE 2.5 have spent many man years pursuing low level process serving architectures. [WB] These are not always necessary requirements in the interim. Highly prescriptive environments can alienate users educated in the culture of open systems and whilst low level architectures may be the ultimate solutions to date they have proved notoriously difficult to perfect. Against this background The IPSYS Process Modelling and Management System (PMMS) has evolved.

3. PMMS IN CONCEPT

PMMS was conceived as an interim solution. The earliest production quality process oriented environments are likely to be anything between three and five years away. Thus PMMS was designed to fill the short term requirements of a company such as IPSYS where existing process automation is rudimentary and work is undertaken on a number of activities concurrently, often by the same individuals!

The aims of PMMS can therefore be summarised as follows:

- Machine encapsulation of concurrent processes
- Engender flexibility in the approach to modelling
- Enable variable levels of policing and control
- A reduction in mis-perception
- Provide planning, monitoring and administration support
- Promote reuse of process models
- Facilitate non-deterministic models

Processes are encapsulated by creating databases composed of tasks that interact within the database and between the databases. Tasks can perform all manner of actions and are capable of policing the compliance of the action to the task specification.

This enables PMMS to act either as the primary agent of interaction between the user and the development environment, replacing the more traditional command line interpreters or shells which normally perform this duty. Or perform a supplemental role in which it acts as a guide to the user by informing them of the tasks assigned, in which order they must be undertaken, who to interact with and which tools they are required to use. This allows users of PMMS to adopt a number of different approaches to the application of the process model. For instance from one approach it is possible to rigidly control the context in which the user operates and police the execution of tasks. However other approaches might desire less formal policing of the process, tasks providing the guidance mechanism for the various stages of the activity.

It is the latter that is the best expression of the thinking behind PMMS: that for a given activity it is not the rigid low-level enforcement of the process that is significant. This argument is premised on the fact that few organisations embark on activities without precedent. A maintenance activity for example is normally one of many and takes place within established organisational parameters. Thus rather than seeking to rigidly police these activities PMMS was conceived as a means of guiding and augmenting them. The user is presented with a series of tasks with clearly delineated dependences and goals, there should be no doubt as to the actions to be undertaken inorder to fulfill the specified requirements. A concomitant of this is the illumination of breaches of the process, and hence the quality standard, thereby gradually reducing error and mis-perception. The user cannot forget the stages of the process, nor with the level of monitoring PMMS enables, need they be allowed to.

The combination of these two approaches enables organisations to implement executable models at a number of application levels and from separate modelling perspectives. Obviously there is a greater initial overhead if the process is to be modelled at the level of, for example, each micro stage of a method. Yet by the same token PMMS promotes the re-use of existing task structures rendering dividends to organisations with clearly defined iterative processes, maintenance being the foremost candidate. It also encourages the incremental development of a process model by the ease with which new task networks can be created or existing models parameterised. Of course the persistent nature of the data associated with the process enables project managers to monitor the execution of the model at all times.

This diversity of approach has been achieved by implementing the mechanics of PMMS via a number of simple concepts and interactions.

4. NOTATION

PMMS lacks a process modelling language akin to P.M.L. in IPSE 2.5., nor does it offer the formalism of the process notations derived from Petri-net implementations. Instead it uses a rule-based notation consisting at the highest level of interacting "roles" which in turn are composed of interacting "tasks" presented in the form of an agenda

4.1. Roles

A role is characterized by the resources and tasks assigned to it, and the roles to which it may delegate tasks. Other than this there is no pre-conceived notion within PMMS as to the usage of the role. Users are assigned to a specific "role database" to which only they and the project authorities have access, this being enforced by a simple set of permissions. Within this database there may be one or several roles defined, these correspond to the different types of activities the user performs within a given project or meta-activity.

The delineation of separate roles within a single users database is to enable the user to clarify the type of tasks associated with a given role. For instance a software engineer may design, code and unit test during a small project. The design process will almost certainly involve the engineer in design reviews and document acceptance procedures. It is perhaps better to split these activities off into a separate role than to mix them with the coding and testing activities also undertaken. One benefit of this division is that a record of the time the user spends in the different types of role activity is immediatly available. A user may obviously be assigned to more than one database and hence can participate in any number of roles.

A role may be granted permission to delegate tasks to other roles within the project. Should this happen the tasks delegated are copied into the recipient role database and the delegated tasks within the delegating role are either marked as delegated, annotated by to whom, when and for what reason, or are removed. The choice of delegation strategy is determined at a macro level during the modelling of the specific activity. The recipient role could if desired report the completion of delegated task hierarchies directly to the delegating role. In this way contracts between roles can be modelled allowing a contract model to be built if desired. By extending this mechanism a full reporting structure can be encompassed within the process model.

The diagram below outlines the interactions between roles and their constituent elements.

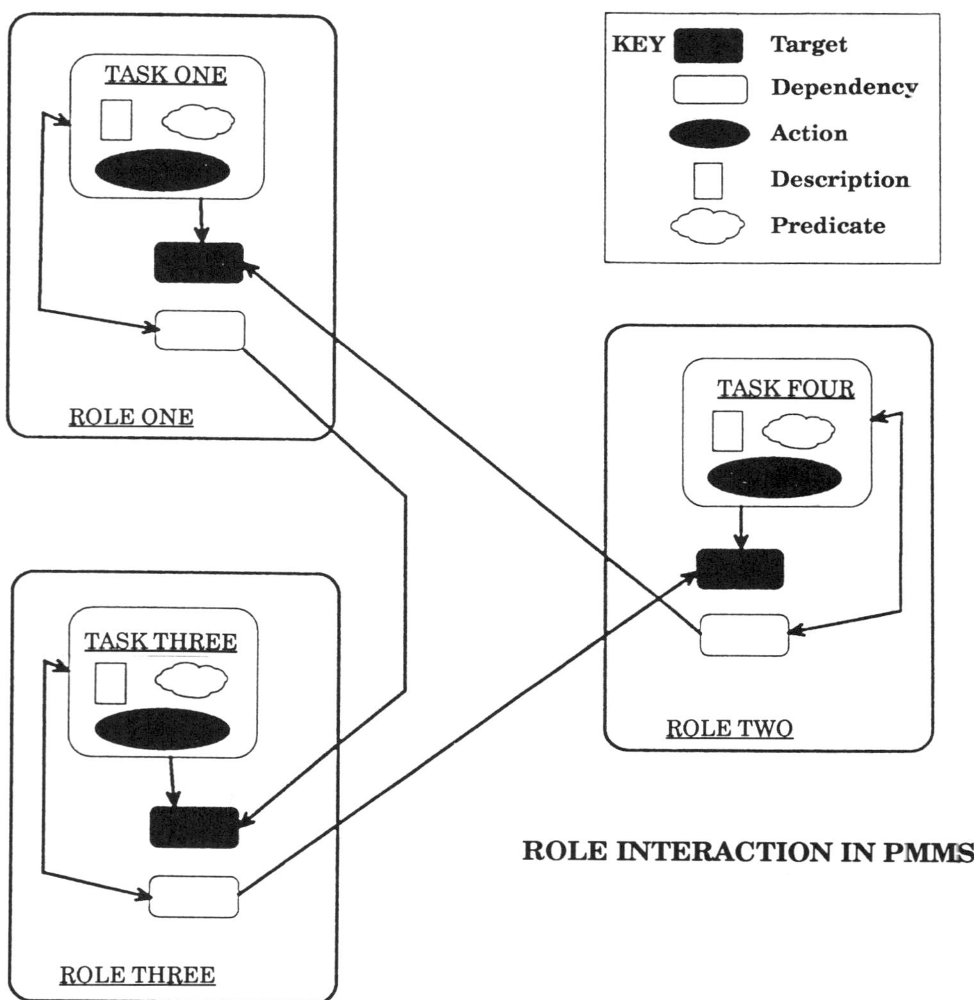

4.2. Components

PMMS models the objects and states encountered in a process via the "Component" annotation. There are two types of component:

- concrete components;

- abstract components.

A concrete component has a representation in filestore, or will have as a result of a tasks action. The concrete component therefore contains a filestore path to indicate the search path for a particular object. A concrete component "exists" simply by being present in filestore, the component itself stores no information about the object. If further information is required about the object such as its currency or ownership this can be retrieved via the "predicate" mechanism described below.

An abstract component has no direct representation in filestore, instead it models the state of an object or process, or a collection of objects and activities, the definition is entirely at the behest of the user. In practice of the two types the abstract component is the most commonly used, its definitional flexibility lending it to a variety of specifications. The abstract component has a status attribute that determines its value. At the simplest level this is just a measure of its existence or otherwise. A recent development has been to provide both concrete and abstract components with a more complex status attribute thereby allowing a component to exist in any one of a number of conditions. This then offers the process specifier far more flexibility, allowing the process to change the relative status of the component.

Components belong to roles but are actually the targets and dependences of tasks. Thus a role will possess only those components upon which its alloted tasks are dependent or which they seek to create or alter.

4.3. Tasks

The task is the central mechanistic concept in PMMS; it states what must be achieved in a particular part of the development and the conditions necessary to achieve it. Although PMMS allows tasks to be decomposed into sub-tasks it makes no assumptions about the relationships between tasks, these are solely determined by the task's targets, dependences and predicate.

A task is characterised by the following attributes:

- descriptions
- a sequence subtasks
- a sequence targets
- a sequence dependences
- predicate
- action
- status
- automation

Each task can have a detailed **description** of the activities associated with it. This is of particular use when task structures are being reused or when staff are assigned to roles outside their usual area of expertise. Provision is also made for the user to add notes to the task. This can serve as additional textual clarification on the part of the users themselves. A more useful function is as an activity record for the user. This allows him to communicate observations about task execution back to the manager who then has a persistent record for evaluation. In a maintenance activity customer problem reports can be placed in the task when the task network to deal with the problem is created. Given the correct linkage completion of the tasks might automatically mark the problem report as resolved.

The **target** is the thing to be achieved, the product of the tasks action, a task may possess more than one target. A concrete target is an actual entity in the underlying database or filestore, which is to be created or modified by the the task. An abstract target has no concrete representation in the database; for example, if the task is to review a document and review records are not stored in machine-readable form, the target "document reviewed" would be abstract. Another example of an abstract target might be the issuing of a purchase order for some additional hardware, it is simply a state of existence. Targets are therefore modelled by concrete and abstract components.

The **dependences** are the objects or states required to create or modify the target of the task. Dependences are normally the targets of other tasks, this provides the foundation for communication within PMMS. Networks of inter-dependent tasks are created, the links in the task network therefore representing information flow in the process model. A tasks dependency on a concrete component is satisfied by the components existence, dependency on an abstract component is satisfied if the state of the component matches that required by the dependency. With relative dependency a task may not have an absolute dependence on the entity modelled by the component. Therefore if the state of the component "at least" satisfies that of the dependency it will allow the action to proceed.

The **predicate** specifies further conditions governing the creation or modification of the target. It may use any information, including the existence, creation time and status of the dependences. Alternatively it may use information held entirely outside PMMS. A predicate may prevent the creation or modification of a target until the conditions are right for its creation, and may prevent iteration of a task if the target exists. Conversely, the predicate may require the iteration of the task if there has been a change in the status of the dependences.

The **action** defines how the target is to be achieved. The action may be concrete, defining precisely the sequence of tool invocations needed to create the target, or it may be abstract, defined by a textual description which allows the user to take whatever steps are necessary to create the target. The user is therefore not constrained in the method of approaching the action other than by the tools and database objects which are provided by that role or are provided in the immediate development environment.

In the current version of PMMS, actions and predicates are coded in EASEL, the data manipulation language of the IPSYS Tool Builders Kit. [TBK] However, a facility is provided to escape from EASEL into the command language or shell provided with the host environment to allow actions and predicates to be completely general. This enables PMMS to control tool invocations and analyse the tools subsequent output or failure. A large number of predefined actions and predicates are provided within PMMS. These are characterised by an activity script which is parameterised by the user and a detailed description of the activity and its intended usage. The user simply chooses the desired action or predicate which is then copied into the action or predicate field of a task. Actions and predicates can be combined and augmented by user defined ones as and where necesary. With due consideration libraries of action and predicate scripts can be built up and enhanced over several process models.

In certain circumstances it may be necessary to perform an action even though the predicate which governs the action may explicitly forbid it. PMMS embodies a *waiver* procedure to handle this case. Whenever a waiver is invoked, the user must give the reason for the waiver, which will be recorded for auditing purposes. It is possible to disable the waiver procedure where it is judged essential that the conditions governing the execution of a task's action must be fulfilled, as might be the case in a project to develop safety-critical software.

A task has a **status** which is the record of its execution. The status is set by the user executing the task, the outcome of the execution determining the new setting.

- Unstarted
- Commenced
- Completed

A task typically begins "Unstarted", is "Commenced" and finally "Completed". Commencement of the task causes it to examine the status of its dependences and then its predicate conditions, failure to satisfy the dependences or comply with the predicate conditions will prevent the execution of its action field and set the status to "Invalid". Successful commencement will cause PMMS to check that the specified targets exist. If they do not the task will be marked as "Invalid". Completion of the task checks that the targets have achieved the required status. Dependent tasks are then free to begin execution. All status changes made by the user are recorded and explained to the user via a shell or activity log. This log provides a detailed account of the failure or success of a tasks execution and therefore plays a significant part in reducing misperception during a complex activity.

At the same time the user may set the status manually to one of several statuses:

- Suspended
- Resumed
- Re-Do

Suspension of a task disables any dependent tasks even if the dependences exist for that tasks execution. Resumption of the task re-activates any dependent tasks. Setting a task to be re-done impies that the conditions governing its former execution have subsequently changed. The effect of a re-do is to trace the target-dependency network resetting the statuses of all dependent tasks.

Changes in task dependency networks caused either through iteration, conscious change as above or mistake are echoed in all dependent tasks by a reseting of the status to one of the following previously described statuses:

- Invalid
- Re-Do

Obviously under certain conditions this can have a major impact on the state of the task network therefore relative as against absolute dependency was introduced to lessen the impact of fine-tuning higher in the task network.

In addition to the attributes mentioned above a task also has a time and date record of all status changes. The date of assignment is also present as are any target dates established as a part of the process. A flag is available to bring attention to tasks that have passed their target dates.

A task can be defined to be **automatic** such that when its dependences and predicate conditions are satisfied it will execute on its own. However this behaviour can only be

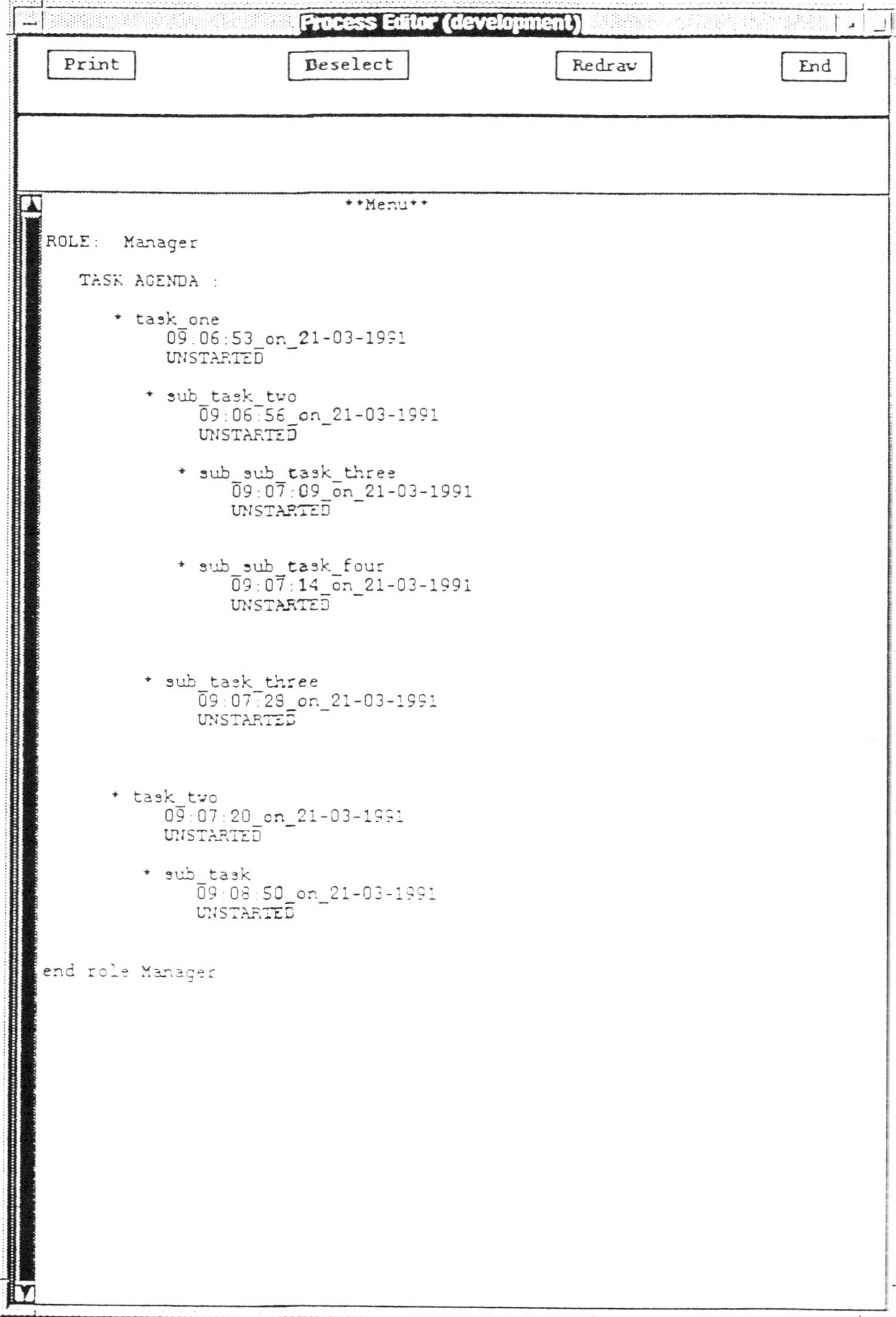

Process Editor (development)
Print   Deselect   Redraw   End
Menu
ROLE: Manager

  TASK AGENDA :

     * task_one
         09:06:53_on_21-03-1991
         UNSTARTED

       * sub_task_two
           09:06:56_on_21-03-1991
           UNSTARTED

         * sub_sub_task_three
             09:07:09_on_21-03-1991
             UNSTARTED

         * sub_sub_task_four
             09:07:14_on_21-03-1991
             UNSTARTED

       * sub_task_three
           09:07:28_on_21-03-1991
           UNSTARTED

     * task_two
         09:07:20_on_21-03-1991
         UNSTARTED

       * sub_task
           09:08:50_on_21-03-1991
           UNSTARTED

end role Manager

6. QUALITY MANAGEMENT

Used to implement a quality standard for a given project the PMMS user's environment would on the face of it look little different from an unregulated one. In each work area would reside a number of role databases to which users would be assigned. Invoking PMMS upon that database would then offer the user, determined by the state of the dependency network, the opportunity to begin task execution. Their working practices are constrained only by the tools and methods the agenda stipulates. The process of creating the model and deriving the role databases is now outlined overleaf. Below is a diagramatic representation of that process.

TEMPLATE INSTANTIATION IN PMMS

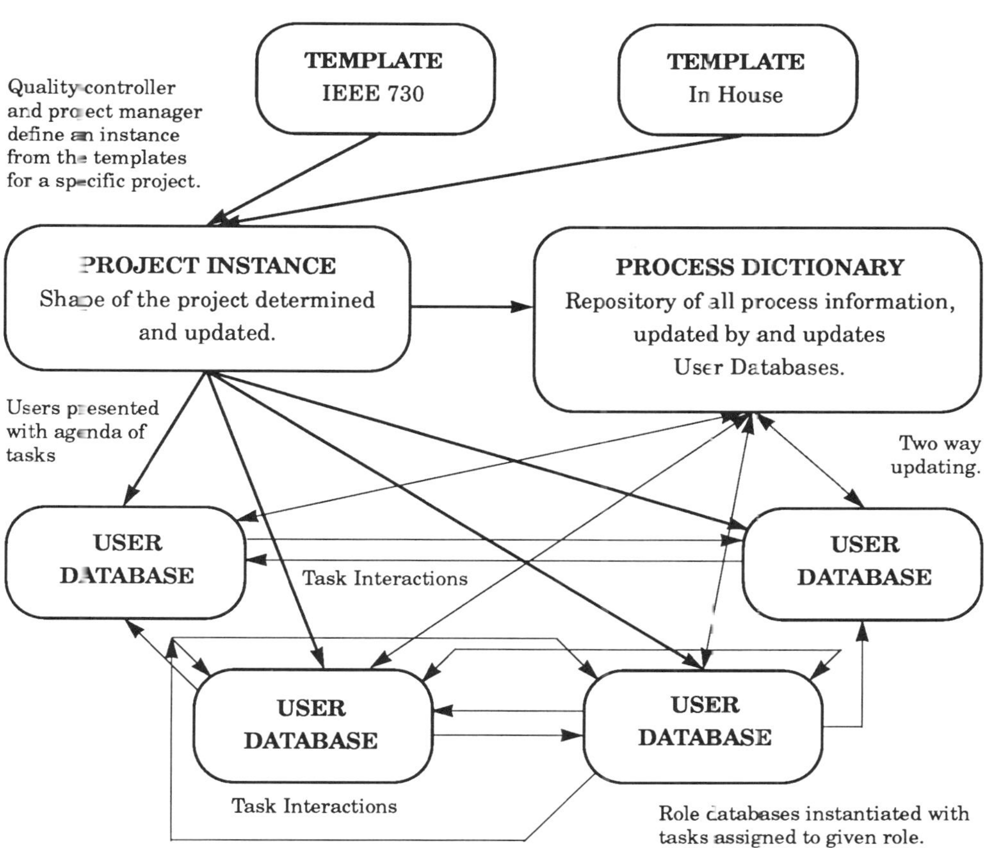

6.1. Templates and Instantiation

PMMS provides the host organisation with a means of defining a series of "quality templates" and instantiating from them a given project instance which is in turn parameterised with the actual requirements of the development. Thus any process can be modelled in outline and reused where necesary with any number of modifications. A template consists of a task network which maps out a given quality standard or procedure. Tasks in the template are known as "task types" because they are neither executable nor specific. An example of the definition of a task type can be seen below, it is in fact the template from which the previous example was instantiated. The stipulations of the standard are encoded in the various fields of the task so that any instance of the task has a description of how the standard defines that activity. An instance of the template would thus consign a given development to progress in the manner encapsulated by the template. The manner of modelling the standard is entirely at the discretion of the organisation: it might break a process down into clearly defined roles within the template or simply build one large task hierarchy with no regard to roles. The roles only being defined during instantiation.

```
        TASK AGENDA :

        TASK TYPE   task_one
          targets: six
          dependences:
          status: UNSTARTED
        end TASK TYPE task_one
```

An instance of the template or a selection of templates is then created and parameterised. Each of the tasks is given a more pertinent name and targets and dependences are renamed in line with the actual objects and states of the project.

The agenda shown below is from the project instance used to generate the examples. The derivation of an executable task from the template has occurred and the target renamed to correspond with a hypothetical project object.

```
        TASK AGENDA :

        TASK TYPE   task_one_type
          targets: six_type
          status: UNSTARTED
        end TASK TYPE task_one_type

        TASK TYPE OBJECT   task_one
          derived from: task_one_type
          targets: real_six
          status: UNSTARTED
        end TASK TYPE OBJECT   task_one
```

From this instance are instantiated the individual role databases with their specific task networks. A given task or tasks may be instantiated many times if necessary along with there attendant targets and dependences. It is these final instantiations upon

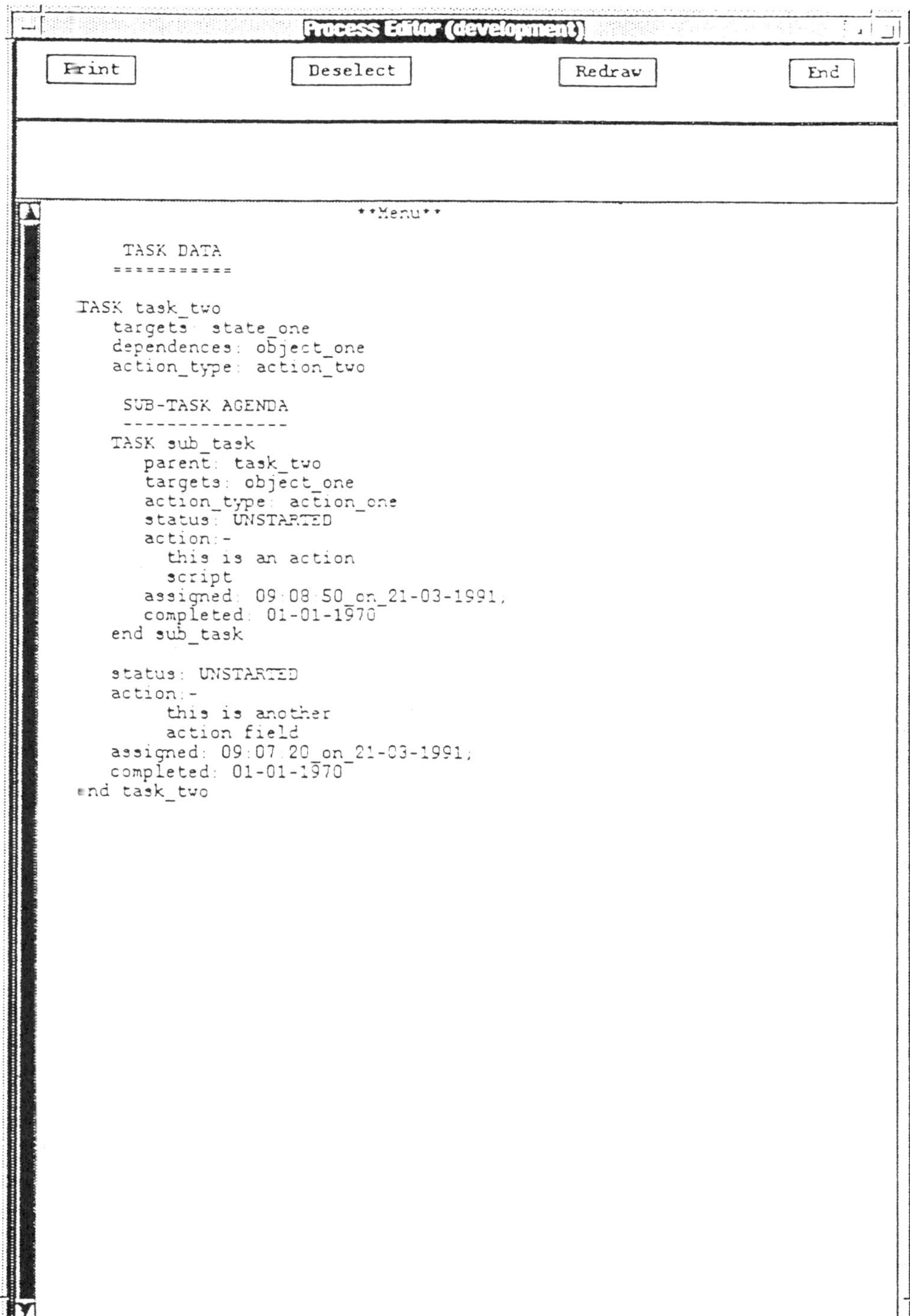
Process Editor (development)
Print   Deselect   Redraw   End
Menu

    TASK DATA
    ===========

TASK task_two
    targets: state_one
    dependences: object_one
    action_type: action_two

    SUB-TASK AGENDA

    TASK sub_task
       parent: task_two
       targets: object_one
       action_type: action_one
       status: UNSTARTED
       action:-
         this is an action
         script
       assigned: 09:08:50 on 21-03-1991;
       completed: 01-01-1970
    end sub_task

    status: UNSTARTED
    action:-
        this is another
        action field
    assigned: 09:07:20 on 21-03-1991;
    completed: 01-01-1970
end task_two

which the individual invokes PMMS, a typical agenda with a selected task is shown overleaf. At the same time a larger database is created into which all the final instantiations are also made. This database acts as a process dictionary providing a project wide record of all task executions. The individual role databases update the process dictionary during each activity and are in turn updated themselves. Iteration of a particular task network is stored in the dictionary as a version with assocated data.

6.2. Dynamic Adjustment

The role databases may then be updated and restructured as necessary during the evolution of the project. This is vital if the inevitable changes that occur within the development context are to be captured by the process model. More importantly this makes the model non-deterministic and enables the project to be modelled initially in outline, detail being introduced as the needs of the process become apparent. Individual users are able to add as many local tasks as they wish and conversely delete them. However they cannot change the relationships demonstrated in the instantiated target/dependency fields nor delete or alter the tasks instantiated into their databases. This ensures, given effective monitoring, that the prescribed process is not circumvented; the user is free to do whatever he likes as long as he ultimately complies with the stated process model.

6.3. Administration

Throughout the process the project managers may avail themselves of a wealth of information on the current state of execution. The time and dates recorded against every status change along with the ability to view the process as a whole present a number of opportunities for chart generation. This is now being pursued as part of the development of a separate management tool.

In combination these facilities provide a sophisticated and flexible means of enforcing and monitoring the adopted quality approach.

7. METHOD SUPPORT

One of the many uses of PMMS is seen as being to provide guidance to users on how to use a method support toolset such as HOOD. The various stages of the HOOD design process can be incorporated in a number of task types and actual task instances created as the design progresses. For example, whenever a new HOOD object appears on the design, tasks to elaborate the new object can appear. In this case the tasks may be created by the toolset itself.

8. DEVELOPMENT OF PMMS

In the interim work on PMMS will concentrate on consolidating the existing functionality. More thought is being paid to the user interface in terms of abstracting a given process model so that as much of the process model as possible is generated automatically. Attention also needs to be given to PMMS's ability to adapt to significant changes in the scale of a project.

Scale and iteration are fundamental issues which the present implementation addresses in a not altogether satisfactory manner. Perhaps an answer lies in the longer term upon the harnessing of other lower level technologies where the role of a tool such as PMMS would be to abstract the process definition. PMMS might then be conceived of as part of an enabling CASE technology rather than a solution in itself. An example of this might be the combination of The IPSYS Tool Builders Kit with something akin to IPSE 2.5. The process serving facilities of the latter could be harnessed via interfaces in the former. Subsequent developments of CASE tools on the Tool Builders Kit could then build in process control as a central part of the toolset. In a more general sense a tool such as PMMS could then be used to generate P.M.L., toolsets built on the Tool Builders Kit could then be controlled by and report via a user-interface such as PMMS, although this to could be left open to user customisation.

9. References

[WB] "The IPSE 2.5 Project: A Process Model Based Architecture", Brian Warboys. In "Software Engineering Environments: research and practice." Ed K.H. Bennett, 1989. Ellis Horwood.

[TBK] "The IPSYS Tool Builders Kit, Version 2.5", Ipsys Software Plc 1991.

[OSF] Motif is a trademark of the Open Software Foundation, Incorporated.

5

Analysis of software process models in the software process management environment MELMAC

Volker Gruhn
Computer Science, Software Technology,
University of Dortmund, PO Box 500 500,
D–4600 Dortmund 50, Federal Republic of Germany

1   Introduction

Recent research efforts [Per90] indicate that models for software processes are regarded nowadays as one of the most essential but still missing parts of software development environments. Software process models are used as means of communication between people involved in software development and for finding potential problems in the planned software development. Thus, they contribute to the increase of software development productivity and of software quality.

Quite a number of research projects have recognized the necessity of including a process model into a software development environment as a means to improve the industrial-like production of software (e.g. ESF [SW88] , ALF [BBC+89], ARCADIA [TBC+88], ATMOSPHERE [BOSV89]).

Since software process models serve for various purposes, we distinguish several phases of managing software processes. These phases are:

- the *modeling* of software processes, i.e. the building of process models which specify a class of software processes,

- the *instantiation* of software process models, i.e. the attachement of tools, initial objects, humans and other resources to the respective process model entities,

- the *execution* of software process models, i.e. the conduction of software processes resulting in assistance of software developers within their work,

- the *analysis* of software process models, i.e. the detection of errors and insufficiencies in process models,

- the *animation* of software processes, i.e. the visualization of project states, and

- the *adaptation* of software process models, i.e. the change of software process models because of evolving software processes.

In contrast to various purely management-oriented plans for software development (such as Gantt diagrams and PERT charts), software process models do not only express ideas about how to carry out software processes, but they are the basis of software processes. That means the information described in a software process model is used for governing real software processes. That is the reason why the analysis of software process model is a promising subject. One can be sure that problems detected in a software process model would eventually affect software processes. Analogously, one can be sure that, if a software process model M is proved to have a certain property (e.g. absence of deadlocks, bounded number of objects of certain object types), then all software processes $S_1, \ldots, S_n$ governed by that model (we write $S_1, \ldots, S_n \in SP(M)$) have that property as well.

Thus, the analysis of software process models contributes to avoid the execution of erroneous software process models. Thereby, software process model analysis helps to save, manpower as well as hardware resources.

Software process models tend to become rather large. Therefore, the analysis of software process models requires tool support. Our approach is to introduce a software process modeling language for which we design analysis facilities and to provide tool support for these analysis facilities.

In more detail that means, that we

- introduce the software process modeling language of **FUNSOFT nets**. This language enables the uniform representation of all software process model entities (objects, activities, persons, roles, etc.). The semantics of FUNSOFT nets is defined in terms of Predicate/Transition nets, which are a standard high level Petri net type [Gen87].

- utilize standard analysis facilities for Predicate/Transition nets in order to obtain software process model specific results.

- develop software process model specific analysis facilities that work directly on FUNSOFT nets,

- implement the developed analysis facilities in the software process management environment **MELMAC**. MELMAC supports all phases of software process management [DG90b, DG90a]. It contains an analysis component - called ANAMEL - that implements analysis algorithms for FUNSOFT nets.

The organization of this paper is as follows: In the next section we introduce the idea of software process model analysis in more detail. Moreover, we distinguish between different techniques of software process model analysis. In section 3 we introduce FUNSOFT nets briefly. Section 4 focuses on the verification of FUNSOFT net properties which are interesting from a software process management point of view. Section 5 is devoted to the implementation of the verification tool for FUNSOFT nets and its embedding into the software process management environment MELMAC. Section 6 sketches how the analysis facilities implemented in MELMAC are exploited in the frame of the ESPRIT project ALF. Finally, section 7 concludes this paper, sketching the focus of our future efforts.

2   Introduction to Software Process Model Analysis

We distinguish two branches of software process model analysis, namely the validation of software process models and the verification of software process model properties.

We validate a software process model M by simulating software processes $S_1, \ldots, S_n \in SP(M)$. A simulation of a software process S corresponds to looking at one specific software process example in detail, it does not show that all software processes of $SP(M)$ have or have not certain properties. Validation of software process models provides a worthwhile contribution to software process model analysis because of the following reasons:

- Validation heightens confidence into a software process model or it reveals errors in software process models quite early.

- Validation can help to examine those software process model properties for which no verification techniques are known, for which verification results are hard to understand and for which verification techniques fails due to software process model complexity.

- Validation can draw software process analysts' attention to software process model properties, which are worthwhile to be checked by verification techniques. Thus, validation can focus verification efforts onto high-risk parts of software process models. If, for example, the simulation of a software process $S_1 \in SP(M)$ reveals that S_1 does not have a particular property it should have (such as the boundedness of number of objects of one object type), it is not worthwhile to try to prove that M is bound. Conversely, the observation that the simulation of several software processes $S_1, \ldots, S_n \in SP(M)$ has revealed that these software processes possess a particular property, suggests to verify this property for M.

The essential weakness of validation techniques is that they do not yield results that are valid for all software processes $S_1, \ldots, S_n \in SP(M)$. Each validation result is underpinned merely by experiments. One cannot be sure that each software process behaves corresponding to the validation results.

Verification[1] of a software process model means to prove that a software process model has certain properties. A software process model M is said to have a property A, if all software processes of $SP(M)$ have property A. In contrast to validation, no individual software process is investigated in software process model verification, but the software process model itself. Thus, results obtained by verifying a software process model M are valid for all $S_1, \ldots, S_n \in SP(M)$.

3   The Software Process Modeling Language of FUNSOFT Nets

FUNSOFT nets are a software process modeling language that can be used as basis of executing software process models just as well as for analyzing software process models. FUNSOFT nets are a high level type of Petri nets whose semantics is defined in terms of Predicate/Transition nets extended by multi-sets [Gen87].

---

[1]The term *verification* stems from Latin. *Verum facere* means to *make true* or in a more abstract sense to *prove*.

For detailed discussions of FUNSOFT nets we refer to [Gru91]. In this paper we give a survey of FUNSOFT nets. In the following we introduce the basic concepts of FUNSOFT nets and all those features in little more detail that are needed in the rest of this paper.

A FUNSOFT net consists of

- a Petri net structure $(S; T, F)$ [Rei86, Pet81, Mur89] (the S-elements are called channels, the T- elements are called agencies, the F-elements are called edges).

- a set of jobs J. A job represents a software development activity, such as *editing of a module, compile a module, meeting with the software development team*. The function T_J attaches jobs to agencies. A job is formally specified by a Predicate/Transition net that specifies the input/output behavior of the activity. The *editing of a module*, for example, accesses a *module* and delivers a *module*, a *meeting with the software development team* reads a *list of agenda items* and produces a *list of tasks* that are forwarded to certain persons. A job is implemented by an executable piece of software, e.g. a program, a shell script or an enveloped tool. The executable part of a job j is executed whenever an agency t with $T_J(t) = j$ is fired.

- a set of object type definitions O. The function S_T attaches object types to channels, if an object type o is attached to a channel s, i.e. $S_T(s) = o$, then s can only be marked with objects of type o.

- a set of predicates P. Predicates define conditions on the objects that can potentially be read by firing an agency. The function T_P attaches predicates to agencies. A predicate can, for example, ensure that a *meeting*-agency[2] can only be fired if the scheduled meeting date is reached. Predicates correspond to precondition of activities as used in MARVEL [KFP88] and ALF [BBC+89].

- an initial marking M_0 that respects the typing of channels. A marking of a FUNSOFT net attaches a set of pairs of objects and natural numbers to channels. The second component of these pairs defines a total order of the tuples per channel. The order of objects marking a channel is significant, since it is needed for accessing a channel in a certain order (channels can be accessed as stack, as queue, or randomly).

---

[2]The notation *xx*-agency is used as an abbreviation of *an agency to which the job xx is attached*.

In order to structure software process models, agencies can be refined. Thereby, it is possible to embed a high level activity like *design* into a high level representation of a software process model, while details of the *design* are hidden in the refinement. This notion of refinement corresponds to the notion of transition substitution as discussed in [HJS89].

Agencies, channels, and edges of FUNSOFT nets have various attributes that contribute to keeping the complexity of FUNSOFT nets (measured in number of nodes) manageable. It is, for example, possible to attach an *access kind* attribute to channels. This attribute determines if a channel is accessed as a queue, as a stack, or randomly. FUNSOFT net edges are typed. Edges from channels to agencies can be of type *IN, CO, ST*, or *STC*. Edges of type *IN* and *CO* are data flow edges, edges of type *ST* and *STC* are control flow edges. Edges of type *IN* implement the reading of tokens in standard Petri nets, if an agency accesses a channel by a *CO* edge, then the read token remains in the channel, it is only copied. *ST* and *STC* edges correspond to *IN* and *CO* edges, but the values of read tokens are without any relevance, just the existence of tokens is important for firing an agency that reads via control flow edges. Edges from agencies to channels can be of type *OU* or *FI*. Both edge types implement the writing of tokens to channels, an edge of type *FI* writes a token that does not carry a value. The function T_{MAN} assigns an automation attribute to agencies. If $T_{MAN}(t) = MAN$ for an agency t, then the firing of t requires human interaction, such agencies are called manual. Other agencies $T_{MAN}(t) = AUTO$ are called automatic agencies. Another attribute that reduces the number of FUNSOFT net nodes is the firing behavior of jobs. In standard Petri nets, each T-element reads objects from all channels of its preset[3], and it puts objects into all channels of its postset. In modeling software processes, it is necessary to introduce more sophisticated firing behaviors. We distinguish the input firing behavior of a job j (denoted by $F_{IN}(j)$) and the output firing behavior of a job j (denoted by $F_{OUT}(j)$). In Figure 1 we sketch a small cut out of a software process model. This cut out describes a simple cycle of *design, edit, compile*, and *link* activities. This example helps to motivate the need for various firing behaviors.

The first agency to be fired out is the *design*-agency t_1. The result of a *design* is a natural number k written to channel s_6, which indicates how many modules the designed system is going to contain. Names of the iden-

---

[3]The preset of a net node n, is the set of those nodes n' for which an edge (n', n) exists, the postset is defined analogously. The preset of a net node n is denoted by $\bullet n$, the postset is denoted by $n\bullet$.

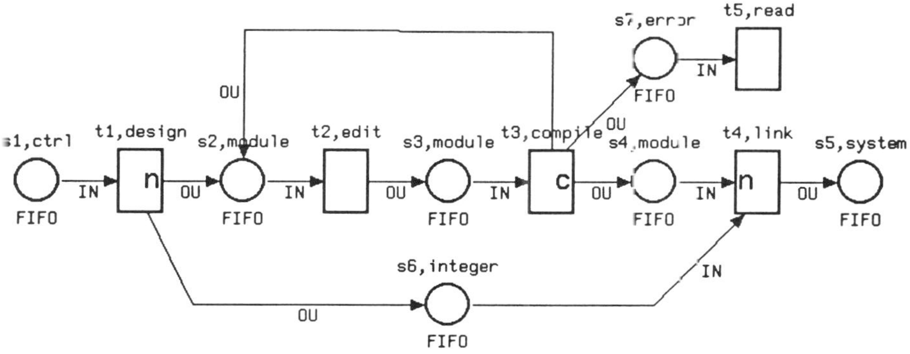

Figure 1: A cut out of a software process model

tified modules are written to channel s_2. Agency t_1 has a *mult* output firing behavior (indicated by the n in the right part of the box representing t_1). That means that the number written to channel s_2 indicates how many objects are written to s_6. For each job with a *mult* output firing behavior the maximal and the minimal number of objects that can be produced within one execution of that job is defined. This number is defined in an <mterm> being part of a job specification. In the given example we assume that the *design*-job produced at least one and at most 10 *modules*.

Designed modules are edited, compiled and linked. The *compile*-agency t_3 has a *complex* output firing behavior (indicated by the c in the right part of the box representing t_3) which is described in detail by the <cterm> (1 AND 2) XOR 3. This term specifies that either the first and second output channel are marked or that the third output channel is marked, i.e. a *module* either can be successfully compiled, or it must be re-edited. In the latter case an additional *failure_report* is produced. The numbers identified in the <cterm> of the *compile*-job refer to unique numbers of edges starting from the *compile*-agency.[4] As initial marking we assume one token in channel s_1. The *link*-agency t_4 has a *mult* input firing behavior (indicated by the n in the left part of the box representing t_4). That means, the value read from the second input channel s_6 determines how many objects are read from the

---

[4] In FUNSOFT nets each edge is uniquely identified. In the FUNSOFT net of Figure 1 these edge numbers are supressed, since the context of all agencies is obvious.

first input channel s_4. In the example this ensures that the *link*-agency can only be fired when all *modules* are successfully compiled.

4   Verification of Software Process Model Properties

First, there are properties which are independent from the initial marking of a FUNSOFT net. These properties are called **structural** properties. Second, there are properties which depend on the initial marking of a FUNSOFT net. These properties are called **dynamic properties**.

Some examples of static properties are enumerated below.

Useless object types From a software process management point of view it is interesting to find out if object types exist for which no objects can be produced and for which no objects exist in the initial software process model. Such an object type is of no use.

Such an object type can be detected by searching source channels. A channel s_1 is called a **source channel** if its preset is empty. If an object type o_1 is attached only to source channels and if all source channels s with $S_T(s) = o_1$ are not initially marked then o_1 is of no use.

For defining the explained property it is at first necessary to define the notion of a source channel. Afterwards the notion of useless object types is defined.

Definition 4.1 source channel:
A channel s of a FUNSOFT net N is called a **source channel** *if the following condition holds:*

$$\bullet s = \emptyset$$

Convention 1 *$SoC(N)$ denotes the set of source channels of FUN-SOFT N.*

Definition 4.2 useless object type
Let N be a FUNSOFT net. An object type $o \in O$ is called **useless** *if the following conditions hold:*

a) $\{s \in S \mid S_T(s) = o\} \subseteq SoC(N)$

b) $\forall_{\{s \in S \mid S_T(s) = o\}} : M_0(s) = \emptyset$

The set of useless object types of a FUNSOFT N can be found out by the algorithm sketched below.

```
useless_list := empty
for each o ∈ O do
    useless := TRUE
    for each s ∈ S do
        while useless do
            if S_T(s) = o ∧ (M_0(s) ≠ ∅ ∨ s ∉ SoC(N))
            /* o is not useless if it is attached to a marked
            channel or to a channel that is no source channel */
            then useless := FALSE
        done
    done
    if useless then append(o, useless_list)
done
```

Unprocessable object types According to the existence of useless object types it is interesting to find out if there are object types for which no objects are processed. Such an object type is not per se useless since final results of a software process are intentionally not processed, but in general it is worthwhile to look at such object types in detail in order to make sure that all unprocessable object types do really correspond to final result types. A similar notion is defined in [LH89]. In [LH89] a project plan is said to be *plan complete* if all not final objects are processed by activities that contribute to the overall project goal.

An object type which is unprocessable since no objects of this type can be processed can be detected by searching for *sink channels*. A channel s_1 is called a *sink channel* if its postset is empty. If an object type is only attached to sink channels one can be sure that objects of that type are not processed at all.

Definition 4.3 sink channel:
A channel s of a FUNSOFT net N is called a **sink** **channel** *if the following condition holds:*
$$s\bullet = \emptyset$$

Convention 2 *SiC(N) denotes the set of sink channels of FUNSOFT N.*

Each sink channel should be contemplated carefully in order to be sure that it is correct that objects arriving at that channel are not processed any further. Moreover, it can be worthwhile to check if object types exist which are only attached to sink channels. Object of such object types are not processed at all.

Definition 4.4 unprocessable object type:
Let N be a FUNSOFT net. An object type $o \in O$ is called **unprocessable** *if one of the following conditions hold:*

a) o denotes a useless object type (cf. definition 4.2)

b) $\{s \in S \mid S_T(s) = o\} \subseteq SiC(N)$

If an object type is useless can be checked as sketched above. The second condition of the previous definition is checked by the following algorithm:

Let N be the FUNSOFT net which is to be examined.

```
unprocessable_list := empty
for each o ∈ O do
    unprocessable := TRUE
    for each s ∈ S do
        while unprocessable do
            if S_T(s) = o ∧ s ∉ SiC(N)
            then unprocessable := FALSE
        done
    done
    if unprocessable
    then append(o, unprocessable_list)
done
```

Infinite numbers of objects From a software process management point of view it is interesting to find out if arbitrary many versions of an object can be produced. Such a situation occurs potentially if an agency t_1 reads an object via a CO edge from a channel s_1 and if t_1 writes tokens to s_1 as well. Such situations are not necessarily faulty since there may be other agencies which read from channel s_1 via IN edges, but nevertheless they represent a potential danger, such that it is worthwhile to look at such situations in detail.

Definition 4.5 statically unbounded channel:
A channel s of a FUNSOFT net N is called **statically unbounded** *if the following condition holds:*

$$\exists f_1 = (s,t), f_2 = (t,s) \in F : F_T(f_1) = CO, F_T(f_2) = OU$$

Statically unbounded channels of a FUNSOFT nets are found by the algorithm sketched below.

```
static_unbounded_list := empty
for each s ∈ S do
    if ∃f₁ = (s,t), f₂ = (t,s) : F_T(f₁) = CO, F_T(f₂) = OU
    then begin
                statically_bounded(s) := TRUE
                append (s, static_unbounded_list)
            end
done
```

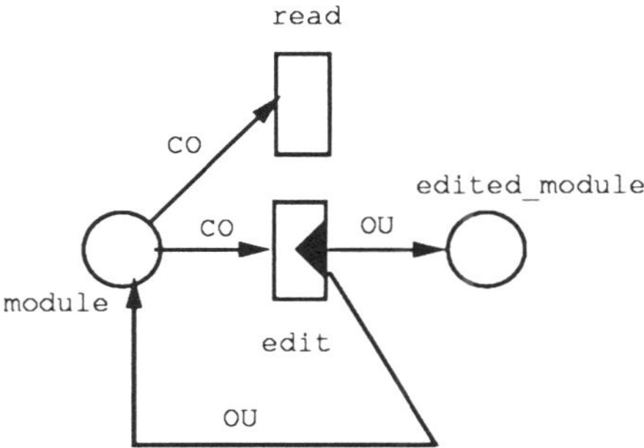

Figure 2: A statically unbounded channel

Figure 2 shows an *edit*-agency which represents the update of modules. The modules are read via a CO edge since it is supposed that the modules must be available for a *read*-agency all the time. The channel storing modules is statically unbounded, since the number of modules is only increased but never decreased.

Permanently enabled activities From a software process management point of view it is interesting to find activities that can be executed permanently. Such activities do potentially consume a lot of resources and thus, they may represent modeling faults.

Activities that can be executed permanently are represented by agencies which have an empty preset. An agency t which accesses all channels in its preset by CO or STC edges is potentially permanently enabled. When such an agency t is enabled once, it remains enabled unless another agency accesses at least one channel in $\bullet t$ by an IN or ST edge. We distinguish two kinds of such agencies. First, we consider manual agencies. Permanently enabled manual agencies are used to model activities that can be executed at any time and for which it depends on the participating software developer when they are actually executed. Thus, there are reasons for modeling permanently enabled manual agencies, but the process modeler should carefully check if there are really no restrictions concerning the execution of agencies. Second, there are automatic agencies. A permanently enabled automatic agency is a modeling fault, since a permanent activation represents a permanent production of tokens and a permanent use of resources. Potentially permanently enabled agencies are of use in very rare situations. Potentially permanently enabled agencies do often indicate that a situation has not been carefully modeled. Thus, the attention of the process modeler should be drawn to such situations in order to check if a potential permanent activation is what he really wants.

Definition 4.6 Permanently enabled agency: *Let N be a FUNSOFT net. An agency $t \in T$ is called* **permanently enabled** *if the following condition holds:*

$$\bullet t = \emptyset$$

Definition 4.7 potentially permanently enabled agency:
An agency t of a FUNSOFT net N is called **potentially permanently enabled** *if the following conditions hold:*

a) t is not permanently enabled

b) $\forall f = (s,t) \in F : F_T(f) \in \{CO, STC\}$

Permanently enabled as well as potentially permanently enabled agencies are detected by the following algorithm.

```
permanent_list := empty
potentially_permanent_list := empty
for each t ∈ T do
    if •t = ∅
    then append(t, permanent_list)
    else begin
                potentially_permanent := TRUE
                for each s ∈ •t do
                    if F_T((s,t)) ∉ {CO, STC}
                    then potentially_permanent := FALSE
                done
                if potentially_permanent
                then append(t,potentially_permanent_list)
    end
done
```

Deadlocks In software process models it is interesting to find out whether objects stored in a particular channel cannot be produced if this channel is unmarked once.

A deadlock - or siphon as it is called in [Mur89] - is a set of channels that, if it is token-free under one marking, remains token-free under all successor markings. From a software process management point of view particular deadlocks with one element are of interest, since they represent channels that must be initially marked.

The notion of deadlock is formally defined as follows.

Definition 4.8 deadlock:
*Let N be a FUNSOFT net. A not empty set of channels $S = \{s_1, \ldots, s_n\}$ is called a **deadlock** if the following condition holds*

$$\forall t \in \cup_{i \in \{1,\ldots,n\}} \bullet s_i : \{s_1, \ldots, s_n\} \cap \bullet t \neq \emptyset$$

Definition 4.9 simple deadlock:
*A deadlock SI of a FUNSOFT net N is called **simple** if the following condition holds:*
$$|SI| = 1$$

The algorithm for finding arbitrary deadlocks in a FUNSOFT net is of time complexity $\mathcal{O}(2^n)$ ($n = |S|$) since it has to check all elements of $\mathcal{P}(S)$. The algorithm is sketched in [Mur89]. Thus, we recommend to restrict the investigation of deadlocks to the search for simple deadlocks. For individual refinements of agencies it is possible to search for not simple deadlocks as well. It is particularly interesting to search for deadlocks of a certain size. The search for deadlocks with at most two elements, for example, can be done in

$$\mathcal{O}(n + \left(\begin{array}{c} n \\ 2 \end{array} \right)) = \mathcal{O}(\frac{n^2}{2}) = \mathcal{O}(n^2)$$

with $n = |S|$.

Besides the examples sketched above, other static properties are related to traps, activities' conflicts, and to the question whether FUNSOFT nets are well-structured [Gru91].

As the sketched examples of static properties show, proofs of such properties are straightforward.

Other static properties are proven on the basis of Predicate/Transition nets. For these properties we use existing tools for checking static properties of the Predicate/Transition net representation of FUNSOFT nets. An example is the tool for calculating S-invariants of Predicate/Transition nets developed by Genrich and improved by Kujansuu/Lindquist [KL84]. By using this tool we are able to show that the number of objects in a certain software process model part remains invariant.

Proving dynamic properties of FUNSOFT nets is more difficult. Generally speaking, it is necessary to consider all markings of a FUNSOFT net that can be reached form its initial marking. The values of most objects produced in a software process depend on human interaction (for example, the text of a program or of a documentation, or the names of software components). Thus, the values of objects of a FUNSOFT nets are unpredictable, they are fixed in the process itself. Therefore, the investigation of dynamic properties of a FUNSOFT net is based on examining quantitative markings of that net. In a quantitative marking only the number of objects stored in a channel are considered, but not their values. Correspondingly, the notion of quantitative coverability trees for FUNSOFT nets is defined. Each node of a quantitative coverability tree represents a quantitative marking. An edge of such a tree is labeled with the name of the agency whose firing transforms the quantitative marking represented by its source node into the quantitative marking represented by its destination node.

Due to the predefined firing behaviors of agencies that can be used in FUNSOFT nets, the abstraction from all object values causes some problems. If we revert to the example sketched above we recognize that the *link*-agency can only be fired, when channel s_4 contains as many tokens as specified by the value stored in channel s_6 (this corresponds to the *mult* input firing behavior of the *link*-job). In order to care for such situations we do not abstract from integer values read by agencies whose jobs have a *mult* input firing behavior. Thus, coverability trees for FUNSOFT nets differ from coverability trees for standard Petri nets. Figure 3 shows a cut out of the quantity restricted coverability tree of a FUNSOFT net shown in Figure 1.

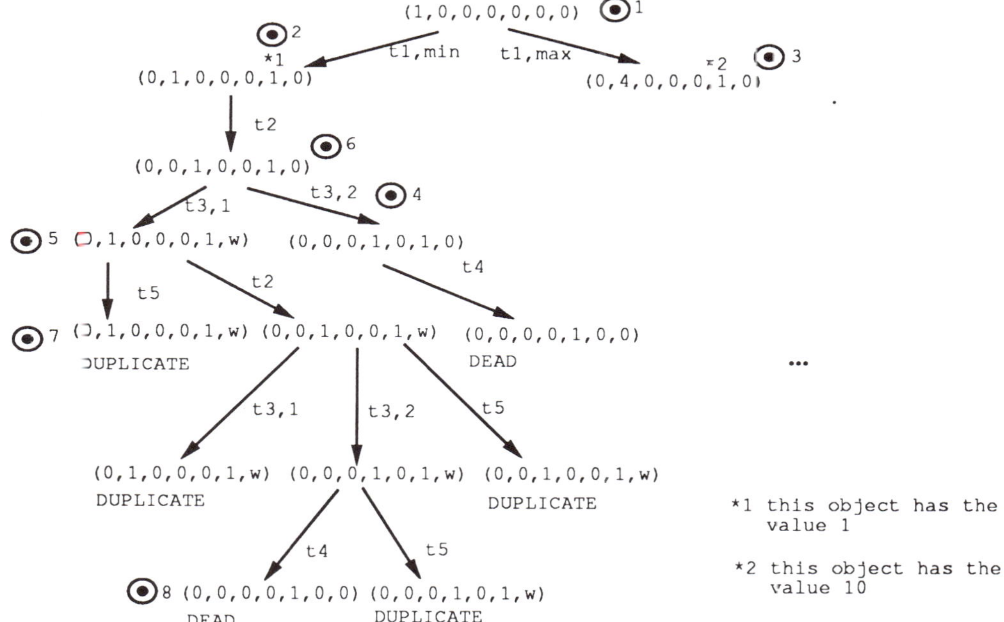

Figure 3: Quantity-restricted coverability tree for a FUNSOFT net N

The example of a coverability tree shown in Figure 3 exemplifies the following features of FUNSOFT net coverability trees:

1. If an agency with a *mult* output firing behavior is quantitative enabled, then two successor markings are generated. In the sketched example the *design*-agency has a *mult* output firing behavior. This agency is

quantitative enabled under the initial marking ($\odot$1 in Figure 3). In one of the two successor markings it is assumed that as few objects as possible are produced, in the other one it is assumed that as many objects as possible are produced. In the sketched example the minimal number is 1 ($\odot$2 in Figure 3), since no further restrictions are specified. The maximal number can be derived from the attached <mterm>. This term specifies that no more than 10 objects can be produced ($\odot$3 in Figure 3). The minimal and the maximal number of objects are stored in the coverability tree, since these values are needed for checking if agencies with a *mult* input firing behavior are quantitative enabled. In Figure 3 only the left branch of the coverability tree is described.

2. If an agency with a *det* or *some* output firing behavior is quantitative enabled, then as many successor markings are pursued as the agency has output channels. In the sketched example the *compile*-agency has a *det* output firing behavior and 2 output channels. Therefore, we pursue two successor markings ($\odot$4 in Figure 3). In one of these successor markings, the output object is written to the first output channel, in the second one the output object is written to the second output channel.

3. The first result of firing the *compile*-agency ($\odot$5 in Figure 3) is derived from its successor marking by adding a token at the second position (*modules* to be edited), by deleting a token at the third position (*modules* to be compiled), and by adding a token at the last position (*failure_reports*). The result looks as follows: $(0, 1, 0, 0, 0, 1, 1)$. This marking covers the node marked with $\odot$2. The value at the last position is actually bigger than the value at the last position of the node marked with $\odot$2. Therefore, this value is replaced by ω ($\odot$5 in Figure 3).

4. One possible successor marking of the node marked with $\odot$5 is produced by considering agency t_5. This agency represents the reading of *failure_reports*. Since the channel storing *failure_reports* is covered by ω anyway and since the arithmetic on $I\!N \cup \omega$ [Mur89] specifies that $\omega - 1 = \omega$, the successor marking ($\odot$7 in Figure 3) corresponds to the marking represented by the node marked with $\odot$5. Therefore, we reached a *DUPLICATE* end, such that we do not consider further successor markings.

5. The node marked with $\odot$8 represents a dead marking, i.e. no transition is quantitative enabled. Thus, no successor markings exist.

We use quantity restricted coverability trees for deciding about

- the deadness and liveness of agencies (corresponding to software development activities which can periodically or which cannot be activated),

- boundedness of channels (corresponding to the number of objects being in a certain state),

- the maximal number of persons that can concurrently work in a software process,

- the potential occurrence of any software process state a software process model analyst is interested in.

5   The Software Process Management Environment MELMAC

Figure 4 shows the architecture of the software process management environment MELMAC.

Within Figure 4 the boxes denote environment components (in the sense of modules [WE86]), the arrows denote a use-relationship.

All components of MELMAC are controlled by the **Control** component. This component ensures that the other components are called in an order that makes sense (the analysis component, for example, can only be called when a FUNSOFT net has been modeled, the net skeleton editor, for example, can only be called when a set of object type definitions and a set of jobs has been chosen). All components of MELMAC are integrated via a common **Window Management System** (WMS). Thereby, it is ensured that all components appear to software developers and project managers in a homogeneous way. All documents (job definitions, object type definitions, predicate definitions, FUNSOFT net skeletons, role definitions, simulation traces, execution traces, analysis results) are displayed by the **Unparser** component. The **Unparser** component displays objects by using the functions offered by the WMS. The different editors access the **Unparser** in order to display certain information.

All documents are stored in an underlying object management system namely in the **GRA**ph Storage System (GRAS for short) [LS88]. This storage system was chosen since it enables a convenient storage of graph-like structures, like FUNSOFT nets.

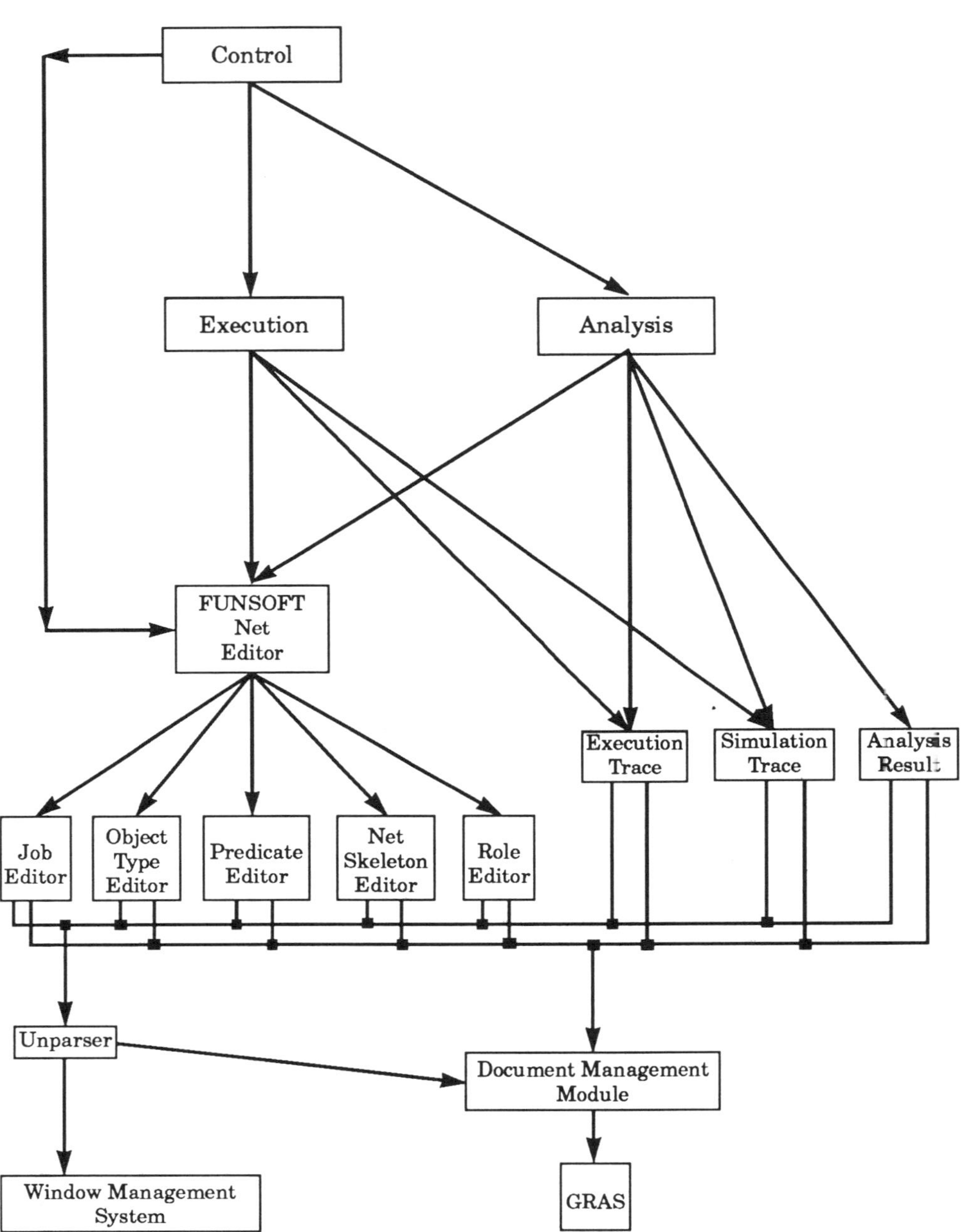

Figure 4: Architecture of MELMAC

We interfaced GRAS with an application-oriented layer which encompasses functions for storing and accessing FUNSOFT components. The interface is implemented by the **Document Management Module (DMM)**. This module provides functions for inserting, updating, and deleting FUNSOFT components in the internal representation of FUNSOFT nets. The basic data model is transformed into the application data model offered by the **Document Management Module**. This means that the data model of GRAS (directed, attributed, acyclic graphs) is transformed into the process management data model (FUNSOFT nets).

The other components of MELMAC implement the functionality of a software process management environment. In the first place, there are some editors used for editing the components of FUNSOFT nets (a **Job Editor** for jobs, a syntax-driven **Object Type Editor** for object type definitions, a **Predicate Editor** for predicates, a **Net Skeleton Editor** for net skeletons, and a **Role Editor** for roles). The **FUNSOFT Net Editor** component manages the access to the various editor facilities. In the second place, there is an **Execution** component, which is used for simulating software processes (i.e. for producing **Simulation Trace**s) and for executing software process models (i.e. guiding software developers in a software process and for producing **Execution Trace**s). In a software process the **Execution** component accesses the **Net Skeleton Editor** in order to animate the current software process state. Thus, not only software developers, but also software process managers are supported in conducting software processes.

Figure 5 sketches the architecture of the analysis component - called ANAMEL. ANAMEL is composed of two subcomponents providing validation and verification facilities. The validation component (ValC) consists of the simulator for FUNSOFT nets. The verification component (VerC) implements the verification algorithms sketched in section 4. Some of the algorithms (the ones that are based on topology checks and quantity restricted coverability trees) operate on the FUNSOFT net representation. These algorithms are implemented in the FUNSOFT Verification component (FUNSOFT VerC). Other algorithm operate upon the Pr/T net representation the FUNSOFT nets have been transformed into. These algorithms are based on the S-invariant analysis method. They are implemented in the Pr/T net Verification Component (Pr/T net VerC). The Pr/T net Verification Component is based on the tool PetSi [KL84].

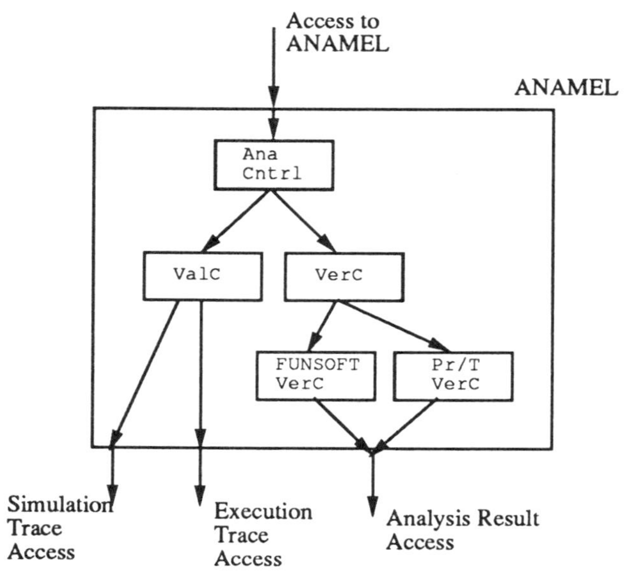

Figure 5: A refinement of the analysis component

6   MELMAC and ALF

The analysis facilities of MELMAC are exploited in the EUREKA project
ESF where the simulation facilities of MELMAC are used for validating software process models and in the ESPRIT I project ALF [BBC+89].

In ALF a software engineering environment that includes software process
modeling facilities is developed on top of PCTE [Cam88]. One major concern
of ALF is to provide assistance and guidance to all people involved in software
development [LBGD90].

In ALF the software process modeling language **MASP/DL** (Models
for **A**ssisted **S**oftware **P**rocesses/**D**escription **L**anguage) has been developed.
The MASP/DL is based on the object modeling faclities of PCTE, on a
textual description of operator types, and on a description of the ordering in
which the operator types have to be applied in terms of path expressions.

These entities build the skeleton of the software process modeling concept,
called **MASP** (Model for **A**ssisted **S**oftware **P**rocesses) and for the soft-

ware process modeling language related to this concept, called **MASP/DL** (**MASP/D**escription Language).

A MASP comprises the following components:

Object Model The object model specifies which object types are dealt with in the specified software process model. Apart from defining the object types, the relations between object types are defined as well. The object model is the object model of PCTE, based on typed entity-relationship diagrams.

Operator Types The operator types specify the names, the signatures, and the pre- and postcondition of operators that are to be carried out in the modeled software processes.

Expressions Expressions appear as part of operator types' pre- and post-conditions, rules, and characteristics. By enumerating and naming them it is possible to refer to expressions without writing them again and again.

Rules Rules describe under which conditions an operator is tried to be executed.

Orderings Orderings describe constraints of the order in which operators are executed. For specifying orderings a path expression like formalism is used.

Characteristics Characteristics describe expressions which have to be true in each state of a software process. Thus, they specify integrity constraints. Whenever a characteristic is violated all efforts are focused on making this characteristic true again.

Crucial parts of MASPs can be translated into FUNSOFT nets. Then these FUNSOFT nets are analyzed by means of the analysis component of MELMAC in order to detect problems and faults of the translated MASP. The translation of MASP components to FUNSOFT nets is described in [Gru90].

7   Conclusion

We introduced foundations of analyzing properties of software process models. Analysis of software process model properties contributes to avoiding the execution of erroneous software process models. By implementing the developed analysis concepts and by embedding the analysis tool in a software process management environment we integrate the analysis of software process models into the management of software processes. This is beyond the limits of most other software process management environments. Our current experience with the developed concepts are restricted to the analysis of academic multi-person software process models. Our future efforts will focus on the analysis of industrial software process models.

Acknowledgements:

First, I want to thank Wolfgang Deiters for his cooperation in designing MELMAC. Moreover, I want to thank the members of the MELMAC group for implementing the MELMAC environment.

The author acknowledges the contribution to this paper from all the members of the ALF consortium, who are: GIE Emeraude (France), CSC (Belgium), Computer Technologies Co. (Greece), Grupo de Mecanica del Vuelo, S.A. (Spain), International Computers Limited (United Kingdom), University of Nancy-CRIN (France), University of Dortmund-Informatik X (Germany), Cerilor (France), Université de Catholique de Louvain (Belgium) and University of Dijon-CRID (France).

References

[BBC+89] K. Benali, N. Boudjlida, F. Charoy, J.C. Derniame, C. Godart, P. Griffiths, V. Gruhn, P. Jamart, A. Legait, D.E. Oldfield, and F. Oquendo. *The Presentation of the ALF project.* In N. Madhavji, W. Schäfer, and H. Weber, editors, *Proceedings of the First International Conference on System Development Environments and Factories*, London, 1989. Pitman Publishing.

[BOSV89] C. Boarder, H. Obink, M. Schmidt, and A. Völker. *ATMO-SPHERE, Advanced Techniques and Methods of System Production in a Heterogeneous, Extensible, and Rigorous Environment.* In *Proceedings of the 1st Conference on System Development Environments and Factories Moretonhamstead UK*, May 1989.

[Cam88] I. Campbell. *Portable Common Tool Environment. Computer Standards and Interfaces*, (8), 1988.

[DG90a] W. Deiters and V. Gruhn. *Managing Software Processes in MEL-MAC.* In *Proceedings of the Fourth ACM SIGSOFT Symposium on Software Development Environments*, Irvine, California, USA,

December 1990. appeared as Software Engineering Notes, 15(6), December 1990.

[DG90b] W. Deiters and V. Gruhn. *Software Process Model Analysis Based on FUNSOFT Nets. Mathematical Modeling and Simulation,* 1990.

[Gen87] H.J. Genrich. *Predicate/Transition Nets.* In W. Brauer, W. Reisig, and G. Rozenberg, editors, *Petri Nets: Applications and Relationships to other Models of Concurrency,* volume 254 of *Lecture Notes on Computer Science.* Springer, 1987.

[Gru90] V. Gruhn. *An Approach to MASP Analysis and Assessment including an Implementation Suggestion.* ALF/UDO-VG/WP-3/5/4-D1, October 1990.

[Gru91] V. Gruhn. *Validation and Verification of Software Process Models (to appear in 1991).* PhD thesis, University Dortmund, June 1991.

[HJS89] P. Huber, K. Jensen, and R.M. Shapiro. *Hierarchies in Coloured Petri Nets.* In *Proc. of the 10th Int. Conf. on Application and Theory of Petri Nets,* Bonn, FRG, 1989.

[KFP88] G.E. Kaiser, P.H. Feiler, and S.S. Popovich. *Intelligent Assistance for Software Development and Maintenance. IEEE Software,* May 1988.

[KL84] R. Kujansuu and M. Lindquist. *Efficient Algorithms for computing S-Invariants for Predicate/Transition Nets.* In *Proc. of the 5th Int. Conf. on Application and Theory of Petri Nets,* 1984.

[LBGD90] J. Lonchamp, K. Benali, C. Godart, and J.C. Derniame. *Modeling and Enacting Software Processes : an Analysis.* In *COMPSAC90,* Chicago, Illinois, USA, November 1990.

[LH89] L. Liu and E. Horowitz. *A Formal Model for Software Project Management. IEEE Transactions on Software Engineering,* 15, October 1989.

[LS88] C. Lewerentz and A. Schuerr. *GRAS - a Management System for Graph - like Documents.* In *Proc. 3rd Int. Conf. on Data and Knowledge Bases,* Jerusalem 1988, 1988. Morgan Kaufmann Publishers Inc.

[Mur89]   T. Murata. *Petri Nets: Properties, Analysis and Applications. Proc. of the IEEE*, 77(4), April 1989.

[Per90]   D.E. Perry, editor. *Proceedings of the 6th International Software Process Workshop*, Hakodate, Japan, October 1990.

[Pet81]   J.L. Peterson. *Petri Net Theory and the modeling of systems.* Prentice-Hall, 1981.

[Rei86]   W. Reisig. *Petrinetze (in German).* Springer, 1986.

[SW88]   W. Schäfer and H. Weber. *The ESF-Profile. Handbook of Computer Aided Software Engineering*, 1988.

[TBC⁺88]   R.N. Taylor, F.C. Belz, L.A. Clarke, L. Osterweil, R.W. Selby, J.C. Wileden, A.L. Wolf, and M. Young. *Foundations in the ARCADIA Environment Architecture.* In *Proceedings of the ACM SIGSOFT/SIGPLAN Software Engineering Symposium on Practical Software Development Environments*, Boston, 1988. appeared as Software Engineering Notes, 13(5), February 1989.

[WE86]   H. Weber and H. Ehrig. *Specification of Modular Systems. IEEE Transactions on Software Engineering*, 12(7), July 1986.

6

Guiding system evolution by task engineering tools

W. Koch, K. Nagel and W. Obst
Technische Universität Berlin, REX-Projekt Sekr.:
MA07E, Straße des 17 Juni 136, D–1000 Berlin 12,
Federal Republic of Germany

1   Introduction

Software Engineering Environments are ensembles of tools that collaborate
to support software engineering manufacturing processes. In this paper we
report on some progress we made in the design and realisation of a software
development supporting toolset. It is built by extending and exploiting the
simple idea of safely triggering development tool applications by interpreting
structural descriptions based on attributed software objects. The toolset is
part of a Software Development Environment supporting activities in distributed system specification, implementation, and maintenance. The work
is based on some years experience in the realization and the use of software
configuration management tools. It is part of the ESPRIT project REX*.
The project context not only enables us to carry on ideas and concrete work
on a system building and a system maintaining toolkit, but also gives us the
opportunity to validate and extend our work in collaboration with people
from areas other than that we have been working in so far.

---

*The project REX (Reconfigurable and Extensible Parallel and Distributed Systems) is
supported by the European Economic Community under the ESPRIT II initiative.
Ten European partners from industry and university research groups are involved. The
project started in May 1989 and is to run for five years.

The second section gives a short overview on the overall working environment and identifies important project work packages.

In the third section the term, the central concept and one basic algorithm of Task Engineering is introduced and explained as a systematic, automatic, and safe support paradigm of guiding software engineering activities.

The last sections collect the tool components necessary to implement Task Engineering. By doing this those scenarios are addressed where task engineering toolkits play their role or will play it in the near future.

2   The REX Working Environment

The work presented here is embedded in the REX project and aims primarily to organize and improve the collaboration of REX tools.

REX's concern is the development of distributed soft/hardware systems. The project's appearance is coined by two areas:

Tool developing area: this encompasses work to develop methods and techniques to improve the construction and the suitable adjustment of distributed application systems.

Application area: the project concentrates on two selected demonstrator application systems, a telecommunication system and an automation system for an industrial repair shop .

Both areas are thought to influence each other during the project life time. In the first project phase of three years the demonstrators are developed in order to set up their more or less complete functionality. Furthermore the hardware constraints will be selected, clarified and built up.

In the area of *tool development* suitable methods, techniques and supporting software tools are chosen. The work in this domain derives its benefits from parts of the demonstrator's functionality in this period. Not only development of new tools but also their integration progressing in the first phase in parallel to the development of demonstrators.
In a second phase the demonstrators themselves are thought of as applications of the developed tools of the first phase. The long living distributed application systems will be reorganized and improved and even reconstructed in parts by the developed tools of the first phase.

The focus of this paper will be the tool developing area.

Many of the partners working together in the project bring in a lot of experiences successfully exploitable for the foreseen goal. But there is no doubt that improvements in software technology play a leading role. On the other hand there is a big variety of methodological domains in the software development process. So the project decided from the very beginning to concentrate to areas specifically necessary and useful for the field of distributed systems. Roughly speaking this comprises configuration management, system specification, design and analysis, and some aspects of programming.

To start with programming, the idea is not to reinvent a complete new programming paradigm, but to adapt as far as possible existing programming languages and their compilers. Much more work is dedicated to improve the initial construction of system components as well as the later reconfiguration of the running system by clear identification and description of interfaces between system parts and exploiting this extracted information by dedicated tools. It is clear that this goal only can be reached by adoption of sound software engineering principles like modularity of system realization, typed component definitions and the restriction to a simple but powerful process communication mechanism.

Up to now there are two important results. On one side an Interface Specification Language (*ISL* [Bieler et al. 90]) is defined separating reusable interface descriptions of the component types as a frame for further fine programming in the selected programming language. On the other side the descriptions of the dynamic setting up of the running system as well as its rearrangement templates while it is running can be expressed in the language *Darwin* [Dulay 90]. This is possible on the basis of programmed reusable system component types. For both languages exist compilers.

The specification, design and analysis area is characterized by a set of powerful mechanisms, ranging from *Petri nets* [Reisig 82], [Genrich 87], [Graubmann 89], [Glaser/Kneisel 89], and *CSP* [Hoare 85], [Reed 88], [Davies 89] descriptions to several other approaches dealing with specification of time behavior and time constraints. Without going into details, we are able to report that there is the general accepted tendency to bring together specification techniques by combining specification expressions of parts of the demonstrator systems behavior. This can be done by transforming those expressions from one specification language to another (e.g. some Petri net expressions to CSP and vice versa). Another approach is to collect and subsume specification components in different languages under the roof of a common system kernel specification and to describe and automatically support the procedures of correctness and consistency. For this the specification frame *Wanda* [Trescher 90] is under development. Furthermore there is ongoing work to integrate (and in this way combine) specification activities of a specific method under a common method describing and guiding toolkit (cf. [Finkelstein et al. 90]).

This project description should give the reader the impression of a variety of working domains and a big variety of supporting tools to be used within REX. There is the explicitly stated project goal to develop a common REX methodology. Therein it should easily be possible to switch between scenarios of work, phases, methods, and tools in order to appropriately construct and maintain system parts in various stages of completeness. This is in our view a challenging organizational problem of system manufacturing.

Following this goal we first try to collect mechanisms and tools which form the basis of a REX Engineering Environment (REX EE) [Koch/Nagel 90].

Before going into details it should be stressed that the heterogeneous REX tools and mechanisms force the supporting environment to support loosely coupled system bricks in most cases. While this is true in general there will be areas of concern (e.g. programming) where a tight coupling of data and tools is possible. Hopefully the number of those areas enabling an automatic configuring support will grow in the further project life time and beyond it.

Moreover the REX EE has to be an open environment in the sense that rapid integration of further tools and other system parts (e.g. document types) should easily be possible. The conclusion is that the REX EE organizational framework can only be supported by some configuring tools which are general enough and therefore based on common properties of *all* system documents and dedicated tools.

The point of main effort of our work will be the integration of tools by describing how they will be automatically triggered by a manufacturing process. That means that we restrict ourselves to a realization of a pragmatic mechanism to describe the macroscopic effects of tool applications as well as the types of software objects involved. The notion of software object in that context is an abstraction of the notion of file which is sufficient to enable the configuration process. For the time being the integration by a low abstraction of object handling is the only one. Perhaps we will adopt later on other integration mechanisms by similar abstractions concerning common user interfaces or message control [Reiss 90], [Cagan 90], [Fromme 90], [Gerety 90], [Mahler/Lampen 90].

Everybody who uses the term configuration management should be aware that this notion is highly overloaded (even in the REX context). What we mean by this is the well defined and elaborated terminology of Software Configuration Management (SCM). The same holds for the term *task* as synonym for the notion of *software development process* which sometimes resides in the process modelling research area.

We try to categorize the constituents of the REX EE into two different areas called Development Environment (DE) and Application Environment (AE). This separation mirrors the fact that the former is a Software Engineering Environment while the latter consists of a very restricted set of tools which are necessary to maintain the *running distributed application system* only.

The REX DE normally is thought to be free of hardware restrictions. A *defining* property of DE is the presence of a management system for software objects. Those objets will normally be system requirement documents, system design documents, software requirement documents, module interface descriptions, several documentations or code in source and transformed or linked form. The whole area of management informations and analysis documents also have to be considered. Those document types and the attached applicable tools (which also are software objects) can be managed either freely in old fashioned way by hand or more safely by configuring tools (like *make* [Feldman 79]) in order to safely apply SE with greater confidence in the construction process itself.

An Application Environment in general will be locally separated from the rest of tools, it normally is located on different hardware (target) platforms and has to consider hardware restrictions and performance very rigidly. It mainly serves to install, dynamically (re)configure, administer and monitor the running code. Often indispensable tools of a DE are absent (like a file system or the like). Insofar it depends heavily on the kind of application and its physical environment.

Despite the separation the DE must be aware of specific settings of the AE (e.g. cross compilers, anticipated configurations etc.). Insofar, the separation is forced by the concrete application restrictions rather than conceptual considerations. Therefore it is often the case that real existing Engineering Environments rarely consist in disjoint host and target system parts. By putting development tools into it the flexibility of the AE is considerably increased.

3   Task Engineering

In this section we give an overview of the concepts of *Task Engineering*. For a more detailed discussion see [Koch et al. 91b]. We use the term *Task Engineering* to define a common frame suitable to integrate tools which can be triggered to achieve a certain result.

All TE activities are determined by a *system description*. The system description consists basically of two parts, which are related to each other:

- the *System Model (SM)*, which is a description of the abstract architecture of the system. It seems to be appropriate to separate the information about version selection or location from the system model itself. This allows parts of the system description to be used as a system structure description by several different tools operating on it [Marzullo/Wiebe 86].

- the *Configuration Description*, which describes a concrete system, e.g. a certain variant, or a certain quality.

The system model and the configuration description is interpreted by an appropriate guiding tool (*enactor*). Enactors support and control the software manufacturing processes according to the following algorithm:
The tool interprets (*enacts*) a *system description*, *checks* which manufacturing steps are necessary, which instances of components are to be *selected* in order to manipulate a concrete system, and passes directives to appropriate "slave" tools, e.g. compilers and linkers. These tools are triggered to perform actions and produce desired results (*derived objects*). We call this systematic and automatic support of tasks and activities *Task Engineering (TE)*. We use the term *task* for a set of activities within a typical working area (*scenario*).

System models are used *on-line*, as means of directing, monitoring, and instrumenting the task. "There is no reason at all why the concept of modelling should solely be applied to the software development process. It can be applied to any activity. And it seems to be especially useful, where activities involve human-computer interaction" [Tully 89], e.g. in configuration management or maintenance activities.

We consider Task Engineering as a highly automatizable process modelling approach based not only on the system model. Other things necessary to achieve good support will be discussed later on in this section.

A good example for the enactability of a model is *make*. The system model supported by make is simple: it is "a special purpose model for describing its domain (configurations), structural properties (dependencies), and methods (build processes)"[Balzer 89]. The user is responsible for setting up the model even if there are tools to generate parts of the model (the dependencies can be derived automatically using a tool, e.g. *makedepend*). The model is interpretable by make. Based on these dependencies actions are triggered, namely if the precondition *a target does not exist or is older than a dependent* is true.

The interpreter itself does not depend on a special method. The interpreter can be used for different models. It is not developed for one special task. By passing the description of a system model to the interpreter the process of building a system can be reused, which "is of greater importance than product reuse", as Tully emphasized in [Tully 89]. As a special and ideal case make does not need human interaction after the system model is created. The whole task can be performed automatically. This is not possible for all imaginable tasks. Consider as an example, the dependency between the documentation and the actual realization of a program: every time, the program has been updated, it might be necessary to update the documentation. This is usually a task, which cannot be performed automatically. But in such a case, we think, at least a reminder service could be helpful.

In order not to mix the work of such "slave" tools and the configuring work performed by the guiding tools (*enactors*) we distinguish between *inner* and *outer* properties of software objects, respectively.

Information about outer properties is stored within attributes attached to software objects residing in an *Attributed File System* ([Lampen/Mahler 88] and [Fralle 90b] see below). While inner properties, e.g. the contents of a source file, are evaluated by tools like compilers and linkers, an enactor of a system model deals only with outer properties stored in attributes. Such attributes contain information about the software objects, e.g.:

quality information like state information *published*, or reported not yet fixed bugs, etc.,

organizational information like the name of the author, or owner, etc.,

history information like version number,

derivation information is attached to derived objects containing information about *how* a derived object has been generated, *which* tools has been used, *which* flags have been passed to those tools, etc.

We use the attributes for different purposes, e.g.:

selection of a concrete instance of an entity, e.g. version 8.3 of foo.c. or last version of bar.c with state *published*,

checking whether or not eventually existing derived objects are *up to date*, which might mean that all of their dependents are older or the derived objects bear appropriate attributes.

We now try to identify those parts that are important for task engineering.
The following picture gives an idea of the essential elements for TE:

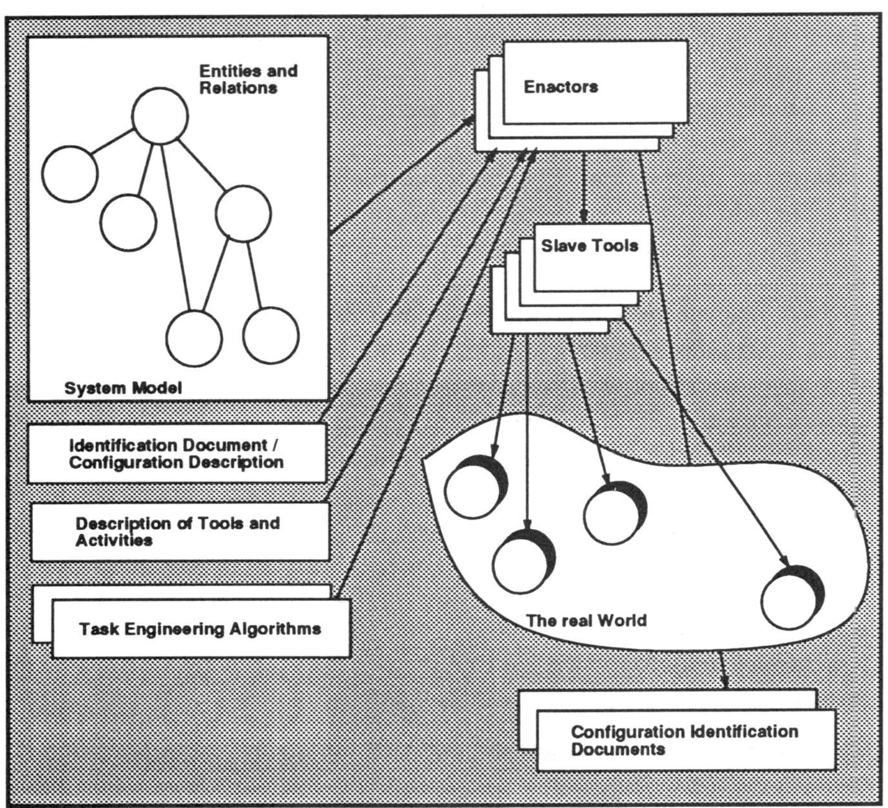

Essential Elements of Task Engineering

These are – in our opinion – the essential parts necessary for TE activities. All activities are determined by the system model, which is a description of the abstract architecture of the system. One or more interpreters are
necessary to enact a model. Each interpreter may have its own view upon
the model. The system model itself consists of so-called *entities*. An entity
may be an abstract *thingee* [Notkin 89], which serves to structure the model,
or represent one or more real world objects. An entity is determined by
the view of the respective enactor. Concrete instances of entities are identified via attributes. *Configuration Identification Documents* describe concrete and bound instances of the system (cf. *bound configuration threads* in
DSEE [Leblang/Chase 84]), [Leblang/McLean 85]. Such configuration identification documents serve to store the information necessary for building a

system, rather than the system itself.

The enactors are parametrizable by TE algorithms in order to define their behaviour within different scenarios. The description of tools and activities serves to enable the enactor(s) to trigger tools in a reliable and safe way.

We developed a language – TELan [Koch et al. 91a] – to be able to describe these parts of TE (see below).

3.1 Task Engineering Algorithms

Different TE algorithms are defineable by combining predefined and/or user written functions. Splitting the functionality of TE enactors into different functions gives the user the possibility to define own algorithms for different purposes. Furthermore, some of these functions can be used in different contexts, if they have been designed carefully. E.g. the function for the selection of concrete software objects can be used by a system building tool, a system model browser, and a retrieval tool operating on the object base.

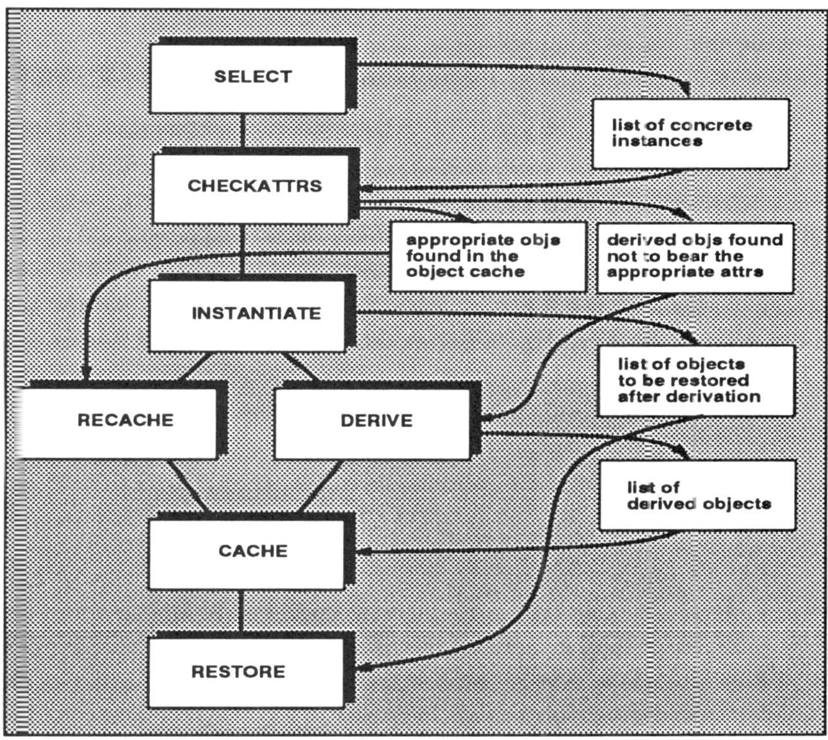

The Basic TE Algorithm for System Building

The picture above sketches the basic algorithm – essentially the algorithm used by shape [Mahler/Lampen 88] – for system building using some of our predefined functions. The select function identifies the concrete instances to be used for system building, e.g. appropriate versions of source files. Check-attrs determines both the objects which are out of date and appropriate – eventually existing – derived objects residing in the derived object cache. If objects have been found to be out of date the concrete instances necessary for derivation are installed and the current user environment is saved by the function instantiate. After this, the necessary derivations or restorations from the derived object cache are performed by derive and recache, respectively. The work is finished by caching the newly derived objects – in order to avoid recompilations – and restoring the former user environment.

In order to give a more complex example, consider the scenario *bug fixing*. Basically, when a bug has been reported, the corresponding release has to be regenerated, the bug has to be fixed, patches have to be generated and to be attached to the sources as attributes. We support this with two functions:

restorerelease restores all objects that constitute a certain release. A release is identified either by an unique symbolic name or by a configuration identification document.

attachpatches generates the differences between original and changed objects (e.g. using the UNIX command *diff(1)*) and stores them as attributes of the respective objects within the object base.

Between these two functions human actions are necessary, for bug fixing usually cannot be performed automatically. Of course, for this step the system building algorithm presented above can be used.

Up to now the predefined basic functions comprise:

select operates on the system model and interprets a selection rule. The function delivers a list of concrete instances of source entities. All attributes are possible candidates to be used for identification.

checkattrs checks whether or not derived objects are up to date, in that sense that it checks if they bear the appropriate attributes; generates both a list of all objects found not to be up to date and a list of objects found in the derived object cache.

checkmtime checks whether or not a derived object is younger than all of its dependents; generates a list of all objects found not to be up to date.

instantiate has as input the list of concrete instances delivered by the select function; saves the current working versions, instantiates these objects, and generates a list of objects to be restored in order to be able to reconstruct the user environment.

derive performs the necessary actions to derive those objects found by a check function not to be up to date.

recache retores the objects found by checkattrs in the derived object cache.

cache is used to store the derived objects into the derived object cache a special pool for storing derived objects to avoid recompilations and mark it with all necessary information to reuse it instead of recreating t.

restore reconstructs the user environment.

attributes delivers both names and values of attributes of objects; this function is necessary to be able to mark derived objects with a set of attributes of their dependents in order to be able to identify them uniquely. Such attributes are for example: name, version, state, etc. *attributes* is used mainly within the definition of derivation rules.

dependents delivers a list of all dependents of an object.

Wth these functions it is possible both to emulate classical system building tools, e.g. *make, shape* and to define a new problem specific behaviour of the eractor. The functionality of *make* can easily be achieved by using the functions *checkmtime* and *derive*.

Of course, the basic functions above are not sufficient for all tasks we want to support. The extension of the list of functions described in this section will be part of future work. Especially, functions to check different kinds of relations between entities, e.g. a function that checks whether or not the implementation meets the requirements of the interface specification.

4   Realization of Task Engineering in the REX EE

The idea of TE arose by designing, implementing and working with the *shape toolkit* for software configuration management support. The *shape* approach makes it possible to have sufficiently integrated tools for engineering software configurations while retaining the flexibility of the basic toolbox philosophy, permitting the use of *off-the-shelf* tools, e.g. editors or compilers.

The shape toolkit consists of an object base for attributed software objects, a version control system and shape, a significantly enhanced *make* program.

The configuration process of *shape* is controlled by four basic components:

- system description,

- selection rules,

- transformation rules and

- variant definitions.

Shape operates on software objects in the object base rather than UNIX[†] files. When building a certain configuration, shape searches the object base for appropriate versions of a software object, installs them temporarily as UNIX files, eventually invokes some of standard tools (e.g. C compiler) on them, and stores the resulting derived objects in the object base.

Besides the development of and the experience with the shape toolkit, several other systems dealing with SCM have been evaluated, e.g.:
Adele [Estublier et al. 84], [Estublier 85], [Estublier/Belkhatir 86],
BUILD [Robbins 85], [Waters 88],
Cedar [Lampson/Schmidt 83], [Swinehart/Zellweger 86],
Crystal [Alperin/Kedzierski 87],
DSEE [Leblang/Chase 84], [Leblang/McLean 85], [APOLLO 85],
Gandalf [Haberman/Kaiser 82], [Haberman/Notkin 86], [Kaiser/Krueger 86], [Staudt et al. 86],
Jasmine [Marzullo/Wiebe 86],
make [Feldman 79], [Fowler 85], [Hume 87], [Feldman 88],
and *Odin* [Clemm 76], [Clemm 84], [Clemm 86], [Clemm 88].
The evaluation results (cf. [Brüning et al. 90]) – especially with regard to their functionality and their linguistic expressions – influenced both the basic concepts of TE and the requirements on TE tools and engineering environments.

The underlying concepts of the *shape* toolkit and the other mentioned systems and their functionality will be *generalized* and *instrumented*. In this process, the deduced principles of TE and the concepts for an engineering environment (e.g. a REX EE) supervised by TE tools are discussed in the

---

[†] UNIX is a registered trademark of UNIX System Laboratories in the USA and other countries.

previous sections. In the following we will describe the tools and prototypes which under development and will constitute a REX EE prototype.

4.1   The Enactors

We see the necessity to realize the REX EE as a Software Engineering support system which not only is a collection of tools but also serves to improve and *automatize* the *correct* and *safe* use of those tools within several software manufacturing processes.

In this context a software manufacturing process is supported and controlled by enactors. As mentioned earlier we provide a set of enactor functions, allowing to build enactors with different functionality.

There exist prototype implementations of enactors for several manufacturing processes, e.g. *system building, maintenance* and *bug fixing*.

The TE browser is a further enactor under development. It serves to navigate through the system model and the object management system using a graphical representation.

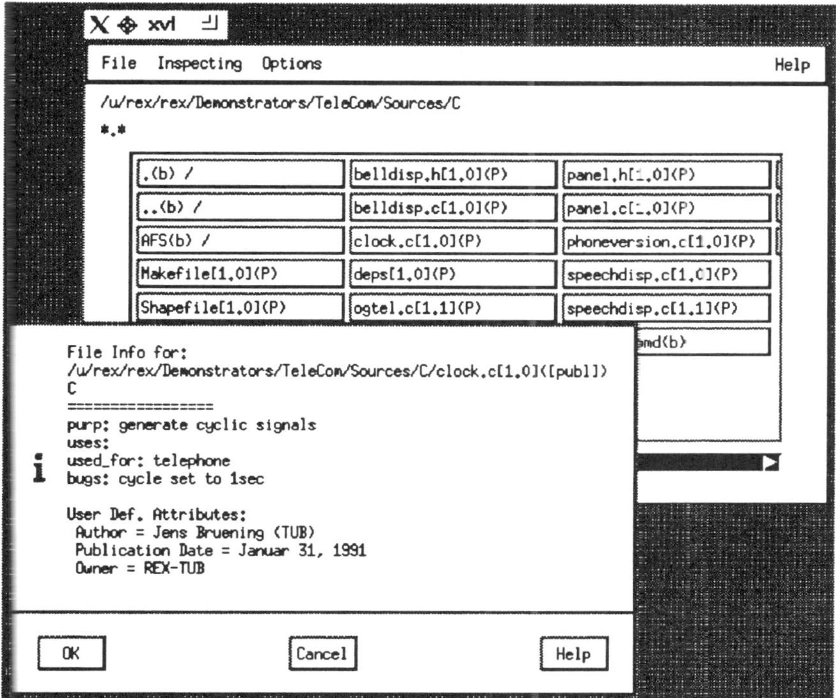

Browsing through the Object Base

Moreover the TE browser serves as an user interface for the REX EE. Based on the system model the different views upon the system model are supported, depending on the selected scenario. E.g. in the specification scenario, only component specifications constituting a system specification are visible. Something similar holds for other scenarios. Moreover, it is possible – depending on a chosen refinement step – to see all entities which constitute a component or all versions and variants of a component. In each case the view upon the system is independent of the directory structure of the underlying file system. Furthermore the TE browser offers – depending on the chosen view and the chosen refinement step – a set of tools which are able to manipulate the components (or entities) and the software objects, respectively.

The Task Engineering Language TELan

The declarative language *TELan* is suitable to deal with all aspects concerning TE activities. TELan offers features to describe both the structure of an application system and the information necessary to guide and assist the process of building configurations in different scenarios in a uniform way.

Both parts of the system description namely the system model and the configuration description are conceptually separated. This is in order to make it possible for different enactors to use to same model as an abstract system srtucture description.

TELan comprises features to describe:

- the structural aspects of a system by using entities and relations,

- definition of new relations between entities of the system,

- derivation rules including "slave" tool application descriptions,

- declarations of the entities,

- functions, e.g. to check relations or to generate a part of the system model itself,

- activities to be performed, if the system or a part of the system is out of date,

- selection rules to identify an instance of an entity (e.g. a certain version of an object).

4.2 The Object Management System

TE tools work on *software objects* only, the underlying concept of which is a generalization of the file concept. Software objects reside in an object management system (*AtFS*) which is an extension of the UNIX file system and allows to fix any number of attributes to software objects.

The principal structures in the object management system are *object histories*, *object versions* and *derived objects*. An object history is a set of subsequent revisions of a *conceptual object* (e.g. program module, documentation, graphics, papers etc.) that result from saving multiply the contents of a conceptual object's busy version. The busy version is a regular UNIX file that can be manipulated by any program that operates on files (e.g. editors, formatters, compilers, linkers etc.). Unlike the busy version, object versions are immutable.

Each object in the storage system is a complex of contents and associated attributes. These objects are called *attributed software objects*. Derived objects reside in a part of the object base which is called derived object cache.

AtFS allows to uniformly access files as well as versions stored in archive files. The object management system predefines a small set of standard attributes, but it can also maintain an arbitrary set of user defined attributes.

The build-in version control system allows storage, retrieval, locking and identification of revisions of source objects as well as multiple instances of derived objects.

4.3 The *slave* Tools

In order to be able to define relevant scenarios (working areas) a first step will be to collect all existing tools and those prototypes under development and to classify them for later arrangement.

General Tools for Structure transforming and changing

This category typically include dedicated text and graphical editors, formatters and browsers.

Tools in the Specification Context

In this area, the *Wanda* compiler under developing could play a very important role.

With the aid of the specification language Wanda it is possible to describe the overall structure of a system specification.

Other important tools of this working area are simulators (e.g. *OOPS* an object oriented Petri net simulator), checkers and visualization tools (e.g. the *Visualizer*,a graphical representation tool designed to support the interpretation of extracted data from analysis tools used during the system specification; in the REX context the main application field of the Visualizer will be the support of the OOPS simulator [Glaser 90]).

Tools supporting the Implementation and Linking Process

The internal structure of an application system is described using a separate explicit configuration language (cf. [Magee et al. 90]). *Darwin* is a configuration programming language developed in the REX project. Programs written in this language can be considered as a set of hierarchically structured and interacting component instances. Two kinds of components are manipulated by Darwin, program components, and configuration components. The interfaces of all kinds of components are described in a uniform manner, as a collection of ports (interaction points).

Components have well defined interfaces specified by the Interface Specification Language. The ISL supports two types of units: components and type units.

The functionality of a component may be implemented in a range of programming languages (e.g. C, C++, Modula 2, etc.) however interaction with other components utilizes communication primitives supplied by the REX runtime system.

Further tools which are supported by the enactors in this area are: implementation language compilers, checkers and linkers.

Tools supporting the Application System

One main topic in the REX project are distributed application systems which can be dynamically reconfigured or extended during their runtime. Therefore configuration managers or configuration agents are available to do that job.

Those tools serve for automatic creation of a consistent state (configuration) of the application system, depending on structural description of the application system and the view onto that structure.

Other tools in this area are dynamic configuration support, selection, monitoring and down loading tools.

5   Outlook

With respect to the project objectives we will exploit at least the following scenarios in which we will apply our TE approach:

- System development and managing process.

- System configuration and dynamic reconfiguration process.

- System maintenance, product and release administration.

Due to the central role of a system model one of the most important requirements is to be able to write safely and simple system descriptions. It is an extremely difficult task to find out, what went wrong, when the system does not yield the expected results and the error is within the model. Even concepts of debugging facilities for the enaction of a system model are not known to us.

One possibility to solve this problem might be a tool to write/generate system models based on a library of model templates, default definitions and standards [Pralle 90a].

We currently evaluate the concepts given in this paper with first prototype tools operating primarily in the system building scenario.

6   Acknowledgement

We gratefully acknowledge the CEC in the Esprit Project REX (2080) for their financial support.

References

[Alperin/Kedzierski 87]   L.B. Alperin, B.I. Kedzierski: *AI-Based Software Maintenance*, IEEE AI Applications Conference, February 87.

[APOLLO 85]   APOLLO: *Domain Software Engineering Environment (DSEE) Reference*, Apollo Computer Inc., July 1985.

[Balzer 89]   R. Balzer: *Process Programming: Passing into a new Phase*, ACM Sigsoft Software Engineering Notes, Volume 14, No. 4, Representing and Enacting the Software Process, Proceedings of the 4th International Software Process Workshop, ACM Press, pp. 43-45, Moretonhampstead, Devon, UK, June 1989.

[Bieler et al. 90]   F. Bieler (editor): *The REX Interface Specification Language*, ESPRIT 2080, Internal Paper, REX-WP2-GMD-035-V1.0, July 1990.

[Brüning et al. 90]   J. Brüning, D. Frädrich, W. Koch, K. Nagel, W. Obst, U. Pralle: *Evaluation of Task Engineering Tools*, ES-PRIT 2080, Internal Paper REX-WP1-TUB-012-V1.C, April 1990.

[Cagan 90]   M. R. Cagan, *The HP SoftBench Environment: An Architecture for a New Generation of Software Tools*, Hewlett Packard Journal, June 1990.

[Clemm 76]   G. M. Clemm. The Odin System: An Object Manager for Extensible Software Environments. *Phd. Thesis at the University of Colorado at Boulder)*, 1976.

[Clemm 84]   G. M. Clemm. Odin - an Extensible Software Environment Report and User's Reference Manual. *Technical Report, CU-CS-262-84)*, 1984.

[Clemm 86]   G. M. Clemm: *The Odin System: An Object Manager for Extensible Software Environments*, CU-CS-314-86, The University of Colorado, February 1986.

[Clemm 88]   G. M. Clemm. The Odin Specification Language. *Proceedings of the International Workshop on Software Version and Configuration Control*, 1988.

[Davies 89]   J.W. Davies, S.A. Schneider: *An Introduction to Timed CSP*, Oxford University Programming Research Group Technical Monograph 75, 1989.

[Dulay 90]   N. Dulay: *A Configuration Language for Distributed Programming*, Ph.D. Thesis, Imperial College, London University, 1990.

[Estublier et al. 84]   J. Estublier, S. Ghoul, and S. Krakowiak. Preliminary Experience with a Configuration Control Program for Modular Programs. *Proceedings of the ACM SIG-SOFT/SIGPLAN Software Engineering Symposium on Practical Software Development Environments SIGPLAN Notices*, 19, 5:149–156, April 1984.

[Estublier 85] J. Estublier: *A configuration Manager: The Adele Database of Programs*, GTE Laboratories, Workshop on Software Engineering for Programming-in-the-Large, pp. 140-147, 1985.

[Estublier/Belkhatir 86] J. Estublier and N. Belkhatir. Experience with a Database of Programs. *Proceedings of the ACM SIG-SOFT/SIGPLAN Software Engineering Symposium on Practical Software Development Environments SIGPLAN Notices*, 22, 1:84–91, December 1986.

[Feldman 79] S. I. Feldman: *MAKE - A Program for Maintaining Computer Programs*, Software - Practice and Experience, Vol. 9, No. 3, pp. 255-265, March 1979.

[Feldman 88] S. I. Feldman: *Evolution of MAKE,* Proceedings of the International Workshop on Software Version and Configuration Control, pp. 413-416, B.G. Teubner, Grassau, West-Germany, January 1988.

[Finkelstein et al. 90] A. Finkelstein, M. Goedicke, J. Kramer: *Methods and Viewpoints in Requirements Engineering,* in Proceedings of 2nd METEOR Workshop on Methods for Formal Specification, to be published by LNCS, (Springer Verlag).

[Fowler 85] G. S. Fowler: *A Fourth Generation Make,* Proceedings of the USENIX Summer Conference, pp. 159-174, USENIX asc., Portland, Or., June 1985.

[Fromme 90] B. D. Fromme: *HP Encapsulator: Bridging the Generation Gap,* Hewlett Packard Journal, June 1990.

[Genrich 87] H. Genrich: *Advances in Petri Nets 1986,* Lecture Notes in Computer Science Vol. 254 / Vol. 255, Springer Verlag, 1987.

[Gerety 90] C. Gerety, *A New Generation of Software Development Tools,* Hewlett Packard Journal, June 1990.

[Glaser/Kneisel 89] M. Glaser, P. Kneisel: *About Specification and Modelling with Petri Nets –* Position Paper, ESPRIT 2080 Internal Paper REX-WP1-UKA-002-V1.0, October 1989.

[Glaser 90] M. Glaser: *The Visualizer: A Graphical Representation Tool,* ESPRIT 2080, Internal Paper. REX-WP4-UKA-017-V1.0, November 1990.

[Graubmann 89] P. Graubmann: *Behavioural Specification of Concurrent Systems –* Position Paper, ESPRIT 2080 Internal Paper REX-WP1-SIE-001-V1.0, October 1989.

[Haberman/Kaiser 82] A. N. Haberman and G. E. Kaiser An Environment for System Version Control. *Dig. Papers Spring Compcon,* November 1982.

[Haberman/Notkin 86]   A. N. Haberman, D. Notkin: *Gandalf: Software Development Environments,* IEEE Transactions on Software Engineering, pp. 1117-1128, December 1986.

[Hoare 85]   C.A.R. Hoare: *Communicating Sequential Processes,* Prentice-Hall International 1985.

[Hume 87]   A. Hume: *Mk: A Successor to Make,* Proceedings of the USENIX Summer Conference, pp. 159-174, USENIX asc., Portland, Or., June 1985.

[Kaiser/Krueger 86]   G. E. Kaiser and C. W. Krueger. *Using the New Gandalf System.* Department of Computer Science, Carnegie-Mellon University, Pittsburgh, August 1986.

[Koch/Nagel 90]   W. Koch, K. Nagel: *Proposal for a REX Engineering Environment - REX EE,* ESPRIT 2080, Internal Paper REX-GEN-TUB-018-V1.0, December 1990.

[Koch et al. 91a]   W. Koch, K. Nagel, W. Obst: *TELan - A Language for Engineering Tasks,* submitted for publication to the 3rd European Software Engineering Conference (ESEC 91) Milano, Italy, 21-24 October 1991.

[Koch et al. 91b]   W. Koch, K. Nagel, W. Obst: *Advancing Software Configuration Management to Task Engineering,* submitted for publication to the 1st International Conference on the Software Process, 21-22 October 1991, Los Angeles, California, USA.

[Lampen/Mahler 88]   A. Lampen, A. Mahler: *An Object Base for Attributed Software Objects,* Proc. of the Fall 1988 EUUG Conference, European Unix systems User Group, Lisbon, Portugal, October 1988.

[Lampson/Schmidt 83]   B. W. Lampson, E. E. Schmidt: *Organizing Software in a Distributed Environment,* Proceedings of SIGPLAN 33 Symposium on Programming Language Issues in Software Systems, San Francisco, June 1983.

[Leblang/Chase 84]   D. B. Leblang, R. P. Chase: *Computer-Aided Software Engineering in a Distributed Workstation Environment,* Proceedings of the ACM SIGSOFT/SIGPLAN Software Engineering, Symposium on Practical Software Development Environments, SIGPLAN Notices, Vol. 19, No. 5, pp. 104-113, ACM, Pittsburgh, PA., April 1984

[Leblang/McLean 85]   D. B. Leblang, G. D. McLean, Jr.: Configuration Management for Large-Scale Software Development Efforts, GTE

Laboratories, Workshop on Software Engineering Environments for Programming-in-the-Large, Harwichport, Massachusets, pp. 122-127, June 1985

[Mahler/Lampen 88]   A. Mahler, A. Lampen: *An Integrated Toolset for Engineering Software Configurations.* Software Engineering Notes, Vol. 13, No. 5, pp. 191-200, ACM Press, Boston, Mass., November 1988.

[Mahler/Lampen 90]   A. Mahler, A. Lampen: *Integrating Configuration Management into a Generic Environment,* Proceedings of the Fourth ACM SIGSOFT Symposium on Software Development Environments (Irvine), ACM SIGSOFT Software Engineering Notes, vol. 15, no. 6, pp. 229-237, December 1990.

[Magee et al. 90]   J. Magee, J. Kramer, M. Sloman, N. Dulay: *An Overview of the REX Software Architecture,* Second IEEE Computer Society Workshop on Future Trends of Distributed Computing Systems, Cairo, Egypt, October 1990.

[Marzullo/Wiebe 86]   K. Marzullo, D. Wiebe: *Jasmine: A Software System Modelling Facility,* Proceedings of the ACM SIGSOFT/SIGPLAN Software Engineering, Symposium on Practical Software Development Environments, SIGPLAN Notices, Vol. 22, No. 1, pp 121-130, ACM, Palo Alto, California, December 1986.

[Notkin 89]   D. Notkin: *Enacting the Models,* ACM Sigsoft Software Engineering Notes, Volume 14, No. 4, Representing and Enacting the Software Process, Proceedings of the 4th International Software Process Workshop, ACM Press, pp. 23-26, Moretonhampstead, Devon, UK, June 1989.

[Pralle 90a]   U. Pralle: *Driving the Software Release Process with Shape,* Proceedings of the Fall 1990 EUUG Conference, European Unix Systems User Group, pp. 27-38, Nice, France, October 1990.

[Pralle 90b]   U. Pralle: *AtFS - The shape Version Control System. Programmer's and User's Guide,* ESPRIT 2080, Internal Paper REX-GEN-TUB-017-V1.0, November 1990.

[REX-TA 89]   REX Project: *REX Technical Annex,* ESPRIT 2080, European Economic Commission, March 1989.

[Reed 88]   G.M. Reed: *A Uniform Mathematical Theory for Real-time Distributed Computing,* Oxford University, D.Phil Thesis, 1988.

[Reisig 82]   W. Reisig: *Petri-Netze: Eine Einführung*, Springer Verlag, 1982.

[Reiss 90]   S. P. Reiss: *Connecting Tools using Message Passing in the Field Program Development Environment*, IEEE Software, vol. 7, no. 4, pp. 57-66, IEEE Computer Society, July 1990.

[Robbins 85]   R. E. Robbins. *BUILD: A Tool for Maintaining Consistency in Modular Systems*. MIT Artificial Intelligence Laboratory, November 1985.

[Staudt et al. 86]   B. J. Staudt, C. W. Krueger, A. N. Habermann, and V. Ambriola. *The Gandalf System Reference Manuals*. Department of Computer Science, Carnegie-Mellon University, Pittsburgh, August 1986.

[Swinehart/Zellweger 86]   D. C. Swinehart, P. T. Zellweger et al.: *A Structural View of the Cedar Programming Environment*, ACM Transactions on Programming Languages and Systems, pp. 419-490, October 1986.

[Trescher 90]   J. Trescher: *Declarative Specification of Parallel Time-Critical Systems*, ESPRIT 2080, Internal Paper REX-WPI-GMD-037-V1.0, December 1990.

[Tully 89]   C. J. Tully: *Introduction*, ACM Sigsoft Software Engineering Notes, Volume 14, No. 4, Representing and Enacting the Software Process, Proceedings of the 4th International Software Process Workshop,, ACM Press, pp. 3-4, Moretonhampstead, Devon, UK, June 1989.

[Waters 88]   R. C. Waters: *Automated Software Management Based on Structural Models*, Software - Practice and Experience, pp. 931-955, October 1988.

Part 2

Invited Speaker

7

Software development environments research projects in the United States

Leon Osterweil
Department of Information and Computer Science,
University of California at Irvine, Irvine, California 92717, USA

ABSTRACT

This talk describes a representative set of research efforts in the United States that are aimed at developing prototype software development environments. The talk will summarize projects supported by the United States government (principally Darpa — the Defense Advanced Research Projects Agency) and by the private sector. The talk will address both technical and organizational aspects of these projects. It will then attempt to indicate how the projects relate to each other, identifying significant ways in which they are similar and in which they differ.

Key Darpa-sponsored projects will include Arcadia, Stars, and Prototech. Key private-sector projects will included Hewlett-Packard's SoftBench project, and the Software Designer's Associate project, being carried out by sda, Inc. Key coordinates along which these projects will be compared and contrasted include process as an integrating theme, control integration through message passing and notification, approaches to data interoperability, and user interfaces uniformity efforts.

1   Project Summaries

1.1   Stars

The Stars project is a collaboration among three prime contractors and approximately 20 subcontractors aimed at building a software development environment featuring 1) superior integration of tools, 2) exploitation of proactive software processes and 3) support for reuse of software components and processes. The first Stars prototype capabilities are to be beta-tested on selected production projects in late 1993. Stars is supported by Darpa ard it is expected that other Darpa-sponsored environment projects such as Arcadia and Prototech will provide Stars with relevant advanced software technology.

1.2   Arcadia

The Arcadia project is carrying out parallel research in five environment infrastructure areas, is coordinating these research thrusts through the development of environment prototypes, and is evaluating this work by using the prototypes to integrate tools in support of Ada language processing and testing and analysis. The five infrastructure areas being explored by Arcadia are: 1) environment architecture, 2) software process, 3) object management, 4) user interfaces, and 5) measurement and evaluation.

It is expected that, within the next several months, Arcadia will have produced a prototype process-centered environment. This environment will integrate comprehensive testing and analysis tools on a very ambitious scale. It will also support software requirements analysis, design, coding in Ada, and limited management and configuration control functions. These capabilities will be directed by a process program. The tools supporting them will be integrated through advanced object management capabilities. The process will be monitored by flexible process measurement facilities, which will feed their measurements back to support process adjustment and improvement. User interface to this environment will be highly flexible and dynamically modifiable.

1.3   Prototech

The Prototech project focuses primarily upon support for the rapid prototyping of software. A major focus of the project is research into languages to support rapid creation of prototype systems. Another major focus, however, is on development of an environment capable of supporting development of systems using that language, and rapid alteration and improvement of those systems. Prototech is a collaboration among five research teams.

The Prototech environment development effort will explore the creation of an environment designed specifically to facilitate creation of prototypes. It will be developed, moreover, as a rapid prototyping activity. It will start with the rapid assembly of existing environment components, and progress by iterative improvement of the components and their integration mechanisms.

Prototech environments will feature: 1) support for multiple languages, 2) powerful Module Interface Facility (MIF) capabilities for integrating environment componentry, 3) support for multiple prototyping processes, 4) powerful measurement and evaluation capabilities, and 5) advanced intelligent editing features.

1.4   SoftBench

The SoftBench project at Hewlett-Packard Corporation has produced a tool integration facility that is seeing use in the integration of commercially available tools. It seems to be an excellent example of a direction that leading-edge CASE vendors might well take in making their tools more amenable to successful integration with each other.

SoftBench exploits a message passing system centered around a broadcast message server whose job is to assure that systemwide events of interest are passed on to tools wishing to know about them. An advantage of the broadcast message server approach is that existing tools can usually be encapsulated to send and receive messages about events. Existing tools can then be integrated into environments with relative little need to modify them. Further, this approach facilitates dynamic alteration of event notification patterns facilitating the alteration of modes of interaction among tools, and therefore the behavior of the toolset and environment.

SoftBench is based upon ideas demonstrated by the Field environment prototype developed by Reiss at Brown University.

1.5   Software Designer's Associate

Software Designer's Associate is being built by researchers at sda, Inc., supported by a consortium headed by Software Research Associates. The goal of this project is to build a process-based environment in which workers are given maximum latitude in selection of tasks that they will perform, but maximum support by tools that might of be use. Processes are designed to be permissive, rather than prescriptive or proscriptive.

2   Analysis of these Projects

These project are most interesting, perhaps, because of certain salient similarities. The talk will identify some of these similarities in an effort to highlight emerging trends in software environment development and architecture.

2.1   Consortium Approach

Virtually all of these projects are being carried out by teams of researchers. There seems to be a tacit assumption that environment development is a very large activity that requires large quantities of resources — both financial and intellectual. Diverse areas of computer science are being synthesized in these projects, necessitating large and diverse teams. Accordingly, there is a correspondingly large amount of effort going into team building and coordination. Often this is at the expense of actual research and development.

2.2   Software Process

Most of these projects are based upon the assumption that some sort of explicit representation of software development processes should be used as a guide to the effective integration of tools and other resources into an environment. Degrees of formality and rigor in process representation vary, but this theme seems nearly universal. Environments are increasingly seen as devices for interpreting and enacting software processes defined by means of formalisms. Increasingly environments are also being thought of as vehicles for developing these process definitions.

2.3   Control Integration

There is a great deal of interest in using message passing among separately compiled modules to control the flow of information and control in these environments. Some message passing is done directly between modules, but increasingly dispatchers and message routing modules are being used to control intermodule communication. This approach facilitates environment flexibility and extensibility to accommodate tools not originally designed as part of the environment. Languages for describing sequences of stimuli and responses are appearing, and promise to bridge this work to software process work.

2.4   Data Integration Frameworks

Interest in software process is inextricably intertwined with interest in software products. Indeed, it is impossible to define software processes without also defining the software products that they produce as final and intermediate products. Thus, these environments generally address the need to define software objects as instances of types, convey these objects between tools, and store the objects in repositories. There is considerable interest in such technical issues as type systems, data interoperability at the symbolic and representation level, and flexibility in repository schemas.

2.5   User Interfaces

In closing it seems important to indicate at least one technical area which is not currently attracting widespread interest — but which should. It is surprising that there is a striking lack of interest in user interfaces. These projects seem to understand that the success of an environment hinges pivotally on the ability of its users to understand the state of the development project, and the role that users are expected to play. On the other hand, most of the projects are not focussing on facilitating user understanding through effective and uniform user interfaces.

3   Conclusion

There is a very great deal of interest in software environment research in the United States. The projects highlighted here were selected to be representative, but certainly not exhaustive. This selection, however, indicates that there is a significant amount of consensus about what the key architectural features of environment must be, and about key technical issues to be addressed in supporting them.

The amount of agreement about environment architecture issues seems to have grown steadily over the past several years, suggesting a maturation of software environments as a research area.

Part 3

Reference Models

8

Using a reference model for CASE frameworks to describe PCTE+

Anthony Earl
Software Environments Group, Hewlett-Packard
Laboratories, Bristol, BS12 6QZ, England

1 Background

The Portable Common Tools Environment (PCTE) project began in 1983
with the aim to produce a public tool interface to be used as a portability
interface and to provide support for the integration of software engineering
tools. The PCTE+ project, beginning in 1987, extended PCTE to make
it suitable for high-security applications, and made a number of other improvements to the original PCTE interface. Technical Committee 33 of the
European Computer Manufacturers Association (ECMA) is developing a
PCTE standard based on PCTE+ issue 3[1], which is the version we review
here. Thomas[2] gives a very good overview of the various PCTE interfaces
and related activities.

When the ECMA Technical Committee for PCTE standardisation was
formed, one of the decisions was to aim to create a CASE envionments Reference Model to assist the standardisation process. A Task Group (TC33-
TGRM) was formed in 1988 to develop a complete Reference Model. During
1989 the first full version of the Reference Model was created, and during
1990 the model was refined further. It is currently being evaluated by applying it to a number of CASE integration frameworks. The reference model
is gaining increasing interest in the CASE community and ECMA TC33-

TGRM believe it merits wider dissemination and publication. The reference model description is now an official ECMA technical report[3].

It should be understood that the reference model is totally independent of PCTE and is in no way biased towards PCTE. The ECMA group see it as an aid in identifying future standards that will be needed in addition to PCTE. It is also a valuable way of describing, comparing, and contrasting CASE environment frameworks. The particular services of the model are described to a degree of detail that is complete enough for the model to be used to describe existing systems and proposals.

Our reference model is designed to cover complete CASE environment frameworks. The clearly stated intent of PCTE+ is that it should be the *basis* for a portable environment. Therefore any incompleteness of PCTE+ with respect to the reference model should not in itself be used as a value judgement against PCTE+.

2   What is a Reference Model?

A Reference Model is a conceptual framework which allows experts to work productively and independently on the development of standards for each part of the domain.

A reference model is *not* a standard itself; it is not to be used as a specification nor as the basis for appraising the conformance of actual implementations. It should identify areas for developing or improving standards, and provide a common reference for maintaining consistency of all related standards.

We developed a list of aims for a CASE environments reference model:

- The reference model should be suitable for being used to describe, compare, and contrast existing and proposed environment frameworks.

- The reference model should provide a framework for the smooth and coordinated evolution of future standards, in particular to ensure that the early standards are developed in such a way that further standards may easily achieve alignment in the sense of upward compatibility.

- The reference model should address interoperability and integration of tools.

- The reference model has to be able to be used to describe a wide range of CASE environment framework designs, but should balance this against

a requirement to be able to define points at which useful standards can
be defined.

- The reference model should be capable of being used as the basis for
  educating systems engineers in the subject of CASE environment frameworks.

- The number of unifying concepts required to describe the reference
  model should be small and the model should recognise the importance
  of the relationships which exist between its elements.

- The reference model should cover all system aspects irrespective of
  implementation techniques or software development methods employed
  by particular CASE environments or systems developed within CASE
  environments.

- The reference model should be compatible with other appropriate reference models.

3   Related Work and our Reference Model Struc-ture

We review the approaches taken by developers of other reference models and
highlight the structural differences between theirs and ours.

3.1   Related Work

Environment frameworks are first discussed in the Stoneman report[4]. Although with its "onion" diagram with minimal and other services centered
around a kernel it has been very influential in the the IPSE community, it is
too coarse-grained to satisfy many of the detailed requirements we placed on
a reference model.

The archetypal reference model is the OSI/ISO 7-layer model for open systems interconnection[5] standards. The **Open Software Foundation (OSF)**
user interface reference model[6] is also layered. We experimented with a
layered approach but found the rules governing it too restrictive to produce
an elegant reference model for our application area.

Another approach to reference models is to describe a whole system from
a set of different standpoints (termed "projections" or "sub-models"). This
approach has been adopted by the ANSA group to describe open distributed

processing[7], and by a working group of CCITT to describe support environments for telecommunication systems[8]. Although this approach has the benefit of being able to concentrate on specific aspects of a whole system (e.g. distribution or security) which are difficult to isolate within a system, that approach has several drawbacks. Firstly, the number of viewpoints is not necessarily small (CCITT has more than 10) and it is not a trivial task to chose the "correct" set. Secondly, the whole system has to be described as many times are there are viewpoints. And thirdly, the relationships and dependencies between the viewpoints have to be discovered. It is our opinion that the multiple-viewpoint approach generates an excessive amount of work to review a system against a reference model.

3.2   Our Reference Model Structure

The CASE environment frameworks reference model is based on grouping sets of services together. Figure 1 shows the overall structure of the reference model. The purpose of grouping the services as they are is that standards will cover at least a whole group. Thus the important interfaces between existing and forthcoming standards can be identified. Some of these groupings also enable various kinds of integration to be discussed: *presentation integration* (user interface services); *control integration* (task management services plus the message services); and *data integration* (data repository plus data integration services).

The diagram should not be interpreted as a set of layers. The ways in which one service can and does interact with another service is one of the most important areas in CASE environment framework development. One reason for its importance is the desire for an *open*, extensible, heterogeneous environment, particularly in the sense that different vendors' hardware and software components can work together effectively. For this reason, the identification and possible standardisation of the relationships between services is important.

This reference model identifies many of the accepted relationships between services. It does not dictate a set of relationships which must exist since current understanding of environment frameworks and the services of which they consist does not allow that. The relationships identified within it should be regarded as sensible ones which can be found in existing systems. Some of these may be considered "layers" but the reference model does *not* impose layering in any sense. Identification of other relationships is encouraged.

The message server services allow two-way communication: service-to-

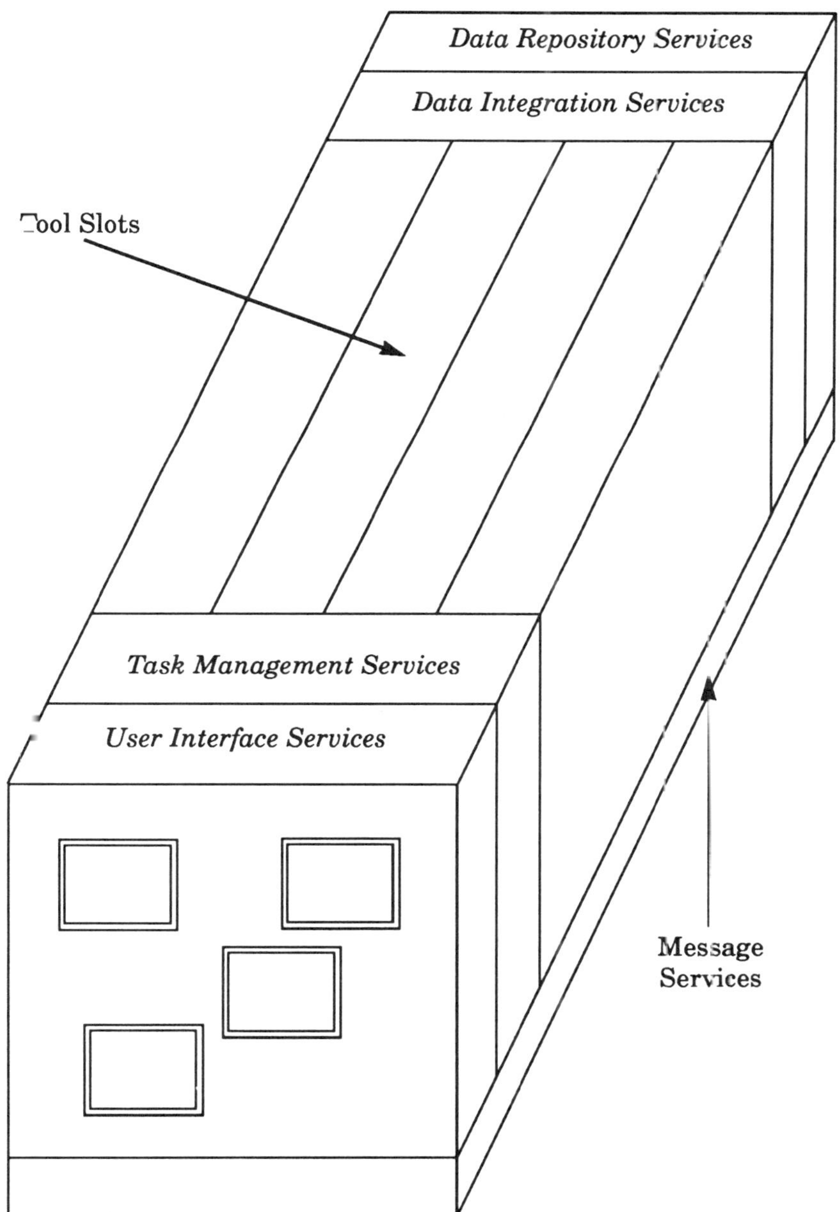

Figure 1: Overall Reference Model Structure

service; tool-to-tool; and tool-to-service. Remember this is not an implementation design.

The tool slots reserve a place for extending the facilities provided by the environment framework with integrated tool sets. The extra tools (or services) available will vary across environments just as database schemas and process programs will be different. The presentation aspects of a tool are deliberately separated from its semantic behaviour as, in general, these are best discussed individually. The classification of tools has not been the primary focus of the reference model but it is a natural extension of the work.

This "Toaster Diagram" (figure 1 by George Tatge of Hewlett Packard) is useful in providing a top level summary of the areas covered by different CASE frameworks and standards.

3.3   Reference Model Dimensions

Despite our model breaking CASE environment frameworks down into about 30 possible services, we found it very useful to structure description of those services to ensure descriptions of systems under review were compatible and comparable, and were clear, precise, and comprehensive in describing what their system did and did not provide. The "dimensions" we chose were those we believe make distinctions clear where it is easy to blur them by using imprecise terminology.

The first dimension is borrowed from the field of data modelling. Its aim is to identify the set of data manipulated by a service, the operations used to do that, and the constraints placed upon the state of the data and the applicability of operations. Our complete review of PCTE+[9] had to include over 200 operations. The second dimension comes from the ANSI SPARC 3-schema architecture[10]. Its aim is to allow separate discussion of what a service is (conceptually), how it is implemented (internally); and the ways in which it is made available (externally).

The third dimension simply aims to ensure a proper distinction is made between instances, types, and information about types (metadata). This distinction is as applicable in the task management and tool areas as in the data management area.

The fourth dimension captures some further points about a service: how well it is understood (e.g. from research topics to part of a tested product); how it relates to other services; and what justification it has for being included in a particular environment.

In this paper we do not make extensive use of our reference model dimensions, mainly because of lack of space, but also because PCTE+ is an interface definition and thus does not aim to cover some dimensions (e.g. internal).

3.4   Using the Reference Model

There is an application technique for using the reference model to analyse CASE environment frameworks. The first step is the acquisition of a set of documents describing all aspects of the system to be evaluated. These may include an interface specification, a user manual, and some internal documentation.

The second step is to identify the services provided by the system. These are then grouped under the relevant service headings of the reference model. This grouping may not correspond to existing documentation of the system and so it is useful to keep a record of which parts of the documentation the services are referenced in.

The next step is to take each reference model service in turn and describe what the system under review does and does not provide. This description is structured by placing points under the relevant dimension headings. The dimensions have been chosen to help clarify such descriptions, and do appear to help in structuring the descriptions, identifying ambiguities and inconsistencies, and providing a checklist for completeness.

A final step is to generate a summary of what has been discovered. It is useful to summarise the degree of coverage systems offer with respect to the overall reference model architecture. Another effective summary is a table showing coverage of the services against the dimensions. In this way for example, an interface specification should stand out as having no coverage of the internal dimension.

4   The Reference Model and PCTE+

We now present very brief descriptions of each of the reference model services (*in italics*) together with the most interesting points as they relate to PCTE+. A full description of the reference model[3] and a separate review of PCTE+[11] are available from the author.

4.1   Data Repository Services

The maintenance, management, and naming of data entities or objects and the relationships among them is the general purpose of the data repository.

Basic support for process execution and control is also addressed here along with a location service to support physical distribution of data and processes.

PCTE+ covers the majority of services in the data repository area. The only omissions are an archive service and a backup service.

Data Storage

The responsibility for storage and access of the objects and entities rests here. This does not imply that the data need actually be stored here but that such operations as "read,", "write", "open", and "close" are provided.

The basic data service entities in PCTE+ are called "objects". Objects have attributes and are typed.

The value types which attributes can have are: integer; boolean; date; float; string; and enumeration. There are a set of predefined attributes which all objects have.

Object types determine if an object has associated "contents". The contents can be one of four kinds: file; pipe; device; or message queue. Contents have separate operations which apply to all kinds but message queues.

Object types inherit attributes in a subtype hierarchy which allows multiple inheritance but is constrained to be a directed acyclic graph. There is a set of predefined object types which partition the inheritance graph (thus preventing, for example, an object being a file *and* a pipe).

PCTE+ objects do *not* have associated operations as in object-oriented models.

Links and Relationships

Links are a common form of implementing relationships. The ability to create, delete, modify and navigate symbolic relationships between entities or objects is assumed.

The PCTE+ relationship service concentrates on links. A PCTE+ "relationship" is a pair of (reversed) links with corresponding sources and destinations.

Links have attributes and are typed but there is no link subtyping. They can have a cardinality of one or many. They are in one of five categories:

- Existence - every object has an existence link to it from another object;

- Composition - used to support composite objects;

- Reference - prevents deletion of the target object;

- Designation - refers to, but does not prevent deletion of target object;

- Implicit - provided by the system to reverse links (other than designation links).

Naming

A "name" is a string of characters associated with an entity. The name service maintains the relationships between surrogates and names. An entity is allowed to have more than one name.

The name service may also support the additional concept of a "namespace". Any surrogate can be associated with a name which is unique within the context of a namespace.

All PCTE+ objects, including processes, workstations, volumes, and SDSs are accessible through a uniform concept of pathname. There are some operations (on SDSs, volumes, and stations) which take shorter names as parameters. This is an external issue. These shorter names are in fact the last components of standard pathnames (respectively starting by the designation of the directory of volumes, of stations, and of SDSs).

PCTE+ does support the surrogate concept[1][12]. Each object has an attribute of name "system-object-exact-identifier". Also, every object has a volume number and an object number. These are not precisely surrogates since they can change when objects are moved from volume to volume but objects can be retrieved using them.

PCTE+ does not allow access by surrogates but through pathnames. Two pathnames designate the same object if these objects have the same exact identifier. With the replication mechanisms, two physically distinct "replicas" may be interpreted as the same logical object.

Backup

A backup is a redundant copy of some subset of the framework managed data. The subset is capable of restoration to active use by a framework implementation, particularly in the event of a loss of completeness or integrity in the data in use by the implementation.

PCTE+ does not provide this service.

Archive

The amount of data which will be associated with a project in a software engineering environment may be more than can be held online. There may be a service which allows online information to be transferred to an offline form.

PCTE+ archiving can be achieved by moving (composite) objects to a new volume which needs to be thereafter copied (physically) onto a tape and unmounted (i.e. the true physical space on the disc can be reassigned to a new volume as long as the volume is considered to be "archived").

---

[1] A surrogate is a unique, system-generated identifier which is never re-used.

This mechanism is implementable through a tool since it is not a PCTE+ service. However, this approach has some limitations.

Data Transaction

A data transaction is a grouping of data operations, including a designated sequence of data operations, which requires that either all of the designated operations are applied or none are; i.e., a data transaction is uninterruptible from the user's point of view.

Concurrency Service

The Data Transaction Service is required to cope with the simple fact that things cannot be guaranteed to work all the time. The concurrency service addresses the extra considerations which have to be managed when more than one transaction can happen at one time.

PCTE+ has transactions (and calls them that). A transaction is a special case of a PCTE+ "activity". An activity is the basis of the PCTE+ concurrency service as well. Thus a transaction implies concurrency control as well (which is not unexpected). Activities can be nested.

Location Service

The location service addresses some aspects of distribution by maintaining a model of the physical components on which the environment framework services run and communicate (e.g. devices, channels, volumes, or peripherals), their attributes (e.g. live or connected), and relationships between them (e.g. the peripherals at a device) In addition to the physical model, the location service can maintain a logical model which abstracts some of the physical details so that e.g. collections of devices can be considered at one "location". The location service maintains a mapping between the logical and physical models.

PCTE+ has operations which provide the means for controlling the status of workstations and for administering volumes and devices.

PCTE+ expects to be viewed as a single transparent distributed system. It consists of a set of heterogeneous workstations connected by a local area network. It is not mandatory for PCTE+ workstations to have physical disks attached to them. It is required that each station has at least an administration volume, but several stations (e.g. a disk server and several diskless bitmap workstations) can share the same administration volume (physically managed by the disk server).

Process Support Service

It is the process support service which provides the basic mechanisms for tools to execute and communicate in a manner independent of the underlying operating system.

The PCTE+ process model provides a complete set of primitives to cover this service.

PCTE+ recognises a range of "foreign systems" from a bare machine which can simply have code initialised by PCTE+, to systems which support PCTE+'s debugging protocol and use IPC mechanisms to allow processes to communicate.

4.2   Data Integration Services

The data integration services enhance the data repository services by providing higher-level semantics and operations with which to handle the data stored in the repository.

Versioning

Support for versions of objects usually assumes at least a tree structure support although some more arbitrary (complex) systems exist. The goal is to be able to revise objects (both new and older) and to be able to maintain a history of the versions of the objects. Versioning is complicated a great deal by relationships. It is necessary to either provide for versioning of the relationships themselves or else to provide automated system support for the tracking and maintenance of relationships between objects as they become versioned.

In PCTE+, objects can be versioned. The general form of the version graph is a directed acyclic graph. (Composite) objects are versioned and the successor (PCTE+) relationship is maintained between all (components of composite) objects.

Configurations

A configuration of objects (or entities) is a set of objects which may be regarded as a single object and thereby support all features thereof. Configurations need to be treated as first-class objects so that they can be created, deleted and versioned as single objects. The component objects constituting a configuration may be of different types, and a configuration is often used as a "baseline" of a system or subsystem.

PCTE+ "composite entities" are defined purely in terms of their constituents and relationships. A PCTE+ composite entity consists of:

- an object, plus

- the set of objects which are in the transitive closure over the composition links starting from the object, and

- the links starting from objects in the composite entity.

Query Service

The query service is an extension to the data storage service's "read" operation. In the general case, it returns sets of values retrieved from sets of entities.

PCTE+ does not have a general query service. There are specific operations among the other services which retrieve particular information.

Metadata

"Metadata" is data about data. Examples would be data about the types, attributes, or relationships held in a database. Names for such data (or where it is held) include "data dictionary", "catalog", or "schema definition". The metadata service provides control and maintenance of metadata.

An example of a metadata service is support for the evolution of types (e.g. adding new attributes) or changing the type of an entity (e.g. a document becomes a secure-document).

PCTE+ has a "metabase" and a (proposal for) Data Definition Language (DDL). There are four types of type (object types, link types, attribute types, and enumeration types) represented in the metabase. These have user-visible surrogates ("definition-IDs") and can have names. Reverse links and the object type hierarchy relationships are held in the metabase. The relationship between key attribute types and link types is held there, but *not* the relationship between attribute types and object types.

PCTE+'s sub-environment service, called "Working Schemas" provides a partial view of the whole database. Working schemas are composed of "Schema Definition Sets" (SDSs). There is metadata associated with each SDS (and about SDSs) which is best considered part of the metadata service of PCTE+.

State Monitoring

The state monitoring service enables the definition/specification of database states and state transformations, and actions to be taken should these states occur or persist. This is sometimes called "triggering". Its usefulness lies in the ways it can help automate the modelling of real-world situations.

The PCTE+ state monitoring service called the "notification mechanism" represents a subset of the facilities described by the reference model.

Sub-Environments

The sub-environment service is an abstraction mechanism to enable a user to see just the data and operations required to carry out the assigned task. A sub-environment will have constraints associated with it to ensure consistent interactions between sub-environments and the maintenance of integrity.

The PCTE+ sub-environment service is called the "schema management service".

There is an overall schema. A working schema gives a partial view of the data types to processes (rather than users or tasks). Just data types, and neither data instances nor operations, are defined by working schemas and the overall schema. Working schemas are sets of "Schema Definition Sets" (SDSs). The overall schema is defined by the complete set of SDSs.

Data Interchange

The data interchange service offers two-way translation between data in the data repository and some format for that data which can be stored on portable storage media.

PCTE+ does not address this issue.

4.3   Tools

The set of environment framework services exist partly to support one another, but mainly to provide a useful interface which can be used in building facilities which support particular forms of software development. The name most commonly used for these facilities is, "tools".

Here, the term, "functional element" is sometimes used and defined in preference to tool. This is because the term "tool" is currently in general use for a whole packaged software product which often consists of a set of co-operating functional elements. A functional element is a piece of software which calls upon the services provided by the CASE environment framework and/or other functional elements. Functional elements "plug in" to the CASE framework and communicate with the services provided by the framework via the message services.

Three kinds of integration are distinguished. They are data integration (covered by the data repository and data integration services in the reference model), control integration (covered by the task management and message services), and user interface integration (covered by the user interface services). It can be seen from their descriptions that some relationships do exist between the different kinds of integration, but it is useful to be able to discuss them orthogonally. Integration of one kind does not necessarily depend on the existence of integration of another kind.

Within each kind of integration, three levels are identified: the interoperability level; the partial-integration level; and the full-integration level. In this case, full-integration depends on partial-integration, and partial-integration depends on interoperability. Degrees of interoperability and integration are allowed. That is, a two or more functional elements (tools or services) may lie somewhere between two of the defined layers for a particular kind of integration.

Thus, to describe to what extent two or more functional elements are integrated, one has to describe their degree of integration of each kind. Functional elements are only fully integrated when they reach that level for each kind of integration.

Integration of tools (and services) is not simply achieved by providing a good set of services. There are many factors, and one of these is a guide for the toolwriter explaining what the services are intended to achieve and suggesting the "common" ways to use them. An example is the PACT Tool Writer's Guide[13].

PCTE+ provides the described set of services to support tools. Otherwise, PCTE+ makes no statements regarding particular tools, kinds of tools, how tools should be regarded. integrated, or encapsulated.

4.4 Task Management Services

The purpose of these services is to provide the ability to insulate the user from the details of fine grain tools in the framework. The task management services[2] provide a layer of abstraction which allows the user to deal with tasks as opposed to accomplishing each job by a tedious series of invocations on individual tools. They also allow for the increase of "intelligence" within the framework so that increased automation of the overall environment may be realistic.

PCTE+ does not provide these services, except for aspects of auditing.

Task Descriptions

Both the user and the environment developer need facilities to describe abstract tasks. These may be programmatic or descriptive. There may be types of tasks and subtasks which have to be made more particular during an instantiation operation before execution.

Task Execution

There may be support for execution, interruption, and termination of tools, services, and processes throughout the system.

Task Transactions

Task transactions are considered separate from data transactions. Whereas one usually desires "all or nothing" in a data transaction, it is usually the case that one does not wish to undo useful work which completed in a task even if the entire task did not complete.

---

[2]Alternative terminology is *software process* management.

Role Management

There has to be visibility and maintenance of information concerning who is responsible for carrying out which kinds of tasks. The role management service exists to handle information about people and roles, and the relationships between them.

Event Monitoring

Support for tasks requires the ability to define triggers based on the start, interruption, or completion of a task, sub-task, or other event.

Auditing

Closely related to task management is the ability for the system to audit events and tasks and to report on them. This requires a facility for description of that which is to be audited as well as description of the reports to be generated.

PCTE+ defines a set of compulsory (security operations, auditing operations, and changing object identification) and selectable (on the basis of a pre-defined set of properties (e.g. user or workstation)) events that are audited whenever the events are detected on a call of a PCTE+ interface function.

The PCTE+ accounting service is modelled in the OMS. The concepts involved are:

- Accountable resources: selected objects like programs, files, pipes, message queues, devices, workstations, or SDSs;

- Consumers: individual users, groups of users, or groups of programs;

- Accounting log.

4.5 Message Server Network

Tool Registration

Registration is required in all classes of message servers so that the communication schemes may be properly implemented. Registration can range from the very simple (e.g. name a location) to the very complex (e.g. all self referencing information of a tool or service).

PCTE+ does not provide this service.

Message Delivery

This is a complex topic and is different for each class of message server. Discriminating message delivery is required for multicast message servers so that only those tools and services which wish to receive a certain type of message do.

The PCTE+ "InterProcess Communication" (IPC) mechanism is based on the idea that processes send messages to queues (not directly to other processes). The messages are typed and prioritized.

4.6 User Interface

The subject of user interfaces is an extremely complex issue which is far more general than integration frameworks. Nevertheless, a consistent user interface service must be adopted for a complete framework. We note the importance of separating the presentation of functionality from its provision.

The CASE reference model offers a summary description of an existing layered reference model for user interfaces. The model is taken from OSF's Rationale Document[6] which is adapted from a draft User Interface Reference Model developed by NIST (National Institute of Standards and Technology), which in turn was based upon a framework developed by X/Open.

The PCTE+ current user interface specification is PCTE1.5 volume 2 which is designed to be portable on the X11 library and offers additional higher level concepts.

4.7 Security

The CASE reference model regards security as a service which crosses many of the boundaries of the reference model divisions. There exists a reference model for security produced by ECMA TC32/TG9, described in [14, 15] and summarised by Cole[16].

PCTE+ supports both mandatory and discretionary security controls. There are many kinds of "elementary access rights" which are controlled. Groups and subgroups are supported.

5 Summary and Conclusion

The review of PCTE+ according to the reference model brings out some interesting points about PCTE+:

- PCTE+ has almost complete coverage in the data repository services and data integration services, especially data storage, links and relationships, security, data transaction, metadata, and sub-environments. It also has good coverage of the distribution services;

- PCTE+ has less complete coverage in other parts of the reference model. In particular it does not address backup services, data interchange services, query services, tools, task management services or message server network services. This reflects the fact that PCTE+ provides lower level services on which it is necessary to build higher level common services and tools.

We have been able to use this review of PCTE+ to study the suitability of uniting other framework standards or mechanisms with PCTE+ to provide more complete functionality. Clearly, other systems which address mainly the data-related services such as Sun's NSE[17] or the CAIS-A standard are more likely to compete with PCTE+ than be complementary to it. An interesting system which does have mechanisms for areas of the reference model complementary to PCTE+ is HP's **SoftB***ench* product. We are currently investigating the possible benefits of combining **SoftB***ench*'s broadcast message server mechanism (providing task management and message services) and CSF/Motif user interface together with the facilities of PCTE.

One measure of success of our reference model is the extent to which it has been found useful to groups outside HP and ECMA. A working group of representatives from three of Europe's largest environment projects (EAST, ESF, and Atmosphere) have measured their proposals against the model to help identify where their projects overlap, and where the projects could work jointly on important areas currently not addressed within any single project.

There are several standards coordination groups in which our reference model is providing the basis for discussion. The CASE'89 conference saw a CASE standards coordination meeting which adopted our reference model framework. At the second invitational workshop on Integrated Software Engineering Environments (ISEE) in December 1989, the National Institute of Standards and Technology (NIST) viewed as their role the coordination of ISEE standardisation efforts. They too have proposed our reference model as a means of supporting this[18]. X/Open are using the reference model in assessing requirements for CASE standards.

Another forum where our reference model partitioning of groups of services has been put to use is the **CAD Framework Initiative** (CFI) which exists to "develop industry acceptable standards, specifications and guidelines for design automation frameworks which will enable the coexistence and cooperation of a variety of tools"[19]. They have split their working groups into the divisions identified by the reference model.

We believe that the model provides an adequate degree of expression to describe environments in a common and systematic way. This enables systems to be more easily and objectively compared and contrasted. The services provide good anchor points at which to discuss portability, interoperability, and intraoperability. Our experience indicates that the model is suitable to describe most aspects of most existing systems and yet identifies interfaces where possible standards could be developed and changed for the future. Its increasing uptake by other groups supports this view.

The reference model focusses on services that are specific to a CASE environment, and does not attempt to tackle in detail more general services such as distribution, security, and user interface. A logical extension to the existing reference model is the classification of tools.

It is our opinion that no existing CASE environment covers all aspects of our reference model. We hope that the concepts described within the reference model can help the evolution of CASE environments in the right direction. We would also welcome feedback on the reference model.

6   Acknowledgements

The work described here is work carried out in association with the European Computer Manufacturers Association (ECMA) Technical Committee's (TC33) Task Group on the Reference Model (TGRM), and has benefitted from discussions with its members.

The author has received guidance and support from others at Hewlett Packard working in this field: George Tatge (inventor of the reference model diagram), Huw Oliver, Ray Crispin, Ian Thomas, and Paul Vickers.

The author also wishes to express his gratitude to Mr. T.G.L. Lyons (of Software Sciences Ltd.) and Mr. R. Minot (of Bull - GIE Emeraude) for their constructive criticism of the review of PCTE+ according to the reference model.

References

[1] PCTE+ Project Team. PCTE+ C Functional Specifications, Issue 3, 28 October 1988.

[2] Ian Thomas. PCTE Interfaces: Supporting Tools in Software-Engineering Environments. *IEEE Software*, 6(6):15–23, November 1989.

[3] A. Earl. A Reference Model for Frameworks of Computer Assisted Software Engineering Environments. Technical Report ECMA/TR/90/55, ECMA, December 1990.

[4] J. N. Buxton. Requirements for APSE - STONEMAN, February 1980.

[5] ISO. International Standard Reference model of Open Systems Interconnection. 1988.

[6] OSF. OSF User Environment Component: Decision Rationale Document. 11 January 1989.

[7] Architecture Projects Management Limited. The ANSA Reference Manual, March 1989.

[8] H. Johansen(ed.). ANNEX 1 to Proposed New Question 6/X for the 1989 - 1992 Study Period. March 1988.

[9] Anthony Earl. A Review of PCTE+ (Issue 3) According to the CASEE Reference Model (draft 3.0). 4 January 1990.

[10] ANSI. Interim Report of the ANSI/X3/SPARC Study Group on Data Base Management Systems. *ACM SIGFIDET*, 7(2):3–139, 1975.

[11] Anthony Earl. A Reference Model for Computer Assisted Software Engineering Environment Frameworks. Technical Report Version 4.0, HP, 17 August 1990.

[12] F. Hall, J. Owlett, and S. Todd. *Relations and Entities*, pages 1–20. North Holland, 1976.

[13] Syntagma. PACT Tool Writer's Guide. Technical report, Syntagma, April 1988.

[14] ECMA. Security in Open Systems: A Security Framework. Technical Report ECMA TR/46, July 1988.

[15] ECMA. Security in Open Systems - Data Elements and Service Definitions. Technical Report Standard ECMA-138, ECMA, December 1989.

[16] Robert Cole. A Model for Security Standards in Distributed Systems. *Computers and Security*, 9(4), June 1990.

[17] E. Adams et al. Object Management in a CASE Environment. In *Proceedings of International Conference on Software Engineering at Pittsburgh*, May 1989.

[18] William Wong and Marvin V. Zelkowitz. A Preliminary Description of an Integrated Software Engineering Environment (ISEE) Reference Model. 23 February 1990.

[19] CFI. Byelaws of CAD Framework Initiative, Inc., 1989.

9

An alternative, object oriented view of the ECMA TC33/TGRM reference model

E. J. Dowling
Ferranti International, Cwmbran, UK

0 ABSTRACT

The ECMA Reference Model for development environment frameworks marks a major step forward in the study and classification of such frameworks. However, it is based on a fundamental split between the services available for data and those for tasks (software processes). This paper proposes an alternative, object oriented view of essentially the same services, which increases uniformity and removes some of the difficulties associated with the basic data/task split. The paper is intended as a discussion document for the next generation of the Model, rather than claiming to present a complete solution.

1 INTRODUCTION

This paper represents the personal view of the author only. Its basis is Version 4.0 of the Reference Model (RM) [1], accepted for publication as ECMA Technical Report TR/55. The RM includes the by-now widely adopted "toaster" model , together with a set of services associated with various parts of the "toaster". The RM as a whole marks a significant step forward in the study and analysis of environment frameworks/infrastructures. The importance of the RM should not be underestimated, and its wide acceptance testifies to its value. The TGRM group within ECMA TC33 that produced the model are to be congratulated on their work. (Although a nominal member of TC33, the author was not able to play an active part in developing the RM).

However, this paper argues, briefly, that the RM has an unfortunate split between data and task services. Many services that the RM places in only one category have direct analogues in the other. Based on this more uniform view of the relevant services, an alternative, object oriented model is sketched.
NB. In RM terminology, a task is what elsewhere might be called an activity or a software process. A typical simple task might therefore be produce_executable, which encompasses the invocation of the edit, compile and link tools. Thus an RM task is at a higher level of abstraction than a program - unlike Ada tasks, for example.

As the RM points out, task services are much less well understood than data services. If for no other reason, it should be stressed that this paper is essentially a discussion document and no claim is made that the ideas have been fully thought out. Rather, the paper contains suggestions for consideration when the next generation of the RM is produced.

2 OVERVIEW

Rather than a proposal that requires the RM to start again from scratch, an evolutionary approach is adopted here. Essentially, this involves a different presentation of the same basic services, but with some of the problems caused by the fundamental data/task split alleviated.

The proposed change is to an object oriented model. This model has the usual perceptional advantages of the object oriented approach, and in addition it highlights some of the weaknesses in the current RM.

An important point to note is that the new model is idealised in the sense that it includes services which can be identified as being useful, but which may not be readily implementable with current technology. This is not seen as a major objection in a reference model, however, since its aim is to clarify concepts and facilitate discussion, and "not to be used as an implementation specification" (section 1.2 of [1]).

3 CURRENT RM SERVICES

The current RM includes the following services, grouped as shown - see section 5 of [1]. Some other services are also identified, but are not discussed here.

Data Repository Services

Data Storage	Relationship	Name
Location	Data Transaction	Concurrency
Process Support	Archive	Backup

Data Integration Services

Version	Configuration	Query
Metadata	State Monitoring	Sub-Environment
Data Interchange		

Task Management Services

Task Definition	Task Execution	Task Transaction
Task History	Event Monitoring	Audit and Accounting
Role Management		

As discussed below, many services that seem just as appropriate for tasks as for data are apparently missing from the RM. For example, relationships, versions, positioning and querying are provided for data but not tasks.

Services may become available if the task services make use of the data services (ie tasks are represented as objects) and can thus obtain them from there, but this assumes a particular implementation strategy - albeit a sensible one. In contrast, the proposed new model identifies the services needed without any assumption about implementation methods.

4 PROPOSED NEW STRUCTURE

The basic object types of interest can be identified and placed in a simple hierarchy as shown below. Services can then be associated with each object type. This clearly has some similarities with the ATIS [2] approach, but really only to the extent that both are object-oriented. A possible hierarchy is

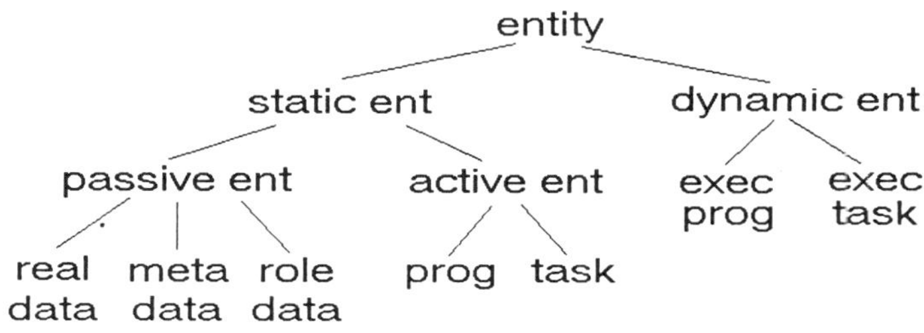

(No doubt with more thought better type names could be identified in the above hierachy!)

The basic type is **entity**. A **dynamic entity** is an executing program or task (ie a task invocation). A **passive entity** is an item of "real" data, metadata or role data. An **active entity** is a task (definition) or a program/executable image. That is, an active entity can be invoked to generate a dynamic entity.

Note that these classes have been selected to facilitate comparison with the current RM; many different models could be devised. In particular, programs, as both active and dynamic entities, could be subsumed by tasks. They are retained here simply because the current RM deals with them separately (in the Process Support service). Role data is identified separately for similar reasons.

The distinction between static and dynamic entities can be a valuable one to make. Because of its current approach, the RM sometimes tends to lose this distinction, for example in the section on Task Services which does not always distinguish between task definitions and task instances (ie executing tasks).

In any framework, a dynamic entity will also have a (static) representation - eg an entry in a process table in a classical operating system, or an Object Management System object in PCTE(+). The distiction between a dynamic entity and its representation is different to that between a dynamic entity and its corresponding active entity, and this paper does not always make the former distinction specific (eg whether a name applies to the entity itself or its representation). However, this is not generally important.

4.1 Brief Comparison With The Current RM

The current RM services are not presented in an object oriented fashion so a direct comparison is not easy. However, broadly, the Data Repository and Data Integration services apply to real data passive entities. The position of metadata passive entities is not entirely clear in the current RM. It would seem sensible that the Data Repository and Integration services should also apply to metadata, yet while the Data Storage service provides update and there is an explicit Query service, the Metadata service includes both update and query operations (section 8.4.3 of [1]).

The Process Support service from the Data Repository set applies to 'processes' and 'static contexts' - ie to executing program dynamic entities and program active entities respectively.

The Task Management services apply basically to task active entities, executing task dynamic entities and role data passive entities.

4.2 Entity Services

Basic services applicable to all entities are discussed below. The services considered are essentially those listed above, together with some additional services not included in the current RM. For each, a brief rationale for the service being provided at the entity level is given; [1] provides fuller descriptions and extra justifications for most of these services. Since nearly all the services are discussed in [1] as they apply to data, the emphasis here is on how they also apply to task definitions and dynamic entities. In addition, the services are relevant not just for "real" data, but for role data too - an aspect missing from the current RM.

Of course, while services might be identified at the entity level, there will often be refinements of them at lower levels in the hierarchy - eg the facilities needed to handle concurrency for tasks will differ in detail from those needed for data. Nevertheless, conceptually the services are relevant for all entities.

The services that apply at the entity level are:

- **Storage**. Both static and (representations of) dynamic entities need to be stored, with operations such as define, create, read, write. Concepts such as attributes, types and so on are just as relevant for task definitions and dynamic entities as they are for data.
- **Relationship**. Relationships may need to be recorded between both static and dynamic entities (including static-dynamic, as well as static-static, etc). For example, a used_in relationship between task definitions, a subtask_of relationship between task invocations, or a generated_from relationship between an executable image and a process (ie executing program).
- **Name** All entities need a user name.
- **Location.** The location service deals with distribution. This is relevant for all entities, and operations such as move and copy may apply just as much to task definitions or dynamic entities as to simple data objects (at least conceptually: moving a dynamic entity may not be simple!).
- **Transaction.** The basic transaction service allows the transition from one consistent state to another. The transition takes place by means of operations on objects, and the transaction service allows these operations to be undone if necessary. The transactions needed for the modification of task definitions are exactly the same as for data. For dynamic entities a similar concept can apply, eg processes A, B and C must either all be running, or none should. As [1] points out, there are issues that arise concerning transactions on data when tasks are involved; this is what the current Task Transaction service addresses. The argument here is that data is not the only possible subject for transactions.
- **Concurrency.** Clearly task definitions need to be protected with concurrent users just like simple data. Control for dynamic entities is equally important, eg if user A needs process P stopped while he does something, but user B needs it to be running while he does something else, concurrency control is needed to prevent their interfering with each others work.

- **Archive**. Archiving is "off lining". Task definitions must be archived along with data. Archiving can also be a valid concept for dynamic entities. For example, a process that is performing some sort of continuous but low-priority activity may be archived from a workstation to a central mainframe, to free processing power - just as data is archived to free storage. Even if the process cannot, or need not, be running continuously, the archive service might provide a 'save context/stop process/move context/start "same" process on different site' facility.
- **Backup**. The backup service deals with recovery after failure. Again, task definitions need to be backed up just as data does. Dynamic entities can be backed up by taking replicate copies (including contexts) on other sites.
- **Version**. Active entities can be versioned (eg two versions of an edit/compile task, one with debugger information and one without), and the corresponding dynamic entities should then naturally be seen as versions of each other. Also, two invocations of the same task by different users could be different versions of the same dynamic entity, or perhaps two invocations of the same task with different parameters (eg edit/compile (A) and edit/compile(B)) might also be versions of the same executing task.
- **Configuration**. The configuration service allows composite objects to be formed from simpler ones and then treated as single items. Composite task definitions may be needed, eg to allow a user to be assigned the role of manager for all tasks in a project (a composite task) rather than to each constituent task individually. Similarly, a composite dynamic entity could be used to suspend all tasks related to a particular project, rather than each individually.
- **Query**. Queries can be relevant for task definitions and (representations of) dynamic entities - eg "list all the tasks currently being executed as part of project P for which M is the manager".
- **Metadata**. [1] explicitly excludes data about tasks from the heading of metadata (section 8.4.6). This is reasonable, but if all entities have a type and attributes, which themselves have a type, metadata is a relevant concept for all entities, and metadata exists for task definitions and dynamic entities. However, it may be more appropriate for this service to be associated purely with metadata, ie at the metadata level rather than the entity level.
- **Monitoring**. The current RM has separate State Monitoring (for data - the 'state' is that of the repository) and Event Monitoring (for tasks) services. This generalised service includes the definition of a repository state or event, and of the action to be taken when the state changes or the event occurs. It encompasses changes to task definitions and events concerning processes, both of which seem to be excluded in the current RM structure.
- **Sub-Environment**. Sub-environments allow complex activities, such as the implementation of a large system, to be broken down into smaller units. Each sub-environment gives a restricted view of the total objects and operations involved in the overall activity. A sub-environment can provide a subset of task definitions and dynamic entities, just as for data.
- **History**. The current RM identifies this service only for tasks (really, task invocations). Operations include defining what is to be recorded, recording it and then answering queries about the record. The concept of history and these associated

operations are equally useful for data, task definitions and other dynamic entities. For data, simple information such as date of creation and date of last update is of obvious interest.
- **Auditing and Accounting.** Again, the current RM associates this service only with tasks, but it is in fact a universal one.
- **State.** The state of all entities is an important piece of information. This new service, not really covered in the current RM, is discussed more fully in section 4.3 below.

4.2.1 Static Entity Services

This is probably the appropriate level for the following service:

- **Data Interchange.** As well as "real" and metadata, there will typically be a need to exchange task definitions and role data between frameworks.

In addition, some refinement of the entity services, to differentiate them from the dynamic form, are necessary. Some obvious examples are the Location, Transaction, Concurrency, Archive and Backup services.

4.2.1.1 Passive Entity Services

There are no obvious new or refined services at the passive entity level.

4.2.1.1.1 Data Services

The various kinds of data entities (real/meta/role) do not need any new services, although they do of course each have refinements of inherited services. For example, the facilities provided for metadata might be a restricted set of those generally available, reflecting the problems normally associated with metadata, as discussed in [1]. Alternatively, there may be a separate Metadata service at the metadata level, as discussed above.

Similarly, all role-related services should already exist at - and thus be inheritable from - higher levels in the hierarchy. For example, the "Person E should never be a programmer" rule supported by the Role Management Service (see section 10.7.4 of [1]) is simply a particular example of a more general constraint facility that could be part of the basic Relationship service and apply much more broadly than just to people and roles.

Thus the Metadata and Role Management services of the current RM may be broadly subsumed by other services in this model.

4.2.1.2 Active Entity Services

Since there are no refinements for passive entities, there are no corresponding refinements for active entities. However, there is an additional service:

- **Invocation**. This service allows a dynamic entity to be generated from an active entity.

4.2.1.2.1 Task Services

Refinement will be needed at the program/task level, eg for Invocation, and also an extra service:

- **Task Definition**. While task definition could be seen as setting up attributes and relationships (between task objects and role data objects), there seems a good case for a separate service that provides a higher level of abstraction.

4.2.2 Dynamic Entity Services

Obviously, the entity services that must be refined for static entities need corresponding refinement for dynamic entities. In addition, the following service is required:

- **Execution**. This service supports the starting, stopping, suspending, etc of dynamic entities. It may also include communication mechanism for the use of executing dynamic entities (this aspect does not seem to be mentioned in the current RM).

4.2.2.1 Executing Item Services

The Execution service, and others, will need further refinement at the executing program/task level, since the execution of tasks will typically be much more complex than that of programs. In fact, this difference may be so great that there is a case for a separate Task Execution service as in the current RM.

4.3 The Entity State Service

A new service proposed here is that dealing with state. Note that the state of an entity is involved here; the current RM State Monitoring service deals with the state of the repository - a related, but different thing.

The state of a data entity in the repository is an important piece of information, for example:

- it is of clear relevance for project management tools.
- transition from one state to another may be a significant event for metrics data collection (eg to record how long it took to test a piece of code).
- transition would also be relevant for entity history maintenance, to record when state changed, who changed it, additional information, etc.
- it can play a part in a general control mechanism, eg the publish operation is only allowable for a document when its state is approved.
- it can be used to enforce procedures, eg a code unit's state can only be set to accepted if it is currently tested, not simply coded.

Operations would typically include

- define state type, consisting of states (eg in_work, coded, tested, accepted) and possible transitions (eg coded to tested and coded to in_work, to allow for tests that succeed or fail). Note that in general the states would form a directed graph, not a linear sequence for which simple promote/demote operations were adequate.
- associate state type with entity type (eg entity type code_unit has associated state type code_state).
- change an entity's state (subject to the defined possible transitions).
- query an entity's state.

There are three possible ways of providing state facilities:

- in a tool
- using existing framework services
- with a new framework service

Tools recording state and offering these kinds of operations already exist in the configuration management area, but as noted above, the applications are much wider than this. Also, state is such a fundamental property that it is more appropriate to handle it in the framework.

State clearly has a lot in common with any other attribute and one obvious course is simply to represent it as an entity attribute. This would have the desirable property of uniformity and would allow services such as Monitoring to be exploited. However, there are issues which need to be considered:

- the state type is not simple - it is a directed graph - and it may not be possible to represent this with an arbitrary Metadata service.
- state is a "universal attribute" which all entities have (allowing for a default, simple one-state case, perhaps).
- if state were an attribute, it would probably require access control mechanisms of sufficiently fine granularity to allow it to be protected while other attributes could be changed. Conversely, it might well be necessary to allow the state to be changed while ensuring that nothing else could be modified.

- to ensure only valid transitions take place, all changes of state must be made using the appropriate mechanism; it must not be possible for any user to change the attribute directly, even if he is authorised to change the entity's state.

While probably none of these difficulties is insuperable, on balance they seem to rule out always having state as an attribute.

Another option might be to have a separate entity representing state, using the Relationship service to associate the state entity with the "real" one.   This would immediately remove the need for fine-grain access control, but the other difficulties would remain.   Thus always having state as an entity is also ruled out.

Just as for entities, it is desirable to be able to record/query the state of a dynamic entity, define valid state transitions, etc.   There is more scope for defining a fixed set of states and transitions, but it may still be better to allow flexibility. It is not abstract enough to assume that there will always be repository entities corresponding to each dynamic entity, so some extra-repository means of providing the facilities is needed.

None of the current RM Task Management services seem to be quite appropriate. Presumably, the definitions handled by the Task Definition service are purely static, so are not relevant for recording current state, although they could define valid transitions. The Task History service could be useful, but would obviously be dealing with a lot of historical information, rather than this single piece of current information. The Event Monitoring service is only concerned with change of state.

The conclusion, therefore, is that a State service is required; it cannot in general be subsumed by other services, and so should be a separate service.

5 SUMMARY

The current RM is a valuable aid to the understanding of environment frameworks. The widespread adoption of its "toaster" model underlines how useful it is.

However, when the RM services are considered, it becomes clear that most apply - at least at some level of abstraction - equally to data and tasks.   The current RM's organisation does not support this fact (except implicitly if an assumption about how task services are implemented is made). An object oriented model seems to offer a much better basis for discussing the broader framework services.

While no claim is made that a full alternative model has been developed here, or that this approach does not introduce its own difficulties, it does seem to be a potentially fruitful avenue to explore.

6 REFERENCES

[1]   "A Reference Model for Frameworks of Computer Assisted Software Engineering Environments".   To be published as ECMA TR/55.   (Also Hewlett-Packard document 'Version 4.0 ECMA/TC33/TGRM/90/016'; August, 1990)
[2]   "ANSI X3H4 Working Draft. Information Resource Dictionary System. ATIS". February, 1990

10

A framework for standardisation and support environment technology

Mark Gibbons
British Telecom Research Labs.,
Martlesham Heath, Ipswich, UK

Abstract

The open systems concept is one of the most important in Information Technology today. A support environment is a system (which may be an open system) in which the process of software development is provided with automated support, in order to produce productivity, efficiency and end-product quality improvements. Concurrent with the idea of open systems is the move to Information Technology standardisation. Many standards organisations now exist, each occupying a different technology niche. As a result, many standards initiatives impinge upon, or duplicate work areas within other similar initiatives. With time, some of these initiatives will gain support, while others will cease to play a significant role.

Developers of open systems (in general) will have to interpret these trends, so that their developed products conform to recognised standards. The nature of the frameworks underpinning support environments means that they too are affected to a greater or lesser degree by each of these standards initiatives.

This paper presents the range of standards initiatives affecting support environments, using examples to demonstrate particular standardisation issues. Support environment types are then considered and the different technology requirements for each type discussed. The paper then looks at how standardisation is represented within reference models prior to placing these standards initiatives into an overview framework. This framework could form the basis of a debate to assess each standard's impact upon support environment technology, and thereby make an assessment of the importance of each of the main candidates.

The standards initiatives addressed are those relating to the supporting technology such as PCTE and ATIS, rather than the standardisation of particular methods such as SSADM (which could be supported within a support environment).

Introduction

The concept of, and requirement for open systems is widely accepted by organisations who develop and use information technology. These organisations wish to protect their existing information technology investments by utilising their computer based systems over their existing (and future) proprietary and heteregeneous networks. Linked with this customer driven move towards open systems, is the major drive towards software and systems standards within a variety of formal and de facto standards initiatives.

A support environment is an example of an application which might be implemented as an open system. McDermid [1] defined a support environment as:

"Support Environments are intended to address the problems (of large software development) by providing a set of tools covering the whole software lifecycle, and supporting many different roles in the development process, within a coherent framework. The framework holds the information necessary to allow the problems of configuration control, change control and so on to be solved more systematically"

That is, a support environment is thought of as a system which provides guidance and direction to users when carrying out the roles and tasks assigned to them; together with access to a variety of services necessary in performing such duties. Such services include data storage, configuration management, project management, system analysis and design support etc.

The support environment of the future is an example of an open system which will be impacted by many of the standards initiatives described within this paper. That is, developments within these standards initiatives will have an important effect upon the decisions made by organisations looking to invest in support environment technology. Indeed, since the development of high quality software systems produced on time and to budget is related to an organisation's competitive edge, high financial and business costs could accrue through making the wrong investment decisions with respect to support environment technology. For these reasons, organisations thinking of investing in support environment technology need to actively track and invest resources into technology relating to standards. This paper will point out practical examples of these issues.

This paper describes the range of standards initiatives and support environment architecture types which are currently in existence. Several reference models are then described and their relationship to the various standards and support environment types considered. Lastly, the document proposes a simple framework in which these various standards and support environments can be put into context.

A Glossary of Terms used can be found at the back of this paper

The Range of Relevant Standardisation

When considering support environment technology, what are the standards initiatives that need to be considered? There are, in fact a wide variety of standards initiatives relevant to the field of support environments. These standards can be sub-divided into several technology areas such as:

    ⊃ Public Tool Interfaces
    ⊃ Open Distributed Processing Standards
    ⊃ Repository Management
    ⊃ Open Operating Systems
    ⊃ User Interfaces
    ⊃ Process Modelling (Task Management)?

There is not enough space to describe all of these areas within the current paper. Therefore, the first three areas have been selected in order to highlight relevant points. For each area selected, a short description of the technology and the initiative is given, followed by a discussion of some of the issues raised by that particular initiative:

Public Tool Interfaces:

A Public Tool Interface (PTI) is a set of facilities commonly required by tools which are made available as a framework for a support environment. Once a PTI has been populated with the appropriate tools, an environment for the development and maintenance of software applications is created.

Recent events in the PTI development and standardisation process serve to demonstrate that, contrary to common perceptions of standards related work, events within standardisation initiatives can move with great rapidity. Less than a year ago, debate within this area was commonly based upon the relative merits of the European offering, PCTE, and the American CAIS-A offering. At about the same time discussions were taking place between American experts to initiate a new work programme, PCIS(Portable Common Interface Set) to develop the next generation PTI. At that time, most American experts saw PCIS as principally involving the merging of PCTE with the best elements of the CAIS-A approach.

However, the adoption of PCTE as ECMA Standard 149 in December 1990 has resulted in PCTE being increasingly seen as the pre-eminent PTI available today. This is witnessed by the increased level of corporate commitment being displayed by the major computer manufacturers and the availability of the first PCTE-compliant tools. Starved of corporate investment, these developments in PCTE have sounded the death knell of CAIS-A. Consequently, the debate with respect to the PCIS initiative has changed greatly. Firstly, European input to the debate expressed the need for PCIS to provide a technological advance as well as simply an amalgam of exisiting technology. At the same time American interest has shifted to viewing PCIS as being a set of interfaces based upon a combination of PCTE and Digital's ATIS proposals. The rest of 1991 will be taken up by a requirements phase to determine both civilian and military needs for PCIS, so further rapid developments in the debate can be anticipated.

Open Distributed Processing Standards

The reality of distributed applications is a direct consequence of the many organisational and technical constraints that arise in the real world. Consequently, many information technology systems which need to be integrated together tend to be geographically dispersed. The Open Distributed Processing standards process is aimed at realising these transparently distributed applications.

Initiatives which are of interest here are:

    ⊙ ISO Open Distributed Processing
    ⊙ OSF Distributed Computing Environment (DCE)

0 The ANSA Project

This area of standardisation also illustrates a number of further issues relating to the decisions that have to be faced by organisations looking at support environment technology.

The formal standardisation process is headed by the ISO body for Open Distributed Processing(ODP). Up to this time, ISO have been concentrating their efforts on developing a reference model for ODP. ANSA was an ESPRIT project which has also been addressing the problem of open distributed processing and with their ANSAware product have developed what is regarded in some quarters as the best current example of the ODP platform of the future. The ISO ODP reference model has been greatly influenced by the work and ideas of the ANSA project. Indeed over 80% of the ANSA architecture, and in particular, ANSA's communication mechanism, known as the Tracer have been adopted by the ISO reference model initiative. The OSF have taken a different, more pragmatic approach to the problem of distributed processing, by building DCE based upon a number of existing products.

So what are the decisions which need to be considered by organisations? It is quite possible that the support environments of the future will be expected to be an application run transparently (to the user) over a distributed network. For this to be made reality sizeable investments in distributed technologies will have to be made. Should an organisation wait until the formal standardisation process has been concluded and standard-compliant implementations of the technology exist? Equally, should an organisation invest in State-of the-Art technology closely related to the likely formal standard, but which is produced within a small consortium? Finally, should an organisation commit to a de facto standard such as DCE, which may be technologically inferior, but which is nevertheless characterised by its pragmatic approach and high degree of industrial and commercial commitment? Because of the scale of the problem, there are no simple answers to these questions, yet the costs associated with making the wrong decisions could be very large.

Repository Management

In order to illustrate both the breadth of standards initiatives relevant to support environment technology and to illustrate the types of issues associated with these standards initiatives; the last area that this paper will look at is that of Repository Management.

Standardisation in the Repository (or Data) Management area provides the means by which tools for Management Information Systems and CASE tools can share common information and thus improve the process of application development.

Repository (or Data) Management is currently handled within the following standards initiatives:

0 ISO Information Resource Dictionary Standards (SC21/WG3)
0 ANSI Information Resource Dictionary Standards (X3H4 & X3.138)
0 IBM's Proprietory Offerings
0 Digital's ATIS Proprietory Offerings

The current ANSI IRDS standard (X3.138) was developed to meet the repository needs of Management Information Systems, and was based upon a somewhat weak entity-relationship data modelling approach. Since the adoption of that original IRDS standard, work has progressed on the development of the next generation standard. This has been due both as a result of the weaknesses identified within the existing standard and also because of the recognition, by experts within this area, of the convergence between the data requirements of Management Information Systems and those of CASE tools.

Consequently, work has progressed both within ANSI and ISO to develop the next generation IRDS standard. In selecting SQL2 as the basis for their Services Interface, ISO have adopted a relational approach to the problem. ANSI, on the other hand have rejected this approach and have been reviewing several proprietory options as the basis of their services interfaces.

So what are the repository management issues which need to be considered by organisations investing in the support environments of the future? In the author's view the following issues occur:

> The problems associated with two major standards organisations adopting very different approaches to the same technology area;
> The involvement of proprietory interest within standards organisations;
> The risk involved for organisations looking for upwards compatibility between their existing data storage systems and the repositories of the future - which could well reside within an organisation's support environment (see next section).
> The need for an organisation to develop a technology migration strategy;
> The need to identify the benefits from adopting a particular technology.

Let's consider some of these points in greater detail:

The keystone of IBM's current and future strategy is AD/Cycle. The Repository Manager represents the central element within this strategy and is currently being developed for their MVS mainframe environment. IBM have therefore sensibly (from a proprietory viewpoint), used the Repository Manager/MVS as the basis of a set of proposals for repository management standardisation.

At the same time, IBM have also developed their Systems Applications Architecture(SAA), which is a proprietory version of an open network architecture. As such, AD/Cycle fits on top of SAA, in much the same way as Digital's Cohesion fits on top of their Network Application Support facilities. SAA provides a set of interfaces for use within the SAA environment, including a Common Programming Interface(CPI) for a repository. Again, IBM have made the repository CPI more general, and used it as the basis for a set of proposals for repository management standardisation.

Although the SAA/CPI proposals can be viewed as a subset of the Repository Manager proposals, and exclude many of the most useful features (eg. object orientation, version control) found within the Repository Manager proposals, IBM proposed the repository CPI to ANSI. The ANSI committee duly accepted these proposals, on the condition that IBM would make them compatible with the existing IRDS standard; thereby creating a third set of IBM proposals. More recently, IBM have withdrawn from the ANSI process, leaving the field open to Digital's ATIS proposals - of which there are also three variants available.

The repository management area demonstrates clearly the level of complexity involved in tracking some of these standards areas. It also demonstrates the high level of proprietory influence often involved in the standardisation process. Finally, it demonstrates the difficulties involved for organisations trying to develop a strategy for upward compatibility for their corporate data resource, and the dangers inherent in adopting the wrong technological approach.

In addition to the three areas of technology addressed here, there are several other areas of standardisation which are relevant to support environment technology, such as user interface standards and open operating systems. The question which might be asked is: Where do they all fit? or rather, Where and how do they interrelate and overlap with one another? We will consider these questions later. Firstly, lets broaden the discussion further.

Support Environment Architecture Types

It is increasingly accepted within the support environment community that support environments are characterised by two very different architectural models. For example, see [2]. These are known as the data-centric approach and the communications-oriented approach to developing support environments. The first of these approaches is characterised by its data integration capability, the later by its handling of control integration.

A data centric support environment is characterised by a single data repository which represents the only data store within the environment. Since each tool within the environment accesses the same data (where appropriate), the system provides very tight integration around the repository with a minimum of data duplication. This type of environment is however, less capable at providing loose tool, or control integration by means of some message passing mechanism.

A communications oriented support environment is different from a data centric support environment in that there need be no central data repository. In its place, there is a communications channel which provides the necessary control integration mechanisms by which tools can successfully interwork and relay data between one another. Data storage can be provided by means of dedicated data storage tools within the environment, or by the individual tools themselves. However, this type of environment is weak in addressing the needs of data integration.

From the above, it can be seen that the two architectural models represent different ends of the spectrum. In the future, it is possible that support environments might be developed which make use of both approaches. Examples of this hybrid approach can already be seen within existing state of the art products. For example, Hewlett Packard's SoftBench product with its Broadcast Message Server could be regarded as a simple example of a communications oriented environment. The hybrid approach can be demonstrated by Hewlett Packard's work aimed at incorporating PCTE within SoftBench. It is believed that Digital are also considering the possibilities for including the Multicast Message Server from their FUSE product within the Cohesion Framework.

Do these different models make the same demands upon the standards that we have considered within this paper? The answer is almost certainly no. The different configurations adopted by the two approaches are likely to impose different constraints upon both the elements within the support environment, such as the data repository; and also upon the underlying platform, such as the provision of open distributed processing.

Reference Models and Standardisation

Earlier on we asked the question as to where and how do all the different standards initiatives fit with respect to each other. The way in which this is commonly presented is through a Reference Model. At this time though, there seems to be almost as many reference models as there are standards initiatives in existence. Several of these reference models are applicable to the debate on support environments. For example:

    0 The ECMA CASEE Reference Model
    0 The ATIS Reference Model
    0 The CCITT SG X Reference Model

Let's consider these in a little more detail:

The ECMA CASEE Reference Model

This model was developed within ECMA to provide a means of describing and positioning PCTE in relation to other relevant technologies such as CAIS-A . The model is commonly known as the "Toaster Model", due to the diagrammatic representation of the model (See Figure 1).

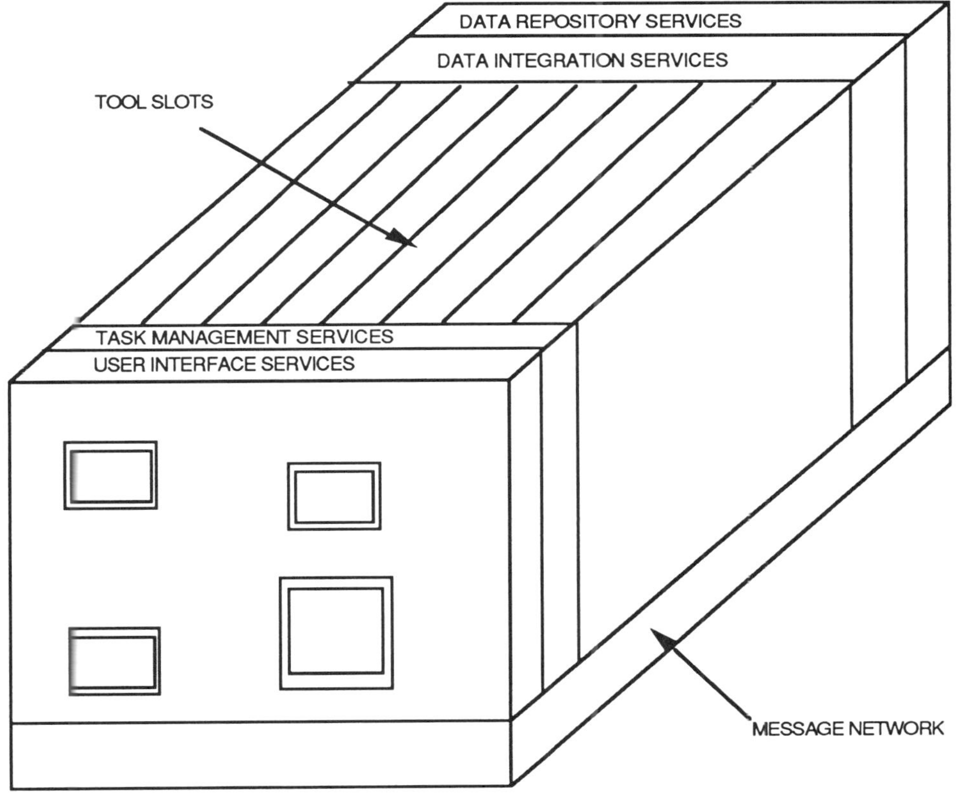

Figure 1

In detail, the model is broken down into the following groups of services:

- 0 Data Repository Services
- 0 Data Integration Services
- 0 Task Management Services
- 0 User Interface Services

The Data Integration Services and the Task Management Services are separated by a number of tool slots, while the whole structure is underpinned by a communication service, known as the Message Network. Within these groupings the various types of integration (presentation, control and data) can be described.

Each of these service groups consists of a set of services. Each service within the group is then described by means of a set of dimensions representing different viewpoints such as the Internal, External and Conceptual views of the service. These services are then used as the basis for the analysis and subsequent informal description of a CASEE, or related product. See [3] for further information on this model.

At this time, the reference model has been used to describe PCTE+, and a work programme is being initiated within ECMA to describe the PCTE standard and the ATIS proposals. The reference model has also attracted considerable interest in America (in particular within the NIST), which is likely to lead to joint work on the further enhancement and maintenance of the reference model.

The ATIS Reference Model

The ATIS(A Tool Integration Standard) Reference Model is a reference model for Repository Management (See Figure 2).

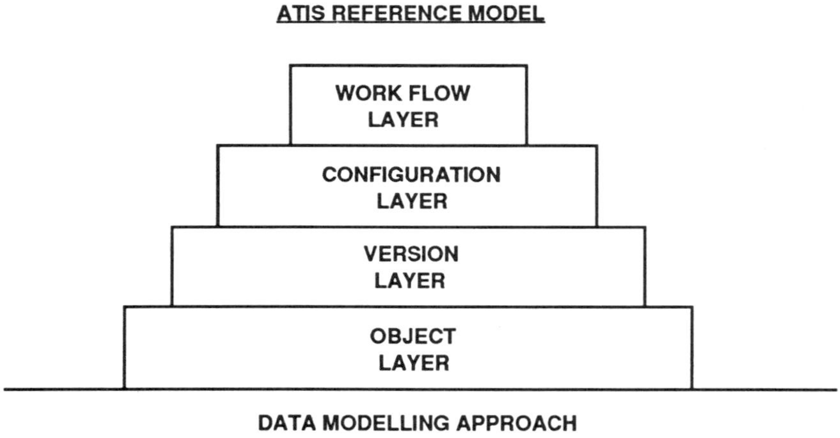

ATIS REFERENCE MODEL

```
                  WORK FLOW
                    LAYER
              CONFIGURATION
                   LAYER
            VERSION
              LAYER
         OBJECT
          LAYER
```

DATA MODELLING APPROACH

Figure 2

The model specifies four levels of service which provide a conceptual and functional framework to describe each system. The layers are:

    0 Object layer
    0 Version Layer
    0 Configuration Management Layer
    0 Work Flow Layer

These layers are all based upon the underlying data modelling approach that supports the repository. Each layer depends upon the lower layers for services and provides additional services to the layers above. As with all reference models, the division of services between the layers is somewhat arbitrary. For further information, see [4].

Initial work undertaken by Digital using this model has demonstrated the degree of correlation which exists between the services provided by PCTE+, ATIS and IRDS, particularly within the higher levels of the reference model. This work proved to be the basis for more detailed consideration of how ATIS and the PCTE standard might be combined within a single system, both as part of the PCIS initiation programme and also in proprietary product discussions within Digital and Atherton Technology.

The CCITT SG X Reference Model

At the time of writing, the CCITT SG X Reference Model is still under development, and as a result is rather less mature than the other reference models discussed here. It is therefore discussed here only briefly. The model differs from a number of other reference models in that it has initially adopted a very broad scope in defining the problem space, which in this case is on what constitutes a support environment. As a result, CCITT SG X considers a support environment as comprising both the automated system and the people interacting with that system. In order to manage this broad scope, much use of process modelling concepts is made within the reference model. The model consists of two parts, the System Architecture Model (which addresses the automation aspects) and the Process Architecture Model (which addresses the human and process aspects). It is likely that the unique aspect of this model will prove to be the interface and subsequent interaction between the two architectural models.

Advantages and Disadvantages of the Reference Model Approach

Reference models have shown themselves to be very worthwhile additions to the debates on the technology niche they address, since they provide experts in the field with a framework and common vocabulary through which to discuss individual technology areas or standardisation programmes. By their very nature they provide a convenient arrangement of technology viewpoints, and these serve to highlight issues relating to that technology which must be focussed upon.

However, using the wrong reference model can lead to significant problems. That is, if a model is inappropriate to the technology under consideration, or if the reference model does not enforce the right level of detail, then use of that model is likely to lead to false confidence in the results produced when using the reference model.

Reference models also contain deficiencies when used to observe the breadth of standardisation initiatives relevant to support environment technology. In this case, the "convenient arrangement" imbued within the reference model fails to demonstrate the idea of how all the relevant standards initiatives inter-relate with one another. This is because none of these reference models are truly generic. This problem is compounded by the fact that most of the reference models have been developed by different communities who have a different view, and hence vocabulary for the problem space in question. In addition, although some of the reference models state that they can be used in conjunction with others, the interface between the models is never defined (even where this is possible). Consequently, none of them allow us to describe all the facets relating to support environments and standardisation that we might wish to within this paper.

Therefore, it is proposed that a simple model is needed to place all the initiatives within a single context, and so act as an umbrella for these overview discussions. This can then be used as the starting point for more detailed deliberations on each technology area. Existing reference models should then be utilised to provide the structure for the more detailed debate on each technology area.

An Overview Reference Framework

So what form might this simple overview reference framework take? Figure 3 provides one possible solution.

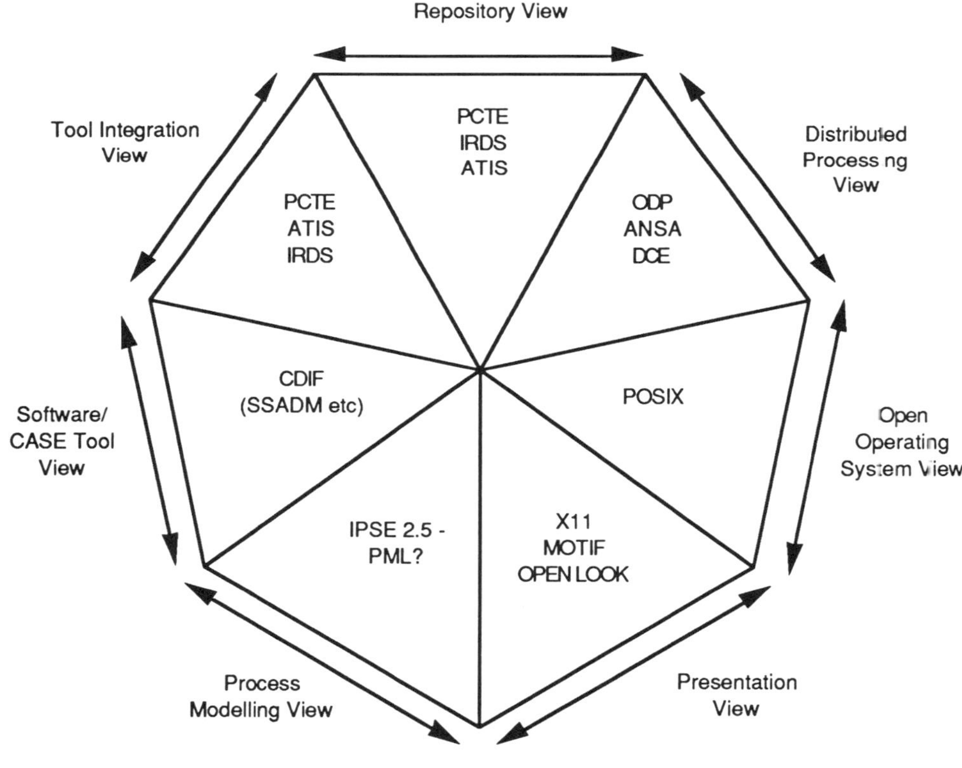

Figure 3

The reference framework is based upon the concept of inter-relating Views, and is depicted graphically by means of a septagon comprising of the following Views:

     0 Presentation View
     0 Open Operating System View
     0 Distributed Processing View

    0 Repository View
    0 Tool Integration View
    0 Software/CASE Tool View
    0 Process Modelling View.

Each View represents a different technology area relevant to support environment technology which is the subject of one or more standardisation initiatives. Individual standards initiatives can be placed within the appropriate Views. Within Figure 3, each of the Views has been populated with many of the initiatives introduced earlier in this paper.

Clearly, the framework is not completely populated, since further standards initiatives could be added to many of the Views. For example, in which View or Views might you allocate the work being performed by the Object Management Group?

Since the reference framework is primarily concerned with the relationships between the various standards initiatives and the identification of possible conflicts of interest, no technology preference is inferred within the framework. Equally, the reference framework implies no layering of individual standards, although the idea of linkage is maintained through the spatial relationships of the Views and the common centrepoint for all the Views. A further benefit of the reference framework lies in its representation of the overlap (in a simple graphical way) between different standards initiatives.

The reference framework can also be easily expanded to include new areas of standardisation relevant to support environment technology, and consequently incorporate them into the discussion on support environments. In Figure 3, this ability for expansion is demonstrated by the inclusion of the Process Modelling View - even though his immature area of technology is not represented by any standards initiative at the current time.

The reference framework forms the top level of a flat heirarchy, in which the leaf level is comprised of all the more detailed reference models such as the CASEE reference model. The reference framework therefore provides a top-level means to initiate discussions on the relevance and impact of different standards initiatives on support environments. More detailed evaluation of a particular standards initiative could then take place by referring to the relevant reference model.

However, the reference framework proposed here should only be seen as a first step. For example, it provides no formal vocabulary (outside of the Views concept) for dialogue between experts and no textual structure is supplied to describe the nature of the interface between the various standards initiatives. In addition, the problem of defining the interfaces between the reference models remains. Further work is therefore needed to fully develop this idea.

Issues Raised By the Overview Reference Framework

A review of the populated overview reference framework in Figure 3 reinforces the visibility of a number of the issues outlined within this paper. These are:

    C The huge number of standards initiatives which have an impact upon support environment technology;
    C The division between formal and de facto approaches;
    C The choice between state of the art technology and commercial commitment;
    0 The overlap and duplication of work between different standards initiatives;

0 The number of difficult decisions facing organisations looking to invest in
  support environment technology;
0 The reference framework itself, provides a simple but useful means by
  which to appreciate the linkage between all these initiatives.

Conclusions

This paper has described some of the standards initiatives and support environment
architecture types currently in existence. Several reference models have been described
and their relationship to the various standards and support environment types considered.

This paper has demonstrated the fact that there is probably no single scenario to describe
the diverse issues affecting support environment technology. However, a simple
reference framework has been proposed by which these various standards and support
environments can be put into context.

It is demonstrated that all organisations need to track and monitor the many relevant
standards initiatives, in order to create the support environment most likely to maintain
their technological and competitive edge. The overview reference framework described
within this paper provides those organisations with a potential starting point, from which
to begin the monitoring of the many standards involved.

Finally, the next step with respect to the overview reference framework would be to
address the issue of describing the parameters governing the relationships between the
various Views within the overview reference framework. However, further development
should be performed in harness with some practical use of the the framework, in order to
identify its strengths and weaknesses, as well as establish the practicality of its usage.

Glossary

ANSA	Advanced Networked Systems Architecture
	(aka Integrated Systems Architecture)
ANSI	American National Standards Institute
ATIS	A Tool Interface Standard
CAIS-A	Common Ada Programming Support Environment Interface Set
CASE	Computer Aided Software Engineering
CASEE	Computer Aided Software Engineering Environment
CCITT	International Telegraph and Telephone Consultative Committee
ECMA	European Computer Manufacturers Association
IRDS	Information Resource Dictionary Standard
ISO	International Standards Organisation
NIST	National Institute of Science and Technology
ODP	Open Distributed Processing
OSF	Open Software Foundation
PCTE	Portable Common Tool Environment
PCIS	Portable Common Interface Set
SAA	Systems Applications Architecture
SSADM	Structured Systems and Analysis and Design Method

References

[1] McDermid J., "Integrated Project Support Environments", IEE 1985.

[2] Kennedy D.M., "The ARISE Project", ESF Seminar, 1990

[3] ECMA "A Reference Model for Computer Aided Software Engineering Environments", ECMA/TR55

[4] Beyer H.R., Chapman K., Nolan C., "The ATIS Reference Model" draft 27/4/90.

Part 4

Integration of Methods and Tools

11

On integration and reuse in a software development environment

Alan W. Brown and John A. McDermid
Department of Computer Science, University of York,
Heslington, York, YO1 5DD, UK

Abstract

While the benefits and advantages of IPSE technology are widely agreed, there appears to be very little commercial use of the IPSEs that are currently available. We believe that much of the reason for this can be traced to overexpectation and misunderstanding within the potential IPSE user communities, and to some extent by IPSE developers themselves. At the root of a lot of these problems appears to be the key issues of *integration* and *reuse*.

In this paper we examine these two key issues, propose a set of semantic levels, or "measures" for each of them, and discuss the fundamental conflict that arises in trying to satisfy the twin goals of tight integration and high levels of reuse within an IPSE.

1   Introduction

It is widely recognised that the environment in which software is developed can have a significant effect both on productivity and on the quality of the software which results. However, there are many conflicting and competing ideas about the best approach to software development support. As a result, it is instructive to take time to examine some attempts at introducing and using Integrated Project Support Environments (IPSEs) within an organisation and to analyse two of the key notions in IPSE philosophy – tool integration and tool reuse. It is widely accepted that integration is necessary to achieve productivity in development and high quality in software products. However, it is also recognised that it is very expensive to develop software engineering tools *ab initio*; hence it is desirable to be able to reuse existing tools. Reuse and integration are often stated as fundamental objectives for IPSEs – indeed, the primary *raison d'etre* for open environments, frameworks, or Public Tool Interfaces (PTIs) such as PCTE+ is to achieve **both** integration and reuse. However, we believe that these notions are in conflict and that some of the difficulties seen in trying to use IPSE systems stem from this conflict. Our aim, therefore, is to throw some light on the notions of integration and reuse, to explicate their conflicting natures, and to illustrate how the failure to recognise their antithetical nature leads to problems in practice.

Section 2 of this paper begins by extracting a number of important issues that have been identified in documented attempts at using IPSE technology, and goes on to show how an understanding of the concept of integration may provide the key to addressing those issues. Section 3 then examines the meaning of integration within an IPSE, identifying a number of views of integration that must be considered. Section 4 provides an initial attempt at a classification of levels of integration within one of the views defined earlier, namely the tool view. Section 5 highlights the conflicts that arise in attempting to satisfy simultaneously the two important requirements within this area – tight integration of tools together with the need to make extensive reuse of tools and tool fragments. This is followed in section 6 by an example of this conflict based on experience with some of our own tool developments. Section 7 discusses ways of (partially) overcoming the conflict by careful choice of the level of integration required for different purposes, and different stages, in the life-cycle. Finally, in section 8 we present a summary of the main points we have raised, and draw some conclusions about the reasons for the relative success of Computer-Aided Software Engineering (CASE) tools and IPSEs.

2   Experiences of Introducing and Using an IPSE

If we wish to investigate IPSE integration, then perhaps the most obvious place to start is to examine discussions on deficiencies with the typical software development process, and reported experiences of the introduction of IPSEs into an organisation and their subsequent use. In particular, such an examination may provide us with an insight into the "real" user requirements for such a system based on the likes and dislikes of the user community when faced with having to use an IPSE for software development. Clearly, such an analysis will be limited in scope, based as it is on the small number of user experiences reported publicly.[1] However, a number of interesting observations can be made.

While many more points are identified in these examples, we highlight three key issues derived from the reports we examined[11, 4, 9, 3, 17, 16]:

1. Management control and organisational issues are at least as important to the success of an IPSE as the technical issues involved with tool support. For example, good support for communication between team members is vital to a project's development.

2. Tool support for individuals through a tightly integrated toolset is often in conflict with the need for (less tightly integrated) tools which facilitate cooperative working between group members.

3. For IPSE technology to be effective it must be well matched to the existing software development processes of the organisation. Without this, individuals will be resentful and suspicious of its imposition, and management will not be supportive of its introduction. This, of course, implies that existing, familiar tools must be reused.

We believe that all three of these issues hinge on an understanding of the concept of *integration* within an IPSE – the major theme of this paper. Furthermore, as a consequence of the three key issues highlighted above, we are able to make the following comments on the role and importance of integration within an IPSE.

The first issue indicates that there may be a number of different dimensions, or *views*, of integration which require investigation. For example, we may wish to discuss how well integrated an environment is from a management view which may tell us little about how well integrated the environment is from a technical view. We need to investigate what these different views of integration might be, and how each view affects the others.

The second issue points to a number of different *levels* of integration within each view. Hence, within a technical view of integration for example, we may identify a spectrum of levels at which the integration of tools within

---

[1]It is clear that many more organisations have experimented with IPSE technology, but in most cases results of their experiences have not been made available due to commercial confidentiality (or, perhaps, embarrassment!).

a particular IPSE can be achieved. Clearly, it would be extremely useful to be able to define such a spectrum of levels in each of the integration views.

Finally, the third issue introduces the idea that an understanding of the software development *process* is an essential precursor to the introduction of a particular software development support solution. From an integration perspective, this highlights the need for an organisation to examine its own methods of developing software to determine where in the development life-cycle particular levels of integration would be most effective and provide most benefit. Based on such an analysis, an organisation would then be able to select an appropriate technology (ie. an engineering solution) which provides such a level of integration. In other words, an understanding of the *semantics* of integration must come before addressing the *mechanisms* of integration. Although this seems an obvious point, in our view most of the work on IPSEs has concentrated on mechanisms without considering semantics. We believe that the focus on mechanisms not semantics is one of the primary technical problems hindering the use of IPSEs.

Pragmatically, the third issue also means that we must consider tool reuse. It is rarely possible to design a process *ab initio* – technical and managerial acceptance is only gained through incremental enhancements from the current state of affairs. However, we believe that reuse and integration are in conflict so that this is a major source of problems in introducing IPSEs, as we shall see in sections 5 and 6. These observations have ramifications not only for those wishing to introduce IPSEs, but also for the current fashion for designing open environments, frameworks, or PTIs. We return to this point in section 8, but first we consider more deeply the concept of integration.

3   What is Integration?

In recent years much attention has been focussed on the requirements for software development environments. It has been found that a key element in providing effective support is the *integration* that is provided within the software development environment. The concept of integration can manifest itself in a number of different ways within the development environment. For example, we could interpret integration as meaning one or more of the following:[2]

- *Interface Integration.* Each tool has the same set of constructs at the user interface (where there is common functionality). Hence, tool users

---

[2]It is difficult to know whether or not this is a "complete" set of views or perspectives on integration. However, we do believe that these are all key aspects of integration.

would find it very simple to move between tools as the ways in which a user interacts with tools is standardised. The Apple Macintosh range of machines and applications are a prime example of integration at the user interface level.

- *Technical Integration.* The environment has been constructed to support a single coherent software development methodology. For example, the Perspective system[5] was designed for supporting the development of real-time embedded software systems, based on variants of MASCOT and Pascal, and was most widely used in avionics systems. In the SAFRA project[17] for example, Perspective was linked to a tool for capturing system requirements in the CORE notation[14] and used for semi-automatically generating software to implement those requirements in an extended form of the Pascal programming language. In addition, Host-Target debugging tools were provided for the object code this language produces. The result was a development environment which was well integrated in the sense that the tools work together with a common understanding of the software development life-cycle supported, and where each stage of the development process supports a single view of the structure of the software system under development. Arguably this view would be better called process integration as there is an integrated process (and we shall adopt this term from now on);

- *Tool Integration.* The environment has facilities to allow tools to share data via a common data format, and preferably one that can be defined for a particular purpose. The most obvious example of this is the UNIX development environment[12] in which all data is assumed to be in the form of a simple stream of bytes. Tools can be combined very easily as a data consumer tool (eg. a printer driver) can expect the output from a data producer (eg. a text processor) to arrive in a predefined form. One alternative way in which this integration may be achieved is via the definition of a schema for a database, and we shall amplify on this topic below;

- *Team Integration.* The IPSE should facilitate inter-working of teams both in the positive sense of ensuring effective communication and information dissemination, and in the negative sense of preventing one user from corrupting the work of another. Environments such as Perspective provide some of the above through a mechanism based on private and shared domains (work areas);

- *Management Integration.* The IPSE should facilitate management control over the *actual* development process, rather than some fictitious reports! This means that management information should be derived from (abstracted from) the technical information produced by the software engineers. We know of no IPSE which provides true management integration.[3]

While all of the above provide interpretations of the term *integrated* with respect to a software development environment, none of them captures completely the notion of integration. In fact, we believe that an IPSE needs to provide integration in *all* these senses in order to meet the requirements set out above. Indeed, we can view these aspects of integration as being "dimensions" in a model of integration. We can illustrate this by considering the tool, managerial, and process views, in figure 1 (five dimensions are too difficult to represent graphically). We can summarise these three views, but

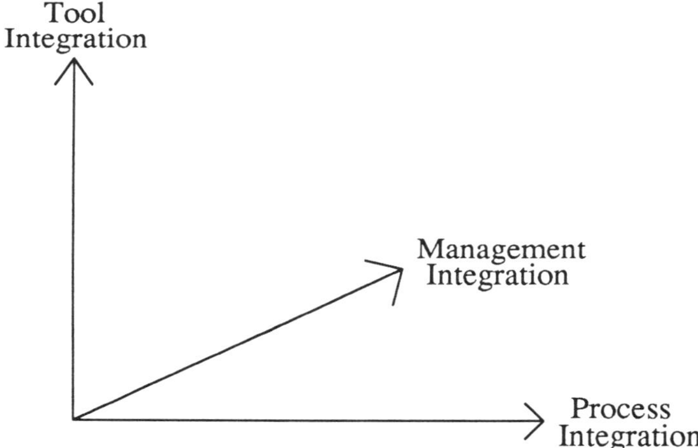

Figure 1: Three Views of IPSE Tool Integration

focussing on tool issues, as:

- *Tool View.* Integration is discussed in terms of how the data is represented and recorded by the tools. This determines the level, or sophistication, of data sharing that is possible between tools.

---

[3]Interestingly, the authors of Stoneman deliberately excluded the notion of management integration as they believed it was beyond the state of the art in IPSE (APSE) design. At least one of the Stoneman authors still holds these beliefs.

- *Management View.* A manager is interested in controlling and monitoring the use of tools. From a manager's perspective, integration of tools into the management reporting and monitoring scheme of a project is the major concern.

- *Process View.* Constraining the order in which tools can be used in processing data is determined by a project's process model. At a simple level this may, for example, involve ensuring that the Ada compiler is only ever invoked on Ada source files. However, more sophisticated systems may, for example, automatically send any re-built software to be reviewed by the quality assurance department.

It is important to note that these views are orthogonal. A set of tools may be well integrated from a tool view, but be poorly integrated from a managerial, or process view.

A limitation of many IPSEs, and certainly IPSE infrastructures, is that they concentrate on only one or a small number of these aspects of integration. Indeed, most infrastructures are aimed almost exclusively at tool integration and, even here, they do not provide the level of facilities which are really required for effective integration, as we shall now illustrate.

4   A Tool Integration Classification

While "integration" is recognised as being of vital importance to the success of an IPSE, there is still much work needed to understand *what* level of integration is required, and *how* that integration should be provided.

The first step to resolving this confusion was to recognise that there are a number of orthogonal *views* of tool integration. Having made this realisation we now need to investigate how to classify the "degree of integration" achieved in each dimension. Whilst we don't believe that there is a clear scientific basis for establishing measures and metrics, we do believe that we can give a useful pragmatic classification of levels or degrees of integration. The utility arises as the classification gives us a basis for comparing and analysing systems (and to some extent interface definitions). We illustrate this by considering the tool integration dimension. We chose this dimension as it seems to be where currently most effort is going in developing IPSEs and defining PTIs.

4.1 Tool Integration

The key to understanding tool integration in an IPSE from a technical point of view, is a recognition that the way in which information is recorded, shared and transferred between tools is the crucial factor in determining how well integrated it is.

To take a step towards a better understanding of these issues, figure 2 presents a proposed classification of a number of levels of tool integration in an IPSE.

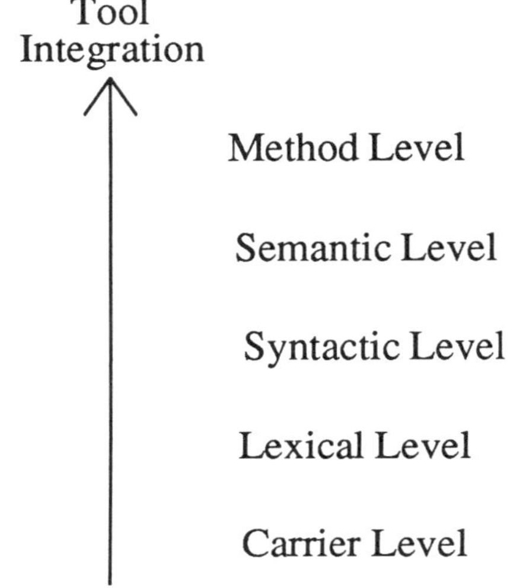

Figure 2: Levels of Tool Integration in an IPSE

We now examine these levels in detail.

4.1.1 Carrier Level Integration

If we consider the UNIX programming environment[12] then it has been possible to "integrate" a set of tools for many years. However, the integration that is provided is a primitive means for simple tool composition by enforcing a single, consistent file format. While the tools themselves are responsible for data structuring, validation, and so on, the tools can share data by taking advantage of the fact that all input/output of tools is in the form of a stream of bytes. There is no co-operation between tools at any deeper level than passing streams of bytes. We can refer to this level of cooperation as *carrier level* integration by analogy with the use of the term in electronic communications. This level, although simple, is non-vacuous as, for example, file formats and character codes are not (normally) common between operating systems.

Useful as this level of integration is, it has been said[8] that in many ways providing only carrier level tool integration is in fact tackling the wrong problem, or at best, tackling the right problem at the wrong level. For example, since there is no common understanding of the data which is carried between tools, then each tool has to analyse its input in its entirety leading to much repetition of processing. For example, Thimbleby[21] implemented a version of Knuth's Web for C by producing a troff[4] pre-processor and found that he needed to replicate much of the troff functionality in the pre-processor in order to encode suitable format information in the byte stream going between the programs. Thus, the simple "plug and socket" view of integration, whilst being necessary and useful, is a long way from providing full integration as it doesn't support establishment of a common view of the semantics of the shared data.

4.1.2   Lexical Level Integration

A partial solution employed by many existing development systems is to tightly couple sets of tools into families (toolsets) which share a common understanding of the lexical conventions of structures which are shared between those tools. We can refer to this as *lexical level* integration. Such tool families share common data formats and operating conventions which allow them to interact in a meaningful way. A typical example is the set of UNIX tools which make up the documenter's workbench[1]. By sharing a common approach to lexis, ie. the use of commands starting with a "." at the beginning of a line, a single document may contain tables, equations, and diagrams and it can be processed by passing it through a sequence of tools (tbl, eqn and pic or ideal, respectively) which understand which of the lexical symbols they are meant to process and know that they should ignore other symbols.

However, the conventions are still embedded within the tools. Thus, to add a new tool to the family would involve understanding the communication and data conventions with which new tools must interact. This could involve re-implementing the checks and structuring operations that already exist in the family. In practice difficulties do arise, and occasional faults arise, due to unwitting sharing of troff number registers and the like when developing new tools.

---

[4]The standard UNIX typesetting program.

At a more abstract level the integration is limited as there is still no understanding of the operations carried out by one tool on the part of the others. Thus, for example, if troff changes the point size of text in a box, pic doesn't know about this (as the change happens further down the pipeline) and won't adjust the box size, with the result that the text may not fit. Making the text and box fit can only be achieved by tedious (manual) iteration through the whole pipeline.

4.1.3 Syntactic Level Integration

A more meaningful level of integration can be provided when a set of data structures, or more precisely the rules governing the formation of the data structures, have been agreed by all relevant tools within an environment. The *syntactic level* of integration provides a much greater degree of cooperation between tools such that many of the repeated actions necessary to analyse, validate, and convert data structures are no longer required within every tool.

The most obvious examples of this level of integration occur in programming environments which are tightly integrated through some common underlying representation such as a parse tree, or symbol table[20]. By agreeing on this common structure, it is easier, for example, to develop a structured editor, compiler, and debugger for a given language syntax. The common representation (eg. a parse tree and symbol table) greatly reduces the amount of work which must be carried out in each tool. These capabilities are commonly found in AI development environments, especially those based around Lisp and (arguably) this is the source of the greatest contribution to productivity when using these environments.

In most existing IPSE's this is the level of integration that is generally supported, typically through a database schema. An initial phase of an IPSE development project is to define the database schema which acts as the focus of tool integration, and such information is recorded in a data dictionary which can be queried by the tools. The work on the Information Resource Dictionary System (IRDS) is very much aimed at this level of tool integration[7].

A crux, however, is the level of detail, or granularity, at which schemas are shared. This should be viewed as a further measure (or gradation of this measure) of integration. If the level is very fine-grained then good co-operation can occur, but the presence of a database is not enough to guarantee good integration if there is no agreed schema at a level "within" what would normally be operating system files.

4.1.4   Semantic Level Integration

To increase tool integration still further, a common understanding of the data structures must be augmented with a common definition of the semantics of those structures. This *semantic level* integration implies that a set of commonly agreed data structure definitions, *and the meanings of the operations on those structures*, is available. This can be achieved in one of two ways:

1. The data structure and operation specifications are defined before the tools are written so that tool writers know what structures are available, how they are named, the meaning of each structure, the effect of each operation, and so on.

2. The data repository in the infrastructure includes information about the data structures and operations which make up the repository. Such metadata ("data about data and operations") can then be queried by the tools.

The latter approach is, of course, much more flexible as it gives the opportunity for extending the toolset once the IPSE is in use.

Most highly integrated toolsets fall into the first class. To return to our troff/pic example, we could automatically adjust the size of a box if we had semantic integration and pic knew of the ramifications of the change in point size from the point of view of space requirements, not details of the characters. Note that this also requires co-operative access to shared data structures, not a simple pipe mechanism.[5]

The ideas of object-oriented databases for IPSEs and knowledge-based IPSEs seem to be aimed directly at the latter class — the difference is between the use of method specifications rather than rules to encode information about operation semantics. In our view, however, no present IPSE achieves integration at the semantic level, although some well-integrated toolsets (perhaps Microsoft Word is a good example) do reach this level.

4.1.5   Method Level Integration

However, by standardising on the data structures available, and even the operations upon them, we have only provided a partial solution. Problems still exist with tools overlapping in their role, being applied in an inappropriate

---

[5]We have achieved similar effects on UNIX via complex sets of pipes, for example in a tool for processing Z specifications[10]. However, conceptually it would have been much easier to achieve the requisite functionality with shared data structures (see also section 6).

order, and leaving gaps with the project life-cycle. Hence, attention is now moving towards *method level* integration by recognising that tools are used, and interact, only within the context of the software development process. This is really a projection into the tool dimension of what we mean by process integration, but it is genuinely a level here as it implies that the tools have an "understanding of the process".

It is necessary not only to agree on the data structures being manipulated and the manipulations, but also on the development process within which the tools are being used. Numerous methods and methodologies exist supporting some part of the project life-cycle. It must be possible to combine methods to produce a consistent view of the software life-cycle, and then to model that view within the IPSE itself, and within the particular tools so that they "know" their role in the process and can interact with other tools — so that they can send messages with meanings such as "you ought to know about this change I've just made" — where appropriate.

This provides the opportunity to constrain the use of tools to the correct point in the life-cycle, to offer positive guidance on what may be the best actions to take at any particular time, and to automate further (consequential) actions, where appropriate. This can be seen as having two forms as discussed for semantic integration — the knowledge of the role in the process is hard coded into the tools, or else it is represented in the repository/database. Clearly, explicit representation within the repository gives greater flexibility, including the ability to change the process.

Method integration is a key issue in providing truly integrated support for software development. A number of research projects are examining the way in which this level of integration can be provided[19, 18]. Some of our own work is looking at the utility of the object-oriented paradigm for achieving this level of integration.

4.1.6   Commentary

The assumption, or belief, behind the levels we have defined is that the higher levels are in some sense "better" than the lower levels. The validity of this view can be seen in terms of some of the above requirements.

For example, consider productivity which relies on efficiency of tool operation (and human tool use). Without carrier level integration then work is needed to convert between the output of one tool and the input of another. With carrier and lexical level integration tools can work together without transformation between formats, but there may still be much re-processing of data both during one combined operation with the tools, and caused by the need to use the tools repeatedly to achieve some desired effect (cf. the comments on the troff document processing tools). At the higher levels of integration the reprocessing is progressively eliminated, thus giving efficiency and productivity. Clearly this analysis is somewhat superficial, but studies of particular tools (eg. Thimbleby's cweb[21]) show that this theoretical analysis is borne out in practice.

We can see similar benefits with respect to other requirements, eg. quality, by considering the scope for errors (and user frustration leading to an acceptance of lower quality results). Thus, we believe that the levels represent a progressive increase in the degree of integration and concomitant improvements for the degree of satisfaction (of at least some) of the requirements on IPSEs.

Similar classifications can be carried out on the other "dimensions", although it is not quite so easy to order some of the levels, eg. for team integration, as there are both positive and negative aspects to this notion. Nonetheless, we believe that it is possible to produce useful classifications of integration from each of these points of view, although space does not permit us to perform the analysis here.

Of course, this ordering of levels of integration cannot be regarded entirely in isolation. Although there are benefits in integration as we go up the levels, there are also costs, eg. the need to take into account several tools when carrying out design work, and the performance costs of interpreting data structures rather than executing compiled code. Thus, for any practical IPSE development, there would be a set of trade-offs made — the benefit of the above classification is that it makes the basis for the trade-offs more explicit.

5   Reuse vs. Integration

In the context of IPSEs it is common to talk about the need for integration and the need for tool reuse. These twin goals are rarely analysed in detail. We believe this is unfortunate as they are, in a fundamental way, in conflict and we need to understand the conflict in order to achieve the right *compromise* between reuse and integration in an IPSE. We consider the relationship between reuse and integration from two points of view: matters of principle and pragmatics.

In principle, to achieve reuse (without major re-engineering) we need intrinsic compatibility between software tools. Perhaps surprisingly, we require *low* integration, eg. carrier or lexical level, in order for one tool to use the output of another without modification (to the data or the tools). This is the basis on which UNIX works, but it can perhaps be seen most clearly by means of a counterexample. Suppose we were to require higher levels of integration (eg. at the semantic level). This would require that the tools were designed with a shared understanding of the data and the operations on the data. Hence, by definition, we couldn't reuse one pre-existing tool in the context of another unless they had already been designed together (in an integrated fashion). This seems to preclude reuse in any meaningful or useful sense. In other words, *unpremeditated reuse*, allowing tools to be designed at separate times, can only be achieved at the expense of integration (happenstance excepted).

The principle is very simply stated. The pragmatic issues are rather more complex to analyse and we first remind the reader about some rather old concepts relating to the properties of module structures.

In the 1970's Myers[15] introduced the twin notions of module coupling and cohesion. Module coupling represented the character of the interaction between modules and cohesion indicated the "conceptual unity" of the module. Myers proposed simple "measures" for these notions, based around the capabilities and limitations of programming languages of the day. It is more helpful to give a simpler and more modern treatment of the concepts.

We follow Buxton and McDermid[2] and choose the following definitions for levels of cohesion and coupling with the implications that the earlier definitions (in the list) are better – from the point of view of code comprehensibility, maintainability, etc.

Cohesion (within a module)

- *Abstract* – object oriented – encapsulating the functions associated with a single class of objects or abstract data type;

- *Functional* – containing a single function;

- *Temporal* – time related functions, eg. all initialisation code;

- *Logical* – logical relationship between functions, eg. all input code;

- *Coincidental* – no good reason for the grouping.

These definitions are meant to be interpreted as implying that "good design" will produce modules which are Functional or Abstract.

Coupling (between modules)

- *Abstract* – by type checked procedure calls on services between modules;

- *Networked* – with import-export interfaces between modules;

- *Block Structured* – nested blocks as in Pascal, etc.;

- *Common* – via common data access as in Fortran;

- *Direct* – unrestricted access to code and data within other modules.

Again the intended interpretation is that "good design" will produce Abstract or Networked coupling.

The levels of integration which we described in section 4 are essentially *semantic* issues, whereas the notions of coupling and cohesion are essentially *mechanistic*. Thus they are, in principle, orthogonal but, in practice, certain mechanisms are better suited to supporting particular levels of integration and this is primarily due to non-functional issues such as timing and resource usage. Two sketch examples should suffice to illustrate this point.

Abstract coupling seems to imply a shared semantic model between the communicating objects – but there is no reason why the parameters might not be byte streams giving no more than carrier level integration. Conversely an AI[6] "blackboard system" might have a shared data area to provide communication, i.e. a form of common coupling – but use this mechanism to provide semantic integration, in the terms of the measure introduced in section 4. Almost undoubtedly, cohesion will be low in such a case. In the blackboard case common coupling is used, at least in part, to achieve better performance than could be realised on the same hardware with a pure object-oriented approach.

Thus, although the semantic measure of integration introduced in section 4 and the notions of coupling and cohesion are logically independent, consideration of issues such as performance often results in designs which have high coupling and low cohesion. It is now instructive to consider the relationship between reuse, integration, coupling and cohesion.

We require high cohesion within units which are to be reused, i.e. they need to carry out a well-defined function to be candidates for reuse. Further, we need low coupling between such units otherwise they will fail to work

---

[6]In our experience AI tools, including development environments, show high levels of integration and we believe that this is one of the main reasons why their use can be so productive.

when moved to another context (this is perhaps most easily seen with direct coupling). This seems to be independent of the dichotomy we are trying to draw between reuse and integration, but there is a link. We pointed out that, in order to achieve efficiency, highly integrated tools tend to have high coupling (and perhaps low cohesion) and this too hinders reuse.

From the above discussion we can see that, in principle, *unpremeditated reuse* is directly in conflict with integration. On the other hand, notions of cohesion and coupling are, in principle, orthogonal to the notion of integration. However, we have established that reuse requires low coupling and high cohesion but, in practice, high levels of integration are often only achieved at acceptable performance through accepting high coupling and low cohesion. Thus, both in principle and in practice reuse and integration are in conflict.

The situation may not be as stark as the above implies because module structures are normally hierarchic. Thus, some modules which are highly coupled and have low cohesion may be linked into a higher level module with the opposite characteristics, eg. the "backboard system" when considered as a whole will have high cohesion and low coupling. As a result it may be possible to achieve integration and reuse in one environment if we work at the right granularity – and this is the point to which we return in section 7.

6   Examples

We can illustrate the conflict between the twin goals of reuse and integration by reference to two simple examples.

The UNIX operating system is often referred to as a "first generation IPSE"[13] consisting of a filing system as persistent store, a set of tools and tool fragments built on a simple system call interface, and a well-defined (and simple) mechanism for communicating between tools using pipes and filters which can be embedded in the shell programming language. However, it is recognised that there is a very low level of integration between tools within UNIX using a simple convention of a stream of bytes passing between processes. This corresponds to the carrier level in our simple classification of tool integration given earlier. Given this low level of integration, how can we account for the high degree of success of UNIX as an IPSE when it runs contrary to the goal of tight integration within an IPSE ? The answer is that the very loose coupling of tools promotes a high degree of reusability. It is this reusability which is a key factor in the success of UNIX.

As a result, when developing a new tool in a UNIX system, invariably the first step is to see if any existing tools can be used in constructing the new tool. For example, a new tool which looks for the existence of a set of documents, edits those documents, sorts them into descending order of date, and mails them to a group of users, could easily be constructed by making use of existing tools for file searching (grep), editing (sed), sorting (sort), and mailing (mail).

However, there are severe limitations to this approach, as described earlier with Thimbleby's cweb[21]. It is illustrative to consider these problems in more detail. We have recently developed CADiZ[10] which is a tool designed to assist in the production of high quality documents containing Z specifications. In developing CADiZ we started by reusing troff, the standard UNIX text processing tool, and a locally developed previewer for troff documents known as *proof*. CADiZ carries out syntax, scope, and type checking on Z specifications, and it was considered desirable that error messages, particularly pertaining to types, should be type set to facilitate their understanding. This lead to the tool architecture shown in figure 3.

Thus far, the level of reuse is high, but the level of integration is still at the lexical level. However, it became clear that it was desirable to be able to interactively inspect displayed, typeset, specifications both to examine errors and to investigate specification properties. This involves selecting specification fragments (eg. disjuncts in a predicate) – but proof did not "understand" the syntax of Z. Hence, modifications to CADiZ were required.

To provide a solution, non-printing characters are included in the specification by CADiZ to delimit syntactic units (eg. predicates), predicate lists and declarations, and to indicate errors. These characters are used by proof to highlight errors and to delimit selections, see figure 4. Thus, new interactive facilities were provided – but by modifying troff and proof to make them more integrated, and in effect, reducing the level of reuse (although much of the code in proof, for example, is unchanged).

However, due to the very close coupling of the various components of the CADiZ toolset, it has proved very difficult to reuse part of the functionality within other tools. For example, when considering a similar toolset for a Macintosh environment, it seems clear that the type checking sections of the toolset *should* be reused, while the input and display facilities should be replaced by Macintosh specific routines. In practice, this separation has proved very difficult due to the very tight integration of the various CADiZ components which now make considerable assumptions about the nature of the processing carried out by other tools in the family.

The moral of this story is simple: the tighter the integration between tools, the harder they are to reuse in another environment. Hence, our theory

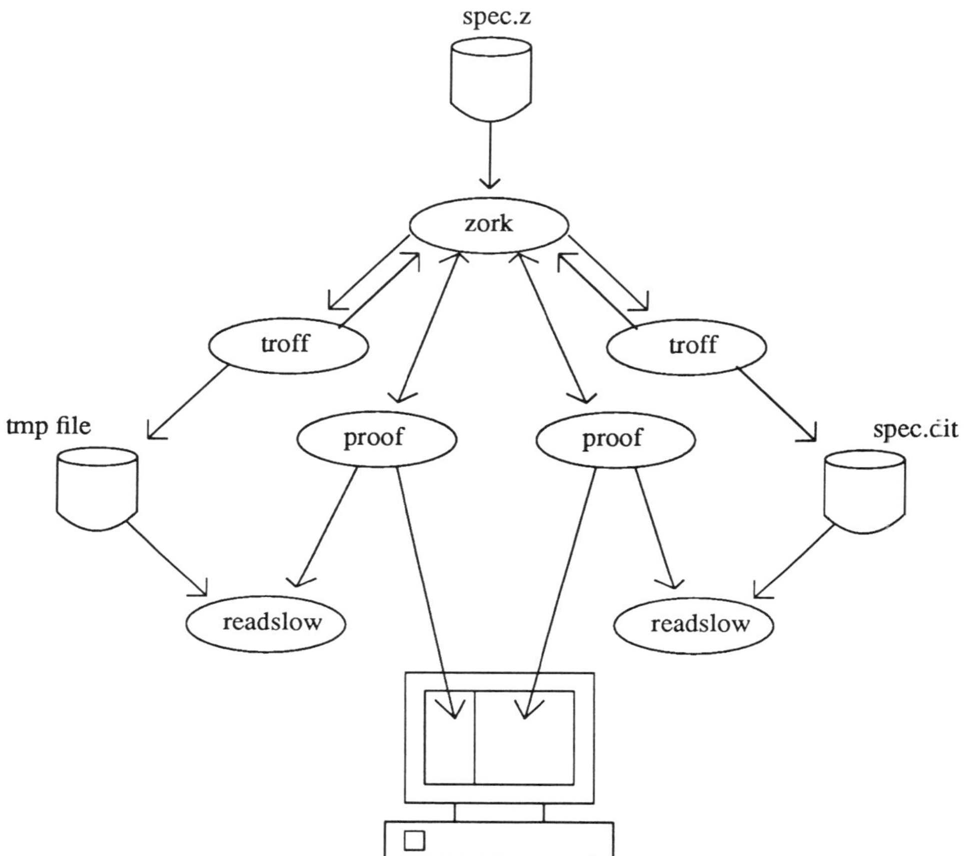

Figure 3: The CADiZ Tool Architecture

is borne out in practice.

7   Integration in the Life-Cycle

In section 6 we made clear that, on both theoretical and practical grounds,
reuse and integration are in conflict − in other words we cannot expect to
be able to reuse tools *and* to achieve integration with minimal effort. This
conclusion holds even for environment infrastructures or frameworks such as
PCTE+ as the problems are essentially semantic issues and are not resolved
simply by the provision of mechanisms, no matter how sophisticated. However, the situation may not be so bad as this conclusion seems to imply −

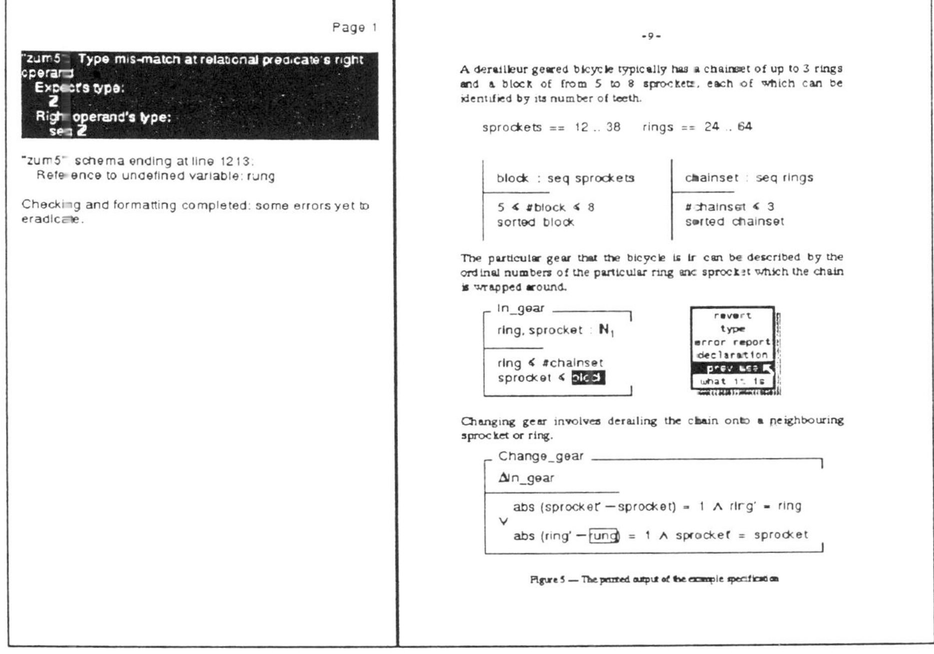

Figure 4: The CADiZ Tool

and the "way out" arises from considering the degree of integration which is appropriate across different stages of the life-cycle.

In fact, we can illustrate the point by considering two separate, but related issues: the necessary degree of integration between stages in the development process, and the integration between technical and managerial activities. The key to the problem is to consider the level of integration required in each case.

The value of semantic and method integration is that they enable different tools in a toolset to operate co-operatively on a problem knowing[7] how to respond to actions and changes in shared data structures made by other tools. For example, this enables compilers and editors to work in harmony to produce quick edit-compile-execute cycles. This level of integration is effective and useful *within* a stage of the development process, i.e. for a coherent set of technical activities, as it gives productivity and reduces the

---

[7]Strictly with their designers knowing, but the anthropomorphism enables us to avoid clumsy circumlocution.

scope for errors, but the same degree of integration is not required between stages.

Looser integration between stages is not only acceptable, but probably essential. Pragmatically we need to be able to produce "baselines" at the end of one stage of the development process to feed into the next. These baselines need to (appear to be) stable and tight integration would (tend to) result in rapid propagation of changes, and hence development instability (in part this depends on the way in which tools are linked at a mechanistic level, but the risk is there). Between stages the key issue is probably traceability, so syntactic level integration – where one tool understands the structure of the product of another – is all that is necessary to satisfy this requirement. In other words we require high levels of integration within toolsets dealing with particular stages of the development process, but relatively weak integration between the tools at adjacent stages.

Similar arguments apply between technical and managerial activities. Managerial activities need only a relatively abstract view of the technical activities as they need to be able to gauge progress, to track the products of the development process, and so on. Here again, low levels of integration – perhaps as low as carrier level – are adequate to meet the managerial requirements. This is true both for certain classes of technical managerial activities, e.g. configuration management, where products can be treated as indivisible entities which simply need to be stored securely, and for more "pure" managerial functions such as progress monitoring.

It is possible to look at this issue from a different point of view. High levels of integration imply high levels (bandwidths) of information exchange between tools. High bandwidths are required within technically coherent groups of activities – but not between such groups (high bandwidths may be needed between humans, but the same is not true between tools which are much more concerned with traceability than semantics).

There is an obvious consequence of the above. It is possible, in principle, to reuse tools and to achieve integration. However, it is necessary to reuse toolsets which are already well-integrated and which give a coherent treatment of all the technical activities at one stage of the life-cycle. These can then be integrated, albeit much more loosely, to span the whole life-cycle and to give an appropriate level of integration within and between stages (and between technical and managerial tools). IPSE infrastructures are quite capable of providing carrier and syntactic level integration, thus they can be employed to provide the links between toolsets and to provide an effective integrated working environment – so long as the toolsets employed are already well-integrated.

8   Summary and Conclusions

We have considered two key issues in IPSE development: integration and tool reuse. We have given an extensive analysis of integration, indicated the different facets, or dimensions, of integration and given what we believe is an effective pragmatic classification of different levels of integration, at least within one dimension. We have also discussed the relationship between reuse and integration and shown that they are in conflict, in the sense that the technical conditions which are necessary for reuse preclude the establishment of the conditions needed for integration, and *vice versa*. We also indicated that the level of integration required between stages in development is much less than that required within stages – and that this gives some opportunity for reusing toolsets which are already highly integrated, then to obtain the necessary (lower levels) of integration between technical stages using some mechanism such as an IPSE infrastructure.

The above analysis is, to some extent, an argument of principle, although we have backed up the principles with a discussion of an example on which we are currently working. However, we started by considering experience in introducing IPSEs into organisations, and it is instructive (and perhaps more convincing) to look at our analysis in the light of this experience.

One of the key requirements we highlighted was the need for a smooth transition between an existing working environment and an IPSE – and this is one of the sources of the requirement for reuse. SAFRA[17] is one of the few examples of a really successful use of an IPSE and, although the IPSE developed was less than elegant in some respects, it did provide this smooth transition (at least in part) by reusing existing tools. Furthermore, SAFRA seems to bear out very strongly our view that tight integration within a group of tools is important, but that lower levels of integration between groups is acceptable and appropriate.

Similarly, considering a system such as ISTAR[6], it is clear that the strategy here was to provide strongly integrated toolsets which could be linked in different ways – and much more loosely – to provide support for different approaches to the technical development activities in the life cycle. This again matches strongly with the conclusions of our analysis regarding integration and reuse.

Saying that our theory is borne out in practice when the practice came before the theory, is perhaps rather a specious claim to verisimilitude – but there are good precedents for such claims in physics and other natural sciences! In some sense we have not discovered anything new – the problems of achieving reuse and integration at the same time have already been recognised – but we believe we have given an explanation why these difficulties are inevitable, i.e. why they are inherent in the concepts, rather than merely being accidents of inappropriate engineering. This is something new and important.

First, this realisation means that we should now treat reuse and integration as being in conflict and decide how to make trade-offs between these two desirable properties, rather than assuming that we can (if we are lucky or clever) achieve them both at once. This is an important piece of information for someone who is designing an IPSE, or who is installing one in an organisation. It also has ramifications for the research and development community.

Infrastructures such as PCTE+ are designed on the assumption that they must be open – to provide reuse – but they must also promote integration. But we now know that we cannot achieve both of these objectives simultaneously – at least not with respect to the same set of tools. Our analysis shows that this aspiration is unattainable and raises a question about the thrust to develop open environments. In contrast, CASE toolsets offer tightly integrated facilities and are now expanding in scope to provide a number of other loosely integrated facilities. They seem to be much more successful (technically and commercially) and are now encroaching on the IPSE marketplace. Perhaps the CASE developers have appreciated that the way to get integrated toolsets is to *design* and develop integrated toolsests, not to provide generic mechanisms and to hope that integration will arise as if by magic. This hope seems, to us, to be a modern day equivalent of the philosophers' stone – and just as unobtainable.

Acknowledgements

We are grateful to our colleague at York, Ian Toyn, who provided a number of helpful comments on this paper.

References

[1] AT&T. UNIX System V Documenter's Workbench – Introduction and Reference Manual, April 1984.

[2] J.N. Buxton and J.A. McDermid. Architectural Design. In *The Software Engineer's Reference Book*. Butterworth, 1991.

[3] P. Cronshaw. The Experimental Aircraft Programme Software Toolset. *Software Engineering Journal*, 1(6):236–247, November 1986.

[4] B. Curtis, H. Krasner, and N. Iscoe. A Field Study of the Software Design Process for Large Systems. *Communications of the ACM*, 31(11):1269–1287, November 1988.

[5] Systems Designers. DEC/VAX Perspective Technical Overview, November 1984.

[6] M. Dowson. ISTAR – An Integrated Project Support Environment. *Proceedings of 2nd SIGSOFT/SIGPLAN Symposium on Practical Software Development Environments*, pages 27–33, December 1986.

[7] L. Gradwell. The Arrival of IRDS Standards. In *Proceedings of the 8th British National Conference on Databases (BNCOD-8)*, pages 196–209. Pitman Publishing Ltd, 1990.

[8] J A. Hall. Databases in Software Development: The Ada Programming Support Environment. In P.J.L. Wallis, editor, *Ada Software Tools Interfaces*, number 180 in Lecture Notes in Computer Science, pages 115–132. Springer Verlag, 1984.

[9] W. Humphrey. Improving the Software Development Process. *Datamation*, April 1989.

[10] D. Jordan, J. McDermid, and I. Toyn. CADiZ – Computer-Aided Design in Z. *Proceedings of the 5th Annual Z Users Group Conference*, December 1990.

[11] P N. Lequesne. Individual and Organisational Factors and the Design of IPSEs. *The Computer Journal*, 31(5):391–397, October 1988.

[12] R. W. Mitze. The UNIX system as a Software Engineering Environment. In H. Hunke, editor, *Software Engineering Environments*, pages 345–357. North Holland, 1981.

[13] D. Morgan. The Imminent IPSE. *Datamation*, 33(7):60–68, April 1987.

[14] G.P. Mullery. CORE – A Method for Controlled Requirement Specification. In *Proceedings of 4th International Conference on Software Engineering*. IEEE Computer Society Press, 1979.

[15] G.J. Myers. *Reliable Software Through Composite Design*. Van Nostrand Reinhold, 1975.

[16] J. Parkinson. Making CASE Work. In *Advanced Information Systems Engineering*, pages 21–41. Springer-Verlag, 1990.

[17] C. Price. *SAFRA – A Debrief Report*. NCC Publications, 1987.

[18] R.A. Snowdon. A Brief Overview of the IPSE2.5 Project. *Ada User*, 9(4):156–161, 1988.

[19] R.N. Taylor and Others. Foundations for the Arcadia Environment Architecture. *ACM SIGPLAN Notices*, 24(2):1–13, February 1989.

[20] T. Teitelbaum and T. Reps. The Cornell Program Synthesizer: A Syntax-Directed Programming Environment. *ACM SIGPLAN Notices*, 14(10):75–95, October 1979.

[21] H.W. Thimbleby. Experiences of 'Literate Programming' using cweb (a variant of Knuth's WEB). *The Computer Journal*, 29(3), 1986.

12

Method integration – principles and problems described by SA/IM

Matthias Hallmann
Systemhaus GEI, Software Tools, Pascalstraße 14,
D–5100 Aachen, Federal Republic of Germany
Thorsten Janning
RWTH, Informatik III, Ahornstraße 55, D–5100 Aachen,
Federal Republic of Germany

Abstract

A method is an engineering discipline which describes guidelines for a user on how to reach a specific conceptual model and to describe it in a corresponding notation. In most big research and development projects (such as ESPRIT ATMOSPHERE and EUREKA ESF) different methods for different phases in the systems engineering life cycle are proposed. Most of the methods are hard-coded in a tool. Specifying a complex system can be seen from very different point of views. But before tool integration can be achieved in a very sophisticated way we have to understand the problems and principles of method integration. In this presentation this is done by describing an example on a very high level. The requirement phase is structured into the dynamic, the functional, the data modelling and the architectural view. Starting with the presentation of the background of method integration two specific methods (Structured Analysis and Information Modelling) will be introduced before their integration is explained.

1   Introduction

The problem of integration appears to be one of the most important issues of the future. The solution of this problem will lead to a new technical revolution in computer science and even in systems engineering. In the last decade this problem has been recognized by more and more software engineers. But everytime a solution was propagated new questions arose. The problem was like Heisenberg's "Indeterminity Relation". The more detailed the solution was formulated (and even implemented) the less clearer became the problem. (In physics this phenomenon can be described only in the language of probability!) No general solution could be proposed. Having entered this decade it seems that the horizon of integration is visible. Integration solutions can only be achieved via evolutionary and incremental steps.

Why is integration so important? And what kind of reasons can be seen? Integration should provide:

- only one mechanism to make increase of productivity easier and training more efficient,

- a canonical model (uniformity),

- consistency, clearness,

- minimization of interfaces, and at a minimum

- coexistence.

To summarize: integration should combine different strengths and eliminate weaknesses. The integration problem can be tackled on different levels. The question which will be answered in this article is: "Integration - of what?" and "What can be achieved in which evolutionary and incremental steps?" The most important aspect in software engineering is the tool integration aspect. But tools cannot be integrated on a semantical level without solving the method integration problem. In most big research and development projects (such as ESPRIT ATMOSPHERE /BOS 89/ and EUREKA ESF/FHT 90/) different methods are used which must be integrated.

In this article principles and problems of method integration are presented. Doing this one (simple) example is introduced. Structured Analysis (SA) and Information Modelling (IM) based on the entity-relationship approach (ER) have become two of the most widespread requirements engineering methods. SA describes the functional behaviour of a software system, ER is well suited to define information models like data base schemes. To enable the user to work successfully with these models it is necessary to integrate them. We describe an integration mechanism for both models and define consistency rules as a basis for a tool analyzing the consistency within the integrated model. The integration approach presented here is the first step, to integrate some more views to the requirements process of a software system in a homogeneous way. But only one example is presented. The question for the future is: does any "meta method" exist for the description of any other method? If yes, principles, problems and consistency rules of method integration have to be specified with such a general method. As there is up to now no candidate, we give in this paper a catalog of guidelines for method integration.

2 Integration Aspects in Systems Engineering

Systems engineering work has only recently started. Initially the generalization of special problems in multiple disciplines will be addressed. Since it is a long-term research mission, real solutions cannot be expected before the year 2000. The challenge will be to overcome the problems in the work areas intersecting different engineering processes like company, project and product management, system requirements, system modelling, system partitioning, software and hardware production, system integration, and system operation. All these processes can in turn be decomposed into subprocesses.

We state, that at this point of time no fundamental concepts for systems engineering exist. This does not mean that no hard/soft-ware system can be built. Indeed in many application areas embedded systems have been built successfully (e.g. aerospace, aircrafts, medical systems, control of chemical processes etc.). However, embedded systems are being built with ever increasing cost and ever increasing problems in managing the complexity of the system for both the engineering process and the product.

2.1 Basic Definitions

The intention of systems engineering is the development and installation of a system. In accordance with other sciences a system can be described on a very abstract level as a seven-tuple.

System S = (X, Y, ST, F, D, P, C) where:

- X is a set of inputs into the system S

- Y is a set of outputs of the system S

- ST is a set of internal states

- F is a description of the transformation of states mapping (X x ST) onto (Y x ST')

- D is a design or structure components of the system S

- P is a set of performance indices consumed by executing the transformation F (e.g. time, resources etc.) and

- C are conditions and limitations, which must be observed during the transformation F

This is graphically presented in figure 1.

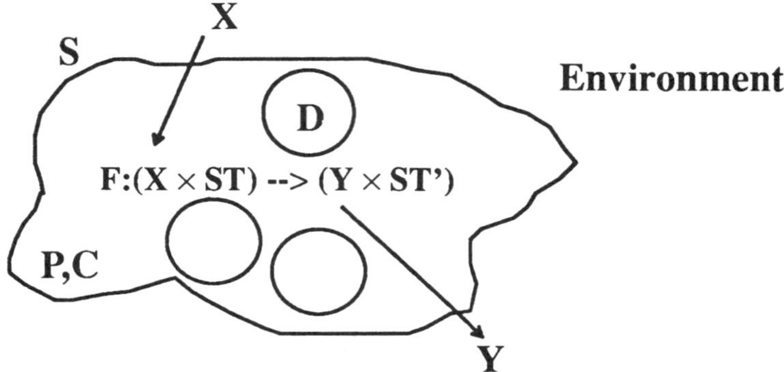

figure 1 : System definition

On a philosophical level it is questioned whether a system S must have behaviour and an environment. The term system is used in social sciences, economics and biology as well as in engineering and astronomy. At the beginning of this century systems theory was founded. Structures, derivation of rules, laws and principles were the areas of interest for researchers like Forrester and Wiener (cofounder of cybernetics). But a detailed definition of the term system was not created. Furthermore, the discussion about behaviour described using states and transformations of states or by differential equations are continued. In this paper a detailed discussion of system dynamics is excluded. The general aim of development work is the production of S if it is not yet existent or reengineering and enhancements of S in the desired form. Doing this you have to define the input X, the output Y, the different states ST, the internal architectural structure D, some performance indices P, and any constraints C. But these steps cannot be seen as isolated activities. These activities must be highly integrated.

Integration is a meta-method (mechanism, technique or concept) which describes how and to which degree components fit together to a whole in a systematic way. These components are:

- architecture D

- functionality F

- data X,Y

- dynamics ST

In the following sections, the functional and the data integration issues are described at a more detailed level.

2.2 The Aim: Process Integration

Building a system means organizing links between different independent processes. This is called "Inter Process Integration". Looking into such a process on more and more deeper levels one can see that many other details must be organized in a proper way.

At the highest level we target the integration of individual software, hardware, quality assurance, and organizational engineering processes. We call this integration approach of multiple disciplines *Systems Engineering*. Many different views exist on the term "System" and the term "Systems Engineering". Hardware engineers are some steps ahead of the software engineering community. Well defined, accepted, and standardized interfaces for that process exist. Hardware components can be described by their structure, their physics, and their behaviour by commonly understood means on several levels. On the logical abstraction level, for example, the structure is described by gates, the physics by cells and the behaviour by boolean equations. The future aim in hardware engineering will solve the limitations of the physical partitions.

The application of software seems not to be constrained by natural physical limitations. Everything seems to be possible and applications are emerging in an ever increasing number of areas in an ever increasing size and complexity. More and more software applications built today are embedded systems, namely software being embedded into hardware (communications hardware, mechanical hardware etc.), software being embedded into a "system". Handling the whole process of managing and producing "software intensive systems" is the challenge of this decade. Software life cycle models were first (and very helpful) attempts to manage the orderly production of software. Resulting from many different critical issues new research activities (like reusability, prototyping etc.) have been addressed. But in hardware and software engineering different methods, tools, languages, models, architectures, production processes, and organizational plans are used. Some research activities are starting now to integrate different views and to produce one global system view. The integration of hardware, software, quality and management processes is called Inter-Process Integration. (The term "inter" means the integration between separate objects.)

2.3 Intra-Process Integration

Realizing that Inter-Process Integration on the system level cannot be achieved in the near future, one should look at the next deeper process level of above mentioned individual disciplines: the *software production process*. This approach is called Intra- Process Integration. (The term "intra" means the internal integration of something which is atomic although it is an isue of abstraction and decomposition.) Different life cycle models have been discussed which focus on the separation of phases (e.g. into requirements, design, and implementation). GEI's system model concentrates on the requirements and specification phase. At least four different views and four different submodels can be distinguished. S can either be a software system for a specific application or a software system for the production of software (Software Engineering Environment).

In the data oriented view the structure of information is described. The functional view completes this by describing processes which work with these data (create, produce, move etc.). The dynamic view addresses temporal issues and describes at which time which process is active and what is going on in sequence and in parallel. The architectural view is used to ensure the use of some basic construction principles. But - using this model different notations, different semantics and different scopes of the four submodels exist. Each of the submodels has different origins. The integration of these submodels must overcome these problem areas.

At the Intra-Process integration level the language, the tool, and the method integration approaches are being discussed. The latter one is the basis for the other two. The interrelationship is described in the following definition.

A **Method** can be defined by a 4-tuple $M = (A, O, B, L_{A/B})$, where

- A is a set of activities a user of a method has to perform

- O is any partial order over the activities

- B is a basic or conceptual model

- $L_{A/B}$ are two description formalisms for the activities A and for the basic model B

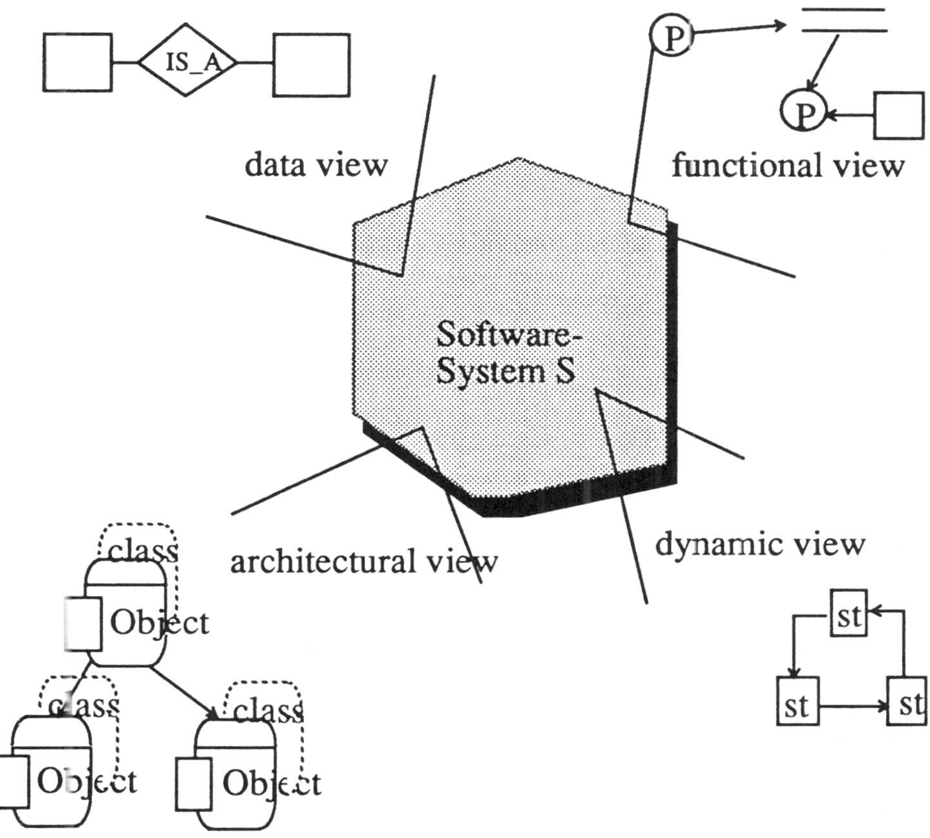

figure 2 : System Model for Intra-Process Integration

In this definition a difference between the abstract model and any description facility is done. This is useful because one abstract model can be described and completed by different languages and notations. A method consists of some guidelines
which guide a user to express her or his problem using a conceptual model by going
through a number of activities in a predefined order. A and O together form a specific process model. Normally A and O are described informally. B describes the
conceptual model (e.g. the relational database model using the the relational calcu-
lus- in this example A and O define the steps the information modeler has to per-

form). L_B is a concrete data definition language (e.g. for DB2). L_A is a language for the informal description of the activities.

This definition of the term method emphasizes the relationship between activities, languages and models. Because this is the basis for tool integration but tool integration is very hard to achieve on an implementation level, we should aim firstly on method integration.

On the one hand method integration deals with the integration of several methods within one phase of the life cycle (e.g. methods which enable a user to describe different views on a requirements model); on the other hand there are attempts to integrate between methods covering different life cycle steps. The first approach is called *"vertical"* the second approach is called *"horizontal method integration"* which is graphically presented in figure 3. Both approaches can be solved by transformation. The methods SA/RT /HP87/ as used in the software engineering environment ProMod /Hr 87/ are an example for the first, and SA - object oriented design /Bo 87/ or SA-Design /JL 90/ are two examples of the second kind of method integration.

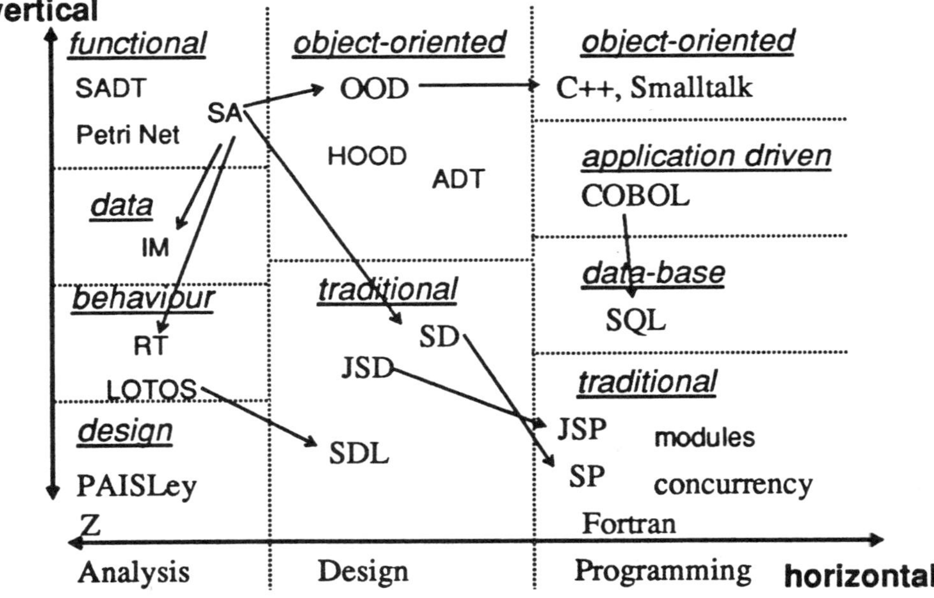

figure 3 : examples for possible horizontal and vertical method integration

In figure 3 this is explained in more detail but please note that this figure is not complete. The horizontal dimension is split up into different phases. The vertical dimension is split up into special categories which are very life cycle phase dependent. Different methods and languages are classified into this schema. The arrows show well known vertical and horizontal integration technology.

The question for the future is if any Meta Methods exist describing principles of any other method.

If the definition of the term integration is mapped onto method integration the "systematic way" will give some hints or guidelines for handling method integration. The following provides some hints:

- identify interfaces, redundancy, desired enhancements, deficits of the methods:

  You should think about the reasons for the integration of method M_1 with method M_2.

- describe the possible working process model:

  How do you currently use the methods (e.g. top-down etc.)? Describe for each method the different activities and the order to perform them. Afterwards you have to define a new working process model which integrates both methods.

- identify a method of principle (if possible):

  Is there any method which is the most important one for your application? This method has some conceptual significance and has influence on the usage of subordinate methods.

- choose any abstract description formalism L_A:

  In the vertical method integration approach you have to define not only new activities and a new order about them but perhaps a new notation or at least a modification of the existing ones.

- describe limitations and dependencies:

  What are the advantages and what are the disadvantages of this kind of method integration. It is impossible to solve all the problems. Some other problems will be created, perhaps only for the customer of the newly created method.

- if vertical method integration is aimed at:

Ensure consistency of information because they will be used in both methods. Specify the time new information will be added.

- notice re-engineering aspects in horizontal method integration:

  Normally the horizontal method integration approach transforms the information gained by method M_1 in the notation of method M_2 whereas M_1 is used as the previous one. If there exists any point of time to go the other way round the linkage between items of method M_1 and method M_2 should be bijective and stored at some place.

3   Integration of SA with IM

The aim of requirements engineering /AM 81/, /Ro 85/ is to define the requirements of a software system, to modify this definition according to information got during realization, or due to changes occurring in maintenance. Therefore, requirements engineering deals with the external specification of a system. The aspects of programming in the large, programming in the small or other working areas of software engineering are only regarded in as much as a requirements definition must be that of an implementable software system. Requirements engineering evidently is an important working area of software engineering as decisions and, therefore also mistakes, determine the system to be developed or maintained.

There are a lot of methods in this area which should provide a basis for providing a complete specification of the requirements. These methods consist of some more or less formal languages, mostly in graphical form, and some informal hints about how to use these languages. These methods are mostly restricted to the so-called functional specification. Nonfunctional parts (user interface style, efficiency parameters, security constraints etc.) are usually given only as plain text.

Therefore, a method for requirements engineering should provide a suitable formal language plus rules about how to apply the language in order to be able to write a complete specification of the functional requirements of a software system. Furthermore, the method should support the writing of readable and maintainable requirements definitions. Finally, "intelligent" tools for the method should be available for editing, maintaining, analyzing, or rapid prototyping of the requirements definition.

Two software engineering paradigms covering the whole life cycle and -with this- the requirements analysis phase have been developed. Structured development methods like Structured Analysis and Structured Design (SA/SD) (/DM 78/, /Yo 89/, /YC 78/) use functional decomposition to conquer even complex software systems. Object-oriented software development on the other side (/Bo 83/, /Bo 86/, / Me 83/) is of more recent origin. Data abstraction and inheritance are the characteristic features of this paradigm.

SA has proved to be very useful to describe the functional requirements of a software system. Therefore, we decided to take a dialect of it for the functional part of our requirements engineering language. Nevertheless, SA has a number of severe drawbacks with respect to its ability to formulate a complete and readable functional specification. Firstly, processes are considered to be implicitly coupled. However, especially in real-time systems, one wants to have explicit control over sequencing, initialization, synchronization of processes /HP 87/. We call this part of a requirements specification the dynamic view of our system.

Secondly, in many applications the logical structure of underlying data is at least as complicated as the underlying process structure. However, describing the data view of the system is done only implicitly in SA , namely by data dictionary entries for data stores and data flows plus consistency rules between them. Therefore, there is a strong need for an explicit information model.

For the design of conceptual database schemas the entity-relationship- model (abbr. ER-model) has proved to be useful. Therefore, we take ER as the basis for our data view considerations. Because ER is a description of types that may have an inheritance hierarchy and a complex structure it may be regarded as a first step towards an object-oriented analysis method.

In this paper we concentrate on the first step of the whole integration, namely on the integration of the functional view and the data view (cf. /De 88/) which is an integration of the structured and the object-oriented paradigm. Recently, there have been several attempts to integrate these paradigms. Bailin (/Ba 89/) for example introduces an "object-oriented specification (OOS)", but by doing so he proposes the modeling of abstract data types during the requirements analysis phase which obviously should be part of the design activity. Ward (/Wa 89/) introduces an object-oriented requirements engineering method based on his real-time extension of SA. Several authors like Page-Jones and Yourdon (/Pa 88/, /Yo 89/) integrated SA with the entity relationship model as an object-oriented requirements engineering method in a similar way as we do but they did not define such detailed consistency rules for the resulting requirements engineering language as is necessary to build sophisticated support tools.

The aim of this chapter is to report about the initial results of an ongoing project which consists of :

1.	the definition of a requirements engineering method integrating functional view, data view, and dynamical view. Furthermore, this method is

2.   to be supported by intelligent tools, where intelligent means that the consistencies between the above different views of a requirements definition are taken into account.

The contents of this chapter is as follows: First we introduce SA as our functional view language. This is followed by an introduction of our data view language which is an extended entity relationship language.

This language introduction is done with the help of a simple example of a small project management support system. Team members and projects have to be managed, i.e. inserted and removed. Furthermore team members can be made responsible for a project and the resulting project costs can be computed (cf. fig. 5).

Afterwards, we explain the integration of SA and ER. Finally, we show how to apply this integrated method.

3.1 A sketch of Structured Analysis

The main components of SA are data flow diagrams (DFDs). Within a DFD a data flow connects a process with any other object, i.e. another process, a data store as a repository for data or a terminator representing elements of the outside world. Processes are the active objects in a DFD using incoming data flows to compute the outgoing data flows. In figure 4 EditStaff or ComputeCosts are examples of processes. ProjectDatabase, Projects, Responsibilities and Staff are data stores, Manager is a terminator.

A process may be refined by another DFD which elaborates the relevant process. In this way a complete system model consists of a hierarchy of data flow diagrams the root of which describes the system in the context of the outside world and, therefore, is called the context diagram. In our example the DFD EditResponsibilities refines the proces with the same name in the DFD ProjectManagement. The detailed functionality of a process may be also described by a mini specification. Mini-specifications use informal text, decision tables or decision trees.

We distinguish two classes of data stores. The stores on the upper levels of our data flow diagram (DFD) hierarchy usually are artificial unifications of data stores of the next lower level in the DFD hierarchy. We call such a data store a unification data store. In our example the ProjectDataBase is such a unification data store. On the other hand there are collections of objects of the same type which are called atomic data stores. They usually appear in the lower levels of the DFD hierarchy. Examples for atomic data stores are Staff, Projects or Responsibilities(cf.fig.5). Data flows must be defined. Those data definitions have a similar syntax as EBNF-rules using sequences, iterations or options(cf. figure 4).

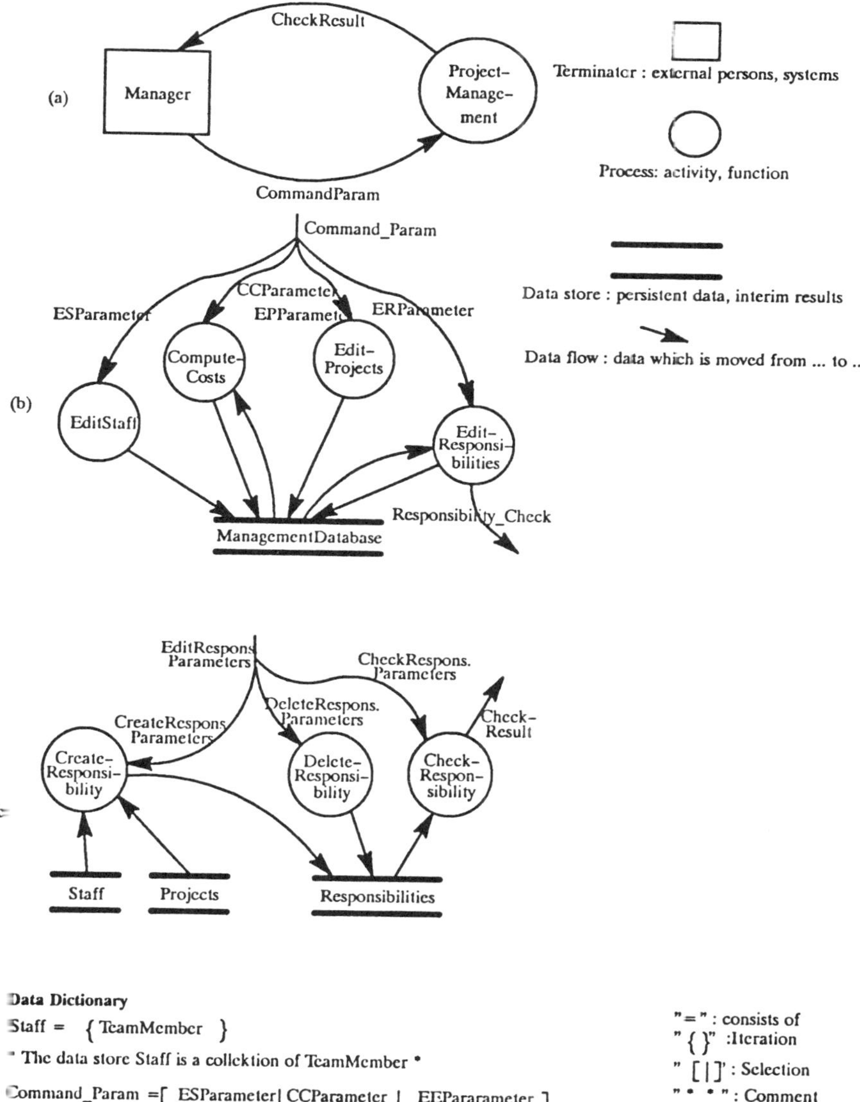

figure 4 : SA-example with context diagram (a) and refining DFDs "ProjectManagement" (b) and "EditResponsibilities" (c)

Unification Datastore:

ManagementDatabase = Staff U Projects U Responsibilities

Atomic Datastores:

Staff = { TeamMember }

Projects = { SoftwareProject }

Responsibilities = { Responsibility }

figure 5 : Different data store declarations

3.2   The data view : Entity-Relationship-Diagrams

The ER-model consists of entity types and relationship types and an attribute
dictionary. To explain it we again give only an example and refer the interested
reader to /Che 76/.

Entity types are homogeneous types describing real world entities, i.e. each instance of the entity type is of the same type and has the same attributes as any other
instance of this entity type. Entity types are associated with each other by relationship types. For example, there is a relationship type, Work, relating the entity types
TeamMember and Project in our example of figure 6.

There have been many extensions of the ER-model (cf. /Che 83/, /Fl 81/, /SS 77/,
/Sch 86/, /Sp 87/). We decided to introduce only a few of them in order to keep our
data view method easy to use. Including these extensions it satisfies the requirements of a data model language.

There may be two or more entity types participating in one relationship type. For
binary relationship types cardinalities are defined. We distinguish 1:1-, 1:n- and
m:n- relationship type cardinalities. The cardinality describes how many instances
of the participating entity types are associated with each other. For example there
is a m:n-relationship between TeamMember and Project. This means that one team
member can take part in several projects and that for each project there are several
team members. But you also see that this relationship is a partial one because a
team member need not take part in any project.

Generalization introduces an inheritance relationship between a supertype and one
or more subtypes. That means that all attributes defined for the supertype are also
defined for the subtypes. The subtypes may add or redefine attributes. In our exam-

ple the subtypes Employee and SelfEmployed inherit the attribute structure of the supertype TeamMember (see figure 6).

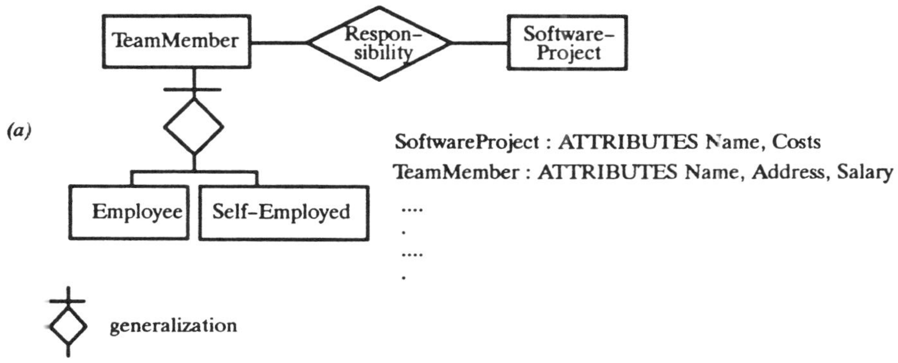

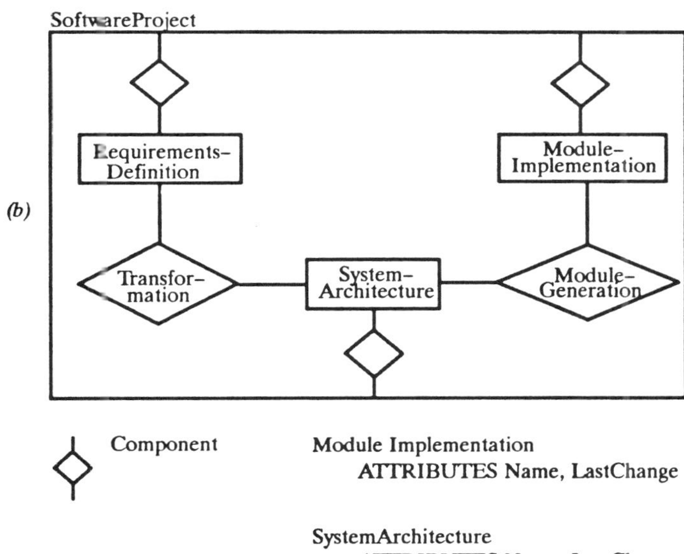

figure 6 : ER diagram with generalization ((a)) and refinement ((b)).

Furthermore, entity types and relationship types having a complex structure may be refined by a complex entity relationship diagram (CERD). Such complex types are called molecule types, the types in the refining CERD are called component types. In our example in figure 6 we have the molecule type SoftwareProject and the component types RequirementsDefinition, ModuleImplementation, etc. The relationship between molecule type and component type has the semantic of "component". It may be specified by the cardinalities 1:n or 1:1. In the first case the component type is called a multiple component type, in the second case a single component type. By doing this we get a hierarchy of CERDs in our data oriented view similar to the DFD hierarchy in the functional view. The top of this hierarchy is the overview diagram. Of course, each type may have attributes with perhaps complex structure which are declared in an attribute dictionary.

3.3   A simple solution for integrating SA and IM

In the previous sections we presented two different views of software systems requirements. With SA we modelled the functional behaviour in a process-oriented way, the information model described the data view in an object-oriented way. Being complementary SA and ER are appropriate candidates for an integration.

If we want to integrate SA and ER we must have a look at the characteristics of both. SA is a model of potential data flows within the modelled system. There are processes and data stores connected by data flows. Data stores are containers for data coming through the data flow channels. ER is a static type definition language. Complex types with attributes of possibly complex structure may be defined.

The integration idea consequently must be the following. We take the data information of SA and replace it with or relate it to the data view represented by ER. We distinguish the object declarations and the type declarations of the old SA data dictionary. The object declarations, i.e. the data store and data flow declarations, become part of the functional view, the type definitons are replaced by the data view.

We have mentioned the existence of two classes of data stores , i.e. the unification data stores and the atomic data stores, and introduced the different declarations for them. Because unification data stores are only an abbreviation for a set of other data stores only the atomic data stores have to related to the data view. They are the collection of instances of an entity type or relationship type and, therefore, have to be related to the corresponding entity type / relationship type declaration within the data view.

Dataflows are marked by types which also have to be declared in the data view. The types of the data flows going into or out of a data store additionally have to be a component of the type of data store entries. For example a data flow going into or out of the data store Staff may have the type TeamMember, Employee, Name, etc..

It is possible to define such a consistency rule by logical predicates but here we want to restrict ourselves to an informal description.

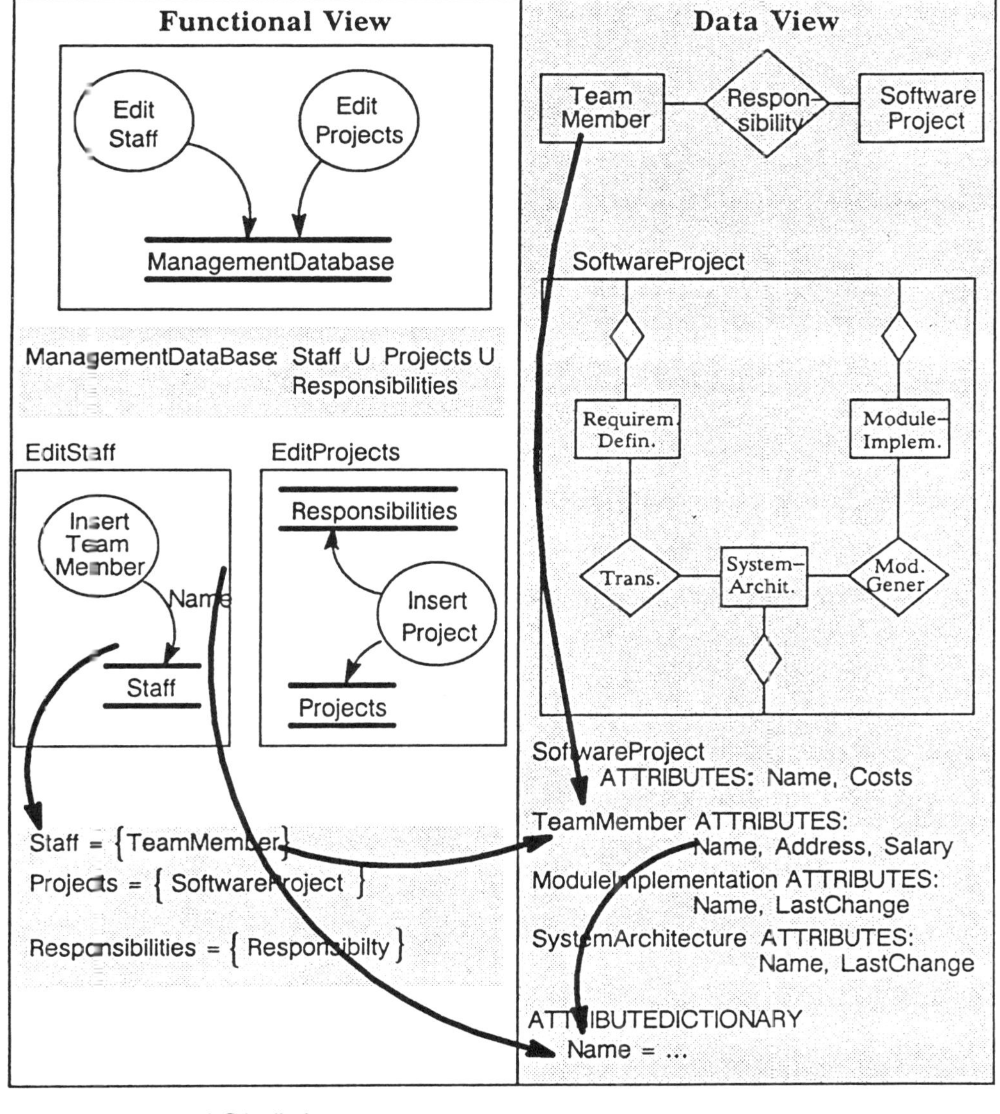

figure 7 : integrating SA and IM

Figure 7 shows this integration idea. We see the two integrated views with the defined relation within each view and between the views represented by the arcs.

In detail we can define the following consistency rules between the two integrated views:

1. Each unification data store is a unification of other data stores

2. Each atomic data store is declared as a collection of instances of an entity type or relationship type

3. Each data flow type has to be declared within the data view, i.e. by an entity type, a relationship type or an attribute type

4. Each type of data flow going into or out of datastores must be a component of the types of the data store entries.

5. Each molecule type is refined by a CERD.

6. The attributes of entity types and relationship types are declared in the attribute dictionary.

3.4 Applying the integrated requirements engineering method

The description of the elements of the integration of functional view and data view alone does not help the user to apply the method. In this chapter we will explain the significant steps of the work with our model.

The strong top down approach of the use of SA has not proved to be very useful. In /MP 84/ the concepts of a "middle-up-middle-down" approach are presented. This means that the system has to be modelled in a middle abstraction level first. After that the user can refine the processes of this level and at last combine processes and data stores to abstract the diagrams of the higher levels. We propose a similar procedure for our model and will explain it with our example.

Step 1: Definition of the data view

The data of the system have to be analyzed. The result is a complete data view to the system.

Step 2: Definition of a context diagram

In this step we model the interaction of the system with the outside world (cf. figure. 4).

Step 3: Definition of a preliminary global DFD

With the help of the information from step 1 and step 2 we define one large global data flow diagram. For each entity type and each relationship type we insert a data store and, later on, the necessary processes and data flows to derive the full diagram.

Step 4 Refinement of the processes of the global DFD

The processes of the global DFD may be complex such that they should be refined. Doing so we have to update the information model.

Step 5: Simplification of the global DFD by process fusion and data store fusion

To reduce the number of processes and data stores in the global DFD we combine correlating processes and data stores to get a DFD of a higher abstraction level like the DFD ProjectManagement in our example. The detailed structure is modelled by refining DFDs like EditResponsibilities for each process of this higher level DFD.

4   Conclusion and open questions

In this paper we have described an integration of structured analysis and information modelling. We related entity sets and relationship sets to data stores and fused the data dictionary and definition dictionary into an integrated requirements dictionary. After that we proposed some guidelines on how to use this integrated requirements engineering method.

Of course, there are some open problems. Firstly, to model large projects, it seems to be necessary to partition ER diagrams to get suitable complexities of them. Secondly, after a formalization of mini specifications it would be useful to be able to check some more rules between SA and the ER-information model automatically. We have to think about the problems (1) whether it is helpful for the user to have that formalization and (2) how to do it.

As global open problems remain the integration of the control model on the basis of /HP 87/ in the same way as we integrated SA and the information model. Furthermore, we are also working on the integration of requirements engineering and software design and how it is possible to support this by software tools

Recommendations

Suppose you are a tool builder and you have to integrate two different methods. This can be achieved by constructing a completely new tool which incorporates these methods or ensure that two tools can interoperate in a predefined order. In the following some problems and principles of method integration are described. This could be read as some guidelines or hints which should be noticed.

- terminology and data reuse

  If you have to use two different methods please note that the identifier of any data can be used in both methods but with different meanings.

- hierarchy

  To structure some kind of entities or components, hierarchies of sub-entities are introduced. Different types of relationships between such sub-entities exist concurrently. Notice that the *used*, the *consist_of*, and the *inheritance* relationships have different meanings.

- two different meanings of consistency

  Consistency between any kind of data must be ensured if the data has any relationship. But note, that redundancy and referential integrity are two different concepts with regard to consistency.

- multi_user

  If the integrated methods are used in parallel by different people you will get some consistency problem. Suppose someone is using SA and the other one is using IM for the same problem domain and some data has been changed. A process model must define when and how the other one will notice these updates.

- modification of items identified in both methods

  This item corresponds to the previous one. Update-operations on data like rename, delete, change, or add should be used very carefully.

- description formalisms and notations

  Choose one common description formalism for the integrated method which can be constructed from different notations. But note that the paradigm behind the notation must be clear for every user of the integrated method.

- loss of information in horizontal method integration

  The transformation of information specified with the help of one method to another one has a big danger that some information cannot be transformed very easily and other information must be added.

- object type / instance distinction

  Types of objects describe some generalities which is common to every instance. Instances have probably some values and types have domains.

- balancing of models

  Suppose decomposition of functionality and/or data is provided by two or more methods. Applying these methods can result in different kinds of parent/child hierarchies which are independent of each other.

- promotion of one method

  In different applications perhaps one of the integrated methods will play a major rule (e.g. in technical CASE you will start with SA and then continue with IM, in business CASE the other way round is probably the better way). Is there any method which is the most important one for your application?

- transformation, reverse-engineering, traceability, analysis

  In the horizontal method integration approach you should take care to come back to the original method.

5 References

/AM 81/ Abbot, R.Moorhead, D.: Software Requirements and Specifications: A Survey of Needs and Languages, Jour. Syst. and Softw. 2,4, pp. 297-316 (1981) ;

/Ba 89/ Bailin, S.C.: An Object-Oriented Requirements Specification Method, Communications of the ACM, Vol. 32, No. 5 (1989);

/Bo 83/ Booch, G.: Software Engineering with Ada", Benjamin/Cummings, Menlo Park (Calif.) (1983);

/Bo 86/ Booch, G.: Object-Oriented Development, IEEE Transactions on Software Engineering, Vol. SE-12, No. 2 (1986);

/Bo 87/ Booch, G.: Software Components with ADA, Benjamin/Cummings, Menlo Park (1987)

/BOS 89/ Boarder, J. Obbink, H., Schmidt, M.: ATMOSPHERE - Advanced Techniques and Methods of System Production in a Heterogeneous, Extensible, and Rigorous Environment, Proc. 1st International Conference on System Development Environments and Factories, Berlin (1989)

/Che 76/   Chen, P.P.: The Entity-Relationship Model: Towards a Unified View
            of Data, ACM Transactions on Database Systems 1,1, pp 9-36 (1976);

/Che 83/   Chen, P.P.: Entity Relationship Approach to Information Modelling
            and Analysis, Amsterdam: North Holland (1983);

/De 88/   Derissen, J.: The Integration of Structured Analysis and Information
            Modelling, Master's Thesis, Aachen University of Technology
            (1988);

/DeM 78/   DeMarco, T.: Structural Analysis and System Specification, New
            York: Yourdan Press (1978);

/Fl 81/   Flavin, M.: Fundamental Concepts of Information Modelling, New
            York: Yourdan Press (1981);

/FHT 90/   Fernström, C., Heße, O.,Thomas, E.R.: An Introduction to ESF Sof-
            ware Factories, Proc. 4th International Workshop on Computer-Aided
            Software Engineering - CASE 90 (1990);

/Ha90a/   Hallmann, M.: Prototyping of complex Software Systems, Stuttgart:
            Teubner Verlag (1990);

/Ha90b/   Hallmann, M.: Platforms, Frameworks, Environments, Factories - The
            horizon of Integration, ESF Seminar (1990);

/HP 87/   Hatley, D.J.Pirbhai, I.A.: Strategies for Real-Time System Specifica-
            tion, New York: Dorset House (1987);

/Hr 87/   Hruschka, P.: ProMod at the age of 5, European Software Engineering
            Conference '87, LNCS 289 (1987);

/JL 90/   Janning, T., Lefering, M .: A transformation from the requirements en-
            gineering into design - the method & the tool, Proceedings of the 3rd
            international workshop on Software engineering & its applications,
            Toulouse (1990) ;

/Me 88/   B. Meyer: Object-oriented Software Construction, Prenctice Hall,
            London, (1988);

/MP 84/   McMenamin, S.M.Palmer, J.F.: Essential System Analysis, New
            York: Yourdon Press (1984);

/Pa 88/   M. Page-Jones: A Practical Guide To Structured Systems Design, 2nd
            Edition, Yourdon Press, NewYork (1988);

/Ro 85/   Roman, G.C.: A Taxonomy of Current Issues in Requirements Engi-
            neering, IEEE Computer 18,4, pp. 14-22 (1985);

/Sch 86/   Schuldt, G.: Structured Database Development: Information Model-
             ling and Access Modelling - A Method presented at SDF VII, Syn-
             chretics Inc., Seattle (1986);

/Sp 87/   Spaccapidra, S. (Ed.): Entity Relationship Approach, Amsterdam:
             North Holland (1987);

/SS 77/   Smith, J.M.Smith, D.C.P.: Database Abstractions: Integration and
             Generalization, ACM Trans. on Database Systems 2, 2, 105-133
             (1977);

/Wa 89/   P. T. Ward: "How to Integrate Object Orientation with Structured
             Analysis and Design", IEEE Software, March (1989);

/Yo 89/   E. Yourdon: "Modern Structured Analysis", Yourdon Press, New
             York (1989);

/YC 78/   E. Yourdon und L. Constantine: "Structured Design", Yourdon Press,
             New York (1978);

13

Integrating visual notations with VDM

Jeremy Dick and Jérôme Loubersac
Bull Corporate Research Center, Rue Jean Jaurés,
F–78340 Les Clayes-sous-Bois, France

Acknowledgement

This work is partially supported by the ESPRIT project Atmosphere, Ref. #2565. The main partners are CAP Gemini Innovation (coordinator), Bull, Philips, Siemens, SNI and SFGL (contractor).

1   Introduction

This paper reports on work in progress to support the creation of formal specifications through the use of diagrams. The terse nature of formal notations, with their frequent use of mathematical symbols, does not provide a good medium for communication with the non-mathematician. We hope to combine formality with visual intuition, alleviate the communication problem with non-specialists, and accelerate the uptake and integration of formal methods into industry.

Other research is being conducted in this area; for instance, work on integrating the Yourdon method with the formal notation Z [SA90]. Our particular focus is on the Vienna Development Method (VDM) [Jones90], and we will discuss two kinds of diagram and their relationship with the VDM specification language.

The ability to present in diagrammatic form the essential structures defined by a formal specification could improve communication. Thus a tool for generating, for instance, Entity-Relationship Diagrams from VDM specifications is an attractive idea. The ability to do the converse - to extract VDM specifications from diagrams - would address another current difficulty: the lack of methodology for the early stages of formal system development. If requirements analysis could be carried out in graphical form, and formal specifications derived, at least in part, from the diagrams, then the route to the adoption of formal methods would be still easier.

It is with these goals in mind that we have set about creating a prototype analysis assistant which can manage the consistency of a VDM specification and a set of annotated diagrams. Such a tool would permit the analyst to create a VDM specification from a collection of diagrams, or to create a set of diagrams showing different aspects of a VDM specification. The tool could also manage changes in text or diagram by performing the appropriate transformations.

Our goal is to find two or three types of diagram, each giving a significantly different dimension of the problem, and yet which, when taken together, give an as complete as possible formal specification. Where information cannot conveniently be represented diagrammatically, annotations will be used to make the meaning of symbols precise.

It is evident that some styles of specification will be a great deal easier to represent diagrammatically than others, especially by automatic translation. Without unduly constraining the analyst, we need to define the styles preferred. These styles will contribute to the methodology imposed by the use of diagrams.

Our role in the Atmosphere project is to demonstrate feasibility rather than provide a production quality toolset. Our approach is therefore to formally specify (in VDM) the transformations required, and make a fully working prototype in Prolog or Lisp. We have adopted the diagraming tools of IDE's "Software thru Pictures" for the creation and editing of diagrams, and our own editor and type-checker for VDM specifications. Using an early prototype, we have already succeeded in generating VDM domain expressions from extended Entity-Relationship diagrams.

In Section 2, we describe how we intend to support the process of analysis, and how the analyst might interact with an analysis tool. In Section 3, we describe a form of entity-relationship diagram ([Chen76]) called Entity-Structure Diagrams used for visualising VDM types. Section 4 describes another form of diagram for depicting VDM operations, Operation-State Diagrams. Section 5 discusses issues relating to the transformations between diagrams and VDM. Section 6 discusses tool support for creating and editing such diagrams, and finally Section 7 draws conclusions and describes the direction of future work.

2 Supporting the Process Of Analysis

The process of requirements analysis involves communication and interaction with the commissioners of the system, collecting, analysing and presenting information in many different forms, until (in this context) a complete formal specification has been drawn up and agreed.

It is our view that there are advantages in being able concurrently to build

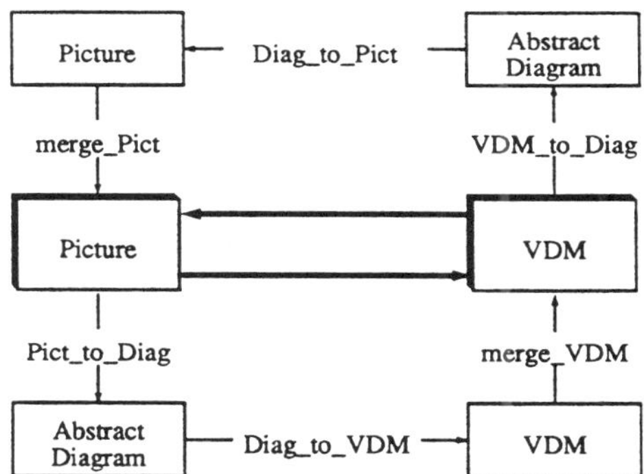

Figure 1: Tool functionality for each diagram

diagrams and formal texts during the analysis process. The diagrams assist in communicating the structure of the system in a clear visual manner, and the formal texts encourage the analyst to ask the right questions to remove inconsistencies and ambiguities from the system description.

We envisage, therefore, analysts working alternately on diagrammatic and textual descriptions of the system. They may choose from one of a number of different kinds of diagram, or the formal text, as the most appropriate medium for developing a particular concept. Tool support, then, should enable analysts to move freely from diagram to text and back again, automatically translating changes as required.

Within this scheme also, several analysts may be able simultaneously to work on different diagrams, developing different aspects of a system, and use tools to bring all aspects together in a unified, structured formal text.

Figure 1 represents the functionality required of a tool for each kind of diagram supported. The boxes and arcs in bold represent the overall functionality required, i.e. the ability to translate from pictures to VDM and back again. The other boxes and arcs represent the smaller steps from which the main transformations are composed. Both transformations pass through an abstract representation of the diagram, and finish with a merge. A set of these transformations is required for each kind of picture used.

Merging is necessary, because there is information contained in both the picture form and the VDM form, not contained in the abstract form, which we wish to preserve across updates. On the one hand, a VDM text may contain operation definitions, for instance, which are not affected by the content of an entity-relationship diagram. The operation definitions should not be lost. On the other hand, pictures carry implicit information about, for instance, the positioning and size of nodes and arcs which we may wish to retain whilst other details of the diagram are altered.

3   Entity-Structure Diagrams

The purpose of this section is to describe Entity-Structure Diagrams (ESDs), an
extended form of entity-relationship diagram that we have chosen to depict the
structure of VDM specifications at two levels: decomposition into modules, and
composite type definitions.

The ability to structure a specification is vital in any software engineering environment. Until recently, the VDM notation has lacked any significant structuring
facilities. A number of proposals for modules are being considered by the BSI committee for the standardisation of VDM, and it is likely that a module structure will
appear as an appendix to the first draft standard. For the time being, we use the
syntax as currently suggested by that committee [BSI90a], and we have in mind the
copy-rule semantics as suggested by [Blaue90].

We shall reflect the structure of a specification by drawing a separate ESD for
each module. We encourage a style in which each module defines a type which
carries the same name as the module. This main type becomes the *central entity* in
the ESD. Other local types (*local entities*) may be defined within the module. Other
modules may be instantiated as *imported entities* referenced by has-a relationships
within the module. In this way, we impose a hierarchical structure on ESDs, and
no single ESD becomes over complex. Circular instantiations are not permitted

In VDM, complex types can be created from certain basic types (Booleans,
Naturals, Characters, Reals, ...) using type constructors such as 'set of', 'seq of',
products, maps and functions. A frequently used construction is the so-called *composite* type, a form of product type with named fields. An example of a VDM
module containing a composite type *Cabin* follows.

```
module Cabin
  interface
    export
      types Cabin
      ....
    instantiations
      instantiate Door
        types Door
      ....
      instantiate Timer
        types Timer
      ....
      instantiate Floor
        types Floor
      ....
  definitions
```

```
types
    Cabin ::
        position : [N]
        speed : R
        dir : Direction
        buttons : set of Button
        door : Door
        timer : Timer
        refers-to : Button ⟵⟶ Floor
                            m

    Direction = { UP, DOWN }

    Button is not yet defined
    ....
end Cabin
```

The fields *position* and *speed* are of types natural and real, respectively. The square brackets round the *position* type indicate that the presence of the value is optional (*i.e.* it can take the value nil.) The field *dir* is of the locally defined enumerated type *Direction* which can take two values. *Door*, *Timer* and *Floor* are external types, mported from instantiated modules of the same name. *Button* is a local type which has no given structure. The mapping *refers-to* relates buttons to floors.

The parts marked .... could be definitions relating to operations which are not relevant to an ESD, and would have to be depicted by some other kind of diagram.

The fields of a composite type may be referenced using a Pascal-like dot notation; *e.g.* if c is of type *Cabin*, one can write *c.speed* to reference the real-valued field of c.

The ESD representing this module is shown in Figure 2. The solid barred rectangles are central entities; dashed barred rectangles are imported entities, and the ordinary rectangles are local entities. Attributes are represented by circles, labeled according to the names of the fields they depict. Imported entities have no attributes, since their attributes are defined on other ESDs.

The oval nodes represent containment, or has-a relationships. They carry the name of the field they depict, and are used when fields themselves have structure, *i.e.* are of a composite type. Types at the end of a has-a relationship are local types or instantiations of other modules. The cardinality on the has-a arc shows the number of instantiations.

The mapping *refers-to* is depicted as a relationship, the diamond shape in the diagram. All relationships must belong to a type, and so the thick arc from the diamond leads to the owner entity.

The informal meaning of the diagram for *Cabin* is as follows: a cabin consists of

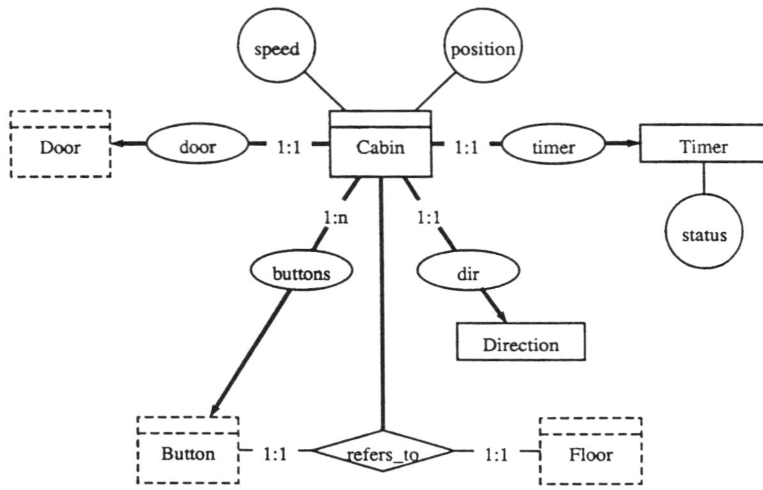

Figure 2: Entity-Structure Diagram for *Cabin*

a single door, a set of buttons and a single timer. It has attributes indicating speed and position, and it has associated with it a one-to-one mapping from buttons to floors.

Another, related, example is as follows.

```
module LiftSys
   interface
      export
         types LiftSys

         ....

      instantiations
         instantiate Cabin
            types Cabin

         ....

         instantiate Floor
            types Floor

         ....

   definitions
      types
         LiftSys ::
            cabs : set of Cabin
            floors : seq of Floor
            is-at : Cabin  ⟶ᵐ  Floor
```

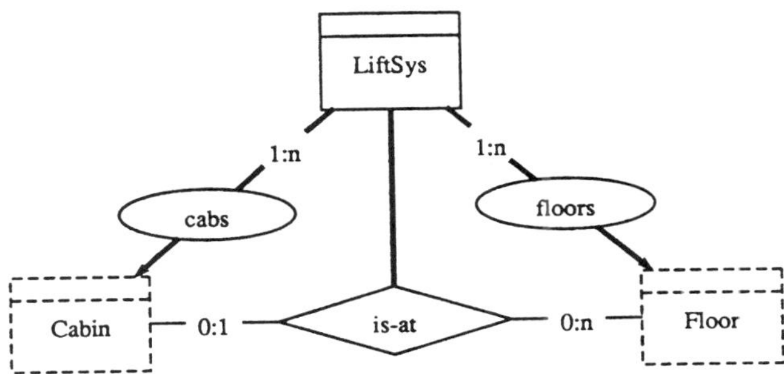

Figure 3: An Entity Structure Diagram for *LiftSys*

....

end *LiftSys*

which defines a new type called *LiftSys* composed of three fields, a set of *Cabins*, a sequence of *Floors* and a mapping representing the presence of cabins at floors. The corresponding ESD is found in Figure 3.

We have chosen not to represent all required information graphically. Examples of this are attribute types, which are left off to avoid clutter, and the optionality of attributes (*e.g.* as in *position*). Another example is whether a cardinality of "1:n" on a has-a relation is intended to be a set or a sequence in the corresponding VDM. Although such aspects are not determined visually, they will be treated by non-visual attributes on symbols.

The order in which the arcs appear on the diagram is, of course, completely arbitrary; an entity, for instance, will be modeled as having a set of attributes, ordering being unimportant. However, the order in which fields occur in a VDM composite type definition is not arbitrary; in the abstract syntax of VDM, a composite type is defined as having a *sequence* of fields. This difference has to be resolved in the transformation between ESDs and VDM modules, and will be handled by the merging process described in Section 5.

We have implicitly suggested here a concrete visual syntax for ESDs, we we have used to motivate the concepts involved. For the purpose of defining formally the transformations between ESDs and VDM-SL suggested in Figure 1, we have created an abstract syntax for ESDs which defines all the information to be represented in visual form and in annotations. The details of this syntax can be found in [DL91].

4   Operation-State Diagrams

Previous sections have discussed VDM type definitions, and how ESDs could be used to visualise them. Here we discuss how Operation-State Diagrams (OSDs) can be used to visualise operations in VDM.

For brevity, we shall only sketch the treatment of operations defined in the VDM implicit style, that is, defined by stating a pre- and post-condition constraining the possible effects of the operation on the state of the system.

An example of an operation *start* on *Cabin* is given below.

$start(\ floor{:}\mathbf{N}\ )$
wr $c{:}Cabin$

$$\begin{aligned}
\text{pre}\quad &c.speed = 0.0\ \wedge \\
&c.door.closed\ \wedge \\
&floor \neq c.position
\end{aligned}$$

$$\begin{aligned}
\text{post}\quad &c.speed > 0.0\ \wedge \\
&c.door.closed\ \wedge \\
&c.dir = \text{if}\quad floor > c'.position \\
&\qquad\quad \text{then}\ UP \\
&\qquad\quad \text{else}\ DOWN\ \wedge \\
&c.position = \text{nil}
\end{aligned}$$

Since *start* has a certain effect on the state of the cabin c, it is tempting to view the operation as a state transition, with the pre- and post-conditions defining the source and target states respectively. The difficulty with this, however, is that pre- and post-conditions allow one to express properties far more general than can be conveniently represented in a classical state-transition diagram. For instance, states are disjoint in state-transition diagrams; that is, only one state can be occupied at a time. But here we wish to handle more complex states, where, for example, the cabin can be moving or not moving, and quite independently its direction indicator may be set to up or down.

Another idea is to use Petri nets, by associating a place to each predicate, and a transition to each operation. Pre- and post-conditions can be decomposed into smaller logical pieces to reflect more closely the complexity of the VDM. Even this, however, does not allow enough flexibility, since we wish to have some operations which have no pre-condition, and, in the case of explicitly defined operations, no post-condition. This would lead to ill-formed Petri-nets. In any case, we feel that to mix the formalism of Petri-nets with that of VDM in this context would lead to confusion.

Instead we have chosen to encourage a particular style of VDM in which states of interest are explicitly identified by auxiliary predicate definitions. These states do not have to be disjoint. We adapt the classical notion of an state-transition diagram by allowing non-disjoint states and operations which are loosely connected to states. The resulting diagrams we call Operation-State Diagrams (OSDs).

First we define some explicit states of a cabin, *idle* and *moving*:

$$idle : Cabin \rightarrow \mathbf{B}$$
$$idle(c) \; \underline{\Delta} \;\; c.speed = 0.0 \;\wedge$$
$$c.door.closed$$

$$moving : Cabin \rightarrow \mathbf{B}$$
$$moving(c) \; \underline{\Delta} \;\; c.speed > 0.0 \;\wedge$$
$$c.door.closed \;\wedge$$
$$c.position = \text{nil}$$

Now we are able to recast the operation *start* making use of these definitions:

$$start(\; floor{:}\mathbf{N} \;) \;\; dir{:}Direction$$
$$\text{wr} \;\; c{:}Cabin$$

$$\text{pre} \quad idle(c) \;\wedge$$
$$floor \neq c.position$$

$$\text{post} \quad moving(c) \;\wedge$$
$$dir = \text{if} \quad floor > c'.position$$
$$\text{then} \; UP$$
$$\text{else} \; DOWN$$

Figure 4 shows what an OSD for the cabin module with a number of operations might look like. States are pictured as circles, and operations as rectangles. Double circles represent initial states. Short, thick lines join sets of disjoint states. Arrows represent dependencies between operations and states as pre- and post-conditions. For instance, the two states *idle* and *moving* are attached to the operation *start* as pre- and post-conditions respectively, as shown by the direction of the arrows, representing the requirement that the operation is only valid on an idle cabin, and the effect of the operation is to leave the cabin in the moving state.

The diagram does not represent all the requirements. Other parts of pre-conditions (for example, that the destination be not equal to the cabin's current position) have to be expressed as non-visual attributes of the operation. Similarly with the details of the arguments of operations, and the other parts of post-conditions.

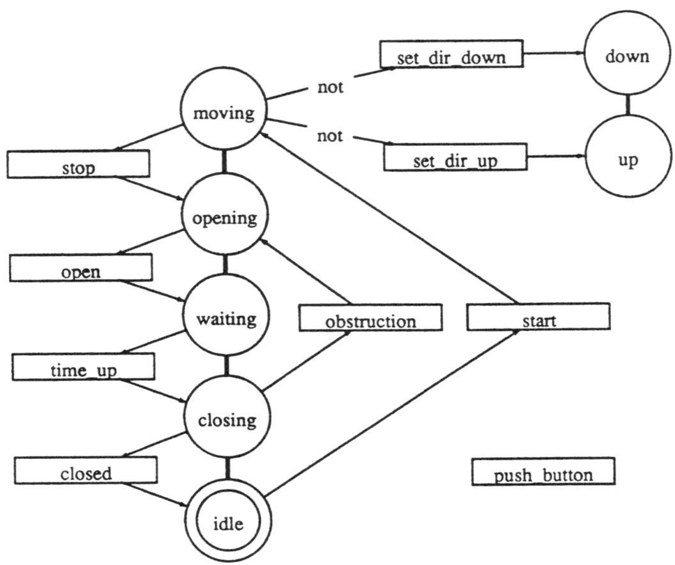

Figure 4: A Operation-State diagram

It is reasonable to interpret the operation *start* in Figure 4 as a state transition, since the states *idle* and *moving* are disjoint. Other operations, however, cannot be so viewed. Take for example the operations *set_dir_up* and *set_dir_down*: these partial operations are only applicable when the cabin is NOT in the *moving* state (as represented by the "not" annotation on the corresponding arrow.) It is clear that the operations in this case cannot be interpreted as state transitions, their only effect being to set the direction, and the states *down* and *up* are independent from the other states.

There is a certain amount of information implicit in an OSD which has to become explicit in a VDM module. For instance, nothing is explicitly stated about how the the moving-opening-waiting-closing-idle state component changes under the operations *set_dir_up* and *set_dir_down*; it is assumed implicitly to remain unchanged. In VDM, every operation has a *frame*, defined by naming those components of the system state that are effected by the operation. A feature of VDM is that, if components of the frame in fact remain unchanged, this must always be stated explicitly. Therefore, in translating operations such as these into VDM, information about the unchanging frame components must be stated.

The disjointness of those states connected by disjointness arcs could be represented in the VDM by an invariant in the composite type (in this case *Cabin*.) It is not clear at this stage how such invariants will be handled in the semantics of

VDM If this would prevent operations from being implemented in a way that allowed the entity temporarily to pass through other states during a transition, then an invariant is not the best way of handling the problem. Another, perhaps better, way would be to generate a proof obligation to show that the various states are disjoint.

Note that the operation *push_button* is not connected to any state. This means, in effect, that the operation is applicable in any state of the cabin, without affecting any of the named states. Its definition must be contained entirely within non-visual annotations.

5　Translation Between Diagrams and VDM

Previous sections have strongly suggested relationships between the elements of diagrams and VDM definitions. We are currently in the process of formally defining these transformations in VDM. Early results of this work can be found in [DL91].

A typical mode of working with the tools would be to create an ESD, extract a VDM module from it, make modifications to the VDM, and recreate the corresponding diagram using the VDM to ESD transformation function. Typical changes to the VDM might be to change the order of fields in a composite type, or add fields to a composite type, or to add operation definitions to the module.

When the diagram is recreated, much of the information has remained unchanged. It is the role of the merge function to take the new version of diagram, and merge it into the old version in such a way as to retain diagram-specific details such as symbol sizes and positions.

A similar merge function must exist in the opposite transformation also, where the transformation of a diagram creates a new version of a VDM module. Here the kind of VDM specific information that should be retained is the order of fields in a composite type, for instance.

The transformation functions will assign default values to variables specific to the target notation. For instance, symbols will be of a default size, and assigned a position according to some predetermined algorithm. Similarly, field orders will depend, perhaps, on the order of creation of the arcs in the diagram. The merge function will then compare the new version with the old, and where common elements can be identified through non-notation specific attributes, the notation-specific values will be copied from the old version. Of course, if the user is not happy with the default values assigned by the tool, the editors can be used to change them.

6　Tool Support

Prototypes of the transformations between ESDs and VDM have been implemented and integrated with the picture editor of "Software thru Pictures" (StP, a product from Interactive Development Environments), which we have tailored to allow the creation and editing of ESDs. Indeed, the figures in the paper where drawn in this manner.

We are able directly to manipulate diagrams by use of the ASCII representation of each diagram provided by the editor. The symbols carry two kinds of attribute: *visible* attributes, shown by shape and textual labels; and *hidden* attributes, made up of structured text which may be inspected and edited separately from the diagram.

It is possible to personalise symbols by redefining the structure of the hidden attributes. StP also provides a mechanism for traversing a hierarchy of diagrams by use of a PUSH-POP function. This allows us, for instance, to move from one ESD to another by following the hierarchy of imported entities.

The hidden attributes of symbols allow diagrams to be linked to an underlying data-base of definitions. Each type of diagram is in essence a different view of the contents of the data-base.

In the work reported here, the role of the underlying data-base is replaced by a collection of interrelated VDM modules. This permits control on consistency, by passing the VDM specification through a type checker. In this way, entities referred to in an OSD but not defined in an ESD, for instance, can be identified. Thus we make no use of the StP data-base.

Our approach to the definition of a concrete syntax for each type of diagram is to first define an abstract syntax for an StP picture. Then we define transformations to and from the abstract syntax of StP pictures and the abstract syntax of each type of diagram. We also define a picture merge function which updates an existing picture from a new version, but retains information such as symbol coordinates and size. Details can be found in [DL91].

7   Conclusions and Future Work

Two visual notations for the expression of aspects of VDM specifications, namely Entity-Structure Diagrams and Operation-State Diagrams, have been described. The transformation of ESDs to and from VDM are relatively simple to specify. The transformations for OSDs are more complicated due to the desire to give the diagrams a rest-unchanged semantics. They also required the VDM to be in a particular style.

We have chosen to depart from the classical entity-relationship and state-transition diagram because neither expressed exactly the kinds of aspects we required for a VDM specification. ESDs allows us to express a containment hierarchy, and OSDs allow us to express non-disjoint states.

For the present, we are continuing with the work of specifying the transformations for ESDs and OSDs. We shall then complete the prototype implementations of the ESD and OSD transformations, and try them out on some case studies.

In due course, other diagrams should be considered as alternatives or as complementary to those described here. For instance, it would be interesting to examine a possible role for data-flow diagrams and structure charts.

We are keen also to look at diagrams for other specification languages, such as the RAISE specification language, which has aspects of process, channel, communication and concurrency not present in VDM. Finding a diagram for representing such aspects is an interesting challenge. Also of interest to us are notations for object-oriented concepts, adding aspects of class and inheritance.

Another very interesting line of work would be to study the refinement of diagrams. Initially, one could study the differences in diagrams of VDM specifications and their refinements, and from there try to devise direct diagrammatic refinement techniques.

References

[Blaue90]   G. Blaue, *A Copy Rule Approach to the Semantics of BSI/VDM Modules*, BSI/VDM N. 195

[BSI90a]   British Standards Institute, *The BSI/VDM Proto-Standard*, Draft of 7 Sept 1990, Brian Richee (Ed.)

[Chen76]   P. P. Chen, *The Entity-Relationship Approach to Systems Analysis and Design*, North Holland, Amsterdam, 1980

[DL91]   J. Dick, J. Loubersac, *A Visual Approach to VDM: Entity-Structure Diagrams*, Bull Research Center Report, DE/DRPA/DMA/91001, Jan 1991.

[Jones90]   Cliff B. Jones, *Systematic Software Development using VDM*, Second Edition, Prentice Hall Int., 1990

[SA90]   Lesley Semmens, Pat Allen, *Using Yourdon and Z: an Approach to Formal Specification*, Procs. Fifth Z Users' Group, (to appear), Springer Verlag, Dec 1990

14

Selecting methods and tools for particular environments: a toolbased approach

Antoinette Kieback
Dornier GmbH, Friedrichshafen, Federal Republic of Germany
Joachim Niemeier
Fraunhofer IAO, Stuttgart, Federal Republic of Germany

1   Introduction

Over the last two decades, formal methods and tools have been introduced into the process of planning, developing, implementing, and managing applications of information technology (IT). For the practical usage existing methods and tools often are seen as incomplete, poorly integrated, often ineffective, and typically insensitive to the application environment. How to make the most of what is available today? Methods and tools to support the newer and more integrated forms of IT applications are still at an early stage of development and are not in common use. A guidance on the selection of methods and tools is needed which shows both what can be achieved now and where developments will come in the future. To a considerable extent the solution of behavioural and organizational design problems are seen as critical. But are methods and tools available for this objective? How to bring together approaches which have so far been pursued along separate paths. The following methods and tools requirements have been expressed in an user organisation (see figure 1). What is the most suitable product supporting the three different environments?

The selection and evaluation of appropriate methods and tools for a specific project in a company requires a considerable effort and is itself a difficult and complex task. There is no single, simple path to excellence. This paper describes a pragmatic and experimental toolbased approach for the selection and evaluation of methods and tools.

	Designer's Workbench Analysis Tool	Programmer's Workbench Code Generators	Integrated Products
Functional analysis	●		●
Data analysis	●		●
Encyclopedia/Repository	●	●	●
Prototyping	●	●	
PC utilization	●	●	●
Mainframe utilization	●	●	●
HW Constraints	●	●	●
SW Constraints		●	●
Symbolic code generator		●	●
Compatibility with internal Standard		●	●
Metalanguage availability		●	●

Fig. 1: Methods and Tools Requirements

2   Background

The HECTOR project (Harmonized European Concepts and Tools for Organizational Information Systems, project no. 2082) was part of the Office and Business Systems area of the ESPRIT II programme of the Commission for the European Communities. HECTOR was a one year explorative action. The term Organizational Informations Systems (OIS) in the project's name was defined as any socio-technical system which supports the work of an organization by facilitating the collection, flow and analysis of information within or between organizations. An organizational information system can include information technology, organizational structure, and work structure.

The purposes of HECTOR have been to determine what is needed in the European marketplace, where opportunities lie to better meet these needs, and to present a framework within which these issues could be studied. This led to the following objectives:

- establish a framework to characterize existing OIS development methods and tools (HECTOR framework of reference);
- use the framework to describe existing methods and tools;
- determine the extent to which these are adequate or inadequate for system improvement projects;
- identify the requirements for integrated methods and tools;
- map out the opportunities for further development;
- recommend and prototype a mean to improve the selection of methods and tools.

A market survey undertaken in several European counties has provided an up to date assessment of the recent and potential uses, of how to select from and make the most of what is available. In most of the cases the choice of methods and tools depends only on the specific knowledge about methods or tools and the past experiences of the analyst/designer. A known method/tool is very often chosen, but normally the problem awaiting for a solution is then adapted to the functionality of that chosen method/tool. This leads in most cases to a situation, in which the wrong problem is solved.

Therefore, tools for choosing methods and tools were seen to be a major field in the future in order to react to the need of finding the appropriate method or tool for a specific problem. Two software prototypes are available at the end of the HECTOR project: SESAM and OISEAU. SESAM (Systematics for Elaboration, Selection and Assessment of Methods and Tools) is a hypertext database of OIS methods and tools. The SESAM database is structured according to the HECTOR framework of reference. OISEAU (Organizational Information System Enhancement Advice Unit) is a prototype decision support system to facilitate the choice of OIS methods and tools. It uses SESAM as a database and several features of the HECTOR framework of reference as parts of its user interface.

In its full form the prototypes would be intended for four types of users:

- The project manger or manager of an OIS user department who wants advice on what would be involved in carrying out possible improvements to the OIS, what methods and tools are available, and which might suit the environment best;
- A consultant employed to assist a user manager to carry out an OIS improvement project;
- A manager in a tool development organization, seeking information on gaps and defects in the OIS tool market which the organization might remedy;
- A researcher interested in investigations in the OIS methods and tools area.

3   The SESAM database

SESAM is a tool designed to gather, characterize and review current OIS methods and tools.

OIS methods are specific or generic methods/approaches covering one or more parts of the process of planning and controlling, building and introducing changes to OIS. In the HECTOR project we have identified eight streams of methods:

- Project management
- System life-cycle support
- Socio-technical or organizational engineering

- Strategic planning
- Economic evaluation
- Configuration of equipment and software
- Management of changes
- Selection and implementation of software solutions

A special effort was made to include methods and tools suitable for OIS improvement which can not be found in existing inventories of available methods and tools. Our initial analyses have identified over 300 tools specifically designed to support one or more parts of the process of planning and controlling, building and introducing changes to OIS. About 250 methods and tools have then been described in the SESAM database, whereas 150 have been classified in such a detail that they are usable for the OISEAU prototype.

The main classes listed below represent a highly fragmented and confused product market:

- Integrated project support environments
- Computer aided software/system engineering tools
- Analyst workbenches
- Modelling tools
- Diagraming tools
- Organizational Engineering tools
- Project management tools
- Portable common tools environment

Several surveys about OIS methods and tools are available on a commercial basis (see for example Ovum 1989, PSI 1989, Balzert 1989). The limitation of these surveys can be seen in the narrowed focus on purely technical tools and the absent foundation of underlying description structure. A methods and tools database should not appear as a paper document, like those studies above, because due to the high dynamics in the methods and tools market a significant portion of information is obsolete the moment a document is printed.

Therefore, SESAM was planned as an online system. During the project SESAM has provided the HECTOR analysts with a complete environment to describe methods and tools. It is implemented as a database using a hypertext system (SuperCard). The philosophy of SuperCard is to represent all screens by cards, with mouse sensitive buttons and graphical backgrounds. Each entry in the database is represented logically by an object and physically by cards. The structure of those cards is described in a mastercard containing all the related information (attributes of the object), physically seen as fields on that card. Each entry is therefore an instance of a mastercard.

The SESAM environment consists of four parts:

- Bibliography
- Analysis
- Configuration
- Glossary

The Bibliography and Analysis card are used to describe a method or a tool. The Bibliography cards allows a quick verbal description of methods and tools whereas in the Analysis card the characteristics of a method or a tool are documented more precisely and in more detail. Configuration defines the contents of the lowest level for the Analysis card (the nominal domains, known as "choice lists"). Glossary refers to relevant terms and can be seen as an online help for the SESAM users.

On the Bibliography card there are a number of fields, in which text can be entered freely:

-       Name
-       Literature/Source of information
-       Last Update (date generated by the system)
-       Keywords
-       Provider
-       Abstract

This card can be thought of as a structured text editor (figure 2).

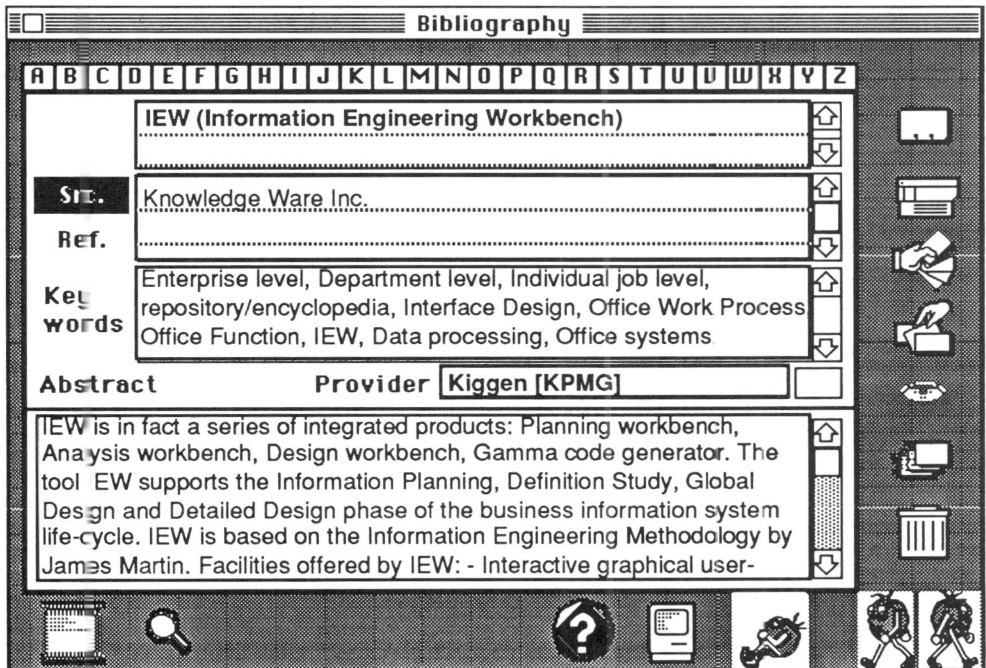

Fig. 2   Display of the Bibliography Card of a SESAM Entry

In contrast to the free text entry on the Bibliography card work on the Analysis card is guided by choice lists. On the Analysis card, methods and tools can be described in three distinct ways: attributes, life cycle support, relationships between methods and tools.

3.1   Attributes

The HECTOR framework of reference is a common basis for classifying and describing all the processes and entities involved in developing and implementing OIS, including OIS methods and tools and their usage. Therefore, SESAM is an application of the HECTOR framework of reference.

Relevant attributes, supported by choice lists, are

-   Name
-   Requirements
-   Application Area
-   Theoretical Model
-   Country
-   Classification

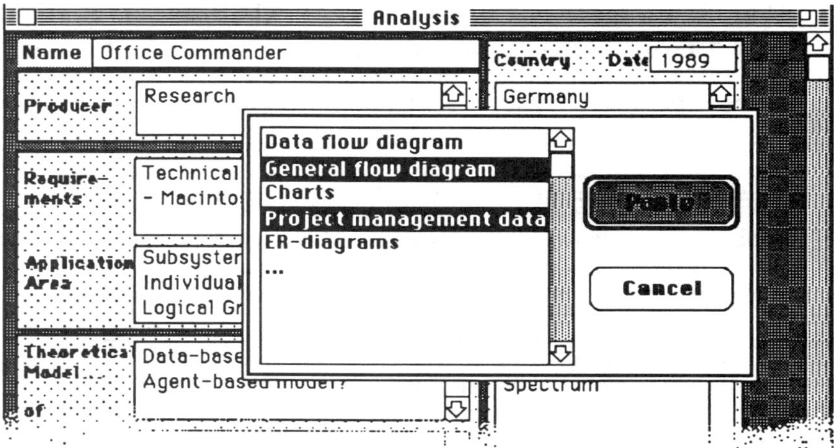

Fig. 3   Display of the Attributes Part of an Analysis Card

3.2   Life Cycle Support

This field contains attributes to provide a global description of the life cycle support. They characterize a method as a black box, and do not reveal any details. In order to break down the method, we have adopted the so called "IAO-step". An "IAO-step" is a triplet consisting of:

Input: a list of information entities to be used in this step.
Action: a verb describing the transformation performed in this step.
Output: a list of information entities resulting from this step.

A specific method can now be described as a set of "IAO-steps". Each step is represented verbal, using as delimiters:

DO: action, IN: list, of, inputs, OUT: list, of, outputs.

This set of steps for each method/tool is partitioned into several phases of the life cycle: analysis, design, implementation, evaluation, maintenance, and project management.

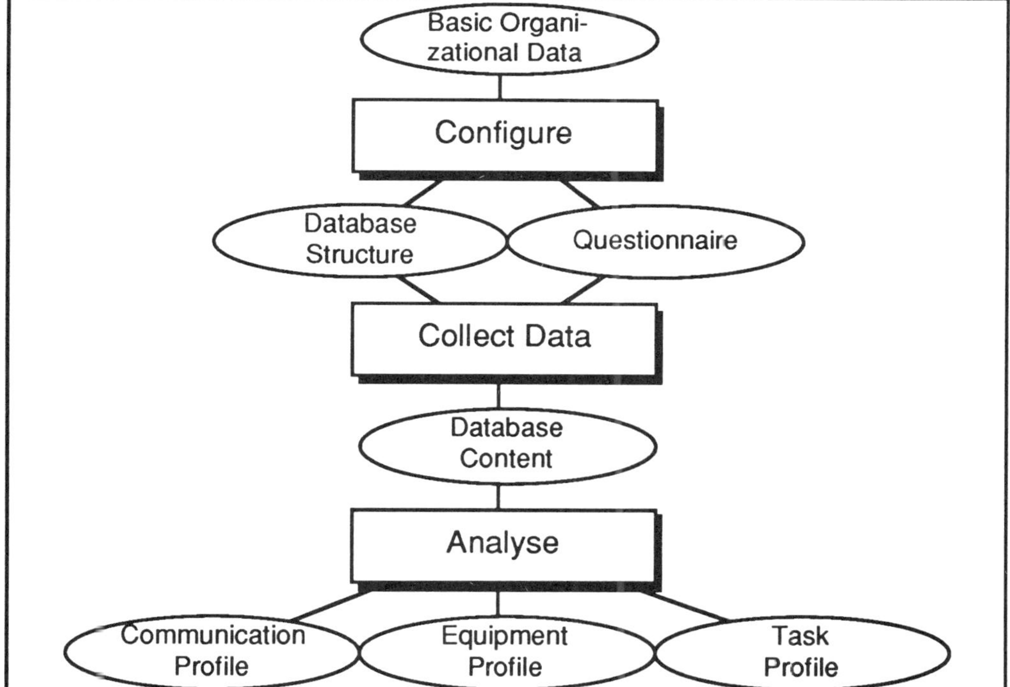

Fig. 4 Example of IAO Description

3.3   Relationships between methods and tools

To capture relations between methods (or between tools or between methods and tools), the relationship field can be used. There are five types of relationships defined:

- **Is similar to:** this method is similar to some other, as judged by SESAM user describing this method.
- **Is part of:** this method is part of a methodology, a method spectrum, or whatever comes to mind.
- **Consists of:** this method consists of another method that is also documented in SESAM.
- **Can be part of:** this method can be used in the context of other methods.
- **Can consist of:** these relationships are similar to the previous two. The distinction is whether the relationship is essential or optional. If optional, then these variant should be used.

The relations are all symmetrical, for example: if A is similar to B, then B is similar to A. Accordingly, entering a relation for method A requires entering the reverse in the description of B.

What kind of analysis can be undertaken on basis of the "IAO (input-action-output)" part of SESAM? Possible questions which could be answered are: "What are possible inputs and outputs of action XYZ (across several methods and tools)?"; "To what extent do existing methods and tools provide the aggregate list of possible inputs and outputs?"; "How rich in useful variants are certain leading methods and tools?"

4   The OISEAU Tool

OISEAU (Organizational Information Systems Enhancement Advice Unit) is a demonstration prototype for a decision support tool to facilitate the selection of appropriate methods and tools within the information systems engineering field. OISEAU is a software tool designed to help users to plan their information system improvement/development project around the critical success factors for their business, bearing in mind factors like their organizational structure and the applications required.

4.1   The Underlying Decision Situation

In daily practice the search for an appropriate method and/or tool is seen very time consuming and complex, depending on the scope of the questions to be answered:

- Does it cover the life cycle phases that are important for system success? Does it cover the relevant subsystems (e.g. organizational design, if appropriate)?
- Is it flexible? Can it be adapted to our organization's needs? Will it accommodate possible changes in system development such as switching to prototyping after a preliminary analysis has been conducted?

- Is the language (graphical and verbal) easy to learn and easy to use? Does it permit to describe all of the details of a system, needed to know, to understand it sufficiently so that it can be improved?
- If the method provides only partial coverage of the situation, is it compatible with the other methods that will be used alongside it?
- Are there tools supporting the methodology or method? Are those tools compatible with each other? Does the expected benefit from their use (higher productivity, better quality results) exceed the various costs (cash outlay, time required to learn to use them, user acceptance)?

This of course is not a complete list of questions, it can only give a taste of the complexity of the decision situation. Fluctuating and conflicting requirements cause additional problems.

4.2   The OISEAU Cycle

Existing system engineering models do not provide enough insight into the real system development processes to guide the selection and evaluation of methods and tools. A typical statement often heard is: "The conditions surrounding our project would not let us work from our model". Therefore, the HECTOR consortium proposed with the HECTOR framework of reference a mean to understand the system development process. In contrast to other frameworks the HECTOR framework of reference provides insight into the environmental conditions and the organizational context of system development.

Based on this framework there are essentially three categories of data relevant to the operation of OISEAU.

- One covers the description of a project's environment, which relates the environment to methods and tools.
- Another category details all of the available methods and tools. This is SESAM.
- The third contains data on the performance of methods and tools in defined environments obtained from completed projects.

The operation of OISEAU is fairly straightforward (see figure 5), though technically far from being simple. The user enter the details of the proposed project into the system. This would include descriptions of:

- the existing OIS,
- the organizational environment (both internal and external) in which the improvement is to take place,
- the nature of the problem(s) to be resolved,
- constraints affecting the project (e.g. budget, deadlines) and the like.

All of these data would be entered by using the HECTOR framework of reference in terms of the variables (characteristics) used and their measurements.

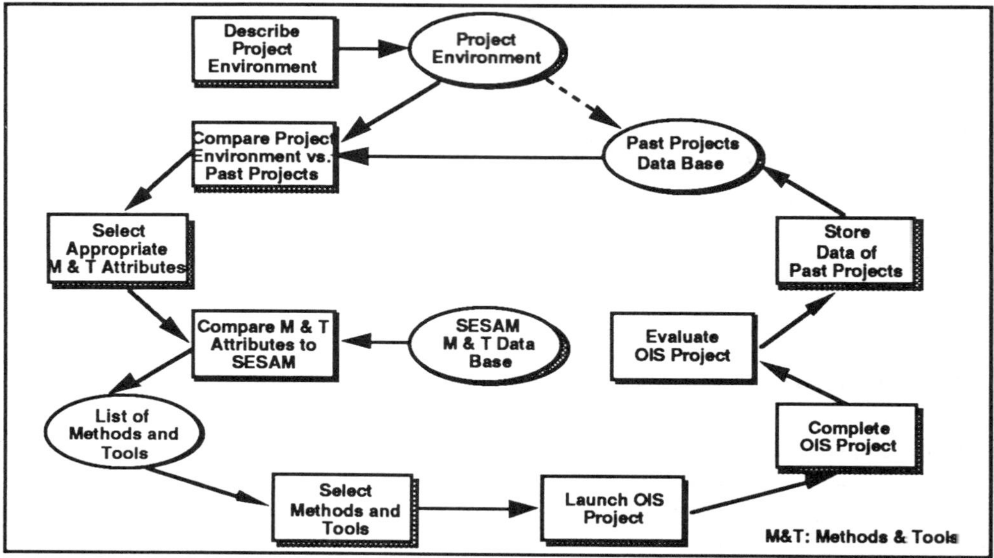

Fig. 5 The OISEAU Cycle

OISEAU would now try to match the current environment with those in its historical database (the database containing how well various methods and tools have worked in different environments in past projects). It would examine similar environments to identify those methods and tools which have performed well, and then deliver a list of methods and tools that would be acceptable (rank ordered when the system has reached that level of sophistication). A choice would then be made by the user of specific method(s) and tools to be used, related to the current project development phase.

To continue the cycle, the project would be launched using the method(s) and tools chosen. After its completion an evaluation would be conducted, especially with respect to methods and tools as far as OISEAU is concerned. Their performance, along with the original environmental data and the methods and tools chosen, would be stored in the past projects database, to be used the next time a project is in the formulation stage.

At present OISEAU exists as a demonstration prototype, developed object oriented using SuperCard on a Macintosh computer. This user friendly interface is used to illustrate the OISEAU functional model guiding the user through OISEAU, and visualize the HECTOR framework of reference for inserting project data. In the SESAM database a tool or method is represented by a card containing all information.

4.3   The OISEAU Demonstration Prototype

This demonstration prototype actually covers that part of OISEAU, that describes the OIS development project, but just with the most important structures of the HECTOR framework of reference, and ends up with a list of methods and tools found in the SESAM database. There is a lack of data on the performance of methods and tools in various environments. What is implemented, however, is a list of keywords connected to each method and tool in the database that indicates the possession of the attributes represented by those keywords. Thus the user can describe the various aspects of methods and tools that are important to an OIS project, and the system will scan the database to see which approach meets the stated requirements/constraints. This is done by means of a predefined check list shown on the screen of the computer, so that all the user has to do is to mark those attributes he seeks. At this point everything available are yes/no measures, which is some distance from the intended long range objectives.

The functional model of the OISEAU demonstration prototype is represented in the following picture. Circles are representing data structures and the SESAM data base is represented by a drum. Rectangles represents processes. OISEAU consists of four parts implicitly shown in figure 6:

- Definition of the OIS project characteristics
- Selection of requirements out of the defined project characteristics using keywords
- Choice of methods and/or tools according to the requirements
- Precision of a method or tool of the choice list, containing the chosen methods and tools

While the prototype does not provide a mean for ranking methods and tools as such, basically because there are no data to do so, it does have an interesting feature which permits an indirect ranking of sorts. The user can add or subtract requirements and constraints according to their relative importance. The greater the number of limitations, the fewer will be the number of appropriate methods and tools. Obviously the reverse is true as well. Thus one can add constraints until there is only one method that satisfies them, or gradually relieve them to see what additional methods are now acceptable.

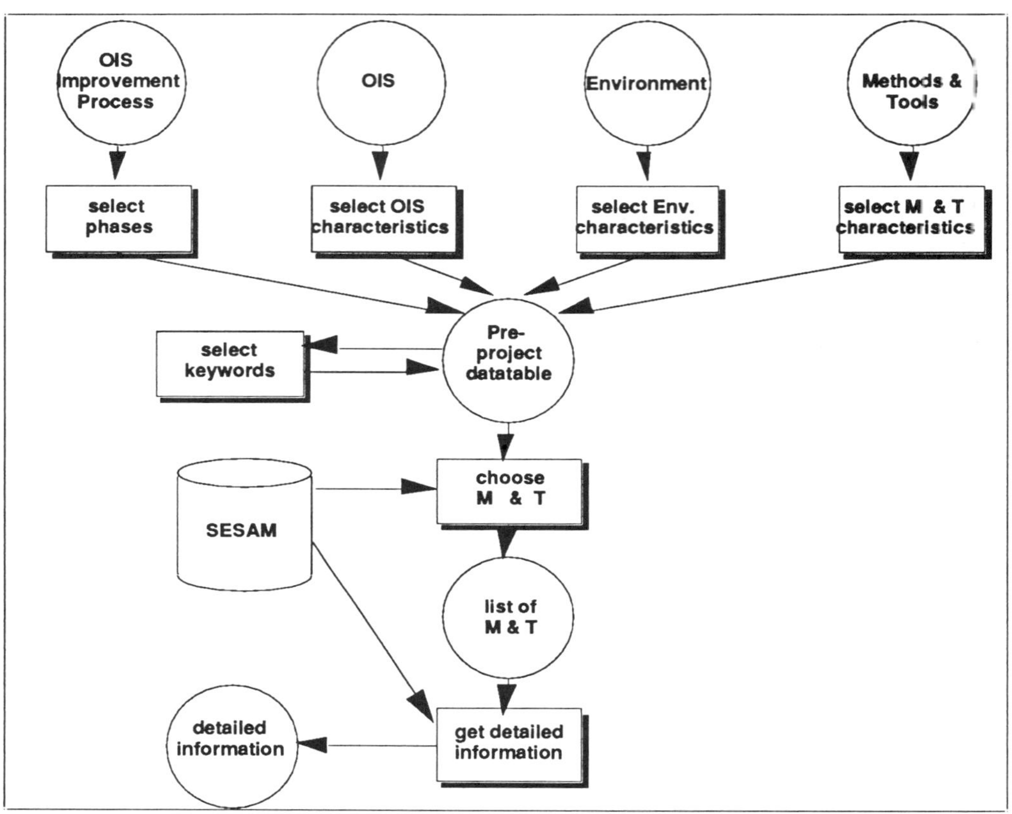

Fig. 6   The OISEAU Demonstration Prototype

5   Discussion and Conclusions

The HECTOR Market Analysis has shown that a good initial choice of methods
and tools is very important presupposed for the success of a project. A wrong
initial choice often leads to the failure of a project or at least to higher costs. A
decision support tool, supported by a comprehensive database of OIS methods
and tools would improve the process of selection and evaluation of organizations acquiring these products.

The prototype allows a first rough selection of appropriate methods and tools
on basis of a maximum of ten project relevant criteria out of 70. It is important
to notice that even the prototype can handle more criteria in contrast to the
number of criteria applied in a "normal" human decision making process.
Results from the HECTOR market analysis show that only one or two criteria
are typically used for the selection of methods and tools. For the final choice the

decision maker can investigate the preselected methods and tools in more depth, e.g. via personal contact to a vendor.

Additional question will be raised like:

- Has the tool vendor an office located in the same region?
- What kind of support is offered by the local office?
- Will the method/tool find acceptance in our organization?
- Is the method/tool already known in our organization?
- Does the method/tool fit to political organizational constraints?
- Which experiences has the project manager?

It is obvious that these factors also strongly determine the final choice. But the relative importance of these factors differ from company to company. It is important to notice that these factors only can complement the preselected decision information produced using OISEAU but never substitute them.

The application of OISEAU in test case scenarios has led to *valid results*. Using OISEAU the possible *solution space is widened*. At the same time *the decision making process is more efficient*: A broader spectrum of possibilities can be checked. The effect of altering the constraints produces shorter and longer lists of acceptable methods and tools. This provides insights in the *robustness of solutions*.

6   Next Steps and Longer Term Issues

Starting from the prototype, OISEAU now needs to be refined with the following improvements in a longer term:

- use improved HECTOR framework of reference as a basement, utilizing sophisticated domains containing weights for the keywords;
- describe and evaluate the environment where the method/tool has been used;
- provide a search mechanism using all defined keywords and rank the result list according to the best choice and indicating, why one method/tool is better than another one;
- take into account the phase, in which the project actually is searching for a tool, in order to be able to use OISEAU in the following phase, without necessarily describing the project again;
- take into account experiences from previous OIS improvement projects, by storing the environmental data about the methods/ tools chosen and information about the evaluation results of the methods/tools used in that environment.

The most important steps to be taken are enhancing the conceptual model of SESAM, to cover performance data, and gathering a sufficiently rich database on the performance of methods and tools in various environments so that OISEAU can operate as proposed. The maintenance of a database like SESAM

is a time consuming task, in a rapidly changing market, and has to be coordinated among several organizations. A high quality of SESAM entry can only be
reached if methods and tools have been tested by a impartial unit.

7 Acknowledgements

The results presented in this paper are mainly derived from the HECTOR-
project (see "List of Final HECTOR Reports" under "References"), wherein six
European countries contributed their work. We thank BIFOA, Cap Gemini
Innovation, CRAI, DELGA Internacional S.A., Fraunhofer-IAO, IOT, KPMG
Peat Marwick McLintock, and PA Consulting Group for their research work on
the European market, CRAI, Dornier, Fraunhofer-IAO, and PA for their work
on the HECTOR framework of reference and the development of SESAM and
OISEAU. We also like to thank the University of Jyväskylä and the University
of East Anglia for their contribution to the market analysis and the HECTOR
framework of reference. All partners supported in gathering and inserting data
on methods/tools into the SESAM database.

8 References

Balzert 1989: Balzert, H.: CASE - Systeme und Werkzeuge, Band 7, Reihe:
Angewandte Informatik, BI Verlag, Mannheim 1989

Ovum 1989: Rock-Evans, R., and Engelien, B.: Ovum, Analysis Techniques
for CASE: a detailed Evaluation, Volume 1 Ovum Ltd, London,
1989

PSI 1989: Woschinski, S. and Warner, A.: PSI, Softwareentwicklungswerk-
zeuge im Vergleich, PSI, Berlin, 1989

List of Final HECTOR Reports

Conrath, Dave; An Overview of HECTOR's Results. Methods and Tools for
Improving Organizational Information Systems

King-Smith, Gavin; Improving Information Systems in Organizations. Methods
and Tools for the 1990s

Hawgood, John, Joachim Niemeier and Edda Pulst; Analysis of Future
Development Opportunities for OIS Methods and Tools

Pulst, Edda et al.; HECTOR's Framework of Reference

González, José L.; European OIS Methods and Tools Vendors Survey

Kieback, Antoinette et al.; OISEAU - SESAM. A Decision Support Tool

Ross, Gordon, HECTOR Market Assessment Report. The Current and Future Markets for Methods and Tools for Implementing Effective Organizational Information Systems

Beslmüller, Eduard et al.; HECTOR Market Assessment. German Country Report

Gaudenzi, Francesca et al.; HECTOR Market Assessment. Italian Country Report

González, José L., Cristina Cabanas, Ramón Monja; HECTOR Market Assessment. Spanish Country Report

Jyväkorpi, Sole, Mauri Leppänen, Vesa Savolainen; HECTOR Market Assessment. Finnish Country Report

Leclerc Annie; HECTOR Market Assessment. French Country Report

Smith, Nick; HECTOR Market Assessment. UK Country Report

15

Integrating COLD and SDL

Gertjan Akkerman
Department of Philosophy, Section of Applied Logic,
University of Utrecht, Heidelberglaan 2, 3584 CS Utrecht,
The Netherlands
Ron Koymans
Philips Research Laboratories, PO Box 80.000,
5600 JA Eindhoven, The Netherlands

Abstract

In this paper we describe preliminary work on the integration of
COLD and SDL. We consider three possibilities for the semantical integration of COLD and SDL: object-orientedness integration, concurrency
integration and data type integration. Before doing so, we will first
explain the relevant features of these specification languages and con-
template on the meaning of method integration. We will then explain
and motivate our course of action.

1   Introduction

COLD is a wide-spectrum specification and design language intended to serve
as the basis of a software development method supporting the use of formal
techniques.   It has been developed at Philips Research Laboratories Eindhoven in the framework of ESPRIT project 432 (METEOR). As a specification language it belongs to the same category as VDM and Z. Fundamental

This work is being done in the context of ESPRIT project 2565: ATMOSPHERE
(Advanced Tools and Methods for System Production in Heterogeneous, Extensible, Real
Environments).
The first author performs this work under a contract with the Dutch Software Engineering
Research Centre (SERC).

to these specification languages is the specification of a system as an abstract
machine, with functions and predicates that can be used to determine differences between states, and expressions (optionally yielding a value) to go from
one state to another. Typical for COLD is the definition of its semantics in a
logical language, being a translation into a special variant of first-order logic.

SDL is recommended by the CCITT as the specification language for use
in telecommunication applications. SDL has a rather operational flavour in
the sense that the system is defined by describing a system in SDL that
behaves the same, as opposed to formalizing it in an axiomatic style. In fact,
we can divide specification languages in two groups, based on the way their
specifications are assigned a meaning:

- The first group is the group of *model class* based specification languages. In this group, the meaning of a specification is the class of its
  (mathematical) realizations.

- The second group is the group of *theory based* specification languages.
  In this group, the meaning of a specification is the set of all its logical
  consequences. (We can think of this theory as the set of assertions valid
  about the specification.)

SDL belongs to the first group while the current semantics of COLD classifies
it in the second group.

Our involvement in the ATMOSPHERE project consists in method integration, in our case integration of COLD and SDL. We consider three
possibilities for the semantical integration between COLD and SDL: object-
orientedness integration, concurrency integration and data type integration.
The first of these possibilities concerns a common feature of COLD and
OSDL, viz. object-orientedness. OSDL is an object-oriented extension of
SDL with the purpose to increase reusability (see section 5). The latter two
integration possibilities aim at the strengthening of one method with concepts from the other. In concurrent systems an important distinction can be
made between data and processes. While COLD is strong in the specification
of data, SDL has a clear notion of processes. Concurrency integration then,
concerns the idea to model processes in COLD and data type integration
looks at ways to enhance SDL with COLD-like features for specifying data
types.

Before looking at these three integration possibilities in section 8 we first
introduce briefly the relevant parts of COLD and SDL in sections 2–5. Section
6 has a more philosophical flavour centered around the concept of method

integration. Mathematical preliminaries are given in section 7. Section 9 ends the paper with some conclusions.

2   COLD

In this section we describe the central COLD notion of classes and their parameterization.

2.1   The Model of COLD

Fundamental to COLD (and similarly VDM and Z) is the specification of a system as an abstract machine, with functions and predicates that can be used to distinguish states, and expressions (optionally yielding a value) to go from a state to another.

A specification in COLD considers a system as an abstract machine, consisting of a set of states and transitions between those states. Such an abstract machine is called a *class*.

2.1.1   Specification of states

The states are mathematical structures, meaning that the extension and values of functions and predicates depend on the state in which they apply. The idea behind this is that states can be distinguished by the predicates and functions, without implying that they are uniquely determined by them: after all one can at any instant define new functions and predicates, creating new distinctions between states.

The following fragment illustrates predicates and functions for assertions about a state:

```
FUNC 0: -> Nat
FUNC s: Nat -> Nat % successor function

DECL m,n: Nat % these variables are implicitly universally
              % quantified in the following

PRED is_gen: Nat
% the following generates inductively all natural numbers
IND is_gen(0);
    is_gen(m) => is_gen(s(m))
```

```
AXIOM 0!; % ! means definedness (NB: COLD uses partial functions)
      s(m)!;
      s(m)/=0;
      s(m)=s(n) => m=n;
      is_gen(n)

FUNC +: Nat # Nat -> Nat
IND m+0 = m;
    m+s(n) = s(m+n)
```

2.1.2 Specification of transitions

If COLD contained only functions and predicates then it would be awkward
to use for the description of current software technology, where many system
components cause state changes in their environment. For this reason, COLD
includes an *expression* language, which is used to name transitions between
states, and to describe which transitions are allowed.

Named transitions are introduced by the definition of procedures. Since
the named transitions will be used to model procedure calls on a module, they
can take and yield values, and therefore we will call them, in accordance
with the definition of COLD, *expressions*. A named expression is called a
procedure. A procedure definition associates an expression with a procedure
name.

There are two ways to describe the effect of expressions: viz. by means
of assertions, and by composing it from other expressions.

In the following fragment we use assertions (taken from dynamic logic,
see [Har79]) to describe the effect of the expression (and procedure) **inc_x**:

```
FUNC x: -> Nat VAR % VAR indicates that x may change over states
                  % (x is a real function and no constant)
DECL y: Nat

PROC inc_x: Nat -> SAT MOD x % inc_x may modify x

AXIOM FIN inc_x(y); % inc_x terminates
      AFTER inc_x(y) THEN x = x'+y
      % the effect of inc_x(y) is that the new value of x equals
      % the sum of its old value (indicated by the ') and y
```

These axioms amount to a definition of **inc_x**.

In the following fragment we use some compositions of expressions, to define a new procedure and to state some facts about our specification.

```
PROC inc_2x: Nat ->
IN y
DEF inc_x(y) ; inc_x(y)


THEOREM AFTER inc_x(y) ; inc_2x(y) THEN x = x'+y+y+y;
        AFTER inc_x(y) | inc_2x(y) THEN (x = x'+y OR x = x'+y+y)
        % | indicates a nondeterministic choice
```

The expression language of COLD is powerful enough to model the structured programming language constructs **if**, **while**, **repeat** and **case**.

COLD is a theory based specification language, with theories built of formulae in the logical language MPL_ω. MPL_ω is an abbreviation for many-sorted partial logic with countably infinite conjunctions, i.e., MPL_ω is a variant of many-sorted predicate logic where functions need not be total, and with countably infinite conjunctions (and disjunctions). Although the semantics of COLD is expressed in terms of MPL_ω theories, it will turn out later that we will want to assign models to COLD specifications.

2.2   Parameterization in COLD

COLD has parameterized classes. The formal parameter is just another class. The signature and theory of the formal parameter impose constraints on the allowable actual parameters, if the specification is to be well formed. Semantically, we have that:

- A (once) parameterized COLD class is a partial function from COLD theories to COLD theories.

- A formal parameter constrains the allowable actual parameters to those of which the theory includes the theory of the formal parameter. This means that the signature of the actual parameter includes the signature of the formal parameter, and that the axioms of the actual parameter (that is, the assertions on the actual parameter) imply all axioms of the formal parameter.

As an example, we consider finite sets.

```
LET ITEM := CLASS SORT Item END
```

```
LET SET[Item] :=
ABSTRACT ITEM
CLASS
  SORT Set DEP Item
  PRED is_in: Item # Set
  FUNC empty: -> Set
  FUNC insert: Item # Set -> Set

  DECL s: Set,
       i,j: Item

  PRED is_gen: Set
  IND  is_gen(empty);
       is_gen(s) => is_gen(insert(i,s))

  AXIOM empty!;
        insert(i,s)!;
        NOT is_in(i,empty);
        is_in(i,insert(j,s)) <=> i=j OR is_in(i,s);
        insert(i,insert(j,s)) = insert(j,insert(i,s));
        insert(i,insert(i,s)) = insert(i,s);
        is_gen(s)

  FUNC remove: Item # Set -> Set
  IND  remove(i,empty) = empty;
       remove(i,insert(i,s)) = remove(i,s);
       i/=j => remove(i,insert(j,s)) = insert(j,remove(i,s))

  FUNC set: Item -> Set
  IND  set(i) = insert(i,empty)

  FUNC select: Set -> Item
  IN   s
  OUT  i
  PRE  s /= empty % COLD supports the pre- and post-condition
  POST is_in(i,s) % style of specification
END
```

Since the parameter is a class, it is possible that it contains axioms (to be
interpreted as requirements). This is for example useful in the specification

of a sorting algorithm, where it can be required that there is a total order on the items in the list being sorted.

3   Inheritance in COLD

In this section we consider the addition of inheritance to COLD as presented in [Jon91]. In his paper, Jonkers makes a careful distinction between the semantics preserving and implementation aspects of inheritance. He uses monomorphisms to represent inheritance, yet appears not to consider implementation at the semantical level. The monomorphisms identify each object in the subsort with precisely one object in the supersort. The definitions of functions, predicates and procedures in the subsort are then required to commute with the identification function and the corresponding functions, predicates and procedures in the supersort.

Similar concepts are used in [BMPW86] to define a fairly general relation of implementation in algebraic specifications. (By algebraic specifications we mean specifications by means of equations.) In particular, there are three aspects to implementation, viz. reduction of the class of models, enlargement of the signature, and splitting of indistinguishable terms. We will briefly consider these three aspects:

- Reduction of the class of models. In a model-theoretic consideration of specifications, the models are supposed to be the realizations of the specification. (The set of models might include realizations that are not practically feasible.) If the class of models of a specification S_1 is contained in the class of models of a specification S_2, then every realization of S_1 is a realization of S_2, and hence we can say that S_1 implements S_2.

- Enlargement of the signature. (By signature, we mean a set of sort and function symbols. "Sort" is just another word for "type".) It is quite acceptable that the internal signature of a module contains new "auxiliary" functions, as long as all configurations reachable from an initial state by means of the exported signature satisfy the required specification.

  This aspect of implementation is covered by a *reduct*, a map from models to models with a restricted signature.

- Splitting of indistinguishable terms. We assume that all modules define equality functions for all sorts defined in them. It is possible that an

implementation is able to distinguish elements (by its larger internal
signature) that the specification does not distinguish, as long as the
exported equality function does not distinguish them. The canonical
example in this case is the implementation of sets by lists: It is possible
to implement finite sets by lists, as long as a suitable "equality function"
is provided that checks that each element that is in one list, is in the
other list as well. This equality function will not distinguish lists where
the elements are only in different order, or lists where some of the
elements are duplicated.

In fact, an implementation of sets by lists can be obtained either by
exporting the list concatenation and insertion functions and a modified
equality function, or by exporting merge and insertion functions that
sort the list elements and remove duplicates and normal list equality.

The equality function is usually given by a surjective homomorphism (a
structure preserving map such that all of the elements in its range are
in the image of its domain), and the stipulation that two elements are
to be considered equivalent when they are mapped to the same element
by the map.

Following the ideas of [BMPW86] in the use of homomorphisms to define
implementation using semantical concepts, we come up with the following
use of homomorphisms:

- Monomorphisms (structure preserving injections) are used to represent
  subsort relationships and inheritance.

- Epimorphisms (structure preserving surjections) are used to model equivalence relations, and therefore (by considering this equivalence relation
  as an equality function) one of the aspects of implementation.

4   SDL

SDL has a notion of processes based on extended finite state machines and
a notion of blocks and systems that hardly transcends the description "a
block/system is an unstructured collection of processes with a can-communicate-
with relation". This is to say, we have more or less described a SDL system
if we have described its processes. This leads us to consider three aspects of
SDL in this section:

1. Data types

2. Processes

3. Parameterization of data types

4.1   Data Types

In general, when data types are specified equationally, there are various possible semantics.

For example, there is a choice between *term generated* and non term-generated semantics:

- In a term generated model, only objects that are denoted by some term constructed from the signature of the specification are supposed to exist.

- In a non-term-generated model, not every object need to be denoted by a term.

Another choice is a choice between *typical* and non-typical models:

- In a typical model, only the objects that are provably equal by the axioms of the specification are supposed to be equal.

- In a non-typical model, more terms may be considered to denote the same object.

Data types in SDL are interpreted using an *initial algebra* semantics, that is, a semantics that considers only models that are both typical and term-generated.

Furthermore, as a methodological constraint, it is forbidden that datatypes that are based on other data types introduce new objects of old sorts, or identify different objects of old sorts. Let us now consider an example:

```
NEWTYPE MyNAT
LITERALS 0
OPERATORS
   s: MyNAT -> MyNAT ;
   add: MyNAT,MyNAT -> MyNAT ;
AXIOMS
   FOR ALL x,y IN MyNAT (
      add(s(x),y) == s(add(x,y)) ;
      add(0,y) == y ;
   )
ENDNEWTYPE MyNAT;
```

Due to these requirements on data type specification in SDL, one is forced to find a signature that generates all the desired terms, and not many more than those. A more liberal data type specification mechanism (using e.g. free semantics, and partial functions as in COLD) might allow the option of postponing this decision on a generating signature.

4.2 Processes

A process in SDL is specified in terms of an *extended finite state machine*, exhibiting the desired behaviour. These extended finite state machines in SDL are based on deterministic and total finite state machines, i.e., finite state machines where the transition relation (between states, on inputs) is a total function.

Facilities provided by extended finite state machines beyond those provided by (ordinary) finite state machines are:

- The possibility of assignments to variables, and choices based on the values of variables.

- Output statements.

- Process creation statements.

- Procedure call statements.

We will now consider some of these extensions:

4.2.1 Output statements

When a system is specified in SDL, it is decomposed into a collection of processes, which interact by sending messages to each other. This collection of processes can be structured by collecting processes in groups. Processes are for example grouped on the basis of their type, or on the block in which they exist (and were declared). Such groups of processes can be nested, when block substructures are used. One cannot easily look at such a group of processes as if it forms a larger process, because processes communicate by directing messages to each other, so that all processes in such a group will still be addressed individually.

Directing a signal to another process is done by means of an output statement.

4.2.2   Process creation

A process creation statement causes a new process to be created, which will
then start to send and receive signals. Processes are always created in the
current block.

4.2.3   Procedure call

A procedure call statement will cause execution of the process to begin at a
separate part of the process graph, only to be resumed at the point of the
procedure call when the execution of this separate part has terminated by
executing a procedure exit.

Procedures may call each other recursively. Whereas the sequences of
states that a finite state machine passes through in its possible executions
form a regular language, the possible sequences of states passed through in
the execution of a process can also be a non-regular context-free language.

4.3   Parameterization

Parameterized datatypes are written in SDL by means of *generators*. Those
generators can have sorts, literals, operators and constants as parameters.
There are no ways to express constraints imposed on those parameters in
SDL.

Uninstantiated generators do not have a semantics in SDL, i.e., the semantics of generators is determined at each instantiation separately. The
instantiation of a generator takes place at text (or lexical token) level.

5   OSDL

OSDL is an extension of the SDL specification language developed in the
joint Nordic research project Mjølner. Added in the transition from SDL to
OSDL to make it more object-oriented were facilities to increase reusability: parameterization, inheritance, and a library facility. Specific features
that were included are *inheritance* and *redefinition of virtuals*. To keep it
type-safe, and to allow separate type-checking, *(specialization) constraints*
on parameters and in definitions were incorporated.

5.1   Parameterization

Constructs can be parameterized over constructs on which they "depend".
For example, blocks can be parameterized over the channels connected to

them, and signal routes over the signals that they carry.

In fact, there are two kinds of parameterization:

- A construct can be parameterized with something it directly depends on: For example, a block parameterized with a channel. This is the proper kind of parameterization, considered in this section.

- A construct can be parameterized with a "smaller" construct. For example, a block parameterized with a procedure. This kind of parameterization is dealt with by means of the redefinition aspect of inheritance.

Parameterization serves the following two purposes:

- It becomes easier to reuse specifications if they are parameterized, because they can then be fitted more easily into their environment.

- Besides, since a library facility effectively takes components out of their context of definition, they *have* to be fitted into their context of application.

5.2 Specialization

There are three aspects to specialization in SDL:

- Inheritance of properties. (The "semantics preservation" aspect.)

- Addition of properties. (The "implementation" aspect.)

- Redefinition of virtual constructs. (The "redefinition" aspect.) I.e., a construct to be specialized can be attributed with *virtual* subcomponents that can be redefined in its specializations.

Specialization is useful for indicating the similarities and differences between components in a compact way:

- The *similarities* are indicated because a component that is defined as a specialization of a parameterized component, inherits all the non-virtual text of that component.

- The *differences* are indicated because the virtual text of a component can be redefined in a specialization.

Many language constructs (viz. systems, blocks, processes and procedures) are extended to include a virtual section, in which virtual subcomponents can be defined. These are typically immediate subcomponents of the constructs. For example, a block may include virtual process definitions.

These virtual subcomponents can be redefined in a specialization of the component, unless they are indicated as **final**. If a virtual subcomponent is redefined, then all references to this component are replaced by references to the redefinition. (This means that an "unfolding" of recursive definitions may only be done with a component in OSDL when code is generated, or when it is declared as final.)

A virtual subcomponent can in a specialization be redefined to a **final** virtual subcomponent, meaning that it may not in further specializations be redefined.

5.2.1   Parameters and specialization

Often, instantiation of generic parameters and specialization go together.

For the instantiation of generic parameters, it is required that the actual parameter is *compatible with the constraint* of the formal parameter. Depending on the kind of parameter, there are usually two kinds of constraints for a generic parameter:

- Immediate constraints, of the form **atleast <identifier>**, where the actual parameter should be a specialization of the formal parameter, and

- Structural constraints, where the constraints on the actual parameter are, based on the structure of the construct, expressed in terms of "smaller" constraints in terms of its subconstructs.

5.2.2   Redefinition in specializations of processes

When components are specialized, their *virtual* subparts can be redefined. In particular, in a process definition:

- a virtual start transition may be redefined.

- a virtual input can be redefined to an input or save.

- a virtual save can be redefined to an input. (Since this would not change anything, it cannot be *re*-defined to a save.)

- procedures can be redefined.

5.3 Library Facility

Components are chosen from a library given the name of the library, the name of the component, and the entity class of the component.

In a *library*, parameterized and to be specialized constructs can be stored. Such components are, so to speak, taken out of their context in the system definition. For this reason, all references to constructs usually in the context of the component must be either via generic parameters, so that they can easily be replaced by references to the actual context, or via library references.

6 Methods and Models

Since this activity takes place in the context of "method integration" we consider in this section how this activity is related to methodology, the study of methods.

Definition: (method)
A *method* is a restriction on the use of a tool or technique.

Example:
An example is *structured programming*. The structured programming method tries to restrict the use of **goto** to where it is necessary.   Such a restriction is of use in practice, because:

1. It contributes to a qualitatively good result.

2. It is an important guiding force in the software development process and may in fact support the developer instead of hindering him.

Is a methodology to be of any use, then it should be based on a model. (The example of structured programming above is based on the correspondence between the structure of programs and the structure of data, and a model that describes data in terms of sequences, iterations and choices. The relation between (data-)structured and **goto**-less programming is that the program structure should not contain **goto**s, since the data structure does not contain them either.)

Good software engineering practices require the use of suitable methods wherever possible. It is to be expected that most systems development projects require the use of more than one method.

Definition: (method integration)
Method integration is the combination of several (not totally unrelated) methods so that they can be used together.

Under the assumption that methods ought to be based on some model, if methods are to be integrated, then the underlying models should be integratable, i.e., it should be possible to look at them as different views on one more complicated model.

Example:
Ward and Mellor (see [WM85]) use three models:

1. Regular expressions for the definition of the data structure.

2. The relational model for the information analysis.

3. Finite state machines for the control flow.

Similar concepts as those used by [WM85] are also present in SDL:

1. Use of deterministic finite state machines.

2. Partitioning of blocks and subblocks and channels and subchannels.

3. Restriction of the communication between processes only allowing it to go via the present signal routes and channels.

Currently, there exists some integration between such models and concepts, but it is expected that more is possible.

We intend to achieve method integration by means of model integration. We will integrate a model of finite state machines with a model of mathematical structures for data types, using an algebraical framework (see section 3).

We will especially pay attention to the model of finite state machines, for the following reasons:

1. We need a formalism to model processes that supports the integration of COLD and SDL. As we have seen in previous sections both specification languages already have an underlying model based on finite state machines.

2. For finite state machines, there exists a well developed theory of homomorphisms, which includes results on composition, decomposition and implementation. We will use it to define inheritance as well.

3. This theory is really used in software engineering.

7 The Mathematical Core

In this section, we give our definitions about finite state machines. The definitions given in this section (FSM specification, FSM model, homomorphism and reduct) are an application to finite state machines of the corresponding concepts of the algebraical framework for implementation of abstract data types (see section 3).

Finite state machines are given by means of finite state machine specifications. Each finite state machine specification has a signature.

Definition: (FSM signature)
A finite state machine signature is a triple $\langle S, I, O \rangle$, where $S = s_1, \ldots, s_i$ are state symbols, the $I = i_1, \ldots, i_j$ are input symbols and $O = o_1, \ldots, o_k$ are output symbols.

Given a FSM signature, we can present FSMs with this signature:

Definition: (FSM specification)
Let $\Sigma = \langle S, I, O \rangle$ be a FSM signature. A FSM specification is a tuple $\langle S, I, O, T \rangle$, where T, the transition function, is a function $T : S \times I \to S \times O$.

Since we want to model the "model inclusion" aspect of implementation, we will now consider models of a specification.

Definition: (FSM)
A FSM (FSM model) is a tuple $\langle \Pi, S_1, I_1, O_1, \sigma_1, \iota_1, \omega_1, T_1 \rangle$, where $\Pi = \langle S, I, O, T \rangle$ is a FSM specification, S_1 is a set of states, I_1 is a set of input signals, O_1 is a set of output signals, $\sigma_1 : S \to \mathbf{P}(S_1)$ is a function assigning sets of states to state symbols, $\iota_1 : I \to I_1$ assigns input signals to input symbols, $\omega_1 : O \to O_1$ assigns output signals to output symbols, $T_1 : S_1 \times I_1 \to S_1 \times O_1$ satisfies: $\forall s_0, s_1 \in S, u, v \in S_1, i \in I, o \in O((T(s_0, i) = \langle s_1, o \rangle \wedge u \in \sigma_1(s_0) \wedge T_1(u, \iota_1(i)) = \langle v, \omega_1(o) \rangle) \Rightarrow v \in \sigma_1(s_1))$

Remark:
Given ι_1 and ω_1, each FSM specification has a class of models with a unique (modulo bijections) minimal model. This minimal model can be built from syntactic ingredients.

The signature enlargement aspect of an implementation is modeled by reducts:

Definition: (reduct)
Let $\Pi_0 = \langle S_0, I_0, O_0, T_0 \rangle$ and $\Pi = \langle S, I, O, T \rangle$ be FSM specifications with $S_0 \subseteq S$, $I_0 \subseteq I$, $O_0 \subseteq O$ and $T_0 \subseteq T$. Let $M = \langle \Pi, S_1, I_1, O_1, \sigma_1, \iota_1, \omega_1, T_1 \rangle$ be a Π-model. Let $S_2 = \bigcup_{s \in S_0} \sigma_1(s)$, $I_2 = \{\iota_1(i) | i \in I_0\}$, $O_2 = \{\omega_1(o) | o \in O_0\}$. Then we define the Π_0-reduct of M as the model:

$\langle \Pi_0, S_2, I_2, O_2, \sigma_1|_{S_2}, \iota_1|_{I_2}, \omega_1|_{O_2}, T_1|_{S_2 \times I_2} \rangle$. We notice that a reduct of a connected FSM may be unconnected.

Surjective homomorphisms represent the allowable "splitting" of indistinguishable elements in implementations:

Definition: (homomorphism)
Let $M_1 = \langle \Pi, S_1, I_1, O_1, \sigma_1, \iota_1, \omega_1, T_1 \rangle$ and $M_2 = \langle \Pi, S_2, I_2, O_2, \sigma_2, \iota_2, \omega_2, T_2 \rangle$ be FSMs. We say that $\langle \phi_1, \phi_2, \phi_3 \rangle$ is a homomorphism if $\phi_1 : S_1 \rightarrow S_2$, $\phi_2 : I_1 \rightarrow I_2$, $\phi_3 : O_1 \rightarrow O_2$, and $T_1(s,i) = \langle s', o \rangle \Rightarrow T_2(\phi_1(s), \phi_2(i)) = \langle \phi_1(s'), \phi_3(o) \rangle$.

Definition: (monomorphism)
A *monomorphism* is an injective homomorphism.

Following [BMPW86] we define implementations as a combination of reducts, homomorphisms and model inclusions.

Definition: (implementations of FSM specifications)
A FSM specification F_1 implements F_2 if there is for every model of F_1 a homomorphism from the F_2-reduct of this model to a model of F_2.

A process is just a finite state machine with a sequence of procedures. Each procedure has a graph, a start state and an end state. We will not do this here, but by incorporating procedures we can define in a similar way as for FSMs process specifications, process models, process homomorphisms and process implementations. For instance, a process model is a finite state machine model where the end states of procedures agree with execution beginning in the corresponding start state.

8 Integration of COLD and SDL

The purpose of this paper is to investigate possibilities for the semantical integration of COLD and SDL. We intend to pursue this integration in three directions: *object-orientedness integration*, *concurrency integration* and *data type integration*.

8.1 Object-Orientedness Integration

For the integration of COLD and SDL with respect to object-orientedness we take into consideration OSDL, the object-oriented variant of SDL (see section 5). Features that were added in the transition from SDL to OSDL to make it more object-oriented are *inheritance* and *redefinition of virtuals*. To keep it type-safe, and to allow separate type-checking, *(specialization) constraints* on parameters and in definitions were incorporated. Due to the fundamental undecidability of these matters on one hand, and the wish to allow effective type checking on the other, these constraints are only checked syntactically, based on the signature of the specification, and not semantically, based on its content. Now, the question arises in what ways the specifier could be restricted in the use of these facilities to obtain a semantical satisfaction of the constraints as well. In our investigations this will be a central question.

The object-orientation of COLD is semantically well founded, as it is based on monomorphisms between algebras (actually, first-order structures). In the addition of inheritance to COLD, a careful separation is made between the inheritance and implementation aspects of object-orientation.

Given this state of affairs, we consider it our goal to investigate the relationship between the semantical base for object-orientedness given in COLD, and the facilities for object-orientation provided by OSDL. In order to do this, we will define monomorphisms (and for a semantically well founded implementation also homomorphisms) for the objects under consideration in an OSDL specification.

Since the concept of processes and parallelism is present in OSDL, but not in COLD, we will have to find a suitable model, equipped with homomorphisms and monomorphisms, for processes. Because the processes in OSDL are extended finite state machines, we will base our considerations on finite state machines. This is advantageous since there already exists a large body of theory on finite state machines, and also because finite state machines are already in widespread use in software engineering. Although we will, for a start, base our considerations on finite state machines, we will eventually extend them to arbitrary OSDL processes.

8.1.1   Redefinition

OSDL offers the possibility of redefining parts of a construct that are designated by the keyword `virtual`, when it is specialized. We consider the aspects *parameterization, constraints* and *defaults* of redefinition.

- Virtual subparts of a construct can be redefined. If a virtual subpart is redefined in a specialization, then all references to this subpart will refer to this new definition. I.e., not only the references in definitions added in the specialization will be altered, but also the definitions in the inherited text. Therefore, we may *not* unfold calls to virtual subparts. We can look at the virtual subparts of a definition as *parameters* of that definition, but these parameters possess *default* instantiations, which apply in case the virtal subpart is never redefined.

- Virtual subparts are, as argued above, just like ordinary parameters except from their having defaults. Therefore, they can be constrained parameters, with the constraints expressing that the actual parameter be of a certain minimal signature for the specification to be well formed.

- If in some use of a component with virtual subparts, some of those virtual subparts are not redefined, then the virtual subpart itself will apply as a default.

After this analysis of redefinition, we will now consider how to model it in COLD.

To model redefinition, we will split it in two of its aspects, viz. (constrained) parameters and defaults. We model these two aspects as follows:

- The parameterization aspect of redefinition is modeled by associating a parameter with every virtual subpart, and letting the component with virtual subparts be parameterized with those parameters.

- The default aspect of redefinition is modeled by associating a mapping from those parameters to their default instantiations with the component. This mapping can be updated if virtual subparts are redefined in a specialization, and it can be applied when finally code needs to be generated.

Example:
Consider the following fragment of an OSDL specification:

```
PROCESS P<>
VIRTUAL
   PROCEDURE VPROC1 ...
   PROCEDURE VPROC2 ...
...
ENDPROCESS P
```

We consider it semantically equal to the (syntactically ill formed) parameterized procedure

```
PROCESS P<PROCEDURE X1, PROCEDURE X2>
...
ENDPROCESS P
```

together with a mapping

```
{ X1 := VPROC1, X2 := VPROC2 }
```

A specialization

```
PROCESS P1<> : P<>
VIRTUAL
   PROCEDURE VPROC1 ...
   PROCEDURE VPROC2 ...
...
   PROCEDURE VPROC1 ... (new body) ...
ENDPROCESS P
```

will give rise to the same P with the old VPROC1 in the map overwritten by
the new VPROC1, while the specialization

```
PROCESS P2<> : P<>
VIRTUAL
   PROCEDURE VPROC1 FINAL
   PROCEDURE VPROC2 ...
...
   PROCEDURE VPROC1 ... (new body) ...
ENDPROCESS P
```

Will be P with X1 instantiated and deleted from the map.

Furthermore, PROCESS P(10) will be PROCESS P<VPROC1,VPROC2>(10),
where the parameterized procedure P is applied to the associated procedures
from the map.

8.2   Concurrency Integration

COLD, as it originally was developed, has in distinction to SDL no special
constructs for concurrency. On the other hand, COLD classes represent abstract machines. Therefore, one can look at a COLD class as if it were a
process, at the imported and exported procedures as if they were communication actions that this process shares with its environment, and at the
imported and exported functions and predicates as if they were inspection
facilities (i.e., not causing state changes) shared with the environment.

Still, those "processes" lack facilities for process creation. Concerning
concurrency integration of COLD and SDL we plan to investigate the relationship between the (extended) finite state machines of SDL and the abstract machines of COLD, and the ways to model process creation by means
of COLD classes.

8.2.1   Processes and classes

Milner (see, e.g., [HM85]) has already used process logic to describe processes. In this approach:

- $p \models [a]A$ means: after every a, the resulting process satisfies A. This action is typically used in the form $[a]$**False**, meaning that whenever an a action is done by the process, **false** holds, i.e., the process allows no a actions.

- $p \models \langle a \rangle A$ means: the process can do a and may then satisfy A.

This process logic is similar to dynamic logic [Har79] which is used in COLD for the specification of transitions between states (see subsection 2.1.2).

The model behind SDL is the model of finite state machines. Common to this model and that of process/dynamic logic, is the view on a system as a collection of states with named transitions between them. These named transitions are called procedures in COLD, and signals in SDL. We will use this fact to describe SDL processes as COLD classes.

Let us consider an SDL process. It is described by a set of states S1, ... Sn, with transitions between those states. Let us consider a transition from S1 to S2 on signal i1 and outputting signal o1.

First, we introduce predicates In_Si for all SDL states Si. We translate this transition into an axiom:

```
AXIOM
   In_S1 =>
      [ i1 ] < o2 > In_S2
```

We can identify the start state S0 by an axiom

```
AXIOM
   INIT => In_S0
```

Of course, we will have to add proper exclusion axioms for all states, to ensure that a process is after a transition in only one state.

8.2.2   Modeling queues and process creation

The above modeling applies to finite state machines, but SDL processes are not finite state machines. However, the modeling of SDL processes incorporating procedures is straightforward given the relationship between our model for finite state machines and that for processes (see section 7).

We will now sketch an answer to the remaining questions of modeling queues (including an example) and process creation:

- Queues are modeled by adding to each COLD class an additional input queue class, which shares a hidden signature with the COLD class. I.e., we split each SDL process in a queue process and an extended finite state machine process reading from this queue. Since those two processes can both have synchronous communication, we can model them in COLD.

- Process creation, and the resulting existence of multiple processes of one process type are modeled by having a *process manager* for each process type. By adding a `Pid` (process identification) parameter to each process variable, we can let this process manager simulate many processes, by making it update only the variables of the process which is currently executing. (I.e., we use an interleaving semantics for concurrency.)

Example:
In this example, we sketch the introduction of queues to a class with synchronous communication. We assume that data is defined in a class `DATA`, that the process is described by means of a class `PROCESS1`, and that data is transferred by means of a procedure `signal:  Data ->` defined in class `PROCESS1`.

The class `QUEUE` has the following structure:

```
LET ITEM := CLASS SORT Item END

LET SEQ[Item] :=
ABSTRACT ITEM
CLASS
   SORT Seq DEP Item
   FUNC empty: -> Seq
   FUNC cons: Item # Seq -> Seq
   ...
END

LET QUEUE[Item] :=
ABSTRACT ITEM
IMPORT SEQ[Item]
CLASS
```

```
FUNC contents: -> Seq[Item] VAR
PROC dequeue: Item -> SAT MOD contents
PROC enqueue: Item -> SAT MOD contents
   . .
END
```

Here, it is assumed that the procedure **dequeue** succeeds only if its parameter
has the same value as the head of the queue. (This is a somewhat unnatural
requirement, stemming from the fact that we want to use dynamic logic to
model process logic.)

Now, we can model addition of queues to a class with synchronous communication by the following operations:

```
LET PROCESS1_WITH_QUEUE :=
  COMPONENT DUMMY SPECIFICATION
  % auxiliary class to get renamings right
  EXPORT PROC enqueue: Data -> % hide PROC dequeue, but
        SIG  DATA, PROCESS1   % make the rest accessible
  IMPORT DATA,
        QUEUE[Data] RENAMING PROC dequeue: Data -> TO signal END,
        PROCESS1
    END
SYSTEM % now comes the class PROCESS1_WITH_QUEUE proper
       % which uses a simple renaming applied to DUMMY
IMPORT DUMMY RENAMING PROC enqueue: Data -> TO signal END
END
```

8.3   Data Type Integration

COLD provides a very flexible and broad range of concepts for the specification of abstract data types. There are no inherent limitations to a fixed
number of constructors (generators) whatsoever. The concepts include parameterization, modularization, first-order predicate logic, partial functions
and inductive definitions.

SDL provides also for abstract data types, but based on a much more
restricted set of mechanisms. For instance, typical SDL abstract data types
are specified by equations only — no first-order quantification, no inductive
definitions. Moreover, traditionally the abstract data types part of SDL is
often hardly used at all.

We feel that the COLD activity could serve as a technology push here.
One obvious experiment is the replacement of the sublanguage of SDL for

specifying abstract data types by a fragment of COLD.

Some advantages we see in such a replacement of the data type specification language of SDL by one based on COLD are:

- Because of the presence of partial functions in COLD, it is no longer the
  case that the term algebra should be a quotient of all terms. That is,
  when describing the domain of a data type, one can use a term model
  which is slightly larger then the intended domain, and let some of the
  terms denote no value. Of course, this feature should not be over-used.

- Because of the presence of existential quantifiers, and of the free (i.e.,
  not term-generated and not typical) semantics of COLD in general, it
  is possible to use objects which cannot (yet) be denoted by a term.
  This feature may be useful in the early analysis stages of systems development, but again should not be over-used.

  Whenever term-generated sorts are required in COLD, this is done by
  inductively defining a predicate (usually called "is_gen"), holding for
  all generated terms.

- COLD has pre-post condition style specifications which allow a detailed specification of procedures, while postponing their design and
  implementation.

9 Conclusions

Although we haven't tackled the semantical integration of COLD and SDL
in full technical details yet, the suggested directions seem promising. In the
case of object-orientedness integration this stems from the idea to structure
the possibilities offered by OSDL to increase reusability along the lines of
inheritance as put forward in COLD. Concurrency integration is based on
the connections between the extended finite state machine model of SDL
and the abstract machine model of COLD. Data type integration has a more
complementary nature: the abstract data type part of SDL can be upgraded
by the possibilities offered in COLD.

On account of the above such an integration effort can result in a benefit
for both formalisms based on a fruitful cross-fertilization which may lead to
a wider scope and stronger application possibilities.

References

[BMPW86] M. Broy, B. Möller, P. Pepper, M. Wirsing. *Algebraic Implementations Preserve Program Correctness*, Science of Computer Programming, Volume 7, pp. 35–53, 1986.

[Har79] D. Harel. *First-Order Dynamic Logic*, Springer Verlag, 1979.

[HM85] M. Hennessy, R. Milner. *Algebraic Laws for Nondeterminism and Concurrency*, Journal of the Association for Computing Machinery, Volume 32, pp. 137–161, 1985.

[Jon91] H. Jonkers. *Inheritance in COLD*, in: J. Bergstra, L. Feijs (eds.), *Algebraic Methods: Theory, Tools and Applications (Part II)*, to appear in Springer Lecture Notes in Computer Science, 1991.

[WM85] P. Ward, S. Mellor. *Structured Development for Real-Time Systems*, Volumes 1–3, Yourdon Press, 1985–1986.

16

Augmenting SDL specifications with LOTOS behaviour expressions

Mark Lindqvist and Heikki Tuominen
Nokia Telecommunications, PO Box 33,
SF–02601 Espoo, Finland

1 Introduction

The CCITT Specification and Description Language or SDL is widely used in
the telecommunications industry to specify telecommunications systems and
software therein [4]. SDL has been successfully applied both in specification
of requirements set for telecommunications systems and in describing their
actual implementation. The major volume of the usage, however, seems to
be in the latter.

In a requirements specification one observes a system from the outside.
Such a specification describes how this system, or even a set of systems,
should behave or what its *observable behaviour* is. This is usually what is
expressed by protocol specifications. The description of how such a protocol
is implemented provides then a view from the inside of the system telling how
the behaviour specified by the protocol is accomplished by a set of processes
or finite state automata executing concurrently. These two system views can
be seen as the two extremes both in which SDL can be applied.

At Nokia Telecommunications SDL has been mainly used in describing the

This work is partially supported by the ESPRIT project ATMOSPHERE, Ref #2565.
The main partners of the project are CAP Gemini Innovation, Bull, Philips, Siemens, SNI,
and STGL.

implementation of telecommunications systems, especially software therein. This also seems to be the case with several other telecommunications systems implementors. What is characteristic for this kind of use of SDL amounts to the following: SDL is used to specify or describe the implementation of software. Actually it is often used as a higher level programming language. The environment where it is used is homogeneous. The systems described are often of a very large scale consisting of even some million lines of source code. To manage a system of this size requires strong mechanisms for structuring and modularisation.

SDL offers some structuring mechanisms – mainly blocks and channels with the substructuring facility. The possibilities to define interfaces between blocks within the document describing the blocks themselves are, however, rather restricted. These are limited to a set of signals defined within a channel. A consequence of this is that the blocks used in SDL to group processes together cannot hide their internal structure. If one wants to communicate with the block in order to benefit from its functionality she or he is forced to deal with the full complexity of the block on the lowest level of detail. What would be needed is something that corresponds to the concept of a *method* in object orientation to hide internal, irrelevant details. Here only a method would not refer to an operation signature but to some defined signal exchange pattern or protocol, i.e. to observable behaviour.

Traditionally signal sequence charts have been used to specify how processes or blocks should communicate with each other. Their shortcomings are, however, well known; the history relation they express is not sufficient to distinguish between systems whose external behaviours differ. As a consequence an enormous amount of such signal sequences or traces might be needed to specify even partially the external behaviour of a process or its interface. A tree like structure should rather be employed. A second possibility would be to have special SDL-descriptions within an SDL-description of the system itself which would be restricted to the external behaviour of the processes. This would not be a part of the actual system description but should be rather seen as another SDL document. A third possibility would be to supplement SDL descriptions with LOTOS [2] expressions. These specifications could be seen as comments even though a full formalisation over their semantics would be available.

In this particular context LOTOS would, strictly speaking, not offer anything that could not be expressed with SDL as well. However, if offers a different view of the system. In addition: being event oriented instead of state oriented as SDL it offers means to write succinct expressions which are fluently incorporated into an SDL document as supplementary information.

The supplementary LOTOS expressions would unambiguously and succinctly specify interfaces or set requirements of how blocks or processes should communicate with each other. The proposed means to do this would be to attach to a channel in addition to a set of signals also a set of these LOTOS expressions called *service definitions*.

In the following we will take a closer look on these service definitions and their use and study the relation between service definitions and SDL processes. The paper is organized as follows: In Section 2 service definitions are introduced in more detail. The relation of LOTOS and SDL is also discussed by introducing a scheme for transforming LOTOS behavioural expression into corresponding SDL processes. This is followed in Section 3 by a detailed example demonstrating the design process of a part of a banking system employing sequence charts, service definitions and SDL descriptions. In Section 4 the formalisation of the semantics of service definitions is discussed. In particular it is discussed what is meant by an SDL process conforming to a service definition. During the discourse it is assumed that the reader is familiar with the basics of LOTOS and SDL.

2 Incorporating LOTOS-based behaviour expressions into SDL

Consider Figure 1. There two blocks A_S and B_S are communicating via a channel. The internals of the two blocks have been described in SDL. The description of the whole system includes also the blocks themselves and the channel. Now, the internals of the blocks can be seen as a description of the implementation of some functions provided by the blocks. When the system is started signals begin to flow back and forth in the channel connecting the blocks. The way these signals flow is determined by the implementation, i.e. by the SDL processes. Suppose now that we want to say something about what is happening in the channel, i.e. what is observed by an observer who is situated outside the blocks. Moreover, we want to be able to tell how to communicate with the block without having to consider the detailed internal aspects present in the SDL process descriptions. The possibilities offered by SDL to do the job are the following:

1. Use the signal set connected with the channel to specify which signals are possible.

Figure 1: Two blocks connected by a channel.

2. Produce an other SDL description to simulate the flow of signals in the channel.

Suppose further we would like to use the above descriptions as a *requirements specification* telling how the blocks should behave when they are observed as black boxes from the outside. The problem with the first suggestion above is that it is not very informative. It does not tell very much of what is actually happening in the channel. To try to formulate when a system conforms to a requirements specification expressed as a set of signals would lead most likely to arbitrary and nonsensical implementations.

The second possibility, the use of an entirely new SDL description, would surely be by far a better alternative. Lets consider processes P_a and P_b which reside in separate blocks and communicate through signals b and a over channel C. In Figure 2 a) we have a description of the implementation of a process P_a. This description contains a lot of actions which are unobservable and irrelevant from the point of view of channel C connecting the blocks of P_a and P_b. In Figures 2 b) and c) we have SDL descriptions which specify only the observable actions in C from the point of view P_a and P_b, respectively. These could then be called the interface specifications of the processes or their enclosing blocks telling exactly how the communication between them takes place. It is clear that having both of these interface specifications is superfluous since they are dual: one of them can be converted to the other by changing the inputs into outputs and vice versa. In addition the states have to be adjusted accordingly. The convention we adopt here is to present such an interface specification from the point of view of the one who inputs the first signal. This signal represents a request made to have some task or service performed. Therefore we may call such a specification a *service definition* and say that the specification is given from the point of view of the service provider.

Even though these service definitions could be very well given in SDL, some shortcomings, not necessarily severe, could be noted:

1. The interface specification SDL would be a separate document from the implementation description SDL and would not be easily incorporated into the latter to provide one handy document.

2. The state oriented style of SDL introduces states into the interface specification which are irrelevant for the purpose and increase unnecessarily the size of this specification.

Now, instead for writing service definitions in SDL also LOTOS could be used. The advantage it offers as an alternative is that the problems listed above would be avoided. LOTOS based service definitions could be attached to SDL channels in addition to the signal sets they carry. They would then be an integrated part of an SDL description and tell how services are offered by blocks and how they can be used by other blocks. When this is done blocks can be interfaced with each other without having to know about their internal implementation. This makes a system highly modular and consequently improves its maintainability.

2.1   How to use LOTOS for service definitions

The use of LOTOS for writing service definitions involves some special assumptions. The communication mechanism in SDL is asynchronous on the contrary to the synchronous communication in LOTOS. Therefore the synchronization mechanisms of LOTOS need not to be employed. In addition, the communication can always be seen as taking place between two parties, the service provider, the system, and the service user, the environment. When only the observable behaviour is taken into account these parties can be assumed to consist of one SDL process each. Therefore no parallelism is present and it is enough to consider only the sequential part of LOTOS. For similar reasons also process instantiation and gate parameters can be omitted.

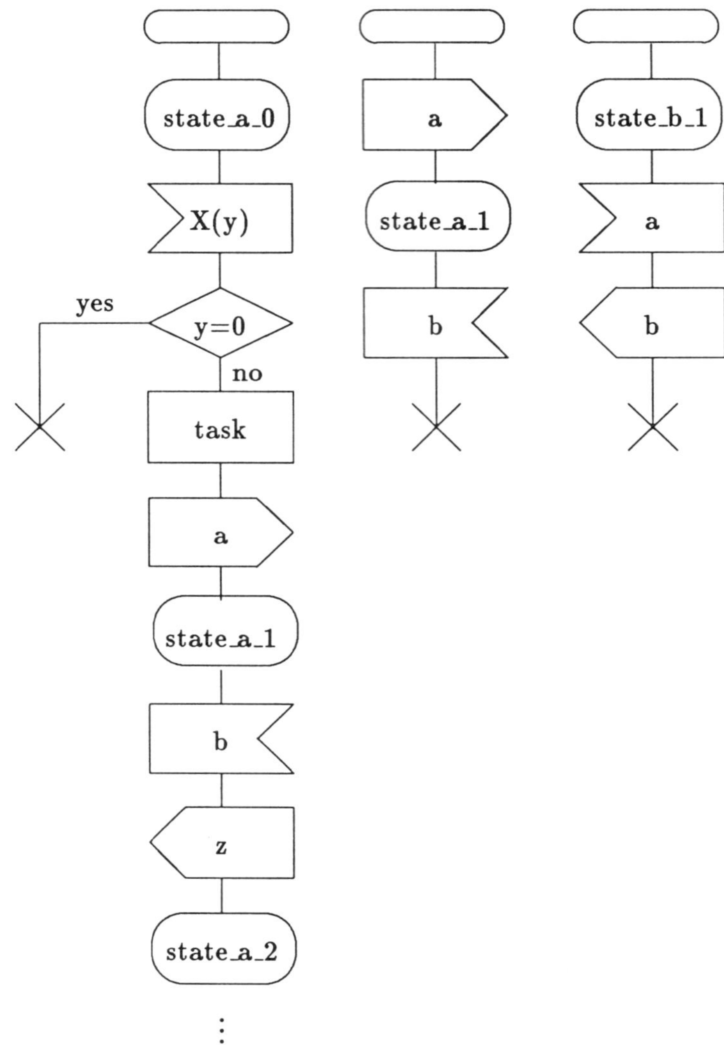

Figure 2: Different SDL descriptions: a) description of the implementation of process P_a, b) the interface of P_a towards P_b and, c) the interface of P_b.

In service definitions we have two kind of events; the input and output of an asynchronous signal. To express this in LOTOS we need one gate name, say g, together with value and variable declarations. Then we have the following expressions corresponding to each other:[1]

SDL	LOTOS
INPUT a	$g\ ?a$
OUTPUT a	$g\ !a$

Since gate g is not synchronized with any other gate nothing prevents us from taking the value and variable offerings at g as the consumption and sending of an asynchronous signal. In the following we will still use a simpler notation and drop the gate name g and simple write $?a$ and $!a$ instead of $g?a$ and $g!a$.

LOTOS offers several operators which come in handy in service definitions. Some of them are straightforward to express in SDL whereas some offer a more compact representation than corresponding SDL constructs.

Action prefix: Action prefix, ;, can be used to prefix an existing behavioral expression with an action. The resulting expression denotes sequentially executing first the action and then the rest of the expression. The service specification of Figure 2 c) can therefore be expressed in the following way: $?a;!b;$stop. In SDL action prefix means simply that events are executed sequentially which is always the case within one process.

Choice: The choice operator [] can be expressed in two different ways in SDL. If there is a choice in signals to be input then this is taken care of by a state and the different inputs connected to it. In other case decision is employed. Since the choice in LOTOS is nondeterministic nondeterminism would also have to be introduced into the decision construct of SDL.

Synchronization and interleaving: As was mentioned earlier we need not employ any parallelism or consider synchronization in service definitions. This leaves us with only pure interleaving, ||| , where the actions of the expressions it connects may interleave arbitrarily. It is an operator which may require several states when expressed in SDL. Consider the expression

$$?a;\ ?b;\ \textbf{stop}\ |||\ ?c;\ ?d;\ \textbf{stop}.$$

---

[1] The expressions are, strictly speaking, not in line with the syntax of SDL nor of LOTOS. A signal in SDL is in a sense both a variable name and a type declaration. In LOTOS we would have to use a list of types and a list of values of the parameters of the signal. Since we are not interested in this level of detail we simply use the name of the signal the meaning of which should be intuitively clear.

The possible traces of this expression are:

$$?a; ?b; ?c; ?d$$
$$?a; ?c; ?b; ?d$$
$$?a; ?c; ?d; ?b$$
$$?c; ?a; ?b; ?d$$
$$?c; ?a; ?d; ?b$$
$$?c; ?d; ?a; ?b$$

An SDL process offering the possible orders of inputing the signals is depicted in Figure 3. As can be seen already eight states are needed.

An SDL counterpart to the interleaving can also be found in the service concept of SDL where the events of the different services (i.e. subautomata) within one process are interleaved. In this particular case we could use services and have one subautomaton for $?a; ?b;$ **stop** and another for $?c; ?d;$ **stop**: clearly a more compact way of describing the same behaviour as in Figure 3. This use of services is, however, straightforward only when signals involved in the interleaved expressions do not appear elsewhere in the LOTOS expression that is to be transformed into SDL. This is not the case e.g. in the expression

$$?a; \textbf{stop} \, [] \, ?c; (?a; ?b; \textbf{stop} \, ||| \, ?c; ?d; \textbf{stop}).$$

Enabling: This is an operator whose meaning is taken care of by SDL states: performing the successful termination action δ by **exit** can be expressed by an SDL process reaching a specific state. This takes also care of the implicit synchronization of δ actions possibly involved in expressions composed by the interleaving operator.

Disabling: Disabling can occur in two ways. It is an interruption caused either by the reception of a signal or by the sending of one. In the former case the interruption originates in some external cause. Here disabling can be expressed in SDL in a handy way by asterisk states. The signal the reception of which causes the interruption of the normal behaviour is connected to all those states where it is to be expected. To do this only one asterisk state is necessary. In the other case, i.e. interruption by the sending of a signal, the originating cause is internal and is expressible by decisions.

Exit and stop: As discussed above the **exit** of LOTOS does not correspond directly to any specific construction in SDL. Its effect is taken care of by states of an SDL process. The SDL counterpart of the LOTOS **stop** is STOP.

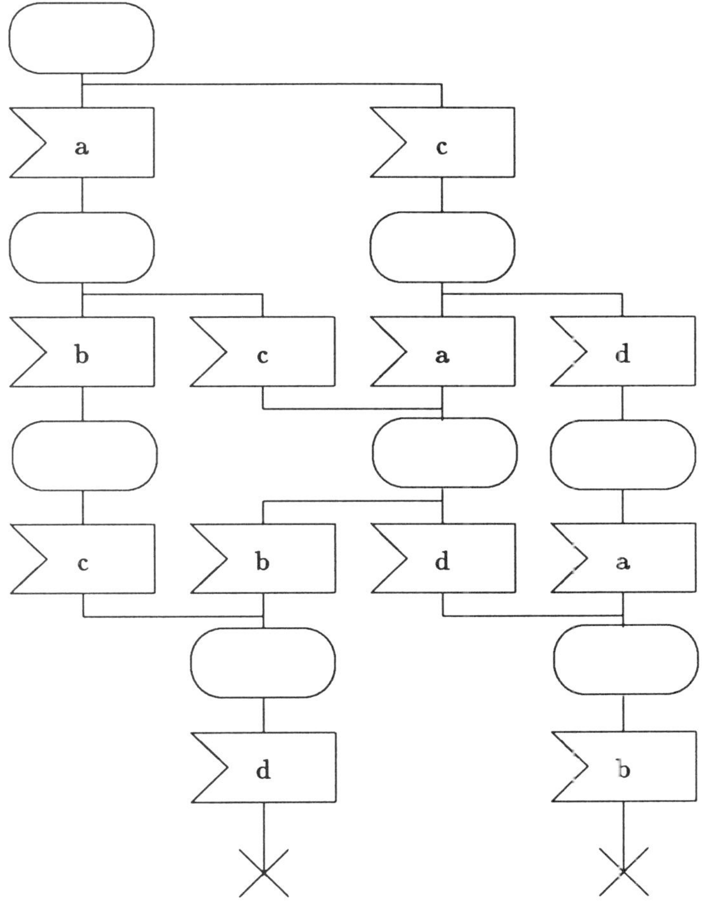

Figure 3: An SDL process which corresponds to the LOTOS expression $?a; ?b$ **stop** ||| $?c; ?d;$ **stop.**

Recursion: recursion can be taken care of by state transitions: after some state transitions an earlier state is entered repeatedly.

Above we have described what the relation between LOTOS behavioural expressions and SDL descriptions is in the particular case of defining the observable behaviour between two communicating entities — the system and its environment. The transformation between the two formalisms is intuitively rather clear when synchronization and parallelism is not considered. This relation between them can also readily be formalized as discussed in Section 4. To carry it further to include also the parallel aspects is, however, not any more easy at all.

The two formalisms considered here are quite different in nature. SDL is state oriented, has an attractive graphical representation and can be used as an implementation driven method. LOTOS, on the other hand, is event oriented and is more requirement driven. Since their relation is quite clear in the sequential world they can be well used together to provide different views of a system under design. An approach incorporating these different views into one design method is described in the next section.

3   An example of the use of service definitions

To illustrate the use of service definitions as requirements specifications for SDL processes we present a part of an imaginary bank automaton. To give a view of the whole design process and the role of service definitions therein we start with sequence charts and move step by step via service definitions into a skeleton of the SDL process. The structure of the system is illustrated in Figure 4, on the main level it consists of the bank automaton and a main computer. The bank automaton is further divided into a control part and a user interface part. We'll give the service definitions for the services provided by the USER_INTERFACE and MAINFRAME processes and further a skeleton of the SDL process implementing the latter.

3.1   Sequence charts

Sequence charts have proved their usefulness in initial phases of system design. A set of sequence charts representing typical signal sequences is drawn to represent the involved processes and their communication on a chosen level of abstraction. Each process participating in the activity is represented as a vertical bar in the sequence chart, time is interpreted to run downwards, and the signals are represented by vertical arrows between the processes. Such

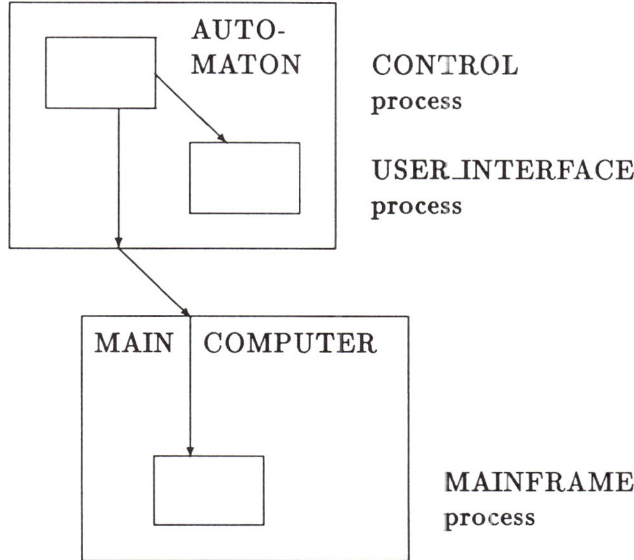

Figure 4: The block structure of the imaginary bank automaton system.

charts provide an overall view of how processes participate in performing some function of the system. There are also different ways sequence charts may be enhanced as discussed in [3].

In the bank automaton example the processes involved are the CONTROL process, the USER_INTERFACE process, and the MAINFRAME process. Perhaps the two most typical cases of signalling are a successful withdrawal of money and a failure due to the unaccessibility of the main computer. Signalling in these two cases is illustrated in Figures 5 and 6. In the first chart the control part asks the user interface to check the password and when it later gets the type of the required transaction it starts communication with the main computer. When the control part gets the permission to give money it forwards the permission to the user interface and sends later an acknowledgement to the main computer. In the second chart the communication starts as in the first one but the main computer is not ready to co-operate and no money can be given to the user.

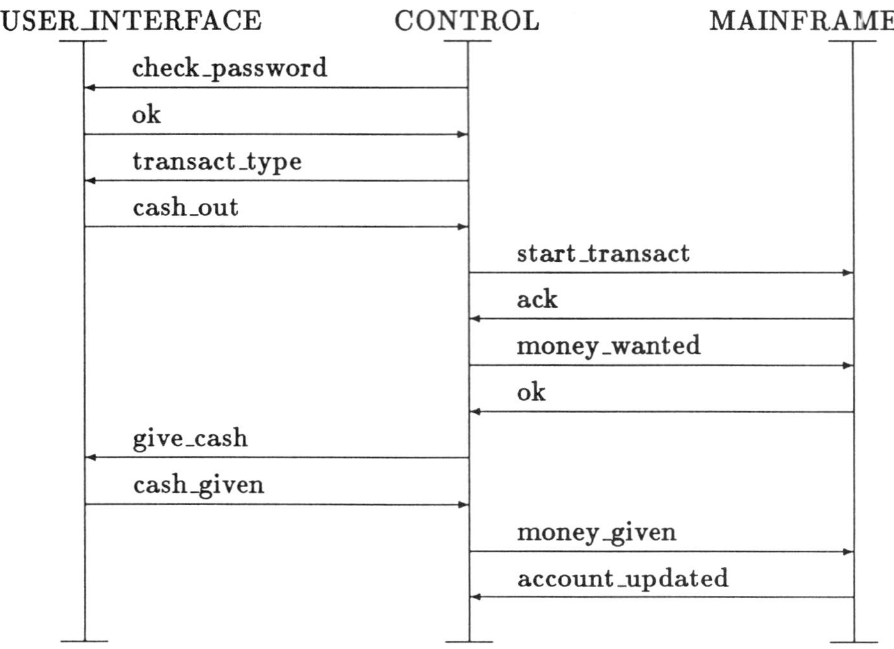

Figure 5: A sequence chart representing a successful withdrawal.

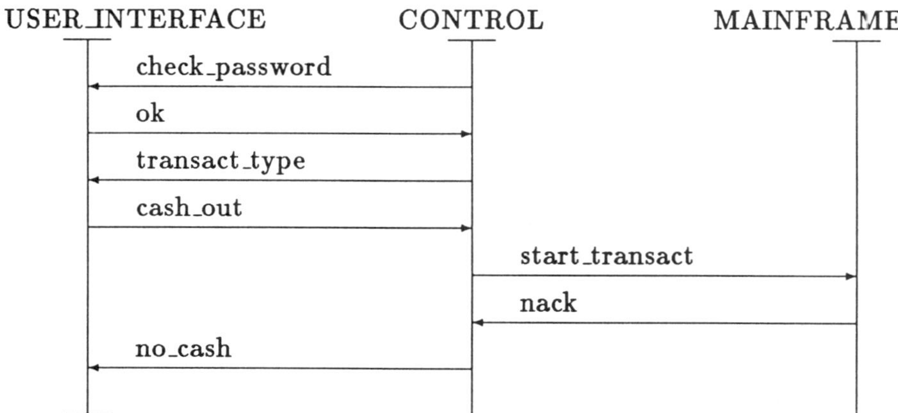

Figure 6: A sequence chart representing a failure due to the unaccessibility
of the main computer.

3.2   Service definitions

The sequence charts do not alone tell very much about how the processes should actually behave, i.e. what the requirements specifications are for them. They only give a rough idea of how the signalling goes in some usual cases. To specify all possible exceptions and special cases hundreds of signalling charts would be needed. However, a set of sequence charts, even an infinite one, can be coded as a few service definitions in a concise way. The main advantage of the service specification over the corresponding set of sequence charts is thus the disjunctive nature of the former.

Usually one service definition is written for each pair of processes having mutual communication. The possible signal sequences between processes specified by service definitions are seen from the perspective of one of the processes, the signals received by that process are prefixed with a question mark and those sent by it with an exclamation mark. We'll write one service definition for the signalling between the processes CONTROL and USER_INTERFACE and one for the sigalling between the processes CONTROL and MAINFRAME. The former will be seen from the standpoint of the USER_INTERFACE process and called **user_transact**, the latter will be seen from the standpoint of the MAINFRAME process and called **system_transact**.

The two service definitions are quite similar, in fact the control process is mainly a communication link between the user interface and the main computer. The control process sends information received from the user interface to the main computer and the other way round. The service definitions look out as follows.

```
user_transact := ?check_password;
                (( !ok;exit [ ] !not_ok;stop) )) ?transact_type;
                  (!account_info;account_information [] cash)) [) interrupt;
account_information := ( ?account_record;!record_ack;account_information
                  [] ?finish;exit
                  )
cash := !cash_out;(?give_cash;!cash_given;exit [] ?no_cash;exit)
interrupt := ?control_interrupt;exit[]!interface_interrupt;exit


system_transact := ?start_transact;
                  (( !ack;exit [] !nack;stop) )) (query []money)) [)
                  break
query := ?status;!account_info;exit
```

money := ?money_wanted; (!not_ok;exit
                          [] !ok;?money_given;!account_updated;exit
)
break := !system_break;exit [] ?user_break;exit

3.3 SDL process

As mentioned above the service definitions can be used as a requirements specification for the USER_INTERFACE, MAINFRAME and CONTROL processes. Actually, a skeleton of an SDL process can be even automatically extracted from the service definitions. The result is only a skeleton because the service definitions do not deal with the data or the internal events of the process. Possible nondeterminism in the definitions is represented in the extracted SDL process by decisions whose expressions are left open. The designer can then add the needed information manually.

The skeleton for the SDL process MAINFRAME is depicted in Figure 7. The process implements the service definition **system_transact**.

3.4 Summary

To sum up the approach to system design outlined in the example above following steps are presented:

1. An overall view of the system is sketched with a set of sequence charts presenting an adequate collection of signalling traces of the usual cases.

2. The interfaces between communicating process pairs are specified formally by service definitions. Sequence charts can be used as guidelines. If desired, the conformance of the service specification to a set of traces presented by signalling charts can be verified by tools.

3. An SDL description of a process skeleton is extracted from the service specification. This step can be automated.

4. The skeleton is augmented to include the data and internal actions. Here other service definitions may be exploited. Also for this step tool support is possible.

5. The final process implementing the service may be verified automatically against the service definitions specifying the services offered and used by the process.

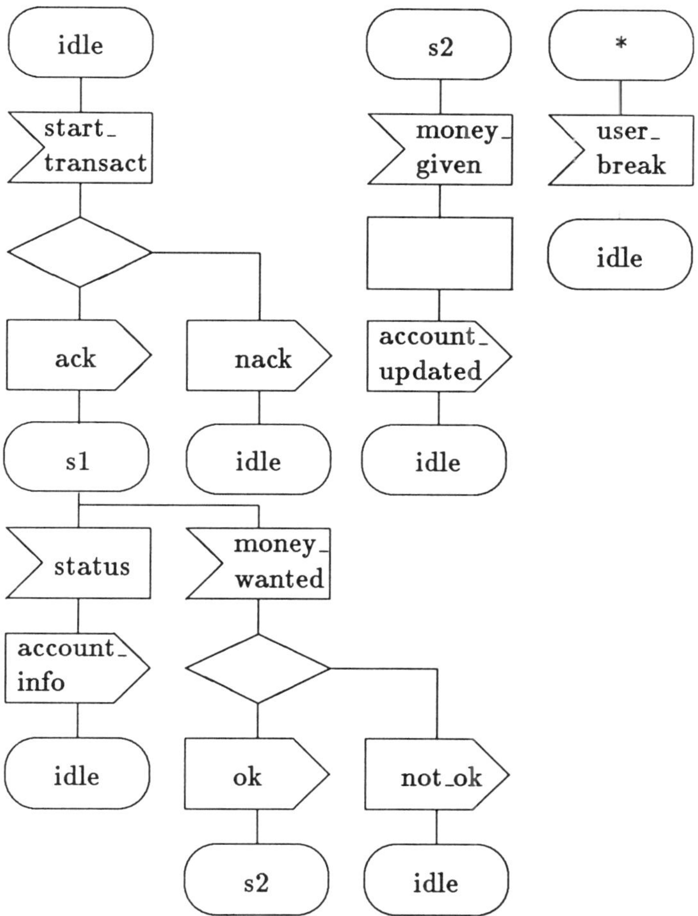

Figure 7: The SDL process implementing the **system_transact** service.

6. Test sequences can be generated automatically from service definitions providing for full covering of the testing of the implemented process.

4 Formalization of semantics of service definitions and conformance

In this section we present the formalization of service definitions and their use as introduced in the previous section. To start we define a model for the observable behaviour of an SDL system and its environment. This model called Asynchronous Communication Tree is based on the Actor model introduced in [1]. After this a corresponding tree model is defined for service definitions. Using these two semantical models the conformance of a process to a service definition can finally be stated formally. Due to the scope of this paper the primary aim here is to demonstrate the intuition behind the idea of conformance rather than to derive its full formalization.

4.1 Asynchronous Communication Trees of SDL systems

In this section we will develop the Asynchronous communication tree to provide a semantical model for a system of SDL processes and its environment. We assume that the environment behaves as the system, i.e. as a set of SDL processes. The approach is based on actor systems and their event diagrams [1].[2] The ultimate goal of this section is to provide the necessary semantical basis needed to formalize the conformance of an SDL process to a service definition as mentioned previously.

In here we will use the word process even though strictly speaking the notion of process instance should be employed. We have also assumed in the model to be introduced that the configuration of the system is static, i.e. no processes are created and none are stopped. Changes in system configuration could be included but would not serve the purpose here. For similar reasons what dynamic process identifiers, $pIds$, are known to a process at a moment and how it gets to know them is ignored.

Notation 4.1 *In the basic notation the following set symbols are used:*

1. $\mathcal{A} = \{a_i | i = 1, \ldots, n\}$ *is the set (alphabet) of signal names and $\mathcal{A}^*$ is the set of strings over $\mathcal{A}$.*

---

[2]The definition of the tree itself follows outline discussed in Contribution D.13/X to CCITT Working Party X/3 meeting in Geneva in November 1989.

2. Π *is the set of pIds and* $\Sigma = \{\sigma_i | i = 1, \ldots, n\} \subseteq \Pi$ *and* $E = \{\eta_i | i = 1, \ldots, n\} \subseteq \Pi$ *are the sets of pIds of the processes of the system and of the environment, respectively.*

3. $S = \{s_i | i = 1, \ldots, n\}$ *is the set of process states.*

The state of the system is expressed as a set of ordered pairs consisting of a *pId* and a state of the corresponding process. It is defined in the following as a function which returns the state of the process whose *pId* is given as the argument:

Definition 4.2 *The state of a system* Σ *of processes is defined as a mapping* $S_\Sigma : \Sigma \to S$ *from the pIds of processes of* Σ *to the set process states.*

When dealing with the overall state of an SDL process the queues containing the signals sent to the process have to be taken into account. The following definition provides the machinery necessary for dealing with queues:

Definition 4.3 *The queues of processes* $\pi \in \Pi$ *is a mapping* $\mathcal{Q} = \Pi \to \mathcal{A}^*$.

1. $\mathcal{Q}(\pi) = q_\pi = \langle a_1, \ldots, a_n \rangle$ *denotes the contents of the queue of process* $\pi \in \Pi$. *Particularly, we write* $q_\pi = \langle \rangle$ *to denote that the queue of process* π *is empty.*

2. *Let* $q_\pi = \langle a_1, \ldots, a_n \rangle, q_\pi \in \mathcal{Q}$ *and* $q'_\pi = \langle a'_1, \ldots, a'_m \rangle, q'_\pi \in \mathcal{Q}'$. *Then* $q_\pi \cdot q'_\pi = \langle a_1, \ldots, a_n, a'_1, \ldots, a'_m \rangle$ *is the concatenation of the two queues.*

Further we use $\mathcal{Q}_{QI} : \Pi \to \mathcal{A}^*$ *and* $\mathcal{Q}_{QS} : \Sigma \to \mathcal{A}^*$ *to denote the input queues of the processes of* Σ *and its environment and the queues of saved signals of processes of* Σ, *respectively.*

A queue of a process is defined as a mapping which returns the contents of the queue of the process whose *pId* is given as the argument. We use the convention that the first signal in the queue is presented as the left most element of a string which is enclosed in $\langle$ and $\rangle$. Also the distinction is made between the input queues and queues of saved signals even though both are similar constructs. To deal with queues and their contents, with states of processes and with sending of signals we will define some mappings to make the presentation more compact in the sequel. Note that we treat the 'state' where a process immediately is after its creation as an ordinary state of the set S. The signals output in a state transition of a process are treated as a queue of signals. The order of these signals is the same as the order in which the output statements sending the signals appear in the transition.

Definition 4.4 *Let $\mathcal{P}(X)$ denote the powerset of a set X. Then we define the following mappings:*

1. *$\underline{\text{start}}, \underline{\text{initial}}$ and $\underline{\text{current}}$ are mappings $\Sigma \to \mathcal{S}$ and denote the starting state, initial state and current state of a process, respectively.*

2. *$\underline{\text{next}} : \mathcal{S} \times \mathcal{A} \to \mathcal{P}(\mathcal{S})$ is the set of states that can be entered after a signal in input in a state, i.e. the set of possible follower states.*

3. *$\underline{\text{input}} : \mathcal{S} \to \mathcal{P}(\mathcal{A})$ is the set of input signals of a state.*

4. *$\underline{\text{save}} : \mathcal{S} \to \mathcal{P}(\mathcal{A})$ is the set of signals to be saved in a state.*

5. *$\underline{\text{output}} : \mathcal{S} \times \mathcal{S} \to \mathcal{A}^*$ is the string of signals output in a transition from a state to another.*

6. *$\underline{\text{sender}}$ and $\underline{\text{dest}}$ are mappings $\mathcal{A} \to \Pi$ and denote the sender and receiver of some signal, respectively.[3]*

7. *$\underline{\text{first}} : \mathcal{Q}_{\text{I}} \to A$ denotes the first signal of some queue.*

Yet we have to be able to manipulate signal queues, i.e. we have to be able to express addition of signals to and removal from queues of the processes of the system. For this purpose two special operators are defined. As is the case with *first-in-first-out* queues signals are always added to the end and removed from the front of the queue:

Definition 4.5 *Let $\mathcal{Q}$ be the queues of processes $\pi \in \Pi$. We define operators $\oplus$ and $\ominus$, addition and removal of signals, in the following way:[4]*

1. *Let $\mathcal{Q}' = \mathcal{Q} \oplus \{\pi, \langle a \rangle\}$ and $\mathcal{Q}(\pi) = q_\pi$. Then*

$$\mathcal{Q}'(\pi') = \mathcal{Q}(\pi') \; \forall \pi' \neq \pi \; and$$
$$\mathcal{Q}'(\pi) = q_\pi . \langle a \rangle.$$

2. *Let $\mathcal{Q}' = \mathcal{Q} \ominus \{\pi, \langle a \rangle\}$ and $\mathcal{Q}(\pi) = \langle a \rangle . q_\pi$. Then*

$$\mathcal{Q}'(\pi') = \mathcal{Q}(\pi') \; \forall \pi' \neq \pi \; and$$
$$\mathcal{Q}'(\pi) = q_\pi.$$

---

[3] Actually, we should be dealing with signal instances here although SDL does not make such a distinction.

[4] Note that we have, formally speaking, treated here the function $\mathcal{Q}$ as its extension, i.e. a set of pairs.

An Asynchronous Communication Tree is defined as a tree with a mapping from its nodes to a triple that gives the states of the processes of the system, the contents of the input queues of the system and the environment and the contents of the queues of the saved signals of the system. Further, there is a mapping from the arcs of the tree to the observable and silent events of the system. Note that only the reception of a signal sent by the environment to a process of the system is observable. Naturally, the internal message exchange of the system is not observable. This is also the case with signals output by the system to its environment. They only have an effect on the queue of some environment process where the signal is queued. Later this signal can be consumed by the environment which results in another silent transition enabling the environment to respond to the consumed signal. The argumentation of this kind of an approach to observable events can be found in [1, pages 117-118, 125].

Definition 4.6 *Let $\mathcal{T} = (\mathcal{N}, \mathcal{E})$ be a tree with mappings $C : \mathcal{N} \rightarrow (\mathcal{S}_\Sigma \times \mathcal{Q}_I \times \mathcal{Q}_S)$ (called a configuration) and $\lambda : \mathcal{E} \rightarrow \mathcal{A} \cup \{\tau\}$ where τ stands for a silent event. Then $\mathcal{T}$ is called an Asynchronous Communication Tree or ACT for short. By $C_\mathcal{S} : \mathcal{N} \rightarrow \mathcal{S}_\Sigma$, $C_{\mathbf{QI}} : \mathcal{N} \rightarrow \mathcal{Q}_I$, $C_{\mathbf{QS}} : \mathcal{N} \rightarrow \mathcal{Q}_S$ we denote the configuration of the processes $\sigma \in \Sigma$, of input queues of Σ and E and of save queues of Σ in some node, respectively.*

After having defined an ACT we now show how to construct the ACT of a given system and its environment. As mentioned before, the model does not take into account creation and stopping of processes nor how processes get to know each others *pIds*. However, there are no technical reasons why this augmentation of the model could not be done. The reasons for this are purely to keep the model from coming too complicated with an negative effect on its comprehensibility.

Definition 4.7 *Let Σ and E be the pIds of processes of a system and its environment. Then $\mathcal{T}$ is an ACT for (Σ, E) iff:*

  1. Initial configuration: *The configuration C of the root node $n_0 \in \mathcal{N}$ is such that:[5].*

     (a) $\forall \sigma \in \Sigma : C_\mathcal{S}(n_0)(\sigma) = \underline{\text{initial}}(\sigma).$

---

[5] Without loss of generality we can assume that there are no decisions, i.e. no branching in the start transitions of processes

(b) $\forall \pi \in \Pi : \mathcal{C}_{\mathbf{QI}}(n_o)(\pi) = q_\pi = \langle a_1, \ldots, a_n \rangle$ and $\forall a_i, i = 1, \ldots, n \; \exists \pi'$
$\in \Pi$ such that a_i appears in $\underline{\text{output}}(\underline{\text{start}}(\pi), \underline{\text{initial}}(\pi))$. Further,
if $\langle a_{i_1}, \ldots, a_{i_k} \rangle$ are signals in q_π such that $\underline{\text{sender}}(a_{i_1}) = \ldots =$
$\underline{\text{sender}}(a_{i_k}) = \pi'$ then the order of their appearance in q_π is the
same as their order in $\underline{\text{output}}(\underline{\text{start}}(\pi), \underline{\text{initial}}(\pi))$.

(c) $\forall \pi \in \Pi : \mathcal{C}_{\mathbf{QS}}(n_o)(\pi) = \langle \rangle$.

2. Input from the environment: *Let $n \in \mathcal{N}$. Then $\forall a \in \underline{\text{input}}(\underline{\text{current}}(\sigma))$
such that $\sigma \in \Sigma$ and $\underline{\text{sender}}(a) \in E$ and $\forall s_{next} \in \underline{\text{next}}(\underline{\text{current}}(\sigma), a)$
$\exists n' \in \mathcal{N}$ such that*

(a) $\mathcal{C}_\mathcal{S}(n') = \mathcal{C}_\mathcal{S}(n) - \{(\sigma, \underline{\text{current}}(\sigma))\} + \{\sigma, s_{next}\}$,

(b) $\mathcal{C}_{\mathbf{QI}}(n') = \{(\sigma, \mathcal{C}_{\mathbf{QS}}(n)(\sigma))\} \oplus \mathcal{C}_{\mathbf{QI}}(n) \oplus \{(\underline{\text{dest}}(a_1), \langle a_1 \rangle)\} \oplus \ldots \oplus$
$\{(\underline{\text{dest}}(a_n), \langle a_n \rangle)\}$ where $\underline{\text{output}}(\underline{\text{current}}(\sigma), s_{next}) = \langle a_1, \ldots, a_n \rangle$
and s_{next} is as above. In addition, if $\underline{\text{first}}(\mathcal{C}_{\mathbf{QI}}(n)(\sigma)) = a$ *then*
$\{\sigma, a\}$ *is removed from* $\mathcal{C}_{\mathbf{QI}}(n)$.

(c) $\mathcal{C}_{\mathbf{QS}}(n') = \mathcal{C}_{\mathbf{QS}}(n) \ominus \{(\sigma, \mathcal{C}_{\mathbf{QS}}(n)(\sigma)\}$,

(d) $\lambda(n, n') = a$.

3. Signal sent from the environment to be saved: *Let $n \in \mathcal{N}$. Then
$\forall a \in \underline{\text{save}}(\underline{\text{current}}(\sigma))$ such that $\sigma \in \Sigma$ and $\underline{\text{sender}}(a) \in E$ then $\exists n' \in \mathcal{N}$
such that*

(a) $\mathcal{C}_\mathcal{S}(n') = \mathcal{C}_\mathcal{S}(n)$,

(b) $\mathcal{C}_{\mathbf{QI}}(n') = \mathcal{C}_{\mathbf{QI}}(n)$,

(c) $\mathcal{C}_{\mathbf{QS}}(n') = \mathcal{C}_{\mathbf{QS}}(n) \oplus \{(\sigma, \langle a \rangle)\}$,

(d) $\lambda(n, n') = \tau$.

4. Consumption of a signal by the environment: *Let $n \in \mathcal{N}$. Iff $\exists \eta \in E$
such that* $\underline{\text{first}}(\mathcal{C}_{\mathbf{QI}}(n)(\eta)) = a$ *then $\exists n' \in \mathcal{N}$ such that*

(a) $\mathcal{C}_\mathcal{S}(n') = \mathcal{C}_\mathcal{S}(n)$,

(b) $\mathcal{C}_{\mathbf{QI}}(n') = \mathcal{C}_{\mathbf{QI}}(n) \ominus (\eta, \langle a \rangle)$,

(c) $\mathcal{C}_{\mathbf{QS}}(n') = \mathcal{C}_{\mathbf{QS}}(n)$,

(d) $\lambda(n, n') = \tau$.

5. Input, saving and implicit consumption of a signal sent by a process in
system Σ: *Let $n \in \mathcal{N}$. If $\exists \sigma \in \Sigma$ such that* $\underline{\text{first}}(\mathcal{C}_{\mathbf{QI}}(n)(\sigma)) = a$ *and*
$\underline{\text{sender}}(a) \in \Sigma$ *then $\exists n' \in \mathcal{N}$ such that*

(a) *if $a \in \underline{\text{input}}(\underline{\text{current}}(\sigma))$ then* *i.* $\mathcal{C}_S(n') = \mathcal{C}_S(n) - \{(\sigma, \underline{\text{current}}(\sigma))\} + \{\sigma, s_{\text{next}}\}$ *where* $s_{next} \in$ $\underline{\text{next}}(\underline{\text{current}}(\sigma), a)$,

    ii. $\mathcal{C}_{\mathbf{QI}}(n') = \{\sigma, \mathcal{C}_{\mathbf{QS}}(n)(\sigma)\} \oplus [\mathcal{C}_{\mathbf{QI}}(n) \ominus \{(\sigma, \langle a \rangle)\}] \oplus \{(\underline{\text{dest}}(a_1),$ $\langle a_1 \rangle)\} \oplus \ldots \oplus \{(\underline{\text{dest}}(a_n), \langle a_n \rangle)\}$ *where* $\underline{\text{output}}(\underline{\text{current}}(\sigma), s_{\text{next}})$ $= \langle a_1, \ldots, a_n \rangle$ *and* s_{next} *is as above,*

    iii. $\mathcal{C}_{\mathbf{QS}}(n') = \mathcal{C}_{\mathbf{QS}}(n) \ominus \{(\sigma, \mathcal{C}_{\mathbf{QS}}(n)(\sigma))\}$,

    iv. $\lambda(n, n') = \tau$ *or*

  (b) if $a \in \underline{\text{save}}(\underline{\text{current}}(\sigma))$ *then*

    i. $\mathcal{C}_S(n') = \mathcal{C}_S(n)$,

    ii. $\mathcal{C}_{\mathbf{QI}}(n') = \mathcal{C}_{\mathbf{QI}}(n) \ominus \{(\sigma, \langle a \rangle)\}$,

    iii. $\mathcal{C}_{\mathbf{QS}}(n') = \mathcal{C}_{\mathbf{QS}}(n) \oplus \{(\sigma, \langle a \rangle)\}$,

    iv. $\lambda(n, n') = \tau$ *or*

  (c) if $a \notin \underline{\text{input}}(\underline{\text{current}}(\sigma)) \cup \underline{\text{save}}(\underline{\text{current}}(\sigma))$ *then*

    i. $\mathcal{C}_S(n') = \mathcal{C}_S(n)$,

    ii. $\mathcal{C}_{\mathbf{QI}}(n') = \mathcal{C}_{\mathbf{QI}}(n) \ominus \{(\sigma, \langle a \rangle)\}$,

    iii. $\mathcal{C}_{\mathbf{QS}}(n') = \mathcal{C}_{\mathbf{QS}}(n)$,

    iv. $\lambda(n, n') = \tau$.

We have now defined the ACT of a given system and its environment. The first item in the above definition tells how to construct the initial configuration referring to the situation where each process is in its initial state after having executed the transition from the start to this initial state. The possible signals output in these transitions are queued as usual. Note that the order in which signals sent by different processes to one process are queued is random. However, signals sent by one process are queued in the order they are sent.

The second item of Definition 4.7 deals with the situation where a signal is expected from the environment. Here it is assumed that any time a signal is expected it also arrives. As a consequence all possible ways the system may evolve are covered in the ACT. There is no need to queue these signals since the resulting information would still be the same. In case the signal from the environment has been saved earlier and is the first in the queue it is removed. As a result of a state transition the saved signals of the process in question are added into the head of the input queue.

The next item deals with the saving of a signal from the environment although it could be stripped from the model without changing the observable behaviour of the system as expressed by the generated ACT. Item 4 is also similar in that sense. It only makes explicit the fact that the behaviour of the environment has to be reconciled to the situation where a signal from the system has been received. It has, however, no effect on the possible future behaviour of the system as expressed by the ACT.

In the last item events internal to the system are considered. Even if these events are considered to be silent they affect the future behaviour of the system in respect to the environment: the resulting changes in states of the processes have an effect on what signals are expected from the environment.

In constructing the ACT the assumption is made that all signals sent are immediately queued in their receiver processes. The takeover possible in SDL is not modeled. Here again there are no technical obstacles, rather it is a restriction made to keep the ACT from growing too complex with even small systems. The way to add this non-determinism caused by the traveling time of signals the queues would be to define the queues as a mapping $Q = \Pi \times \Pi \to \mathcal{A}^*$ rather than $Q = \Pi \to \mathcal{A}^*$. A process would have an separate input queue for each process and it would be free to choose from which to consume the next signal. This way all possible orders in which signals could be queued would be taken into account.

4.2   Construction of the Asynchronous communication tree for a service definition

In order to define conformance between service definitions and SDL processes we have to define the corresponding Asynchronous Communication Trees also for the service definitions. We use the labelled transition graphs of LOTOS specifications as intermediate steps to make the construction more intuitive.

For the operational semantics of LOTOS on which its labelled transition graphs are based we refer to [2]. Intuitively the paths of a transition graph represent the action sequences allowed by the corresponding behavioural expression. The only deviation from the operational semantics of LOTOS is done with respect to the disabling operator ([>). The original definition goes as follows

- if $B_1 \xrightarrow{\mu} B_1'$ then $B_1 \ [> \ B_2 \xrightarrow{\mu} B_1' \ [> \ B_2$

- if $B_1 \xrightarrow{\delta} B_1'$ then $B_1 \ [> \ B_2 \xrightarrow{\delta} B_1'$

- if $B_2 \xrightarrow{\mu^+} B_2'$ then $B_1 \ [> \ B_2 \xrightarrow{\mu^+} B_2'$

However, in order to adopt the notion of transition in SDL a received signal can cause an interrupt only in a state, not between an input and an output or between two outputs. Unfortunately this means breaking the clear semantics as follows

- if $B_1 \xrightarrow{\mu} B_1'$ then $B_1 \ [> \ B_2 \xrightarrow{\mu} B_1' \ [> \ B_2$

- if $B_1 \xrightarrow{\delta} B_1'$ then $B_1 \ [> \ B_2 \xrightarrow{\delta} B_1'$

- if $B_2 \xrightarrow{!a} B_2'$ then $B_1 \ [> \ B_2 \xrightarrow{!a} B_2'$ for $a \in \mathcal{A}$

- if $B_2 \xrightarrow{?a} B_2'$ and $B_1 \xrightarrow{?b} B_1'$ then $B_1 \ [> \ B_2 \xrightarrow{?a} B_2'$ for $\{a, b\} \subseteq \mathcal{A}$

In addition, because we interpret the expression only to specify possible signal sequencies the i transitions representing internal actions are just ignored in the conformance definition.

The transition graph gives an operational semantics for the service specification, i.e. it defines the possible action sequences of the service. The nodes of the transition graph are labelled with behaviour expressions and the edges by atomic actions, i.e. elements from the set $\{\delta, i\} \cup \{?a | a \in \mathcal{A}\} \cup \{!a | a \in \mathcal{A}\}$ where δ is the action leading from **exit** to **stop** and i the internal action. Given a node labelled with a behaviour expression the transition system semantics of LOTOS defines which actions are possible and what are the resulting behaviour expressions. The generation of the graph is started with a node labelled by the original behaviour expression, the possible actions in that expression are computed and a new node is generated for each successor. Then the procedure is repeated recursively for the new nodes. To make the construction finite in some cases, nodes with equal labels are identified in the construction as soon as detected. More formally the labelled transition graph of a service definition is defined as follows.

Definition 4.8 *An initialized labelled graph G is a labelled transition graph of the service definition B_0 if and only if*

1. *the initial node of G is labelled by B_0 and*

2. *for each node n of the graph labelled with a behavioural expression B the following holds: n has the successors $n', n'', \ldots, n^{(m)}$ labelled with $B', B'', \ldots, B^{(m)}$ such that the edges $(n, n'), (n, n''), \ldots, (n, n^{(m)})$ are labelled with actions $g', g'', \ldots, g^{(m)}$ respectively if and only if the operational semantics gives to B exactly the possible transitions $B \xrightarrow{g'} B', B \xrightarrow{g''} B'', \ldots,$ and $B \xrightarrow{g^{(m)}} B^{(m)}$.*

The next step in defining conformance between the service definitions and SDL processes is to transform the transition graphs to corresponding ACTs. We suppose that the transition graph is given in the form of a tree, a transition graph can always be unwound to an equivalent transition tree. The ACT differs from the labelled transition tree only in the sense that sending signals is given less emphasis in the former.

As in the case of SDL the nodes of the Asynchronous communication tree are labelled with configurations of the system. However, in the case of service definitions our knowledge of the system is very limited and the configurations cannot be as detailed as in the case of SDL.

The service definition divides the universe into two parts, the provider of the service and the user of the service. Following the construction of ACTs for SDL processes we can here interpret the system to consist of the provider process σ and the environment of the user process ν. The internal structure of σ and ν are not known on basis of the service definition, we only know that their mutual communication should follow the service definition. Comparing with the construction of the ACT for an SDL process it is obvious that the only information we are able to include in the configuration labelling node is the input queue of the service user ν, denoted by q_ν.

The definition of the ACT corresponding to a labelled transition tree can now be given. Roughly speaking there are two differences between the two trees, the output edges of G are replaced with corresponding τ-edges (silent transition) in the ACT and the nodes of the ACT are labelled with queues which represent the queue of the environment.

Definition 4.9 *The ACT corresponding to the labelled transition tree G has exactly the same structure as G and the labels of its nodes and edges are defined as follows:*

1. *The initial node of the ACT is labelled with the empty queue.*

2. *If there is an input edge labelled with ?a in G between two nodes n and n' then in the ACT n and n' are labelled with the same queue and the edge (n, n') has the label a.*

3. *If there is an output edge labelled with !a in G between two nodes n and n' then in the ACT n' is labelled with the queue of n appended with a and the edge (n, n') is labelled with the silent transition τ.*

4. *If there is a δ-edge or an i-edge in G between two nodes n and n' then in the ACT n' is labelled with the same queue as n and the edge (n, n') is labelled with τ.*

4.3   Conformance

Because of the differences in the communication mechanisms in SDL and LOTOS we have to set two additional requirements for an SDL process implementing a service definition. The conditions are used to force the process to consume the signals sent by the user of the service in their order of arrival and not to miss any signal sent by the user of the service. Stated in SDL terms the conditions are the following.

1. The SDL process must not contain states which have a SAVE for some of the signals sent by the user and an INPUT for another signal sent by the user.

2. All states of the SDL process which do not have INPUTs for signals sent by the user must have SAVEs for all the possible signals sent by the user of the service.

Intuitively, to conform with a service definition we want an SDL process to fulfil three conditions. Firstly, everything the SDL process can do must be allowed by the service definition. This is the normal relation between a specification and an implementation. Secondly, the SDL process should at any time be ready to accept any signal which the user of the service according to the definition can send to it at that time. Thirdly, we want the SDL process to carry out its task to an end, i.e. it is not allowed to stop any time it decides to.

To capture the three aspects of conformance we first have to define the observable actions in the Asynchronous communication trees. Because the ACT for the service definition contains only information about the messages input or output by the provider of the service we restrict the observable actions in the ACT for SDL to the corresponding actions. At present assume that the user of the service is behaving correctly, i.e. it is always ready to accept the signals sent by the provider. The notation used in defining conformance is adopted from [2] where it is used to define observational equivalence of LOTOS behavioural expressions.

Definition 4.10 *The observable actions in an ACT for an SDL process are*

1. input from the environment and

2. consumption of a signal by the environment.

The first ones are interpreted as actions ?a where a is the input signal and the second ones as actions !a where a is the consumed signal.

The definition means that actually we interpret the ACT to have the $?a$ and $!a$ labels on the edges corresponding to the observable actions and τ as the label on the other edges corresponding to unobservable actions.

Definition 4.11 *The observable actions in an ACT for a service definition are*

1. *input by the provider of the service and*

2. *output by the provider of the service.*

The first ones are interpreted as actions $?a$ where a is the input signal and the second ones as actions $!a$ where a is the output signal.

Next we define a relation between nodes in an ACT, $n \stackrel{s}{\Longrightarrow} n'$ to mean that there is a path from the node n to the node n' which contains exactly the same observable actions in the same order as s which is a sequence of observable actions. Any number of unobservable actions is allowed on the path before and after any of the observable actions in the sequence.

The ACT of an SDL process conforms to an ACT of a service definition iff there exists a conformance relation R such that the roots of the trees in that order are in the relation R. The concept of a conformance relation is defined as follows.

Definition 4.12 *A binary relation R between nodes of ACT trees is a conformance relation iff for any pair (n_1, n_2) of nodes in R and for any string s of observable actions whenever $n_1 \stackrel{s}{\Longrightarrow} n_1'$ then $n_2 \stackrel{s}{\Longrightarrow} n_2'$ for some n_2' such that*

1. $(n_1', n_2') \in R$,

2. *the set of signals on input edges which can be reached from n_1' by the symmetric, transitive closure of the relation induced by the unobservable actions is the same set as the corresponding set for n_2', and*

3. *if there is no node n_1'' such that $n_1' \stackrel{s'}{\Longrightarrow} n_1''$ where s' is a non-empty sequence of observable actions then there is no node n_2'' such that $n_2' \stackrel{s''}{\Longrightarrow} n_2''$ where s'' is a non-empty sequence of observable actions.*

The different parts of the definition correspond to the three intuitive requirements given to conformance. In the general case an additional problem might be caused by the configurations of the initial nodes of the trees. The label of the initial node of the ACT for the service definition is defined to be the empty queue but in the initial node of the ACT for the SDL the process can already have been sending messages to the queue of the environment. However, a service is defined always to start with an initial message from the user of the service which means that the provider of the service cannot in its start transition send signals to the user.

5   Conclusions

The work presented here is intended to be taken as a stimulus for a discussion on what the relation between LOTOS and SDL is and how they could be used together to the benefit of the people dealing with these formalisms in their everyday work. In an attempt to achieve this we have presented how LOTOS can be transformed into corresponding SDL constructs. A method was also presented on how LOTOS can be incorporated into SDL to provide means to succinctly specify interfaces between SDL processes or blocks of them. These interfaces can also be seen as requirements specifications to blocks. The interface specifications are expressed as LOTOS based behavioural expressions, called service definitions, which can be attached as annotations to an SDL channel that specify, so to speak, the grammar of the signal exchange in that channel. Service definitions thus also tell how the blocks connected by a channel should communicate.

A method how to use service definitions in system design was described in an example. Service definitions provide a requirements view of the system and make the transition from sequence chart descriptions to describing the actual SDL process easier and more rigid. The information they contain can be fully exploited when the actual SDL processes are constructed. Furthermore, service definitions provide several ways that help to modularize and manage a large system. What was not discussed here was their use in automatic test case generation and testing.

In the last section the formalisation of semantics of service definitions was discussed together with concept the of conformance. It is possible to state formally what it means that an SDL process conforms to requirements specifications expressed as service definitions. This lays also the basis for automating the extraction of SDL process description skeletons from service definitions, the checking of conformance and the verification of correct communication when using a service.

References

[1] Agha, G. *ACTORS: A Model of Concurrent Computation in Distributed Systems.* The MIT Press, Cambridge, Massachusetts, 1986.

[2] Bolognesi, T. and Brinksma, E. Introduction to the ISO Specification Language LOTOS. *Computer Networks and ISDN Systems 14* (1987), 25–59.

[3] Grabowski, J. and Rudolph, E. Putting Extended Sequence Charts to Practice. In *SDL '89 The Language at Work (Proceedings of the Fourth SDL Forum, Lisbon, Portugal, 9–13 October, 1989)*, O. Færgemand and M. Marques, Eds., North-Holland, Amsterdam, 1989, pp. 3–10.

[4] Saracco, R., Smith, J., and Reed, R. *Telecommunications Systems Engineering using SDL.* Elsevier Science Publishers B.V., Amsterdam, 1989.

Part 5

Environment Projects

17

An ESF pilot factory for real-time software

Christer Fernström
Cap Gemini Innovation, Grenoble Research Centre,
Grenoble, France

Abstract

The aim of the Eureka Software Factory (ESF) project is to provide the necessary technology in order that software factories may be constructed and tailored from components marketed by independent developers. Over the last three years the project has focused on the definition and the development of the three following aspects of integration technology: *process modelling* as a support for teams and cooperative working, *user interaction technology* supporting the integration between individuals and their support environment and *software bus* as a support for integration of the components of the factory. The emerging technology has consistently been applied in full scale integration experiments. This paper describes one such experimental integration activity, which has resulted in a pilot software factory devoted to the development of real-time software systems. This factory, which has been developed under the working name of "ESF Mini", comprises more then twenty components from eight different development organizations. Integration is supported by prototype versions of a software bus, a factory process engine with tools for process definition and a user interaction environment manager.

The ESF Mini pilot factory supports many common activities of software production, including document preparation, project planning, configuration management, software design, programming and quality control. Furthermore, it supports reuse and the modelling of documents, working procedures and products. Special care has been devoted to the problem of users' interaction with their support environment. The ESF Mini supports process guided user interaction through the concept of "User Work Contexts", which extend the user interface with knowledge about the process in which the user is currently taking part.

1. Background

The Eureka Software Factory (ESF) project [Fernström et al. 89] aims at creating an adequate technical foundation to allow software producers to construct software factories, tailored to meet their specific needs, from components available on the market and provided by independent developers. Over the last three years the main thrust of the ESF project has focused on the definition and the development of the three principal aspects of the ESF integration technology: *process modelling* as a support for teams and cooperative working, *user interaction technology* assisting the integration between individuals and their support environment and *software bus* as a support for integration between the components of the factory.

As a complementary activity, the ESF project has set up a track where the emerging technologies are applied in full scale integration experiments. This track has resulted in several factory demonstrators, including one focussing on information flow between individuals [SI89], one devoted to process guidance and component interoperability [Hubert et al. 90] and one oriented to supporting the development of commercial applications [PEBA90]. This paper addresses the most ambitious work in the experimental track of ESF, which has resulted in a pilot software factory devoted to the development of real-time software systems. This pilot factory, which was developed under the working name of "ESF Mini" was publicly demonstrated in November 1990 [Bégou et al. 90]. It comprises more then twenty components from eight different development organizations of the ESF project. Integration is supported by prototype versions of a software bus, a factory process engine with tools for process definition and a user interaction environment manager.

2. Support Scenario

The ESF Mini pilot factory was constructed over a period of eighteen months. Its aims are twofold: to demonstrate the potential user support in ESF software factories and to validate the architectural principles of ESF in a realistic situation with integration of full fledged CASE tool components. The choice of user support functions was guided by a wish to support a wide range of activities within a realistic software development model, while at the same time limited to functions supported by tools provided by ESF partners.

As a first step, a support scenario was established, describing a realistic development situation where a team of software engineers, managers, quality assurance specialists and documentalists are to develop a fairly complex multi-user application with certain real-time constraints. A fairly simple development model for object oriented development of software for real-time applications in Ada was constructed, based on an example from Booch [Booch87].

The example from Booch was chosen for several reasons: its scope fitted well with the planned support functions of the factory (object oriented design, Ada programming), its was of manageable size but still complex enough to make it interesting (programming-in-the-large) and it was fully documented with its documentation in the "public domain". On the other hand, its focus was merely on pure development activities: requirements specification, design, programming and integration, while management and quality control activities were absent. The original model was thus extended in several ways, mainly with respect to documentation and quality control during all activities, re-use of design and program code, and to the constant interplay between production teams and management.

The final model was subsequently enriched with user functions, mapped to activities and objects to give a clear indication of where data and control integration was necessary. In this way, it could serve as a guideline for the integration work.

3. Factory Functionality

3.1 Roles Supported

The pilot factory is organized around *roles* and *tasks* of software production. A role defines a set of responsibilities within a project context and defines the characteristics a person must have in order to take on the role. Tasks are the activities a role player may be involved in and for which work support is required. The following roles are supported in the Mini pilot:

- **Methods Manager**. Is responsible for defining the development methods (i.e. modelling the process)
- **Project Manager**. Is responsible for workbreakdown, planning, resource allocation, monitoring and tracking of projects.
- **Software Reuse Librarian**. Is responsible for maintaining the library of reusable elements of design and code.
- **Quality Manager**. Is responsible for defining the quality control criteria of all items delivered by the factory.
- **Software Designer**. Is responsible for producing software designs from specifications and requirements.
- **Design Reviewer**. Is responsible for reviewing design documents according to defined quality criteria
- **Programmer**. Is responsible for producing and testing individual code modules from designs, specifications and requirements according to defined quality criteria.
- **Quality Controller**. Is responsible for measuring and controlling the defined quality criteria of code modules.
- **Product Manager**. Is responsible for builds and configurations of products built from code modules and documents.

3.2 Support Functions

Table 1 gives an overview of the support functions available in the ESF Mini factory. The functions are grouped into the three categories: process modelling, process instantiation and process execution. These concepts will be further detailed below (see Section 4.3). For now it is enough to know that "process modelling" refers to the activities of describing the procedures and methods to be used in the factory, "process instantiation" to the act of binding real tasks, people and tools to the models described, and "process execution" to the actual carrying-out of the development tasks.

Modelling	Instantiation	Execution
Development process Documentation Product configurations Coding standards Factory configuration	Workbreakdown, scheduling and resource allocation	Process visualization Document editing Documentation management Product configuration management Object oriented software design Reuse Ada programming in the small Ada programming in the large Coding standards verification Factory configuration management ... (Desktop support from Unix utilities)

Table 1. User support functions in the ESF Mini factory.

4. Inside the Factory

4.1 The Factory Support Environment

The scope of a software factory includes not only the computerised support, but also the organisation, the methods employed by the organisation, the people involved and all the rules that govern the software development process (e.g. quality control criteria). This section describes the inside of the factory: its computerised support - the Factory Support Environment, FSE.

Although in principle applicable to any size of projects and organisations, the principles of ESF software factories are most useful when applied to large project teams, where informal practices for information flow are insufficient. The most appropriate underlying support for such teams is in our opinion based on distributed computing where individual work is supported by workstations (or powerful personal computers) and where work coordination is managed through globally available "services" for configuration management, electronic mail etc.

Requirements for inter-operation and integration between the various parts that together make up the team support environment are very different for different parts of the system. Individual work is characterised by frequent shifts of focus between detailed tasks, each one of which is supported by one or more tools. Shift of focus and information flow between different tools need therefore to be very efficiently supported. From the point of view of individuals it is equally important that redundant re-entry of information is kept to a minimum.

It must also be possible to introduce new tools with minimum effort, i.e. without the need for updating global schemata or recompilation of global system information. The individual work support environments can be seen as islands of tightly integrated parts where global synchronisation with other parts are kept to a minimum.

Between these islands of tight integration circulate information, the flow of which must be carefully controlled and managed by the global rules of the factory. Here, the requirements for integration and inter-operation are more oriented towards access and authentication management and transaction control, and less towards instantaneous interaction. The principal characteristic of the information that flows on this level is its global nature and the fact that it is related to the work of several people.

FSEs are built on a platform that efficiently supports and controls communication of information. All components have programmatic interfaces. In the case of the ESF Mini pilot factory, which mainly is built on Unix, components are Unix processes and their programmatic interfaces consist of procedures which are callable via Remote Procedure Calls (RPC). Component interfaces are described in a "component description language", CDL. It is a longer-term objective that the Software bus should generates the necessary interface code and adapter components from the CDL descriptions of the available components. In the pilot factory these have however been hand crafted and the role of the Software bus is limited to run-time support.

Following the view-model of ESF [ESF89], a software factory can be described in three different views, representing three different perspectives:

- The User View, representing the interaction between the individual and the FSE.

- The Process View, representing the functionality available in the factory, the roles and the tasks.

- The Structural View, representing the internal structure of the FSE: the building blocks, their relationships and their interoperation.

These views represent in turn the perspectives of the individual user, the organization which is supported by the software factory and the two roles of tool provider ("component builder") and integrator ("FSE builder").

4.2 The User View

The User View of the ESF Mini is based on the concepts of *User Interaction Environment* and *User Work Context*. A User Work Context is a user, role and task specific collection of data and tools which may be used and customized (e.g. in terms of look-and-feel) by any individual allocated to the role. The User Interaction Environment is the set of all User Work Contexts available to a user at one point in time, see Figure 1. The ESF Mini features a User Interaction En-

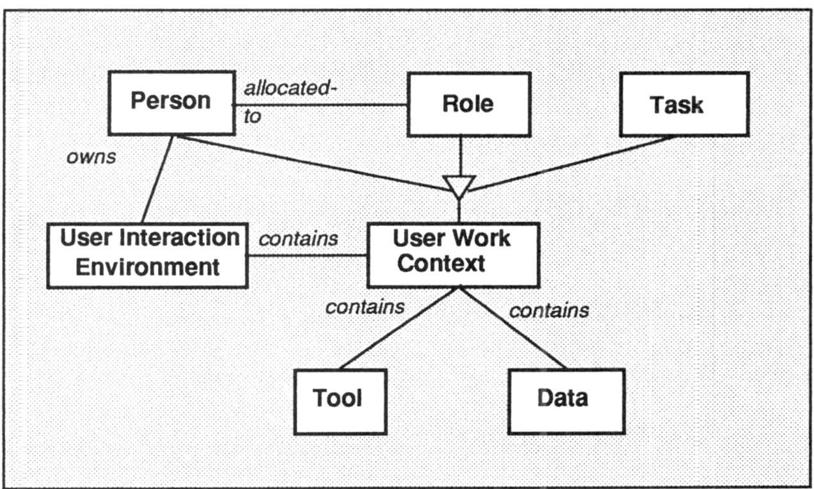

Figure 1.   The User Work Context binds tasks, roles and users
to the adequate tools and data

vironment Manager which allows the creation, the modification, the presentation, the activation, the de-activation and the deletion of User Work Contexts. User Work Contexts are treated as "first-class objects" and may as such be sent between users by means of electronic mail or dispatched to specific users from the "Factory Process Engine" (see 4.3.3). Delegation and subcontracting of work is thus fully supported: if delegation of a task is permitted, this is simply accomplished by sending the corresponding Work Context

The User Work Context is the heart of the user interaction system in the Mini pilot and provides the necessary information to build the advanced user desktops, which are tailored to fit the work the user is currently involved in. The User Interaction Environment Manager is the overall manager of User Work Contexts on the user's workstation and provides a consistent look-and-feel for manipulation of the desktops available to the user.

4.3   The Process View

4.3.1   Modelling the Process

The Process View of an ESF software factory shows the factory support environment as a programmable system; how it is customized to fit the methods of organizations and projects and how the users are to be actively supported, e.g. through the automatic provision of User Work Contexts. Methods are described by means of *Process Models* which describe the relationships between entities of types *Role, Task, Activity, Tool* and *Object* and which serve as templates for task descriptions. The generation of specific descriptions from such templates is referred to as the *instantiation* of Process Models and the result as *Process Programs*.

The Process View of the ESF Mini is supported by a set of tools for manipulation of Process Models and Programs. Activity models are created and modified by means of the OPIUM graph editor. Here, activities are modelled by Petri-net graphs and individual tasks (the atomic elements of OPIUM process models) are linked to object types and tool types. Activities are generic in the sense that they have parameters (e.g. the objects produced by the activity).

4.3.2   Instantiation of processes

Instantiation of task models involves parametrization and binding to the real persons that will work on the tasks. In the Mini pilot, instantiation of task models is done by the PC-PIMS project management support toolset. Workbreakdown in PC-PIMS is done according to the tasks that have been modelled with OPIUM. When resources have been allocated to a task, an instance of the corresponding task model, with all parameters bound, is created and sent to the process execution manager, the *Factory Process Engine*.

4.3.3   Process execution

Process programs are compiled and executed by the Factory Process Engine of OPIUM. As soon as a task becomes active (e.g. is started by the project manager), task information and a description of its default User Work Context is sent to the User Interaction Environment Manager of the concerned users. Project events (e.g. start of task, end of task, synchronization of tasks, exceptions) are processed by the OPIUM Factory Process Engine and, when appropriate, additional information is sent to the concerned User Interaction Environment Managers in order to provide dynamic updates of the users' User Work Contexts.

OPIUM also provides a Process Viewer which serves as a "project cockpit" by allowing to visualize the state of all active Process Programs in the factory.

4.4 The Structural View

The Structural View of the factory describes the implementation of the various building blocks within the framework of an open systems interaction model. The ESF reference architecture is communication oriented, based on client-server and peer-to-peer interoperation. The various functions are provided by *Service Components* which are entities with private address space and which may be allocated over a computer network. The interaction between users and the functions provided by the Service Components is handled by *User Interaction Components*, which are software entities running locally at the users' workstations. Tools in the traditional meaning do not exist as distinct entities, but could be seen as compositions (or bindings) between User Interaction Components and sets of Service Components.

The various aspects of integration between components is managed by the *Software Bus*. This includes:

- the matching of services that are required by one component to those offered by another one

- the provision of new services through combination of services already available

- the communication between components with little structural and semantic loss of information, across heterogeneous language and system platforms

One important question the ESF Mini has tried to address is the degree of coupling that is necessary between components. For various reasons the degree of coupling is inverse to the degree of flexibility: as the coupling becomes tighter, the flexibility with respect to system reconfiguration is reduced. In order to illustrate this, the ESF Mini features two different Software Bus implementations. One providing a high degree of coupling, based on a commercially available, highly efficient Remote Procedure Call mechanism (SUN-RPC); the other which stresses "pluggability" of components and loose coupling, is the result of one of the experimental Software Bus prototypes developed by ESF: HAPPI.

HAPPI uses a Frame based representation mechanism (borrowed from well-known mechanisms of knowledge representation in artificial intelligence) to describe required and offered services, data representation formats, communication primitives and service requests. In the heart of HAPPI sits a Lisp based evaluator of service request which provides dynamic binding between clients and servers. A service request triggers daemon functions of the Frame system, resulting in the correct server binding and transformation of data format as necessary. Once this has been accomplished, the request is forwarded to the server via message passing.

5. Scenario

As an example we will briefly describe the "Ada cluster" of the ESF Mini pilot factory. This denotes of a collection of components that together give comprehensive support for design, re-use, coding and quality control of Ada programs. The overall schema of the Ada cluster part of the ESF Mini is depicted in Figure 2.

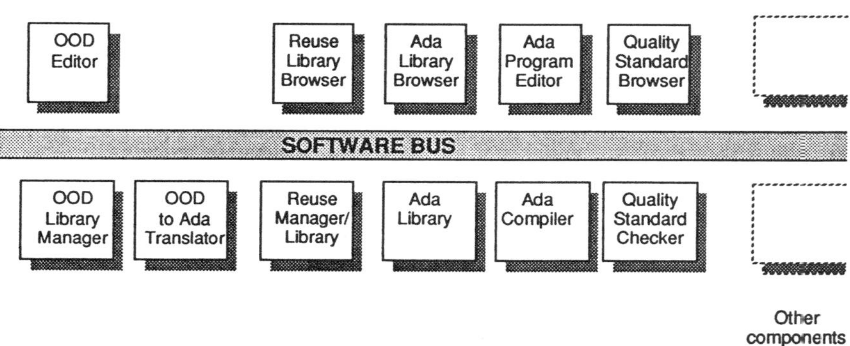

Figure 2.   The components of the Ada Cluster in the ESF Mini. User Interaction Components above the Software Bus and Service Components below.

A graphical object oriented software design support tool is provided through the components *OOD Editor* and *OOD Library*. This tool, which has been built by the ESF FERESA subproject, provides certain extensions to the

HOOD design method. OOD designs are translated into Ada package specification skeletons by means of the *OOD to Ada Translator*.

The Ada reuse tool (components *Reuse Library Browser* and *Reuse Manager/Library*), which has been developed within the ESF subproject ROSE, supports classification, storage, retrieval and integration of Ada reusable elements. Main emphasize has been put on making the retrieval and integration facilities efficient and attractive to use by programmers. Accordingly, the retrieval mechanism accepts Ada package specifications as input (which may have been automatically generated by the *OOD to Ada Translator.*). In order to satisfy a retrieval query, the matching function performs a number of non-trivial transformations on the reusable elements in the library, including instantiation of generic packages, renaming and composition, and reports the most economic combinations of instantiated, renamed packages that satisfy the request. If accepted by the user, the result is forwarded to the Ada editor.

The set consisting of the four components: *Ada Library Browser*, *Ada Program Editor* (for which there in fact are two variants - a syntax directed editor and a standard text editor), *Ada Library* and *Ada Compiler* constitute the principal support for Ada program development in teams and is provided by the EASE subproject of ESF.

Quality control of Ada code is supported by the *Quality Standard Browser* and *Quality Standards Checker* from the SQAW subproject of ESF. This comprises support for verification of user definable coding standards and a number of software measures, including call graphs, control flow analysis, etc.

6. Conclusions

The ESF Mini pilot software factory, which has been built over a period of eighteen months was successfully demonstrated in November 1990. It incorporates more then twenty components provided by eight organizations in the ESF project and gives a realistic view of what a software factory according to the principles of ESF might be. Furthermore, it provides valuable validation of the ESF integration mechanisms, by putting prototypes of these mechanisms into use in a full scale experiment.

The integration mechanisms used for building the ESF Mini pilot factory were those available in the ESF project by early 1990. Since then, considerable progress has been made both in terms of extended functionality and better implementations. A good overview can be found in [ESF90].

Acknowledgements

The list of persons who have positively contributed to the ESF Mini is long:
Karl Hettling, Andrej Mraz, Gro Oftedahl, Claudia Ruf and Anne-Lise Skaar
lay out the initial foundation. Frederic Le Diberder and Pierre Martin did a great
job in early prototyping and clarified the interplay between the Software Bus
and the Process Engine. Didier Bloch, Gerald Perdreau and Bertrand Rousseau
designed and implemented the HAPPI software bus. Frederic Fournier and Lau-
rence Hubert designed and implemented the OPIUM process support functions.
Anders Bremer and Norma King designed and implemented the User Interaction Environment Manager. The difficult task of making the Mini work converge into one integrated system was successfully managed by Philippe Bégou
and Eric de Torcy. Numerous other people were involved in building components or re-engineering existing CASE tools to fit into the ESF Mini. For this
important contribution the following ESF subprojects are recognised: EASE,
FERESA, HAPPI, ROSE, SCM, SQAW and TWIST.

References

[Bégou et al.90]   Philippe Bégou, Eric de Torcy, *ESF Real-Time Factory*, ESF Seminar,
                      Berlin, November 1990. ESF, Hohenzollerndamm 152, D-1000 Berlin
                      33, West Germany.

[Booch87]   Grady Booch: *Software Engineering with Ada*, 2nd edition, 1987.

[ESF89]   ESF Technical Design Group: *ESF Technical Reference Guide*, Version
                      1.1, ESF project technical report, 1989, ESF, Hohenzollerndamm 152,
                      D-1000 Berlin 33, West Germany

[ESF90]   ESF, *ESF Project Report,* November 1990, ESF, Hohenzollerndamm
                      152, D-1000 Berlin 33, West Germany.

[Fernström et al. 90] Christer Fernström, Lennart Ohlsson, *ESF - An Approach to Industrial
                      Software Production*, in Software Engineering Environments-Research
                      and Practice, ed. K.H. Bennett, Ellis Horwool Books in Information
                      Technology, 1989

[Hubert et al. 90]]   Hubert, L., Perdreau, G.: *Software Factory: Using Process Modeling for
                      Integration Purposes*, First International Conference on Systems Inte-
                      gration, Morristown, April 1990

[PEBA90]   PEBA: *ESF Business Factory*, ESF Seminar, Berlin, November 1990.
                      ESF, Hohenzollerndamm 152, D-1000 Berlin 33, West Germany.

[SI89]   SI: *SITE - SI Team Environment - How to Support Cooperation in
                      Teams*, Technical Report May 1989, SI, P.O Box 124 Blindern, 0314
                      Oslo, Norway.

18

ESF/PEBA A flexible and integrated factory
to support business application production

Marcel Franckson
Sema Group SA, 16 Rue Barbès, F–92126 Montrouge, France

1. Context and Objectives of ESF-PEBA.

1.1 Introduction.

ESF, the Eureka Software Factory project is a major European project in the area of software engineering.

Fourteen European companies and research institutions of 6 European countries have built a consortium to tackle the strategic problem of improving the efficiency and quality of software production. They aim at bringing to the market place a comprehensive set of products and solutions in an open environment.

One sub-project of ESF is PEBA (Production Environment for Business Applications), which has the objective to build comprehensive, flexible and integrated factory support environments supporting many methods, based on the ESF architecture and technology.

1.2 Context of ESF-PEBA.

A high percentage of the currently developed software belongs to the area of business applications (banking, insurance, manufacturing, trade and distribution, administration, governmental agencies, utilities, etc.). Several inter-related problems have been identified in this area: the difficulty to produce efficiently good quality software, the difficulty to control and manage projects, the backlog, the shortage of programmers, the lack of software reuse, the difficulty to codify and communicate the know-how ...

It is now recognised that this software crisis can only be overcome by a software industrial revolution [COX]. A comparison with similar situations in other industries [SHA] has suggested that this revolution should be characterised by the emergence of a true Software Engineering discipline. Such an engineering discipline is characterised by a synergy between commercial practices and a sufficiently mature science.

The same study [SHA] states that although "software engineering is not yet a true engineering discipline, it has the potential to become one" and we are close to the point where commercial practices may benefit from scientific knowledge. ESF PEBA provides a meeting point where this merge of science and industry will happen. PEBA offers a unique opportunity to gather the most advanced scientific knowledge existing within ESF and the most valuable commercial experience brought by the PEBA partners.

1.3   Objectives and characteristics of PEBA.

One of the notorious problems that keep development cost high and efficiency low is that comprehensive and flexible tool support for development is still rare. There is currently no integrated computer system supporting the complete software development process. Moreover, most tools are not adaptable enough to the wide variety of methods that can be found in software development organisations.

The main objective of PEBA sub-project is to create an integrated factory support environment (in short FSE) suitable to business application development, built upon ESF architecture. PEBA FSE is designed to fulfil an organisational objective: efficient production of quality software. Possible customers of PEBA FSE will be software houses as well as end users who develop their own software.

Within the overall PEBA universe, we distinguish between two large areas of concern: the production environment in which PEBA itself runs, and the target environment in which the software produced by a PEBA FSE runs. PEBA will provide a comprehensive, integrated and adaptable FSE for common business application production, keeping in mind possible target environments.

The components of the PEBA FSE cooperate in order to support the three basic functions of a software production factory:

- software production which is the objective of a factory;

- software production control;

- management of information about the produced applications and the projects.

These functions may be more or less automated, ranging from fully automated activities to interactive aids to the PEBA FSE user. The PEBA sub-project focuses mainly on the functional integration of components of the FSE and the additional functions that can be implemented thanks to the integration. The improvement of the components is also addressed in PEBA, although it is not its primary objective to develop components. Indeed, there are several strategies to get components: get them from other ESF sub-projects, from the partners, from the market, or develop them within the PEBA sub-project itself.

The characteristics of a PEBA FSE are full integration of its components, adaptability to various methods and software development process models (at least Merise, SSADM, and any European Standard Method that could appear in the early 90's), open-endedness to components coming from the market or the partners, comprehensibility (coverage of the whole life cycle and activity types), user-friendliness, compliance with ESF standards and kernel components, support of evaluation of its instances.

The other important objective of PEBA sub-project is to contribute to the requirements to other ESF sub-projects and to provide a validation of ESF concepts, standards and architecture.

PEBA is research and product oriented. The research mainly concerns the integration of components and requirements for plug-in mechanisms. The products appear at three different stages:

- demonstrators based upon existing products.

- PEBA for the ESF mini, which is a first version of a complete FSE based upon existing products;

- first PEBA production version which fully conforms with ESF architecture.

2. The Factory Model according to the General System Theory.

2.1 Introduction.

The General System Theory addresses the issue of complex system modelling. Important contributions have been made by Von Bertalanffy, K.E. Boulding, H. Simon, H. Von Foerster, E. Morin, J.L. Lemoigne, J. Meleze, etc... According to this theory, a System is [LEM]:

- an identifiable and structured thing,

- acting in an environment,

- according to some goal (finality) with respect to the environment,

- stable but nevertheless evolving in order to preserve its capability to reach its goal.

Beyond a certain level of complexity, the System must be controlled by a sub-system able to make decisions on its actions and its evolution. These decisions are made using symbolic information stored in a memory. The cycle information-decision-action-information ensures a feedback which allows the System to achieve its goals and to be preserved in a changing environment.

A Software Factory is such a System: it is an organisation of people and computers for which the goal is software development. According to the General System Theory, it contains:

- a **Production System** - its purpose is to fulfil the goals of the whole factory with respect to its environment.

- a **Decision System** - its purpose is to control, regulate and adapt the Production System through feed-backs of information produced within the Production System and the environment,

- an **Information System** - its purpose is to manage the information about the factory and its environment necessary for the Decision System to play its role. It is the interface between the Production System and the Decision System.

Each of these sub-systems, in its turn, may be considered as a System and can be represented as containing a production system, a decision system, and an information system. The model looks like a Russian puppet.

The General System model has to be taken as a conceptual framework and does not necessarily match the physical structure of the factory, namely its decomposition into components. But this conceptual framework is a very rational and useful support for understanding and designing a factory.

2.2 The Factory Model.

The model described here is using a data flow diagram technique adapted from Meleze [MEL].

Four types of flow are used:

- **technological flows**: they carry the products that are transformed, assembled, decomposed or produced by the Production System; although in a Software Factory, everything is "information", they may be considered as the flow of material undergoing a transformation from the raw material up to the finished product.

- **operational flows**: they carry the information which is necessary or useful to perform the activities of the Production System, like the required knowledge, some information about the execution of an activity which impacts another activity, some information which helps in executing an activity although it is not part of the technological flow.

- **informational flows**: they carry information about the products and the processes of the System; most of them are going to or coming out of the Information System.

- **control flows**: they carry the decisions sent by a Decision System to a Production System or to a lower level Decision System.

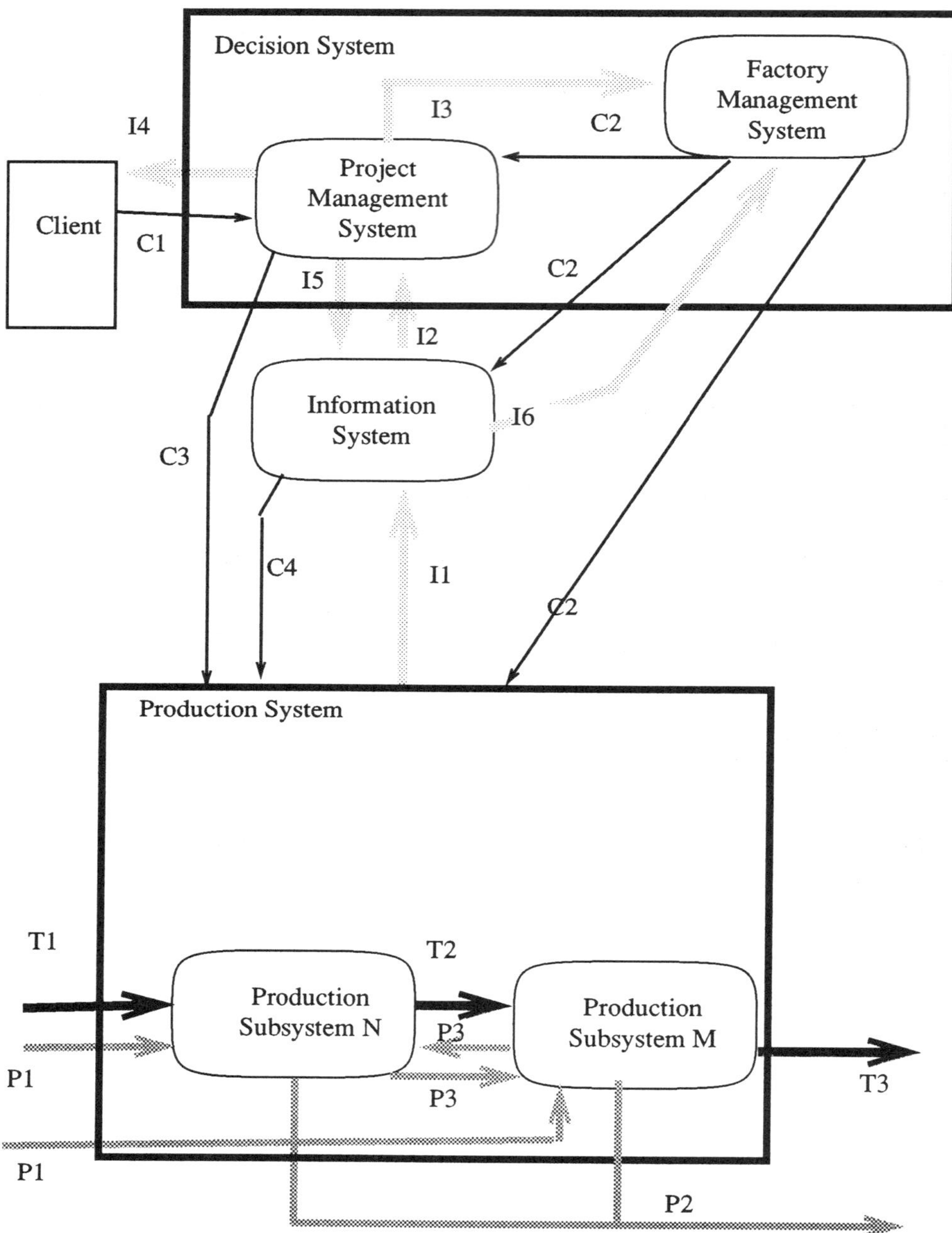

Decision System
Factory Management System
Project Management System
Client
Information System
Production System
Production Subsystem N
Production Subsystem M
I4
I3
C2
C1
C2
I5
I2
C3
C4
I6
I1
C2
T1
T2
T3
P1
P1
P3
P3
P2

2.2.1   Description of the Main Technological Flows.

T1:

main technological flow going from the environment to a Production Subsystem (requirement analysis function and other functions needing inputs from the environment);
Typical information contained:
- existing systems of the end-user (usually the client) and their environment;
- end-user requirements.

T2:

main technological flow between Production Subsystems.
Typical information contained:
- products resulting from a production activity and required by another production activity.

T3:

main technological flow going from a Production Subsystem to the environment.
Typical information contained:
- products going to the end-user (usually the client) and possibly the environment

2.2.2 Description of the Main Operational Flows.

P1:

operational flow going from the environment to a Production Subsystem.
Typical information contained:
- operational information about existing systems of the end-user (usually the client) and their environment;
- operational information about the end-user requirements;
- operational information about the available technology.

P2:

operational flow going from a Production Subsystem to the environment.
Typical Information contained:
- operational information about products or activities necessary or useful for the end-user, which are not part of a technological flow.

P3:

operational flow between the Production Subsystems.
Typical Information contained:
- operational information about products or activities necessary or useful for a future activity, which are not part of a technological flow.

2.2.3 Description of the Main Informational Flows.

I1:

informational flow going from the Production System to the Information System.
Typical Information contained:
- information about products;
- information about activities;
- information about resources.

I2:

informational flow going from the Information System to the Project Management System
Typical Information contained:
- information about products;
- information about activities;
- information about resources.

I3:

informational flow going from the Project Management System to the Factory Management System.
Typical Information contained:
-report on the use of the methods, tools, etc...

I4:

informational flow going from the Project Management System to the Client
Typical Information contained:
- project report;
- quality report.

I5:

informational flow going from the Project Management System to the Information System.
Typical Information contained:
-    objectives and constraints on the products (characteristics, quality, time schedule, etc...);
- decision about the high-level processes (plan, time schedules, costs, etc..);
- decisions about resource allocation.

I6:

informational flow going from the Information System to the Factory Management System.
Typical Information contained:
- statistical data related to product types and process types.

2.2.4 Description of the Main Control Flows.

C1:

control flow going from the Client to the Project Management System.
Typical Information contained:
- objectives and constraints on the project and on the products.

C2:

control flow going from the Factory Management System to the Project Management System, to the Information System, to the Production System.
Typical Information contained:
- methods (process models, techniques, models, rules, heuristics, knowledge,
standards, metrics, quality plan, ...);
- organisational structure;
- tool support.

C3:

control flow going from the Project Management System to the Production System.
Typical Information contained:
- objectives and constraints on the products (characteristics, quality, time
schedule, etc...);
- resource allocation;
- high-level processes (plan, time schedules, costs, etc...)

C4:

control flow going from the Information System to the Production System.
Typical Information contained:
- objectives and constraints on the low-level processes (characteristics, sequence constraints, time schedules, etc...), which constitute the process guidance.

2.3 The Production System.

The production system fulfils the goals of the factory.
It supports through its **sub-systems** the following tasks: requirements analysis,
specification, logical design, physical design, code production and integration,
tests, implementation, maintenance, and analytical quality assurance.

The following typology of activity is established :

1. Requirements analysis.
Collects and structures the requirements.

2. Design.
Makes models of a system (software application).
It contains the following sub-types of activity :
Creating, modifying - creates and modifies a model,
Mapping - translates a model into a lower abstraction level (code generation is a special case of mapping),
Reverse engineering - translates a model into a higher abstraction level,
Refining - details some part of a model in another model,
Integrating - makes a model of an aggregate using the models of its components,
Reusing - reuses a model into another one,
Analysing - ensures that the model is syntactically correct,
Cross-checking - controls consistency between two different types of model,
Tracking - ensures consistency between models of different abstraction levels,
Testing - generates test data and test environments and execute tests,
Evaluating and optimizing - evaluates a model against some pre-defined criteria, and optimises the model after evaluation,
Simulating - simulates the functioning of a model.

3. Analytical Quality Assurance.
Controls the products to meet the specified quality standards.
It contains the following sub-types of activity :
Static Analysis - measures the system up according to given metrics measurements,
Checks - reviews, inspections, walk-through,
Dynamic Analysis - functional, performance, reliability tests,
Simulation - helps to consolidate the requirements or verifies the feasibility of the product.

2.4 The Decision System.

The decision system controls, regulates and adapts the production system through feed-backs of information produced within the production system and the environment. It is frequent to have hierarchical decision systems. In a factory three levels are recognised :

1. **Factory Management**: responsible for the adaptation of the factory.
It includes:
- **The definition of the method** - process models, techniques, models, rules, heuristics, knowledge, standards, quality properties assigned to product types, metrics, quality plan.
- **The definition of the organisational structure of the factory;**
- **The definition of the FSE** (Factory Support Environment) including the tool support.

2. Project Management: responsible for the high-level control of the software production project. It may also perform some adaptations (method, organisation, tool support) specific to the project.

It involves miscellaneous activities: planning, scheduling, allocating resource, budgeting, forecasting, evaluating, estimating risk, simulating the consequences of decisions, monitoring, controlling cost, controlling the quality of the products, etc..

3. Process Guidance: responsible for the low-level control and regulation of the software production project. It is usual to include it in the Information System because it involves generally decisions of an algorithmic nature.

2.5 The Information System.

The information system is gathering, managing and storing information on the products and the processes of the system. This includes information about configuration and version of the products and quality data associated with the products.

The information is used for three purposes:

1. To support and to guide the processes of the production system by simulating and anticipating its normal functioning: this is the Process Guidance;

2. To provide the information required by the project management system to perform his activities (current state of the project and history, statistics, etc...).

3. To provide the information required by the factory management system to perform his activities (tuning of methods and tools, etc...).

3. Requirements to an ESF-PEBA FSE.

The previous section was concerned with Software Production Factories; this section is concerned with Factory Support Environments abbreviated as FSE. The FSE is defined in the ESF Technical Reference Manual [ESF].

"The collection of all computerized support available to a person in a Factory is called a user support environment. Through the user support environment, the user is able to perceive and, with appropriate tools, manipulate the different objects he needs to perform his tasks....The term Factory Support Environment, or FSE for short, is the collection of all, possibly overlapping user support environments in a Factory." [ESF]

PEBA has established requirements to a FSE for Business Application Production.

The main requirements to a PEBA FSE are the following:

1) it enhances development **productivity** and target software **quality**.

2) it is fully **integrated**: the components cooperate with each other and with other ESF components in the framework of ESF architecture (Software Bus, Factory Process Engine, User Interface Services).

3) it is **open**: it can be extended to other components coming from the PEBA partners or from the market; components may be substituted with new versions or different

components fulfilling the same function; in other words, components are pluggable to the FSE.

4) it is **open to the future**: no future technological advances are excluded from PEBA; in particular it should be possible to include components based upon artificial intelligence technologies.

5) it is **comprehensive**: it addresses all classes of functions that are used over the entire development life cycle. Not only production functions, but also management functions and quality assurance functions are addressed.

6) it is **flexible**: it is adaptable to the application developer methodology and environment; in particular it does not impose any constraint on the use of the methods and formalisms that are currently found in the business application production area (Merise, SSADM, SA/SD, etc.); neither does it impose any constraint on the software development process (waterfall model, evolutionary model, transform model, spiral model, fountain model, etc.); it must then be designed with a great genericity.

7) it provides a **flexible guidance**: it offers a control of the software development process (process guidance and project management), but the level of guidance, from strong to weak, may be customised; it is considered that helping the users of the FSE is better than controlling them.

8) it is **user-friendly**: user interfaces must be seamless and consistent if required. User-friendliness means also a possibility to tailor the FSE to the type of user: application developer, project manager, quality controller, end-user, etc.

9) it is **reliable**: PEBA FSE makes use of the ESF mechanisms to ensure reliability, security, confidentiality and integrity of the products.

10) it supports **reusability**: it uses ESF (and industry standard) mechanisms aimed at reusability of software components.

11) it supports **measurements and evaluations**: it contains a set of components in charge of measuring and evaluating a specific software production environment.

12) it can support **complex factories**: the FSE supports multi-users, multi-roles, multi-sites, multi-projects factories.

13) it is **product-centric and not process-centric** [COX]: the products of a process and its goals in terms of product characteristics are considered more important than the process itself; although this statement is rational, it is not shared by the whole software community; however, process-centric software universe is more and more criticised [COX] and modern methodologies like SSADM Version 4 [SSA] are definitely putting more emphasis on products than on processes.

14) it supports an **integrated product and process management including configuration and version management**: although the FSE is product-centric, the processes are not ignored, but they have to be related with the products.

These requirements may be summarised by saying that PEBA FSE is user-centric and product-centric, integrated and flexible.

4. Architecture of PEBA FSE.

PEBA FSE is based on the ESF architecture. It demonstrates advanced ESF technology for integration from three points of view:

Interaction: human to technology. Integration between people and tools. The FSE user gets its objects in his working context. He/she can only perform the available actions on them according to the object state, his/her role and authorisations. Once the action has been selected, the appropriate tool is executed.

Interworking: human to human. Integration between people by coordinating their development process.

Interoperation: technology to technology. Integration between tools by sharing data via the Inter-Component Data Transfer.

All 3 aspects of integration technology put requirements on components to be used in an ESF context.

ESF tools separate concerns for user interaction, implemented in User Interaction Components (UIC), from functionality, implemented in Service Components (SC). ESF tools are built by configuration of inter-operating components, which communicate via the Software Bus (SWB).

The control of the software development process and the integration of the user interface are respectively performed by two Components, the User Interaction Environment (UIE) implemented within PEBA FSE through the Process Guidance Interface and the Factory Process Engine (FPE) implemented within PEBA FSE through the Process Guidance Monitor.

The ESF PEBA FSE is one of the first software factory prototypes which realize the ESF architecture.

5. Bibliography.

[COX] Brad J. Cox, "Planning the Software Industrial Revolution", IEEE Software ,November 1990.

[ESF] ESF Technical Design Group, ESF Technical Reference Manual, Version 1.1, ESF paper (1989)

[LEM] Lemoigne J-L, "Theorie du Systeme General", P.U.F., (1984)

[MEL] Meleze J., L'analyse modulaire des systemes de gestion. A.M.S", Edition Hommes et Techniques

[SHA] Mary Shaw, "Prospects for an Engineering Discipline of Software", IEEE Software, November 1990.

[SSA] SSADM 4 Reference Manual, NCC Publication, (1990).

19

An overview of the Mjølner BETA System

Lars Bak, Claus Nørgaad and Elmer Sandvad
Mjølner Informatics ApS, Science Park Århus,
Gustav Wiedsvej 10, DK–8000 Århus C, Denmark

Jørgen Lindskov Knudsen* and Ole Lehrmann Madsen*
Computer Science Department, Århus University, Ny Munkegade 116,
DK–8000 Århus C, Denmark

* Also at Mjølner Informatics

Introduction

The Mjølner BETA System is a highly integrated programming environment
for object oriented programming. The objective is to support development
of large, efficient industrial programs. The Mjølner BETA System is a result
of the Scandinavian research project Mjølner.

The Mjølner BETA System includes an implementation of the BETA
programming language [8, 7]. In addition it includes a set of grammar-based
tools, which can be used for any formal language that is defined by a context-
free grammar. The grammar-based tools include a hyper structure editor, a
metaprogramming system, and a fragment system.

The BETA programming language is a block structured, strongly typed
object oriented programming language. The language supports procedural,
object oriented, concurrent and to some extent functional programming.

The hyper structure editor is an integrated text and syntax-directed editor with extensive facilities for abstract presentation, browsing, and hypertext. The hypertext facility combined with structure editing of documents
makes the editor particularly well suited to support program documentation. Furthermore, an graphical extension to the hyper structure editor is
currently being developed such that the editor can be used as an integrated

diagram editor, too. The diagram editor will inherit all facilities from the hyper structure editor.

The fragment system makes it possible to split a program into arbitrary modules called fragments. This is used to share code in the form of libraries. In addition it is used to split a program into an interface part and an implementation part. For a class it is thus possible to separate the description of the interface from the description of the implementation. Since a fragment may have several different implementation parts, the fragment system also supports having several variants of a program.

The metaprogramming system defines a unique representation of programs in the form of a set of classes defined by the abstract syntax of the language. This makes it possible to write programs that manipulate other programs. In addition application programs may manipulate programs by means of this representation. The metaprogramming system has been designed to allow for "Lisp-like" representation of programs as data.

The system includes a system browser, a source level debugger, a graphics system, an user interface system, an application builder, a general interface to the underlying operating system and interface to external routines.

The Mjølner BETA System is grammar-based, implying that most components of the system exists in the form of tool generators, that given a context-free grammar for a language, will generate a language specific tool.

All tools in the Mjølner BETA System (including the compiler) are written in BETA (except the run-time system and a few other routines written in C and assembly language). The Mjølner BETA System is implemented under Macintosh and UNIX workstations. The Macintosh version is implemented under MacOS and MPW for MacII series workstations. The UNIX versions uses the X Window System and is available for SUN3 series workstations, Apollo DN3500 series workstations and HP9000 series workstations.

1 Overview of the Mjølner BETA System

The Mjølner BETA System is an *integrated* and *interactive* programming environment with support for industrial object oriented programming.

The integration of the various tools in the Mjølner BETA System is established by insisting that all tools in the system utilizes one single representation of the program. This representation is abstract syntax trees (ASTs). All manipulations of the ASTs by the various tools are done, utilizing the metaprogramming system, which defines an interface to the AST, and ways to manipulate the AST. The overall structure of the Mjølner BETA System

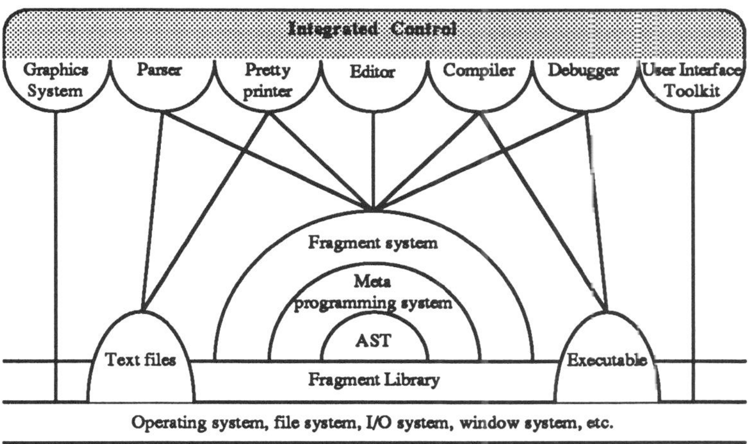

Figure 1: Mjølner BETA System overview

is illustrated in figure 1.

The Mjølner BETA System is based on the notion of *program fragment* (or just *fragment*). The notion of fragments is based on the context-free grammar for the programming language. In principle, any sentence derived from any nonterminal in the grammar may be a fragment. Nonterminals are the natural units of the syntax-directed editor. Fragments and nonterminals are the units of manipulation in major parts of the entire system, and the BETA compiler translates BETA fragments into native code. The system is also using fragments as a powerful notion of separate compilation, that enables the system to ensure full consistency across compilation units. This enables the programmer to make changes to the program, and the system will only compile or check the affected compilation units.

The hyper structure editor is a highly interactive tool for manipulating fragments. The user interface toolkit and graphics system is available to the application programmer in order to support the development of highly interactive and graphical applications by means of the Mjølner BETA System.

2   A Grammar-based System

Major parts of the system (e.g. editor, parser, pretty-printer, metaprogramming system, fragment system) are grammar-based in the sense that tool generators exists that given a specific grammar for a language will define

a specific tool, that is able to manipulate programs written in that specific
language. Such language specific tools have been generated for the BETA language, and form the basis for the Mjølner BETA System. Furthermore, the
generators have been used to create tools for Simula, Modula, SQL, OSDL,
Pascal, FelixPascal and others.

A variant of context-free grammars, called *structured context-free grammars*, are used for specifying the context-free syntax. Structured context-free
grammars are like ordinary BNF grammars except that productions must be
one of:

```
<A>    ::=    w0 <t1:A1> w1 ...   <tn:An> wn    construction rule
<A>    ::|    <A1> | <A2> | ...  | <An>          alternation rule
<A>    ::*    <B> w                              list zero rule
<A>    ::+    <B> w                              list one rule
<A>    ::?    <B>                                optional rule
```

where `<A>` denotes nonterminals, `<t:B>` denotes nonterminals with a tag-
name, and `w` denotes terminals. A construction rule specifies that the nonterminal on the left-hand side of the rule may be replaced by the string `w0`
`<t1:A1>` `w1` ...   `<tn:An>` `wn`. An alternation rule specifies that the nonterminal on the left-hand side of the rule may be replaced by either of the
nonterminals `<A1>`, ..., `<An>` on the right-hand side. A list zero rule specifies
that the nonterminal on the left-hand side of the rule may be replaced by
zero or more instances of the nonterminal on the right-hand side, separated
by the string `w` (i.e. nothing, `<B>`, `<B>` `w` `<B>`, `<B>` `w` `<B>` `w` `<B>`, etc.). A
list one rule is like the list zero rule, except that there must be at least one
element in the list. An optional rule specifies that the nonterminal on the
left-hand side of the rule may either be replaced with nothing or by the nonterminal on the right-hand side. A nonterminal may only appear once on the
left-hand side of a production.

In the rest of this paper, we will use the BETA language as the vehicle
for all examples and describe the grammar-based tools by describing the
BETA specific tools, generated from the tool generators. Nearly all that
is said about these tools apply to all tools being generated from the tool
generators. The exceptions are the static semantic parts and the integration
with the BETA compiler. This implies, that in order to create a highly
integrated environment based on these tool generators (like the BETA specific
environment), one needs cooperation with the compiler.

An example of a BETA program is given in figure 2. The program defines
three identifiers: **Private**, **Push** and **Pop**. **Private** is a static object (caused
by the **©**), and **Push** and **Pop** are routines. **Push** takes one **integer** argument. Special grammar symbols are shown enclosed by `<<` and `>>`. These

```
(#
  Private: @<<SLOT Private:Descriptor>>;

  Push: (# e: @integer
         enter e
         do <<SLOT Push:Descriptor>>
         #);
  Pop: (# <<Attributes>> <<...ActionPart...>> #);
  <<Attributes>>
#)
```

Figure 2: Example of a BETA program

symbols are called *placeholders*. Placeholders are always associated with a
nonterminal of the grammar. A placeholder may have a tag-name in order to
be able to distinguish between several instances of the same nonterminal in
a program. I.e. `<<Push:Descriptor>>` is a placeholder, where **Descriptor**
specifies the syntactic category and **Push** is the tag-name.

Generally, programs may contain placeholders of three different types:
nonterminals, slots or *contractions*. Nonterminals and slots denote unex-
panded nonterminals of the underlying grammar, whereas contractions denote expanded nonterminals.

Nonterminals (e.g. `<<Attributes>>`) are indications that these parts of
the program have not been specified yet. The ability to handle nonterminals
in a program is the means for allowing syntax-directed editing.

Slots (e.g. `<<SLOT Push:Descriptor>>`) are indications of parts of the
program that deliberately have been kept open. Slots are the means for
modularization of a program in order to support information hiding and
separate compilation. The program parts to by located in slots will reside
in another fragment. The fragment system for BETA (which takes care of
slots) will be described in section 3.

Contractions (e.g. `<<...ActionPart...>>`) are placeholders indicating
that this part of the program, derived from the nonterminal, is not shown.
I.e. contractions are a means for suppressing details that are present in the
program. Note that contractions may suppress other placeholders, i.e. within
a contraction, nonterminals, slots and other contractions may reside.

3   The Fragment System

The foundation of the fragment system is syntax-directed program modularization as described in [6]. Syntax-directed program modularization is a very general principle for program modularization. The fragment system is a concrete, but limited implementation of syntax-directed program modularization, applied to the BETA programming language. The aim of the fragment system is to support modularization, information hiding and separate compilation of programs.

The basic level of the environment is the fragment library, that is the storage system for fragments. The fragment system is language independent implying that modularization, information hiding and separate compilation need not be defined as part of the programming language.

The fragment system supports:

Modularization and Information Hiding: The fragment system enables the programmer to define the granularity of modularization and information hiding that suits his particular problem. Fragments are the modules of the Mjølner BETA System and fragments are any legal derivation, implying that both coarse- and fine-grained modularization is possible.

Separation of the interface and the implementation: The programmer may define fragments containing the interface definition of a program part and other fragments defining the implementation part. One implication hereof is that the interface of a class may be separated from its implementation.

Variant control: There may be several implementation fragments corresponding to, say, a class specification. This facility may be used to support variants of a program.

Separate compilation: Fragments are the basic entities handled by the compiler. Fragments may be separately compiled. When a fragment is compiled, all fragments it is depending on will be checked for modifications in the source code since last compilation of these fragments, and if such changes have been made, these fragments will be automatically recompiled.

Code sharing: In general the mechanism is useful for splitting programs into parts that may be shared by several other program parts. This is a useful and orthogonal feature to the class/sub-class mechanism.

3.1   Fragments

The modularization language is called the *fragment language*, since it describes the organization of programs in terms of *fragments*. (The notion

	Nonterminal	Derived string
1.	<<Attributes>>	P: (# a,b: @char #);
2.	<<Descriptor>>	(# a,b,c: @char enter(a,b) <<DoPart>> exit c #)
3.	<<DoPart>>	do a*b->c

Figure 3: Nonterminals and corresponding derived forms

```
Foo: (# a,b,c: @char
       enter(a,b,c)
       do a*b->c
       exit c
     #)
```

Figure 4: The Foo form

of fragment will be introduced below.) The fragment language is used for communicating with the fragment system, which is the component of the Mjølner BETA System that handles storing and manipulation of fragments. The terms fragment language and fragment system are used interchangeably when this causes no confusion.

The fragment language is independent of the language that is used for specifying the programs that are manipulated by the fragment system. The principles behind the fragment language can be used to describe modularization of most programming languages. The fragment language is *grammar-based*. The idea is that any correct sequence of terminal and nonterminal symbols defined by the grammar is a legal module (i.e. fragment). The fragment language describes how such strings may be combined into larger strings. The fragment language is presented here using a graphical syntax, though the fragment language also has a textual syntax which is currently used by the Mjølner BETA System. A future version of the Mjølner BETA System will include support for a graphical syntax like the one used in this paper.[1]

3.1.1   Forms

A string of terminal and nonterminal symbols derived from a nonterminal **A** is called an **A**-*form*[2] or sometimes just a *form*. The derived strings in figure 3 are all examples of forms.

Forms are the basic elements used to define modules in the Mjølner BETA System. Consider e.g. the forms 2 and 3 in figure 3. By substituting the DoPart nonterminal of form 2 by form 3 we get the form in figure 4.

---

[1] In addition to the use of graphical syntax, the fragment language described in this paper is slightly more general than the actual implementation. For details, see the Mjølner BETA System manuals.

[2] In formal language theory, this is called a *sentential form*.

```
<<form Counter:Attributes>>
Counter: (#
  Up: (# n: @ Integer
        enter n
          <<SLOT Up:DoPart>>
        #);
  Down: (# n: @ Integer
          <<SLOT Down:DoPart>>
        exit n
        #)
#)
```

Figure 5: `Counter` fragment form

```
<<form Up:DoPart>>
do n+7->n
<<form Down:DoPart>>
do n-5->n
```

Figure 6: A fragment group

3.1.2 Slots

In the Mjølner BETA System, several tools manipulate forms, but not all
nonterminals are necessarily to be used by the fragment system. The nonterminals used by the fragment language are the *slots* since they define openings
where other forms may be inserted.

Forms may contain slots, and the fragment langage contains constructs
for binding slot names with forms, thus combining forms into composite forms
and eventually complete programs.

Slot names and program names belong to different languages. There is
thus no possibility of confusing program names and slot names. In figure 5
there is a routine called `Push` and a slot called `Push`. As we shall see later it
is convenient to use identical names in this manner.

3.1.3 Fragment Form

In the fragment language, each form must be given a name and its syntactic
category must be specified. A *fragment form* is a form associated with a
name and a syntactic category. Figure 5 shows a fragment form. `Counter`
is the name of the fragment form, `Attributes` is the syntactic category, and
`Counter:  (# ...  #)` is a form (i.e. a string of terminal and nonterminal
symbols derived from `Attributes`).

3.1.4 Fragment Group

It is often convenient to define a set of logically related fragment forms together. For this purpose it is possible to define a group of fragments, called
a *fragment group*. [3] The syntax of a fragment group is shown in figure 6. It

---

[3]The term *fragment* will be used to refer to either a fragment form og a fragment group.
No confusion should be possible.

```
 location /home/smith/CounterBody
 origin /home/smith/Counter
 <<form Up:DoPart>>
 do n-7->n
 <<form Down:DoPart>>
 do n-5->n
```

Figure 7: The `CounterBody` group

```
Counter: (#
  Up: (# n: @ Integer
        enter n
        do n+7->n
        #);
  Down: (# n: @ Integer
          do n-5->n
          exit n
          #)
#)
```

Figure 8: Extent of `CounterBody`

defines two fragment forms. The name of fragment forms are Up and Down, both with syntactic categories DoPart and the actual fragment forms are do n+7->n and do n-5->n.

3.1.5 Fragment Library

The fragment system handles the storing of fragments in a library, called *the fragment library*. The fragment library is usually implemented on top of a file system or a data base system. The fragment language refers to fragments stored in the fragment library. A fragment resides in a specific *location* in the fragment library. Fragments are named using a hierarchical naming scheme in the style of UNIX or Macintosh file systems. The location of a fragment is given by means of a hierarchical name. The name /home/smith/Counter denotes a fragment Counter. Counter resides in the directory /home/smith. In the following examples, the location of a fragment will often be given together with the definition of the fragment as shown in figure 7.

3.1.6 Origin of a Fragment

The *origin part* of a fragment specifies a fragment that is used when binding fragment forms to slots. Consider figure 7. The origin of CounterBody is the fragment /home/smith/Counter (c.f. figure 7). The origin must have free slots corresponding to Up and Down. The origin construct specifies that the fragment forms Up and Down are substituted for the corresponding slots in Counter. The result of this substitution is a form, called the *extent* of the fragment. The extent of Counter is shown in figure 8.

Extent

A fragment defines a unique form, called the *extent* of the fragment. The extent of the above fragment is a combination of CounterBody and Counter.

```
location betaenv
<<form betaenv:Descriptor>>
{*** The basic BETA environment ***}
(# Put: (# ch: @ Char enter ch ... #);
   PutInt: (# n: @Integer enter n do ... #);
   PutText: (# T: @Text enter T do ...#);
   NewLine: (# ... #);
   PutLine: (# T:@Text enter T do T->puttext; newLine #);
   Text: ...;
   File: ...;
   Integer: (# ... #);
   Char: (# ... #);
   ... {Definition of other standard attributes}
   <<SLOT Lib: Attributes>>
do {Initialize for execution}
   <<SLOT Program:Descriptor>>;
   {Terminate execution}
#)
```

Figure 9: The basic BETA environment

The combination is obtained by filling in the slots in the origin with the
corresponding fragment forms.

3.1.7 The Basic Environment

The Mjølner BETA System provides a basic environment that defines the
most important standard patterns and objects. In addition, this environment initiates and terminates the execution of any BETA program. The
basic BETA environment is the fragment **betaenv**[4] shown in figure 9. This
fragment defines a number of standard patterns. In addition, the fragment
has two slots: **Program** and **Lib**.

Simple programs

A complete BETA program that makes use of **betaenv** may be defined by
specifying the **Program** slot. The fragment form in figure 10 is an example of
a very simple BETA program.

The extent of the fragment **mini1** is shown in figure 11. The **Program** fragment has been substituted for the **Program** slot in **betaenv**. In the **Program**
fragment it is therefore possible to use any name which is visible at the point

---

[4]In the rest of this paper, simple names (i.e. without any directory specified) are used
for specifying locations of fragments

```
location mini1
origin betaenv
<<form Program:Descriptor>>
(#
do 'Hello world!' -> PutLine
#)
```

Figure 10: mini1 program

```
{*** The basic BETA environment ***}
(# ...
   PutLine:...
   ...
do {Initialize for execution}
   (#
   do 'Hello world!' -> PutLine
   #)
   {Terminate execution}
#)
```

Figure 11: Extent of mini1

```
location mylib
origin betaenv
<<form Lib:attributes>>
Hello: (# do 'Hello' -> PutText #);
World: (# do 'World' -> PutText #)
```

Figure 12: mylib library

```
{*** The basic BETA environment ***}
(# ...
   Hello: (# do 'Hello' -> PutText #);
   World: (# do 'World' -> PutText #)
do {Initialize for execution}
   <<SLOT Program:Descriptor>>;
   {Terminate execution}
#)
```

Figure 13: Extent of mylib

of the **Program** slot in **betaenv**. **PutLine** is visible at the **Program** slot and is therefore visible in the **Program** fragment. It would also have been possible to make use of patterns like **Integer**, **Char**, **Text**, etc.

Simple libraries

The **Lib** slot in **betaenv** is intended for making a set of general patterns to be used by other programs. The difference between such a library and a program is that the library is a list of patterns whereas the program is a single object descriptor. Figure 12 contains an example of a library consisting of two patterns. By substituting the **Lib** slot in **betaenv** with the **Lib** fragment form, we obtain figure 13.

The library patterns are inserted at the point of the **Lib** slot. This means that in the **Lib** fragment form it is possible to see all names visible at the point of the **Lib** slot in **betaenv**. Note that the extent of **mylib** is not an executable program, since the **Program** slot has not been defined.

3.1.8   Include

When making libraries like **mylib**, we need a mechanism for combining several fragments into one fragment. The **include** construct makes this possible. Figure 14 contains a program that makes use of the library **mylib**.

```
location mini2
origin betaenv
include mylib
<<form Program:Descriptor>>
(#
do Hello; World; newLine
#)
```

Figure 14: mini2 program

```
{*** The basic BETA environment ***}
(# ...
   Hello: (# do 'Hello' -> PutText #);
   World: (# do 'World' -> PutText #)
do {Initialize for execution}
   (#
   do Hello; World; newLine
   #)
   {Terminate execution}
#)
```

Figure 15: Extent of mini2

The effect of **include mylib** is that the patterns defined in **myLib** can be used in the **Program** fragment form. Formally, the fragment forms of **mylib** become part of the fragment **mini2**. In the above example, **mini2** may be understood as a fragment group consisting of the fragment forms in **mylib** and the **Program** fragment form. This implies that the extent of **mini2** is obtained by substituting the **Lib** slot in **betaenv** by the **Lib** fragment form in **mylib** and by substituting the **Program** slot in **betaenv** by the **Program** fragment form in **mini2**. This gives the form in figure 15.

Since the patterns in **mylib** are inserted at the point of the **Lib** slot, they are visible at the point of the **Program** slot. This is where the **Program** fragment form in **mini2** is inserted. I.e. the patterns **Hello** and **World** are visible inside the **Program** fragment form.

A fragment form may have more than one include. This makes it possible to use several library fragments in the same fragment (c.f. section 3.4).

3.1.9 Body

When defining a fragment it is often desirable to be able to specify one or more fragments that always must be included when using the fragment. This is often the case when a fragment is separated into an interface fragment and one or more implementation fragments. Here we introduce the construct for specifying this; but delay further explanation until section 3.2. The **body** construct specifies a fragment that is always part of the extent. Consider figure 16. The **counter** fragment has a body specification that specifies that a fragment called **counterbody** is always part of the extent of **counter**. The **counterbody** fragment could be described as in figure 17. The **counter** fragment could be used as illustrated in figure 18.

The extent of **mini3** is obtained by combining the **Program** fragment form in **mini3**, **origin betaenv** and **include counter**. In addition, the **body counterbody** in **counter** implies that the **counterBody** fragment is also in-

```
location counter
origin betaenv
body counterbody
<<form Lib:Attributes>>
Counter: (#
  Up: (# n: @ Integer
      enter n
        <<SLOT Up:DoPart>>
      #);
  Down: (# n: @ Integer
        <<SLOT Down:DoPart>>
        exit n
        #);
  Priv: @ <<SLOT Priv:Descriptor>>
#)
```

Figure 16: Using body

```
location counterbody
origin counter
<<form Up:DoPart>>
do n+7->n
<<form Down:DoPart>>
do n-5->n
<<form Priv:Descriptor>>
(# V: @ Integer #)
```

Figure 17: A body fragment

```
location mini3
origin betaenv
include counter
<<form Program:Descriptor>>
(# C: @Counter
do 3->C.up; 6->C.down
#)
```

Figure 18: mini3 program

cluded in the extent. The resulting form looks as in figure 19.

As stated earlier, the patterns defined in **Lib** are visible in **mini3** through the use of **include**. However, the **counterbody** is not visible from **mini3**. This means that an evaluation like `C.Priv.V+1->C.Priv.V` is not possible within **mini3**. That is even if the extent of **mini3** includes the **counterbody** fragment, it is not visible within **mini3**.

Domain

The *domain* of a fragment **F** is the part of the extent of **F** which is visible within **F**. The domain of **F** consists of the fragment forms in **F**, plus the domain of the origin of **F** plus the domain of possible included fragments. The domain of **mini3** is the form shown in figure 20. The domain of **mini3** is constructed as follows:

- The domain of **mini3** consists of the **Program** fragment form in **mini3**, plus the domain of **betaenv** (its origin), plus the domain of the included fragment **counter** (c.f. figure 20).

- The domain of **betaenv** is the form in figure 9.

- The domain of the **counter** fragment consists of the form defining the pattern **Counter**, plus the domain of **betaenv**. Note that the **body** part of **Counter** does not contribute to the domain.

```
{*** The basic BETA environment ***}
(# ...
   Counter: (#
     Up: (# n: @ Integer
          enter n
          do n+7->n
          #);
     Down: (# n: @ Integer
             do n-5->n
             exit n
             #);
     Priv: @ (# V: @Integer #)
     #)
do {Initialize for execution}
   (# C: @Counter
   do 3->C.up; 6->C.down
   #);
   {Terminate execution}
#)
```

Figure 19: Extent of `mini3`

```
{*** The basic BETA environment ***}
(# ...
   Counter: (#
     Up: (# n: @ Integer
          enter n
          <<SLOT Up:DoPart>>
          #);
     Down: (# n: @ Integer
             <<SLOT Down:DoPart>>
             exit n
             #);
     Priv: @ <<SLOT Priv:Descriptor>>
     #)
do {Initialize for execution}
   (# C: @Counter
   do 3->C.up; 6->C.down
   #);
   {Terminate execution}
#)
```

Figure 20: Domain of `mini3`

3.2 Separation of Interface and Implementation

Encapsulation and separation of interface and implementation saves compilation time. In the Mjølner BETA System, as in many other systems, fragments
(modules) can be separately compiled. A change in an implementation module can then be made without recompilation of the interface module and
modules using the interface module. This can yield significant savings in
compilation time. On the other hand, a change in an interface module implies that all modules using it must be recompiled. This can be extremely
time consuming. The fragment system manages these dependencies between
fragments automatically and the BETA compiler utilizes this information to
reduce recompilations to a minimum.

Programming takes place at different abstraction levels. The interface
part of a module describes a view of objects and patterns meaningful at
the abstraction level where the module is used. The implementation level
describes how objects and patterns at the interface level are realized using
other objects and patterns.

The fragment language supports encapsulation and separation of interface and implementation. One fragment defines the interface while others
define the implementation. The `Counter` fragment in figure 16 is an example of one such interface fragment, and the `CounterBody` fragment in figure 17 is an example of an implementation fragment. The fragment system
ensures (in cooperation with the compiler), that the fragment `mini3` in fig-

```
location stack
origin betaenv
<<form Lib: Attributes>>
Stack:
  (# Priv: @<<SLOT Priv:Descriptor>>;
    Push:
      (# e: ^ Text
      enter e[]
      <<SLOT Push: DoPart>>
      #);
    Pop:
      (# e: ^ Text
      <<SLOT Pop: DoPart>>
      exit e[]
      #);
    New: (# <<SLOT New: DoPart>> #);
    isEmpty:
      (# Result: @ Boolean
      <<SLOT isEmpty: DoPart>>
      exit Result
      #)
  #)
```

Figure 21: The interface part of pattern Stack

```
location libuser2
origin betaenv
include stack
<<form program:Descriptor>>
(# T: @Text; S: @Stack
do  'To be or not to be' -> T;
    T.reset;
    Get:
      cycle
      (# T1: ^ text
      do &Text[] -> T1[];
         T.getText-> T1;
         (if T1.empty // True then
            leave Get if);
         T1[] -> S.push
      #);
    Print:
      cycle
      (# T1: ^ Text
      do (if S.isEmpty // true then
            leave Print if);
         S.pop -> T1[];
         T1 -> puttext; ' ' -> put
      #)
#)
```

Figure 22:   A fragment using the stack interface

ure 18 cannot utilize the information located in the implementation fragment
(CounterBody).

3.2.1   Abstract Data Types

One of the fundamental concepts in program development is the notion of
abstract data type. In the context of BETA, an abstract data type is a class
pattern whose instances are completely characterized by a set of (procedure)
pattern attributes — sometimes referred to as its operations. These operations constitute the outside view of the objects whereas reference attributes
and details of the pattern attributes belong to the inside view (the implementation).

The fragments in figure 21 and figure 23 shows an example of an abstract
data type in BETA. The fragments define the interface and implementation
of a stack of text references. A stack is completely characterized by its operations Push, Pop, New and isEmpty. The stack may be used as shown in
figure 22. Note, that libuser2 is not a complete program, since no implementations for stack are specified yet.

```
location arraystack
origin stack
<<form Priv:Descriptor>>
(# A: [100] ^ Text;
   Top : @integer
#)
<<form Push:DoPart>>
do Priv.top+1 -> Priv.top;
   @[] -> Priv.A[Priv.top] []
<<form Pop:DoPart>>
do Priv.A[Priv.top][] -> @[];
   Priv.top-1 -> Priv.top
<<form new:DoPart>>
do 0->Priv.top
<<form isEmpty: DoPart>>
do (0 = Priv.Top) -> result
```

Figure 23: Array implementation of Stack

```
location listStack
origin stack
<<form Priv:Descriptor>>
(# head: ^ elm;
   elm: (# T:^ Text; next: ^ elm #)
#)
<<form Push:DoPart>>
do (# R: ^ Priv.elm
   do &Priv.elm[] -> R[];
      Priv.head[] -> R.next[];
      @[] -> R.T[];
      R[] -> Priv.head[];
   #)
<<form Pop:DoPart>>
do Priv.head.T[] -> @[];
   Priv.head.next[] -> Priv.head[];
<<form new:DoPart>>
do NONE -> Priv.head[]
<<form isEmpty:DoPart>>
do (NONE=Priv.head[]) -> result;
```

Figure 24: List implementation of stack

Since the domain of **stack** does not include its implementation, the stack can only be used by means of its operations. It is good practice to define most class patterns as "abstract data types", i.e. restrict their interface to be pattern operations. In some languages, e.g. Smalltalk, class patterns are always abstract data types.

3.3   Alternative Implementations

It is possible to have several implementations of a given interface module. In general this means that different fragments may define different bindings for slots in a given fragment.

Suppose that we want to define an alternate implementation of the **stack** from the previous section. In the alternate implementation, **stack** objects are represented as linked lists. The list implementation is shown in figure 24.

Selecting the proper **stack** implementation is done by means of a **body** specification as illustrated in figure 26. Naturally, this **body** specification could have been given in **libuser2**, but then would all **libuser2** programs be using the **arrayStack** implementation.

```
location libuser3
origin betaenv
include stack
include counter
body liststack
<<form program:Descriptor>>
(# S: @ Stack;
   C: @ Counter;
do 3 -> C.up;
   'Top of stack' -> S.push;
   ...
#)
```

Figure 25: Example of a fragment using more than one fragment

```
location libuser4
origin libuser2
body arrayStack
```

Figure 26: A complete **stack** program using the array implementation

```
location libuser5
origin libuser2
body listStack
```

Figure 27: A complete **stack** program using the list implementation

```
location libuser6
origin libuser2
body  Array ⇒ arraystack
      List  ⇒ liststack
```

Figure 28: A complete **stack** program with two compile-time variants

3.4   Using Several Libraries

The examples of libraries until now have only shown how to use one library from a program. The syntactic category of a slot like `<<SLOT Lib:attributes>>` describes a list of declarations. It is thus possible to bind an arbitrary number of `Lib` fragments to such a slot. Figure 25 shows a fragment that includes two libraries.

3.5   Program Variants

Often several variants of a given program are needed. This is usually the case if variants of a given program have to exist for several computers. The major part of the program is often the same for each computer. For maintenance purposes it is highly desirable to have only one version of the common part. In the Mjølner BETA System, program variants can be handled in the same way as alternative implementations of a module are handled. That is, different variants of a module bind some of the slots differently (as illustrated in figure 26 and 27).

However, often one wants to specify that a given fragment can have several variants (i.e. alternative **body** specifications), and postpone the decision on which variant to select until compile-time. This is done by a special **body** specification (as shown in figure 28). When compiling a program, it is possible to specify a set of tokens (e.g. **Array**) and the compiler will then select those bodies, that correspond to the specified tokens (e.g. **arrayStack** for token **Array**). Program variants can in this way be maintained and produced efficiently.

3.6   Current implementation

The most important limitations of the present implementation of the fragment system in Mjølner BETA System are:

It does not support all nonterminals of the BETA grammar. Only two nonterminals of the BETA grammar are supported, namely **<Attributes>** and **<Descriptor>**.[5]

The naming scheme for fragments is a direct reflection of the file system, such that locations are specifications of files in the underlying hierarchical file system.

The selective **body** directive is currently only implemented for machine dependent tokens like **Sun3**, **HP**, **Mac**, etc. with the compiler automatically selecting the proper variant (identical to the machine type the compiler is running) unless the compiler is asked to cross-compile to another machine type.

It is important to note, that the fragment system in the current Mjølner BETA System implementation is able to handle large program, and supports the separate compilation of these large systems. The best proof of this is that the entire Mjølner BETA System is managed using the fragment system. The system consists of more than 1.000 fragments, distributed in more than 220 fragment groups, with a total of more 64.000 lines of BETA code. The fragment system is used in the Mjølner BETA System implementation to enable the automatic administration of machine specific fragments for four different target architectures on the same physical file system.

A full description of the fragment system as implemented in Mjølner BETA System can be found in the Mjølner BETA System manuals.

4   The Hyper Structure Editor

The editor has the following characteristics:

---

[5] This restriction is not a serious limitation in practice

Structure and text editing: The syntax-directed editor is fully integrated with a text editor, allowing the user to switch freely between structure
and text editing.

Incremental Parsing: The editor makes use of an incremental parsing
algorithm when switching from textual editing to syntax-directed editing in
order to ensure that the text being edited (by text editing) is syntactically
valid within the given context. Only the edited text needs to be considered
by the incremental parser to ensure this consistency.

Adaptive pretty-printing: The internal representation of a program
is an abstract syntax tree (AST) as defined by the Mjølner BETA System.
Pretty-printing, i.e. textual presentation of the AST is done adaptively,
which means that as much as possible is printed on each line in the editing window. The adaptive pretty-printing can be controlled by the user by
tailoring the editor to conform with his needs.

Hyper Linking: The editor supports various types of hypertext facilities. These facilities include program semantical links, links to comments,
links to other program fragments, links to text documents, etc. The linking
facilities are fully symmetric.

Annotation: Comments in a program are handled as links to text
objects. Instead of mixing comments with the program text, comments are
presented and manipulated in separate text editing windows. Comments may
also be included directly in the program text in the form of ordinary program
comments.

Abstract presentation and browsing: Abstract presentation is provided by supporting placeholders of type contraction. Abstract presentation is similar to the ability to compress a whole sentence into one word
(holophrastic). Abstract presentation has two applications: browsing and
documentation. Browsing is supported by letting the user selectively go into
further details of contractions. Printing a program at different abstraction
levels provides good documentation facilities for e.g. functional specifications.

Grammar-based: The editor is grammar-based, which means that it
may support any language that can be described by means of a context-free
grammar.

Metaprogramming system: The editor is built upon the metaprogramming system, which is available for the user (see section 5). The user
has the possibility to program her own metaprogramming tools. Due to a
high degree of tailorability in the editor, it is possible to integrate such tools
with the editor or simply to add functionality to the editor. This tailorability
is available in the editor by providing special hooks to be expanded by the

user and in general by the object oriented implementation language (BETA) of the editor [11].

The editor makes use of almost all other tools in the system: the BETA compiler, the pretty-printer, the parser, the user interface toolkit, the metaprogramming system, and the fragment system.

4.1   Syntax-directed Editing

Syntax-directed editing is supported through placeholders of kind nonterminals. During the editing of a program, nonterminals may appear, either specified explicitly by the user or as a result of another syntax-directed editing command. When a nonterminal is selected, the editor offers the possible derivations of that nonterminal as templates (i.e. the right-hand sides of all productions with the selected nonterminal on left side). This is done in a pop-up menu. If one of these productions are selected, the editor replaces the nonterminal with the right-hand of the selected production and editing may continue by selecting nonterminals in this template or by other editing tasks.

If a terminal in the program is selected, the smallest sentential form containing this terminal is selected. If a sentential form is selected, it may be deleted (i.e. replaced with the nonterminal from which it was originally derived). Special treatment is offered for nonterminals that are defined by optional or list zero productions.

4.2   Text Editing

Textual editing can be performed at any time instead of structural editing. Any sentential form can be selected for text editing, and when the textual editing of the sentential form is completed, the modified text is parsed according to the syntactic category of the sentential form. The parsing of the modified text is done using incremental parsing techniques.

4.3   Hyper Structure Editing

The editor supports hyper structure editing in four different ways:

Abstract Presentation: Most non-trivial fragments are normally too big to fit into a window on the screen, even if the window occupies the whole screen space. Abstract presentation can be considered as supporting intrafragment organizational links. The user has the possibility manually to substitute any structure in the fragment by a contraction, which acts as a link to the suppressed details. Abstract presentation of a program fragment or a documentation fragment has several advantages:

Overview: It provides an overview of the document. The whole document can be surveyed at once in one window without scrolling through pages of text. This facility is also known in some word processing systems as outlining.

Browsing: Browsing is done by interactively detailing parts of an abstract presentation. If the document is a technical report with chapters and sections and the like, the highest abstraction level can actually be an interactive table of contents.

Documentation: Snapshots of a program at different abstraction levels can be very useful for documentation purposes. The user can select an appropriate abstraction level by detailing or abstracting the relevant constructs of the document and save the actual abstraction level including comments on textual form.

Annotations: Comments in a program are handled by means of links to simple text objects, so-called annotations. Any point in the program can be linked to a text object. If a construct in a program fragment is selected, a text window can be opened and the annotation can be entered. After finishing the annotation a special annotation mark (*) is inserted in the construct to indicate a link from the construct to a text object. Whenever the user selects a program construct with a annotation link, a text window can be activated (e.g. by double clicking with the mouse) and the annotation can be read or modified. Annotations may also be included directly in the program text in the form of ordinary program comments.

Program Semantical Linkage: The program semantical links are used to reflect the static semantic information of a program. For example definition-use relationships and super-/subclass relationships. Such relationships are automatically deductible from the program. In the Mjølner BETA System, program semantical links are set up by the checker. These links are used in the checking and coding processes, but are also available to the user in the editor. When a construct is selected in a program fragment a menu presents the available links from that construct (if any). Note that program semantical relationships go across the fragment structure.

Interactive program analysis is normally not considered being part of program documentation, but language specific inspection of a program is often useful when trying to understand it. This kind of program traversal can be considered as non-hierarchical browsing.

Documentation Linkage: Documentation links are used to support all other kinds of relationships between documentation fragments mutually

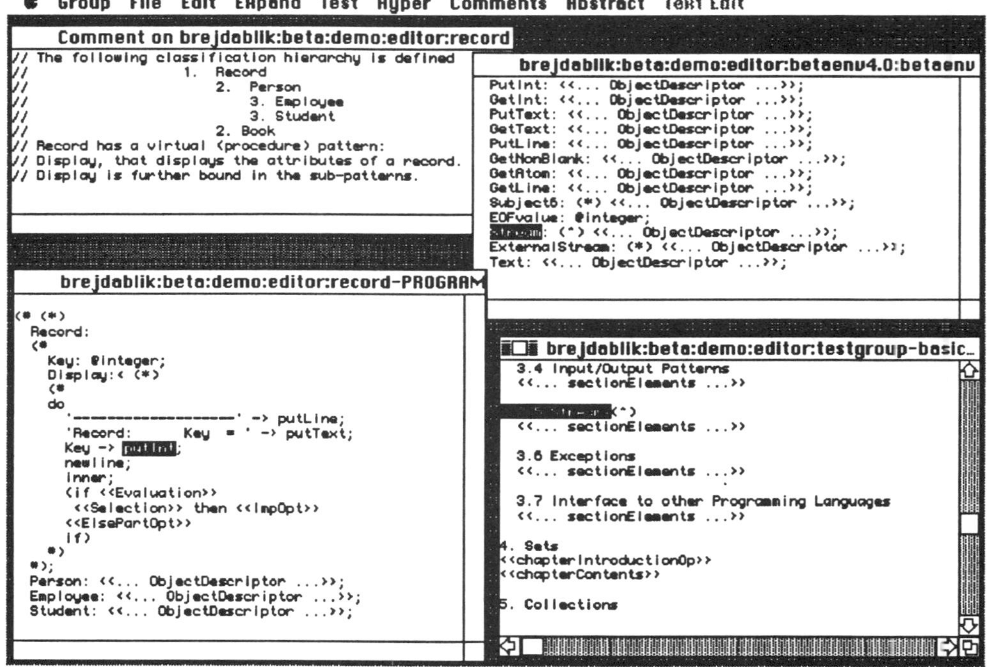

Figure 29: Editor User Interface

---

and between documentation fragments and program fragments. This link
type is manually created by the user. The documentation link type is the
basic mechanism for supporting integration of program and documentation.
Any point in a program or fragment can be linked to another point in the
same or another fragment. When a construct in a fragment is selected, the
construct can be marked as a link source. The link destination is chosen by
selecting another construct in the same or another fragment (possibly after
activating an editor instance on the destination fragment) and then make it
the link destination. A link mark (^) is inserted in the source construct as
well as the destination construct. A descriptive text can be associated with
either end of the link. The hypertext facilities of the editor is based on the
ideas presented in [13].

Figure 29 illustrates these linkage facilities. The lower left window is an
editor window, showing the program being edited. The upper left window
shows the comment annotation that is indicated just before Record in the
editor window. Having followed the program semantic links from putInt in

the editor window, have resulted in the upper right window, showing part of the basic BETA library. **PutInt** is defined in the first line shown (which was automatically selected when the **putInt** link was followed). In the upper right window, the hyper link shown at **Stream** has been followed, resulting in a document editor being opened in the lower right window, where the destination link is shown immediately after **Stream** in the text. Notice that the lower right window is a structure editor on the documentation. The structure editor for documentation is based on the hyper structure editor with the facilities for abstract presentation (which in this case will work like a outline processor), browsing, linking, etc.

With the graphical extensions currently being developed (and discussed shortly in section 6.8, the Mjølner BETA System will support an integrated editor for text, programs and documentation with support for graphical, structure, and text editing of all three types of documents, and with full support for linkage between internals of all three document types. Furthermore, the editor supports abstract presentation, browsing and annotation of all three document types.

4.4   Tailorability

The editor is implemented in BETA and the advanced user is supposed to have programming experience in BETA. If the user wishes to make "real" extensions to the editor, some knowledge of the metaprogramming system and the BETA user interface toolkit is required.

The tailorability of the editor is obtained mainly by applying object oriented design principles extensively throughout the entire editor. In fact, the editor is designed as a class, and major tailorability is often made by creating a subclass of the editor and specify the tailoring in the subclass. The BETA editor is an example hereof, see section 4.5. For a more detailed discussion of tailorability of the Mjølner BETA System, see [11].

4.5   The BETA Editor

The BETA editor is an example of extensive tailoring of the general structure editor in order to fully support handling BETA programs. The BETA specific extension of the hyper structure editor provides the following additional facilities:

Automatic abstract presentation of BETA programs: When editor instances are activated with BETA program fragments, these are presented abstractly. The abstraction levels are object descriptors, attribute lists and imperative lists. Contractions explicitly defined within the AST are preserved across editing sessions.

Integration with the BETA compiler: Each BETA editor instance is able to activate the BETA compiler and to activate the resulting executable BETA program. Notice that the compiler does not have to perform lexical and syntactical analysis but uses the AST that the editor has produced. When the compiler is activated, the current fragment is marked as changed. The whole fragment group, which this fragment is a part of, is "delivered" to the compiler. If there are static semantic errors, the user can browse through these.

Simple static program analysis: The checker part of the BETA compiler sets up static semantic information in the AST, (e.g. references from name applications to the corresponding declaration). This information can be used from the editor by means of the program semantic linkage facilities. E.g. if a name application is selected, the corresponding name declaration can be found. If the name declaration is located in another program fragment, the editor is able to open another editor instance on it.

A more thorough description of the hyper structure editor can be found in the Mjølner BETA System manuals.

5   The Metaprogramming System

One of the objectives of the Mjølner project has been to obtain some of the flexibility of Lisp environments. One of the most significant features of Lisp is the fact that Lisp functions are represented and manipulated as data. This makes Lisp an excellent language for writing programs that manipulate other programs, i.e. metaprograms. In a program environment it is essential to have strong support for metaprogramming.

All metaprogramming tools in the Mjølner BETA System manipulate programs through a common representation that is abstract syntax trees (ASTs). The common representation eases the integration of different tools in the environment e.g. the static semantic checker and the code generator. This well-defined representation also facilitate construction of metaprograms seen from the users point of view.

An AST is modeled as an instance of a class. The classes describing the ASTs are organized in a class hierarchy, which makes it possible to access an AST at 3 levels:

Tree level: The most general set of classes describe the AST as a traditional data structure in the form of a tree with the usual operations.

The operations defined by the classes from the tree level includes operations
to enable the substitution of one subtree in the AST with any other AST,
irrespectively of the syntactic vadility of that substitution. This level is used
by tools that need not know details about the AST. Using only the tree level
enables the editor tool to be language independent. Accessing ASTs at this
level corresponds to manipulate *S-expressions* in Lisp.

Context-free level: This level imposes a context-free structure on
the AST. The operations defined by the classes from the context-free level
includes operations to substitute one subtree of an AST with another AST
with ensurence that the substitution corresponds to a syntactically legal substitution of the grammar. Tools using this level allow only syntactically legal
operation on the AST. The context-free level is generated from the grammar
of the language. The set of classes are subclasses of the classes from tree
level. The interface is uniquely determined by the grammar and the generated classes need not be consulted since the grammar may function as a
specification of the interface.

Semantic level: The semantic level makes it possible to add semantic
attributes and operations to the AST. As an example the static semantic
checker of the BETA compiler use this level to decorate the ASTs with static
semantic information.

5.1   ASTs and Classes

The tree level classes are predefined classes, corresponding to the five types of
productions: construction, alternation, list zero, list one and optional. Given
a specific grammar, the context-free level is defined by subclasses of these
tree level classes, since any nonterminal will be modeled by a class that is a
subclass of the tree level class corresponding to the production rule applied
in the grammar.

The tree level classes are predefined and context-free level classes are generated automatically from the grammar specification. The semantic level is
somewhat different. Instead of defining the semantic level as subclasses to
the classes from the context-free level, the semantic level is defined by augmenting the automatically defined context-free level classes with attributes
containing the semantic information.

To illustrate the correspondence between a grammar and the generated
the class hierarchy, a simple grammar is given in figure 30.

The nonterminals <NameAppl>, <NameDcl>, <Type>, and <Exp> will not
be defined.   This grammar gives rise to the class hierarchy in figure 31.
Indentation defines the subclass relation and the attributes of each class are

```
<Block>     ::= begin <DclPart: DclLst>
                do <ImpPart: ImpLst> end
<DclLst>    ::* <Dcl> ;
<Dcl>       ::| <VarDcl> | <ProcDcl>
<VarDcl>    ::= var <Name: NameDcl>: <VarType: Type>
<ProcDcl>   ::= proc <Name: NameDcl> <Body: Block>
<ImpLst>    ::* <Imp> ;
<Imp>       ::= if <Cond: Exp> then <ThenPart: ImpLst>
                            else <ElsePart: ImpLst>
            endif
<Assign>    ::= <Var: NameAppl> := <Value: Exp>
<ProcCall> ::= <Proc: NameAppl>
```

Figure 30: Simple grammar

```
Cons (...)
  Block (DclPart: DclLst, ImpPart: ImpLst)
  Dcl
    VarDcl (Name: NameDcl, VarType: Type)
    ProcDcl (Name: NameDcl, Body: Block)
  Imp
    IfImp (Cond: Exp, ThenPart: ImpLst, ElsePart: ImpLst)
    Assign (Var: NameAppl, Value: Exp)
    ProcCall (Proc: NameAppl)
List (...)
  DclLst
  ImpLst
```

Figure 31: Simple grammar hierarchy

---

shown in parentheses. The attributes of the classes **Cons** and **List** are defined
by the metaprogramming system. In these classes, several mechanisms for
manipulating the AST are also defined.

For a more thorough description of the metaprogramming system, see [9].
The metaprogramming system is among others inspired by the GRAMS system [3].

6   Other Tools in the Mjølner BETA System

To complete the overview of the Mjølner BETA System, the remaining parts
of the system are shortly described.

6.1   The BETA Compiler

The BETA programming language supports the object oriented perspective on programming and contains comprehensive facilities for procedural and functional programming. Research is going on with the aim of including constraint oriented constructs. BETA replaces classes, procedures, functions and types by a single abstraction mechanism called the *pattern*. It generalizes virtual procedures to virtual patterns, streamlines linguistic notions such as nesting and block structure, and provides a unified framework for sequential, coroutine, and concurrent execution. BETA is a modern language in the SIMULA tradition. The resulting language is smaller than SIMULA in spite of being considerably more expressive. A full description of the BETA programming language is outside the scope of this paper. The language is described in detail in [8, 7].

The compiler for BETA is an effective implementation of the BETA language (except concurrency). The major effort have been put into creating a production compiler for the sequential and alternation parts of the language in order to offer an effective implementation vehicle for the Mjølner BETA System.

The main components of the BETA compiler are the *semantic analyzer* and the *code generator*. The semantic analyzer checks the correctness of the context sensitive syntax (static semantics) of an AST, and performs storage allocation. The code generator translates an AST into executable code (native machine code). The code generator is divided into two components: the *synthesizer* and the *coder*. The synthesizer contains a machine independent model of the code generation, and the coder takes care of the machine dependent parts of the code generation. The synthesizer is the largest part of the code generator. This implies that porting the compiler to another machine can be done with a reasonable effort.

A symbol table is constructed during semantic analysis. The symbol table is defined by means of the semantic level of the metaprogramming system. I.e. the AST decorated with semantic attributes. In this way the symbol table information is an integrated part of the AST and thereby available for other tools accessing the AST (e.g. the editor).

In order to manipulate the ASTs, the compiler makes extensive use of the metaprogramming system. Furthermore, in order to generate ASTs from textual program representations, the compiler makes use of the parser. Finally, the compiler makes use of the pretty-printer to generate a textual representation of parts of the AST (e.g. in order to indicate program errors).

The runtime system for the BETA language is based on garbage collection. The garbage collection scheme is based on generation scavenging.

The compiler uses the fragment system to enable programs to be divided into smaller fragments for separate compilation. The compiler makes an automatic dependency analysis on the fragment structure. When a fragments has been changed, the system keeps track of the dependent fragments that must be recompiled.

6.2   The Source Level Debugger

Mjølner BETA System contains a source level debugger for the BETA language. It contains facilities for specifying break-points, single stepping, inspection of object states, inspection of the run-time organization, etc. The debugger is available both with a command-driven interface and with a graphical interface.

6.3   Parser and Pretty-Printer

Two tools exist for converting between textual and abstract syntax tree representations of a program. Both tools are grammar-based and can be applied to any language with a context-free grammar. The *parser* translates a text stream into an AST and the *pretty-printer* translates an AST into a text stream. The parser is based on LALR(1) parsing algorithms and the BOBS compiler generator system [5]. The pretty-printer is an adaptive pretty-printer based on the adaptive algorithm presented in [12]. The pretty-printer is using a pretty-printing specification to guide the format of the output. For each production in the grammar, pretty-printing directives are given on the layout of sentences, derived from that nonterminal. This specification can be specified by the user. Both tools are used by the compiler and the editor.

6.4   The BETA User Interface Toolkit

Two object oriented user interface toolkits are available: MacEnv for the Macintosh Toolbox and XtEnv for the X Window System. They provide high level interaction concepts, such as hierarchical windows, icons, menues, dialog boxes, etc. The reason for having two different toolkits is that we want application writers to be aware of the limitations and to be able to utilize the strengths of each user interface system. It is planned to create specializations of XtEnv to support Motif and OpenLook/OpenWindows in the future. Furthermore, it is planned to create a platform independent user interface toolkit for easy portability of applications (using the program variant facility of the fragment system to select proper implementation platform). However, it is forseen that this toolkit will be some sort of minimal toolkit for creating relative simple applications.

6.5   The Bifrost Graphics System

The Bifrost graphics system [2] is a device independent, interactive, extensible and tailorable graphics system based on the stencil & paint imaging model. The graphics system supports graphics modeling, interaction with graphics (creation, reshaping, translation, scaling, and rotation), graphics contexts (local, shared and global), and automatic damage repair.

Besides being a fragment library available for programmers, a MacDraw-like drawing application has been build based on Bifrost.

6.6   The Ensemble

The Mjølner BETA System has an object oriented interface to the operating system called the ensemble. The ensemble has three major goals:

1. To access the file system.
2. To control processes in the operating system.
3. To communicate between these processes.

The ensemble is written in BETA, and is therefore accessible to application programmers. The ensemble consists of a operating system independent part and several operating system dependent parts. A UNIX ensemble is extensively used in the UNIX implementations of the Mjølner BETA System, and a MacOS ensemble is used in the Macintosh implementation. For a full description of the Mjølner BETA System manuals.

6.7   Interface to Other Languages

Besides the ensemble interface to the operating system, there exists interfaces to routines written in C and Pascal. This interface enables the programmer to invoke routines written in these languages. Furthermore, there are interfaces to data structures in C (`struct`) and in Pascal (`record`). Furthermore, there are support for call-back from C or Pascal routines to BETA routines.

These interfaces defines a clean interface to these languages, and enables reuse of existing systems, written in other languages. An interface exists also for specifying machine code as part of the actions of an object. These interfaces are sufficient general that interfaces to other stack-based languages can be created with reasonable effort.

The existence of the ensemble and the extern routine interface makes the Mjølner BETA System highly portable across platforms.

6.8 Graphical Hyper Structure Editor

In order to support graphical editing of programs and fragments, and in order to support object oriented analysis and design, a graphical editor is being developed, partly based on a proposal for a syntax-directed graphical editor with extensive support for object oriented analysis and design, see [14, 15]. The editor is developed on top of the hyper structure editor, and will therefore facilitate abstract browsing, documentation, and hyper linking within graphical documents as well as symmetric linkage between programs, documentation and design diagrams. Furthermore, since the editor will use the same underlying structure for programs, documentation and design diagrams, consistency between these documents can easily be ensured. This tool will be a valuable CASE tool for object oriented analysis and design.

6.9 Application Builder

An application builder for the integrated construction of the user interface and functionality of an application is being developed. The user interface is constructed using direct manipulation, and the application builder generates BETA code that makes it easy for the designer to insert his own application code using the hyper structure editor. The generated code and the application code are kept separated using the fragment system. Furthermore, the application builder will enable the modification of the interface code through the application builder while preserving the application code.

6.10 Future Developments

The Mjølner BETA System will be further developed in the future. Several new developments are under consideration:

Incremental Compilation: The present system supports only separate compilation. Incremental compilation techniques, as those developed in the Swedish part of the Mjølner project [10] will be examined in order to investigate their application in the Mjølner BETA System.

Dynamic Linking: Dynamic linking is one technique to minimize startup time for large programs and to minimize storage consumption of programs.

Persistent Objects: One of the very active research areas within object oriented programming is persistent objects. Presently, we are examining several approaches to persistent objects in the Mjølner BETA System, one of which is the use of extensible programs as the vehicle for persistence [1].

Extensible Programs: The ability to specify additional program fragments during run time of a program, and compile and link that fragment into the running program is currently under investigation [1]. Currently an experimental implementation of this technique have been completed with promising results.

Acknowledgements

The work reported here has been partly supported the Nordic Mjølner project. The Mjølner project [4] is funded by the participating organizations and supported by grants from *The Nordic Fund for Technology and Industrial Development*. The Danish team consisted of the authors, Ole Agesen, Peter Andersen, Karen Borup, Svend Frølund, Kim Jensen Møller, Claus H. Pedersen and Per Fack Sørensen. The BETA language design team consists of Bent Bruun Kristensen, Ole Lehrmann Madsen, Birger Møller-Pedersen and Kristen Nygaard. Finally, we would like to express our thanks to Apple Computer for supporting the Macintosh implementation, and to Apollo Computer and Hewlett-Packard for support at various stages in the project.

References

[1] O Agesen, S. Frølund, M.H. Olsen: *Persistent and Shared Objects in BETA*, Computer Science Department Technical Report IR-89, Aarhus University, April 1989.

[2] P. Andersen, K. Jensen Møller, J. Rask: *Bifrost: An Interactive Object Oriented Device Independent Graphics System*, Computer Science Department Technical Report IR-100, Aarhus University, February 1991.

[3] R.D. Cameron, M. Robert Ito: *Grammar-based Definition of Metaprogramming Systems*, ACM Transactions on Programming Languages and Systems, Vol. 6, No. 1, January 1984.

[4] H.P. Dahle, M. Løfgren, O.L. Madsen, B. Magnusson (eds): *The Mjølner Project*, In Proceedings of EUROSOFT '87, London, June 1987.

[5] S.H. Eriksen, B.B. Jensen, B.B. Kristensen, O.L. Madsen: *The BOBS System*, Computer Science Department Technical Report PB-71, Aarhus University, March 1977.

[6] B.B. Kristensen, O.L Madsen, B. Møller-Pedersen, K. Nygaard: *Syntax-directed Program Modularization*, In P. Degano, E. Sandewall (Eds.): *Interactive Computing Systems*, North-Holland, 1983

[7] B.B. Kristensen, O.L. Madsen, B. Møller-Pedersen, K. Nygaard: *Object Oriented Programming in the BETA Programming Language*, Book Draft, Computer Science Department, Aarhus University, January 1991.

[8] O.L. Madsen, B. Møller-Pedersen: *Basic Principles of the BETA Programming Language*, In Gordon Blair et. al (Eds.): *Object Oriented Languages, Systems and Applications*, Pitman, 1991.

[9] O.L. Madsen, C. Nørgaard: *An Object Oriented Metaprogramming System*, In B.D. Shriver (ed.): *Hawaii International Conference on System Sciences – 21*, IEEE, January 1988.

[10] B. Magnusson et al.: *An Overview of the Mjølner/ORM Environment: Incremental Language and Software Development*, TOOLS'90, Technology of Object Oriented Languages and Systems, Paris, 1990.

[11] C. Nørgaand, E. Sandvad: *Reusability and Tailorability in the Mjølner BETA System*, TOOLS'89: Technology of Object Oriented Languages and Systems, Paris, Nov. 1989.

[12] D.C. Oppen: *Prettyprinting*, ACM Transactions on Programming Languages and Systems, Vol. 2 No. 4, Oct. 1980.

[13] E. Sandvad: *Hypertext in an Object Oriented Programming Environment*, Woodman'89: Workshop on Object Oriented Document Manipulation, Rennes, May 1989.

[14] E. Sandvad: *Syntax-directed Graphical Editing*, Computer Science Department, Aarhus University, June 1989 (DRAFT).

[15] E. Sandvad: *Object Oriented Development — Integrating Analysis, Design and Implementation*, Computer Science Department Technical Report PB-302, Aarhus University, April 1990.

20

Digital's COHESION™ environment

Tom Welsh
Digital Equipment Co Ltd., PO Box 110, Reading, RG1 3JJ, UK

1 Introduction

Digital s COHESION environment for software engineering has attracted a lot of publicity and speculation, but many people are still uncertain just what it amounts to. Is there anything really new and better coming, or is it just another wave of hype? Why that particular name, and what does it mean? How does COHESION fit in with other Digital architectures such as NAS; with what other vendors are doing; and with standards such as PCTE+, OSF, IRDS, and OMG? How does it all work?This paper sets out to give a brief overview of why COHESION became necessary, and what it consists of, as well as looking at the repository-based integration framework around which COHESION will develop in the future.

2 The Requirements

During the 1980s, the VMS operating system was a popular choice for software development. This was due to a number of factors, including

- Relative cheapness and flexibility of hardware platform (a program compiled on any VAX computer would run on any other VAX computer);

- The interactive environment, allowing programmers to work at their own speed;

- The multi-language programming environment, which allowed code from languages like Ada, BASIC, C, COBOL, FORTRAN, Pascal, PL/I, LISP and OPS5 to interoperate easily within the same program, thus facilitating reuse;

- Built-in software development tools, such as the Run Time Library, Librarian Debugger, and editors such as EDT and TPU;

- Layered software "productivity tools", including VAXset and the CDD (Common Data Dictionary), which worked with all the programming languages.

However, as the 1980s drew to a close, it became apparent that there was more to life than VMS. Driven by the rapid advance of technology and by the growing need to cut costs and justify expenditure, more and more organisations were adopting a computing strategy characterised by

- Open systems - usually some brand of UNIX^{TM}, or MS-DOS, or a mixture of the two.

- Hardware from different vendors.

- Local and wide area networks, connecting the various workstations, servers, PCs and larger computers.

This left the traditional set of CASE tools, limited to VMS, looking increasingly irrelevant to market requirements (although a large number of organisations still felt that the advantages of VMS outweighed its limitations). Clearly, there was a need to offer CASE tools which would work not just on VMS (or just on UNIX or PCs), but in a *heterogeneous distributed environment* - a network connecting all sorts of more or less standard software running on a mixture of equipment.

There was another consideration, too. The VMS tools had been mainly directed to the small-to-medium size of project (loosely, up to about one million lines of code). But today the largest projects run to tens or even hundreds of million lines. At the same time, reliability was becoming more important than ever: governments were demanding traceability, systematic documentation, and audited adherence to a prescribed methodology. All of these requirements pointed to the need for an IPSE (Integrated Project Support Environment). Such products had been launched before, without any particular commercial success.

3 What is COHESION?

3.1 History

COHESION was "program announced" in June 1990. This was a major announcement as it identified CASE as one of Digital's top priorities.

3.2 Components

COHESION consists of four main components:

- Services and Support

- Architectural Foundation

- Integration Framework

- Comprehensive Set of Tools

Although all four are equally important, we will concentrate mainly on the Integration Framework, as this is the Software Engineering Environment for COHESION.

3.3 Services and Support

Properly understood, CASE consists of the automation of some of the tasks of software engineering. This implies that there are certain prerequisites for the successful adoption of CASE technology, including:

1. Skillful, experienced and motivated people

2. Appropriate software engineering procedures, such as project management, requirements analysis, regression testing, structured walkthroughs, etc. (These sets of procedures are also known as "methodologies").

3. Techniques or methods for specific activities such as analysis and design, coding, configuration management, project management, testing, documentation, etc.

This is why no vendor can satisfy customers, or hope to be successful in the long run, simply by selling software. What organisations really need is not just technology, but expertise and advice. A well known recipe for failure is to take experienced COBOL programmers, send them on a one-week Ada course, and ask them to write an application in Ada. Similarly, giving untrained people powerful workstations with graphic tools may please them, and may result in superficial productivity improvements, but it is not in itself sufficient to guarantee successful projects.

For these reasons, COHESION includes a strong emphasis on providing appropriate learning opportunities. The traditional classroom training course is becoming an expensive luxury, so there will be increasing emphasis on videos, in-house workshops, and computer-based instruction. The DECwindows Bookreader allows users to study manuals on-line, and some COHESION products (such as DECdesign) include step-by-step tutorials in Bookreader format.

Organizational consultancy is another important aspect of COHESION. Two new consultancy packages are available: "CASE Assessment and Review", and "CASE Environment Planning and Design". These allow customers to enlist the help of Digital consultants in deciding where they are today in software engineering terms, and planning how best to make progress.

3.4 Comprehensive Set of Tools

There seems to be a consensus that the most sophisticated IPSE would be of little practical value unless it were populated with a complete set of reliable, cooperating tools. However, it would also be inadequate for a single vendor to offer an environment with a closed, "proprietary" toolset, as customers would be locked in and would not be able to choose the best tools for their own purposes.

For these reasons, it is one of the goals of COHESION to provide a comprehensive set of tools, sufficient to all the needs of software development and maintenance. This gives customers the option of "one-stop shopping". However, COHESION includes open, documented interfaces so that anyone who wishes to can either write tools, or modify existing tools, to operate in the COHESION environment. These interfaces are OSF/Motif and ATIS. Motif provides presentation integration and client-server functionality; ATIS is the repository interface, which provides data and control integration. As a result, it is anticipated that in the foreseeable future each Digital tool will be "shadowed" by a sheaf of tools from independent software vendors. Many customers will choose these, on various grounds - whether because they have become familiar, been enshrined as standards, cost less, or are simply seen to be better.

It is worth noting that, as of 1991, all major new CASE tools from Digital will appear on VMS and ULTRIX simultaneously. Existing VMS-based tools will be ported to ULTRIX (and possibly other platforms) as early as consistent with the relevant quality standards. For example, CDD/Repository and CDD/Administrator will become available on both VMS and ULTRIX at approximately the same time, although in the first release the repository will not be able to be distributed from one operating system to the other.

3.5 Architectural Foundation

The architectural foundation is provided almost entirely by NAS (Network Application Support). NAS is a set of services, based on industry and de facto standards, which enable application interoperability and portability across hardware and software platforms from multiple vendors. COHESION and NAS are interdependent, as

NAS provides the services to allow COHESION tools to work in heterogeneous distributed networks, while the COHESION tools generate the correct calls for the NAS interfaces.

Figure 1 shows the different platforms that are pulled together by NAS.

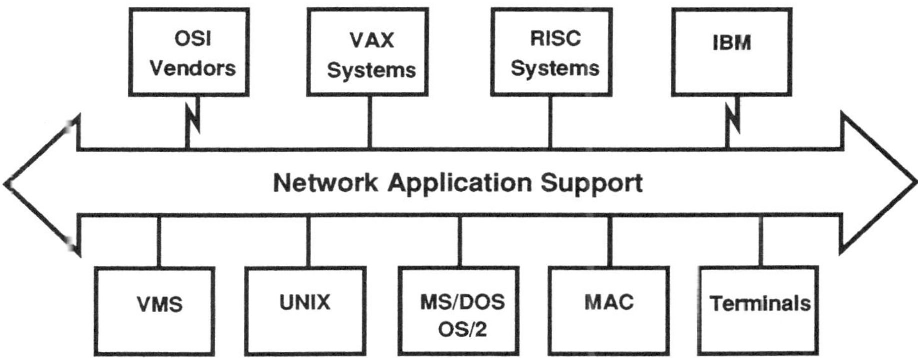

Figure 1   NAS Clients and Servers

The arrow does not correspond to any physical channel or logical protocol. It shows graphically how NAS allows various platforms to interoperate, using such services as DECwindows/Motif, SQL, Repository Services, and LiveLinks. The boxes below the arrow correspond to client or desktop platforms, while those above are servers. (Adopting the more intuitive convention which associates the user with the client, and the computer with the server, rather than the perverse X Window System convention which is the other way round).

The diagram tells us that we can sit in front of a workstation running VMS or UNIX, a PC running MS-DOS or OS/2, a Macintosh, or a character-cell terminal, and operate software which resides on either a VAX system running VMS, or a RISC system running ULTRIX. It is likely that other server platforms will be added in the course of time. Moreover, IBM and other OSI-conformant systems can already be accessed for limited server functionality. As an example, you could sit at a PC and run Paradox or dBase IV (using NAS SQL Services) to access an Rdb/VMS database on a VAX. Moreover, that Rdb database might actually be a DB2 database accessed transparently through VIDA. Another example would be using the POSIX interface on VMS to write applications that will run on UNIX systems - or vice versa.

4 Integration Framework: the Repository

4.1 The Repository of the 1980s: CDD/Plus

Radical advances are exciting, but experience shows that evolutionary progress is
much safer - especially in territory as little understood as integrated CASE. So it's re-
assuring that the integration framework for COHESION will be based on an upgrade
to the existing CDD/Plus, which is being used at thousands of sites around the world
today. Because of Digital's commitment to preserving customers' investment in applications they have already written, this product has remained upward compatible for
ten years, and will continue to be upward compatible in its next release.

The original CDD (Common Data Dictionary) goes back to the early 1980s, when it
complemented the Datatrieve 4GL and the DBMS Codasyl database. As time went
by, CDD was used for more and more different things: ad hoc queries and simple reports with Datatrieve, database definition with DBMS, then central definition of data
structures with BASIC, COBOL, FORTRAN, and other 3GLs. The Rdb relational database was tied in, and the FMS and TDMS forms products. Already the CDD was
the central hub of software development, but only in the data-oriented world of commercial applications. Developers of technical software didn't bother much about their
data, usually defining it on the fly as they wrote their code.

By 1987-8, it had become clear that an active, distributed repository would be essential in order to provide not only data integration but control integration as well. So
with the release of Version 4, CDD got a new name: CDD/Plus. While stable users
went quietly on using the product in their accustomed way, more powerful features
became available. CDD/Plus was layered on Rdb, for a start, so it inherited the power
and the security/integrity features of a leading relational database system. It became
distributed: this meant that a project could set up a "virtual repository" consisting of a
local repository "hiding" a central one in the background. References were resolved
in the same way as they would be in a block-structured language. It became active:
instead of users having to find out for themselves the effects of a change, CDD/Plus
would propagate them automatically. Moreover, it could do "impact analysis" by
showing "what would happen if..." something were changed.

As CDD/Plus became more capable, more and more products chose to integrate with
it. In addition to the 3GL compilers, databases, forms products and query tools, there
were now 4GLs and analyst workbenches. Moreover, in a most significant development, other vendors began to tie their products into CDD/Plus - products such as Excelerator and Smartstar. Many of them had their own "repositories", but these were
really little more than dictionaries, because they were limited to working with one
product, or at most one vendor's products. CDD/Plus, on the other hand, was *the*
central Repository, through which all the other tools could talk to each other.

It now became possible, for example, to use analyst workbenches like DECdesign or

Excelerator to define data fields or aggregates, and place these directly into the Repository, where they could be "seen" by 3GL or 4GL languages, and used in conjunction with forms and procedures which had been defined using different tools. Because of the distributed capability, it now became possible for an organization to have a single set of definitions on which to draw for all software projects worldwide.

4.2 The Repository of the 1990s: CDD/Repository

CDD/Repository V5 will continue the CDD tradition by providing upward compatibility for the approximately 40,000 customers currently using CDD/Plus V4. Applications using the DMU and RDO interfaces, as well as the V4 callable interface, will go on working unchanged.

However CDD/Repository will provide a new interface: ATIS ("A Tools Interface Standard"). ATIS is an object-oriented interface with extensions to support the entity-relationship model as well.

The principal benefit of moving to an OO interface is that it gives much greater flexibility in tool integration. The ER model aims to make all information about an entity explicit. This is a valuable asset in the world of data management in which ER was first applied: data definitions remain relatively static, and it is feasible to modify entities and relationships on the infrequent occasions when definitions do change.

In the world of CASE matters are very different. In a busy development shop, code is being written and changed hourly. New programs and tools may have to be installed and existing ones modified. Relationships between data entities, forms, procedures, queries, and files can change from minute to minute. But it is impossible to be forever rewriting the tools which make up a development environment. How can tools and applications be made independent of the form in which data is stored? The object-oriented model addresses this problem by hiding the exact representation of an object from the client. The object responds to messages; the client depends on the messages supported by an object but not on the implementation of those messages. In the ER model the same concept may appear as an entity, a relationship, or an attribute depending on a number of considerations. An object-oriented interface hides such differences behind a consistent set of methods. If code has to change in response to changes in data format, objects handle the situation by exporting changed behaviour.

All the changes are made in one place, and moreover once made in a given type they are inherited - propagated - to all subtypes of that type. This feature bestows on both code and data (alias behaviour and state) valuable guarantees of consistency similar to those provided (for data only) by the triggers of modern relational database management systems, as well as greatly encouraging reuse.

As a result of all this, the ATIS interface makes it possible to integrate a new tool into the repository environment with a minimum amount of change to its code. In fact, only for full integration is it necessary to make any changes at all.

4.3 The Integration Framework

An ATIS-based Repository, together with a Motif-based user interface, provides most of what is needed for an IPSE. Figure 2 shows how the ability of NAS to put users in touch with the services they need across a multi-vendor network is carried across to the Repository environment. This is because Repository Services and Motif are both built into NAS, so when you use them you automatically inherit the distributed capabilities of NAS.

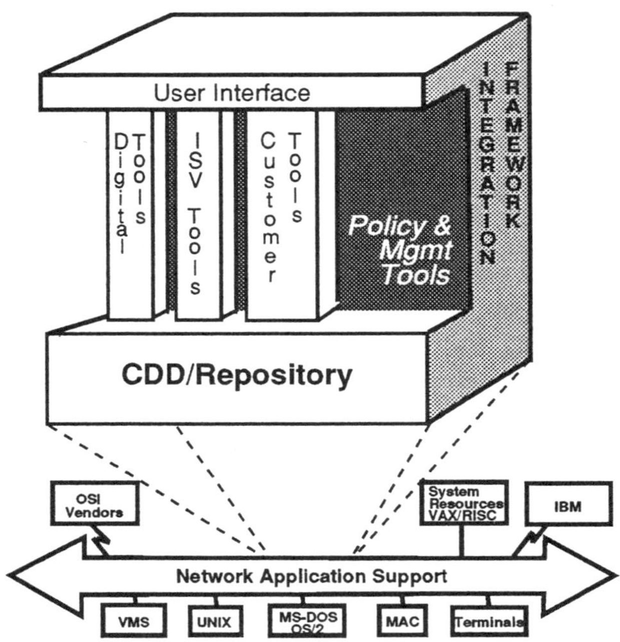

Figure 2

To translate this into concrete terms, you can sit down at any of the NAS client devices and log into the Repository environment, using one or more repositories on VMS or ULTRIX servers. If the repository administrator has set up a distributed repository, its consistency is safeguarded by all the integrity features of a fully distributed relational database management system with two-phase commit capability, journalling, on-line backup, etc.

As described above, any tools can be made available provided they communicate with users through the OSF/Motif graphical user interface (GUI), and with the repository through ATIS.

Between them, these two standards deliver presentation integration (Motif), data and control integration (ATIS), and client-server distribution (Motif and ATIS).

5 ATIS

5.1 Background

The story of ATIS began early in 1988 when Digital and Atherton Technology drafted a proposal to establish a vendor-neutral specification for a CASE tools integration interface. This was originally derived from the Atherton Software Backplane, but there has been substantial divergence since then. In May 1988, ATIS was presented to a group of American organisations including systems houses, tools vendors, research groups and user consortia. Soon after, Digital presented ATIS to the committee of ECMA (the European Software Manufacturers' Association) responsible for the development of the PCTE+ standard. It was apparent that some kind of convergence between ATIS and PCTE+ was extremely desirable, so that there could be a single standard CASE tools interface in the USA and Europe, for civil and military use, in all sorts of software development projects, from data management systems to embedded systems.

In December 1988 the American group was named CIS ("CASE Integration Services") and set up several working groups to address different issues concerning the definition of ATIS. Later, Digital proposed ATIS to the ANSI committee responsible for the IRDS (Information Resource Dictionary System) standard, in the belief that the object-oriented model could offer a new dimension to the development and management of database and transaction processing systems. An approach was also made to the ISO IRDS committee.

In June 1990 Digital announced its intention to deliver a new major release of CDD/Plus which would support the ATIS interface. This would be known as CDD/Repository V5, and would be accompanied by a flexible window-based tool for repository administrators, called CDD/Administrator.

5.2 Some Fundamental Concepts

ATIS introduces four important new concepts. These are *contexts*, *roles*, *collections*, and *partitions*. We will briefly examine each of them, and consider a simple scenario in which a user logs on to a repository-based environment and starts work.

A *context* is a view into the repository, which restricts the owner of that context from accessing any files, tools, reports, or baselines which are not included in the context. Only one user can be in a given context at a time. It is a much more powerful abstraction than an account, a directory, or a username. For instance, a given user may be editing a source file as part of a particular baseline. Suppose that user leaves the system, goes home, and goes on holiday the next day. Someone else will be asked to finish that piece of work. Just by logging into the same context, the replacement worker can be sure of finding everything exactly as his predecessor left it.

A *role* is perhaps the easiest concept to understand. Examples of roles might be "programmer", "analyst", "technical writer" or "project manager". Clearly, these four types of user would have quite different requirements and privileges in an automated project support environment. The programmer would need to have access to the source code and possibly the documentation for the baseline being worked on. He would also need certain tools, including editors, compilers, debuggers, builders and testing tools. In order to assure consistent results, it might be desirable that he would only have access to a certain specific version of, say the FORTRAN compiler. The technical writer would not have rights to modify the source code, but would probably be allowed to read it. On the other hand, he would be allowed to modify the documentation, which the programmer could only read. And so on. The project manager would have access to none of the files and tools mentioned so far, but would be allowed to use estimation, planning and tracking tools, and would see statistical data on project metrics gathered from the programmers, designers and writers, but probably hidden from them. It is quite possible that the same person may be able to choose different roles at different times.

A *collection* corresponds to the familiar idea of a baseline or baselevel. For instance, it is similar to a "class" in VAX DEC/CMS, Digital's current version management system. A collection consists of a number of different elements (some of which may themselves be collections), but only one specific version or "generation" of each. When a given milestone in development is reached, the code written to deliver the required functionality can be compiled and tested. If it passes all the regression tests, the baselevel is declared and frozen. That is when a collection is created. A context grants access to one or more collections, among other things.

A *partition* is involved with the concept of work flow control. A project might have partitions called "Work In Progress" and "Approved Code". Programmers would be given modify access to certain files in the "Work In Progress" partition, but read access only to everything in the "Approved Code" partition. Source files would be "promoted" from "Work In Progress" to "Approved Code" by passing through some sort of "gate" - this would probably include the successful running of certain sets of regression tests, and perhaps sign-off by responsible individuals.

Now we can perhaps see how these rather unfamiliar concepts would work together. Choosing a role from the menu offered in response to our username and password, we are admitted to a well-defined context. This affords us access to some files and tools, while denying us the right to modify, to see, or even to know about the existence of others. Access in this environment is based in general on the "need to know". The context uses another menu to prompt us to choose from the one or more pending work items for which we are responsible. This usually involves reserving one or more elements, or even a whole collection. If we decide to perform the "modify" operation on a source file, the system will automatically perform the appropriate configuration management transaction, call the editor, and position the cursor at the next piece of work to be done. When the edit is finished, the source file will automatically be replaced in the repository, and the changes will be recorded. Finally, if the current deliverable is now complete, some series of actions may lead to its being promoted into a new partition - yet another small contract completed on the way to a successful project.

5.3 ATIS Models

ATIS defines the following models which we shall briefly describe:

- Base Object Model
- Versioning Model
- Configuration Management Model
- Work Flow Control Model
- Tool Integration Model

5.4 The Base Object Model

In ATIS, objects are known as *elements*, and the classes are called *types*. An element is manipulated through the services interface using a unique identifier called an *element-id*. Attributes are called "properties".

The ATIS schema is self-defining, and thus doubles as a "meta-schema". The object types are themselves first class objects and can be manipulated in the same way. This allows for dynamic extension of both schema and behaviour.

Over and above the pure object-oriented schema, ATIS supports the ER model. This is necessary for upward compatibility with CDD/Plus V4 and IRDS.

ATIS is currently a single inheritance model (unlike, for example, PCTE+). However, it is possible to change ATIS to support a multiple inheritance model compatibly with the current specification and without affecting the behaviour currently defined.

The ELEMENT element type is the root of the ATIS type hierarchy. All other types are subtypes of ELEMENT.

It is worth mentioning that methods can have *preambles* and *postambles*. These allow for modification of behaviour without actually changing the method in question. This technique lends itself to activities such as the collection of metrics.

5.5 The Versioning Model

The aim of the versioning model is to record changes in the state of elements over time. Compound elements (*aggregates*) can also be versioned.

Since ATIS is aimed at major development efforts, it is essential to have provision for concurrent development by many different software engineers. This requires the concepts of *branch* or "variant", and *merging* branches back together again.

A number of different versioning models are possible with ATIS. These include

- Check In - Check Out (CICO). ATIS uses the CICO model by default.

- The traditional CMS model in which the users are responsible for arbitrating conflicts at replacement time (whereas CICO forces creation of a variant line of descent).

- Checkpoint (CP). There is no concept of a variant, new generations simply being saved with a unique identifier.

- Hybrid. All of these models can be used simultaneously.

5.6 The Configuration Management Model

Configuration management builds on version control to model system structure and the idea of a baseline. ATIS handles configuration management using the VERSION, CONTEXT and COLLECTION element types.

5.7 The Work Flow Control Model

This deals with the facilities provided by ATIS to model and automate the chosen lifecycle methodology (or "process") of a given organisation. It is important that the work flow model be flexible, giving the users freedom to "do things our way". It has been learned that forcing users to conform to a rigid and inflexible system is one of the quickest paths to failure in CASE.

The work flow model provides levels of change approval (often called change control). With this model, when a change is approved by one or more individuals, it is *promoted* to the next higher level. Promotion must take place one level at a time.

Partitions are named divisions of the repository that model work flow levels. A version of an element exists in exactly one partition. A user views the repository through a *partition list*, an ordered list of partitions which act as "panes of glass": only element versions in a partition on the user's list will be seen when scanning a directory or walking element versions.

It should be understood that the process of setting up the work flow model to reflect a given lifecycle methodology may demand considerable time and effort.

5.8 Tool Integration

There are four different levels of tool integration:

- Non-integration. This does not mean a tool cannot be used in the repository environment. It does mean that the user must fetch or reserve elements from the repository, operate on them with the tool, and then replace them himself. This could be inconvenient, and certainly sacrifices most of the integrity and dependency checking features of the environment. However it does mean that any tool can be used productively without delay.

- Registration. This makes known to the system new element types, messages and methods, but does not require any modification to the new tool's source code. The drawback is that, once started, the tool is on its own. An editor, for instance, could be started up to edit a file obtained through the repository, but during the editing session it would not be possible to "include" other files through the repository.

- Registration with Enclosure. This is a technique whereby a "shell" is written for the tool. The shell program can use knowledge of the files the tool operates on to create traceability links in the repository or otherwise provide information at a fine level of detail.

- Full Integration. This requires that the tool's source code be modified to make calls to the environment's services, and linked against the environment's run-time library. The tool can then make full use of environment services, create and modify elements as necessary, etc.

6 The Repository Information Model

Although, as we have seen, ATIS is self-describing and dynamically extensible, it is extremely undesirable that it should be extended ad-hoc. If every tool which seeks to integrate with the COHESION environment adds its own set of elements and relations to the repository schema, it will not take long for things to get out of hand.

Moreover, the fundamental idea of having a dictionary or a repository is that things should be done in only one place if at all possible. It would be ironic and disappointing if the repository itself did not conform to this principle.

For these reasons, it is necessary to provide a public information model which goes a good way beyond the basic ATIS schema. This model should deal, not in elements, versions, relations and partitions, but in the kind of entitities used for business modelling and systems analysis. Ideally, the model should be rich enough and consistent enough that the authors of any tool which is to be integrated into the repository environment can find the entities that they require, already defined for their use. Categories of tools (such as analyst workbenches, 4GLs, DBMS, and forms products) should use the repository and its contents in set ways, using well-defined and agreed semantics, in order to obtain consistent results and avoid unexpected discrepancies.

Digital is in fact working with leading software vendors to define a comprehensive Repository Information Model (RIM). However for various reasons, it has not yet been possible to publish very much about this process and the results obtained. Digital expects to ship a full specification of the RIM with the first release of CDD/Repository, and the model would remain upward compatible from that time on so as to guarantee the work that is based on it.

The Context Diagram presented in Figure 3 is a tentative snapshot of a dynamic process. There is no guarantee that the diagram resembles what will eventually be provided - indeed, it is likely that there will be substantial differences. The intention of Figure 3 is simply to give some insight into the level of abstraction being contemplated, the types of entities and relationships that are involved, and the fact that this kind of model focuses on business issues more than technical details. It is at this level that it becomes apparent why the repository can aptly be described as "the first corporate CASE tool".

PERSONNEL
MISSION
B
PERFORM
IDENTIFIES, SCOPES, PRIORITIZES
PORTFOLIO
SATISFIES
MANIPULATED BY
A
REQUIRE-MENTS
ASSIGNED TO
USED BY
INPUT TO
DEFINE
PROJECT MANAGE-MENT
GOVERNED BY
SYSTEM LIFECYCLE
B
C
STEWARDS
CONSISTS OF
C
GUIDES, CONSTRAINS
GUIDES, CONSTRAINS
PROCESS
TRANSFORMS
GUIDES
DATA
ALLOCATED BY
ALLOCATED BY
CONSTRAINED TO RUN ON
A
DISTRIB-UTION
RESIDES
MANAGES
PLATFORM
SPECIFY

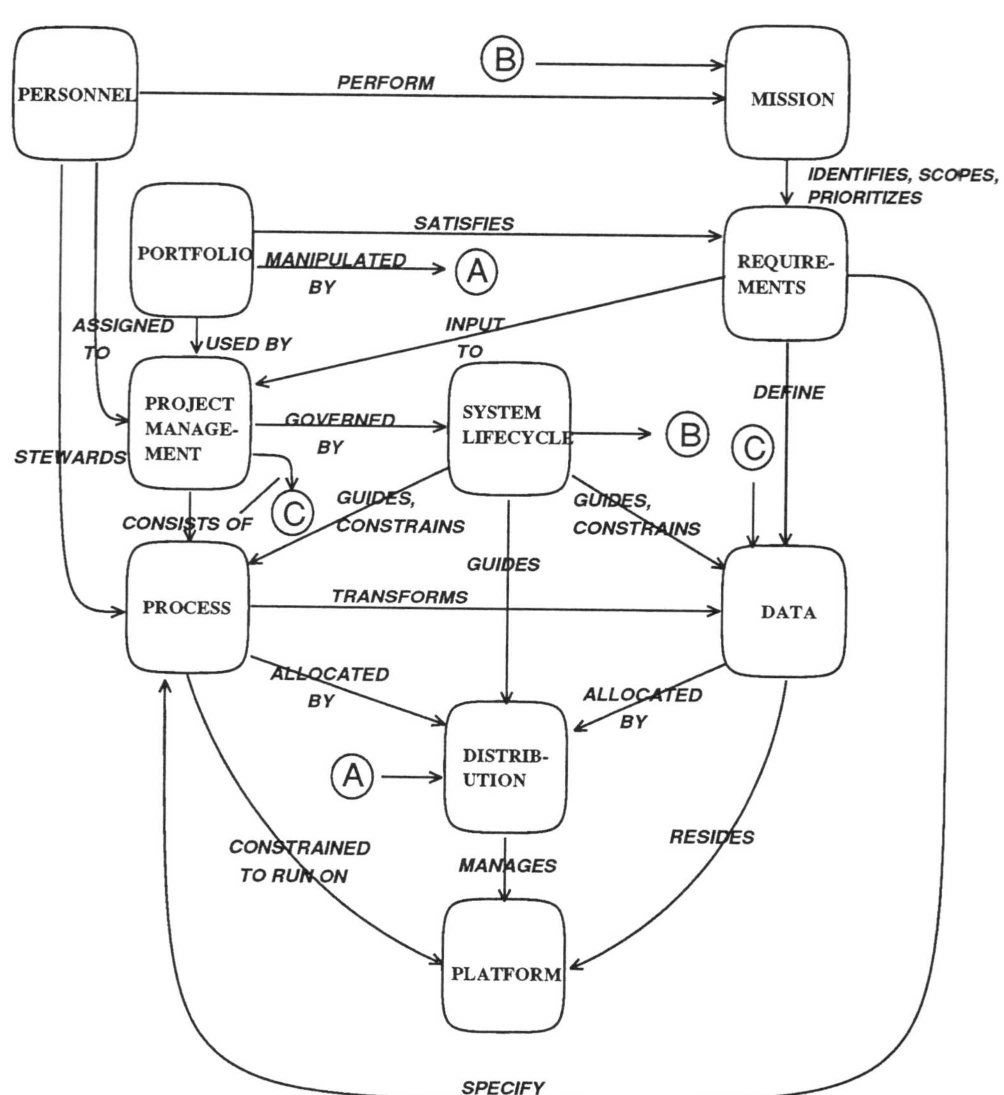

Figure 3

7 Summary

We started out by observing that "closed" proprietary CASE environments, no matter how productive, have decreasing credibility in the marketplace. With the advent of the 1990s software development organisations are more and more looking to open, distributed, multi-vendor systems for the best price/performance and the greatest freedom to adopt new technology as it becomes available.

COHESION is Digital's programme to provide CASE in the context of NAS, which meets these requirements for openness, distribution, portability and interoperability. COHESION has four main aspects:

- Services and Support

- Architectural Foundation

- Integration Framework

- Comprehensive set of tools

After briefly looking at the other aspects, we examined the integration framework based on CDD/Plus and CDD/Repository. It became clear that this environment, defined by OSF/Motif and ATIS, meets the requirements of today's CASE market, and additionally lays the foundations of an Integrated Project Support Environment (IPSE) which would be appropriate for the development and maintenance of very large software systems by teams of dozens or hundreds of developers.

This framework will (over time) be fully populated with tools from Digital, but as soon as it is available it will be open to anyone who wishes to make their tools "plug and play", providing an environment which combines full presentation, data and control integration with an open market in CASE products.

References

Digital Equipment Corporation. *ANSI X3H4 Working Draft Information Resource Dictionary System ATIS. Technical Report ANSI X3H4/90-187, ANSI, 14 February 1990*

Digital Equipment Corporation. *Proposal for Extending Dictionary Standards to Support CASE.*

Digital Equipment Corporation. *Digital's CDD/Repository Information Model.*

Trademarks

The following are trademarks of Digital Equipment Corporation:

CDD, CDD/Plus, COHESION, DECdesign, DECwindows, LiveLink, NAS, Rdb/VMS, ULTRIX, VAX, VAX DATATRIEVE, VAX DBMS, VAX DEC/CMS, VAX FMS, VAXset, VAX TDMS, VIDA, VMS

DB2, IBM, OS/2, PS/2, PC are trademarks of International Business Machines Corporation

dBase is a trademark of Ashton-Tate Corporation

Excelerator is a registered trademark of Index Technology

Macintosh is a registered trademark of Apple Computer, Inc.

MS-DOS is a trademark of Microsoft Corporation

OSF/Motif, OSF/1 are trademarks of the Open Software Foundation Inc

SMARTSTAR is a registered trademark of Signal Technology, Inc.

Software Backplane is a trademark of Atherton Technology, Inc.

UNIX is a registered trademark of UNIX System Laboratories Inc.

X Window System is a trademark of M.I.T.

Parts 6

Standards
and Reuse

21

ECMA PCTE

John Dawes and Hugh Davis
ICL Secure Systems, Eskdale Road, Winnersh,
Wokingham Berkshire, RG11 5TT, UK

1 Introduction

PCTE is a major focus of activity in the field of Public Tool Interfaces, and the publication of Standard ECMA-149 in January 1991 was a significant event. The standardization activity has several aspects of interest, notably the presentation as an abstract (i.e. programing-language-independent) specification and dependent bindings to programming languages (in this case Ada and C). The benefits of this approach were widely (though not universally) recognised at the outset, and it is believed they have been largely realised.

The starting point for the standardization was PCTE+ issue 3 [PCTE+a, b], itself a significant development from the original PCTE [PCTE86], especially for operating-system independence, features for mandatory and discretionary security, and self-referentiality. These improvements have been retained in ECMA PCTE, and a number of others made to rectify deficiencies or to improve functionality. A standardization programme is not the right place for research and development, however, so many good ideas have not been taken up. These have not been lost; they have been recorded as "deferred issues", and it is intended to reconsider them in the future.

The authors have both been actively involved in the PCTE standardization from the beginning; John Dawes was a member of the PIMB Abstract Specification Task Group whose report laid the foundation for the standardization, and is Convenor of the Task Group TC33-TGEP that has carried it out; Hugh Davis is a member of TGEP, and is ICL representative on TC33 and its liaison officer for POSIX. Their previous paper [DaDa89] was written at a stage when it was clear what needed to be done; this paper reports the results of actually doing it. The views expressed in this paper are those of one or both of the authors and not necessarily those of ECMA, TC33, TGEP, or ICL.

Some examples from the PCTE Standards are given at the end.

2   A Brief History of PCTE

PCTE originated in the ESPRIT project 32, part funded by the Commission of the European Communities (CEC), called "A Basis for a Portable Common Tool Environment". That project produced a specification for a tool interface in the C Language, and an initial implementation and some tools. A number of versions of the specifications were produced, culminating in "PCTE Version 1.4" in two volumes: volume 2 covering the user interface and volume 1 covering everything else [PCTE86]. Subsequently the CEC commissioned Ada versions of the two volumes [PCTE87] and a formal definition using an extension of VDM [VIPK88].

The CEC established the PCTE Interface Management Board (PIMB) in 1986 to maintain PCTE and promote its use. Through its subsidiary PCTE Interface Control Group (PICG) PIMB conducted a widespread public review, and published a revision known as PCTE 1.5.

PIMB established an ad hoc task group to consider the form of the standard; this group reported in June 1988 [ASTF88], strongly recommending that the standard should comprise an abstract (language-independent) specification and separate dependent bindings to whatever languages it was desired to support.

In 1986 several nations of the Independent European Programme Group, under Technical Area 13 (IEPG TA-13), embarked on a collaborative programme to enhance PCTE to make it equally suitable for military as for civil use. This project is called PCTE+; the result of the definition phase is an enhanced specification called PCTE+ issue 3 [PCTE+a, b; BGMT89], published in October 1988. This consists of both Ada and C versions of volume 1, volume 2 being the same as PCTE 1.5 volume 2. PCTE+ issue 3 is being assessed by implementing it independently with a variety of tools on two different operating systems.

Upon request from the PIMB, ECMA undertook to continue the development of PCTE to bring it into a form suitable for publication as an ECMA Standard. ECMA TC33 was formed in February 1988 with this objective. Initially it was intended to base ECMA PCTE on PCTE 1.4, but this was soon changed to PCTE+ issue 3. The report of the PIMB task group on the form of the specification [ASTF88] was accepted by TC33, and a task group (Task Group for ECMA PCTE, TGEP) was formed in November 1988, charged with producing the Abstract Specification and bindings for Ada and C.

TC33 established an ad hoc Task Group to consider the question of the user interface for ECMA PCTE, and in April 1989 accepted its recommendation that X-Library should be the portability platform for PCTE-based tools with respect to the User Interface. Accordingly work on volume 2 for ECMA PCTE was abandoned. TC33 also agreed to TGEP's recommendation that ECMA PCTE should be presented as three distinct standards: the abstract specification and the bindings for Ada and for C.

The Abstract Specification was accepted by the General Assembly of December 1990. The Ada and C Bindings are scheduled for consideration by the ECMA General Assembly of June 1991.

3   The Present Status of ECMA PCTE

The Abstract Specification is available as Standard ECMA-149. Application should be made to:

ECMA Headquarters,
Rue du Rhône 114,
CH-1204 GENEVA.
Switzerland

Phone: +41 22 735.36.34
Fax: +41 22 786.52.31
Telex: 413237

It was hoped to produce a Rationale for the ECMA PCTE Standard, giving a rather full account of the reasons for PCTE being the way it is, and for it not being the way it isn't. Unfortunately resources did not allow this, and all that can be done is to produce a record of the reasons for the decisions to make changes from PCTE–. If this is concatenated to the PCTE+ Rationale [RAT03], itself a rationale for changes from PCTE 1.4, then a rationale for differences between PCTE 1.4 and ECMA PCTE should result. There is a gap at the base of this structure, however, as there is no rationale for PCTE 1.4 itself. The ECMA PCTE Rationale will be published either as a Technical Report or as a TC33 Working Paper. It is hoped that future funds will allow the production of a complete Rationale for ECMA PCTE.

One further ancillary document seen as within the scope of TGEP is an introductory document, like [PCTE89]. Other than those, a large number of specialized documents can be identified aimed at particular audiences, but it is not the intention of TGEP to get involved as a Task Group.

The possibility of errors being found in the Standards and other documents cannot be ignored. The Abstract Specification is the biggest and most complex standard published to date by ECMA, and no sophisticated mechanisms exist for such maintenance matters as comment handling. Accordingly TGEP is setting up a system and a procedure; see section 5.1.

4   Technical Aspects of the Standardization Process

4.1   Abstract Specification

4.1.1   Advantages of the abstract specification

The report of the PIMB Task Force on Abstract Specification [ASTF88] distinguished between formality and abstractness of a specification such as PCTE: formality is to do with rigour and precision, whereas abstractness is to do with freedom from implementation-dependent detail. The Task Force recommended an informal abstract specification as the PCTE standard, i.e. one expressed largely in natural English, at a level of abstraction above the details of the programming language bindings, for the following reasons.

(1)   To provide a single authoritative standard.

(2)   To provide a reference source for future language bindings.

(3)   To reduce duplication of work between the various language bindings.

(4)   To provide a firm basis for considering the consistency of different bindings.

(5)   To conform to the preferred approach of standardization bodies.

These reasons have been largely vindicated in practice. (1) is hardly disputable. (2) will be demonstrated when a new binding is produced; preliminary work has begun on a C++ binding, and it appears that no changes are needed to the Abstract Specification to allow such a binding to make full use of the object-orientedness of C++ with no changes to the Abstract Specification. (3) and (4) have been borne out by the work on the C and Ada bindings, which were developed in parallel with each other and the Abstract Specification. Although they revealed some problems in the gap between the assumptions made by the Abstract Specification and the abstraction level of the bindings (see below), both bindings took a fraction of the time to produce that would have been required without the Abstract Specification. It can also now be demonstrated that the C and Ada bindings (and any future bindings) are consistent in a well-defined sense, both being related in defined ways to the same specification, this consistency being guaranteed by the conformance requirements. (5) was perhaps rather anticipatory at the time (June 1988) but it is now accepted practice; for example, POSIX is moving in that direction.

The ASTF decision to advise against a formal definition was not unanimous. A minority (including one of the authors) believed that not only was a formal definition possible and desirable, but that it would actually take less time to produce than an informal one, and could then be the basis of an informal translation of high quality; but this minority failed to carry the day, so the standard is not formal. However, partly as a result of a presentation of the results of the VIP project [VIPK88], which impressed the members of TGEP a good deal, formal methods were used in two ways: VDM-SL notation was used for parts of the specification internally, and later externally; and more importantly, it was agreed that the specification should have the form of a formal definition: that it should appear to be an English version of a VDM specification. This was taken very literally in early drafts, which had a state definition, type definitions, and operation definitions, clearly separated. Later the type definitions and operation definitions were grouped into chapters concerned with specific aspects of the functionality (this is not easy to do in VDM-SL), and related function definitions were added; but the state definition remained and formed the heart of the foundation chapter.

Looking back, the authors believe that achieving clarity and simplicity through abstraction was more important for technical understanding and consensus than achieving rigour through formality, and that the path taken was probably correct.

Also, not having to satisfy the constraints of a formal definition language has allowed a clearer modular structure for the specification. Still, the authors believe that the addition of a formal definition would enhance the usefulness of the Standards even now.

4.1.2 Data Abstraction and Self-referentiality

One of the innovations of PCTE+ was its almost complete self-referentiality: most PCTE entities are represented by objects in the object base. Thus processes, workstations, activities, volumes, and so on, all have their specific object types. There are some variations: locks are represented by links; working schemas are represented by sets of links; and types are represented by several objects: a "type" object for each type, plus a "type in SDS" object for each schema definition set containing the type. This self-referentiality gave rise to considerable discussion about the relation of the entities themselves to their representations. It seemed that for all entities, whether an apparently concrete entity such as a workstation or an abstract entity such as a process, there are three levels of abstraction to be considered: the "real world" where a workstation is a physical entity made of metal, glass, and plastic and a process is an operating system artifact; the PCTE conceptual level where a workstation or a process is an abstract entity with various properties defined by the operations one may perform on it; and a PCTE representational level, where a workstation or a process is an object of type "workstation" or "process" with certain attributes and links to other objects. The "real world" is of no direct concern to the PCTE specification: a PCTE operation cannot be defined in terms of physical connections of physical workstations, for who knows what implementation with virtual workstations sharing physical resources may not be possible? Of course, a knowledge of the likely physical implementation on present-day equipment guided the specification throughout, one overriding concern indeed being that the specification should be practicably implementable, but the fact remains that the world defined by the PCTE specification is a conceptual world.

The relation between the conceptual and the representational levels caused a good deal of discussion. Essentially there were two views: one view (the "two-worlds view") was that the two levels were completely distinct, and that the specification should define the effect of every operation call on both; the other view (the "one-world view") was that they were two descriptions of the same set of entities and it was a design choice which description was used in any particular case. A focus for the discussion was provided by the decision to use the Data Definition Language (DDL) as an essential part of the specification notation. DDL had been described in PCTE+, but mainly as a notation for the user to define object types; and it was not given any semantics. This notation was tidied up a bit and adopted by TGEP to define the representational level. At the same time, VDM was used to define the state, and a start was made on defining the rest of the conceptual level in VDM. The question then became: what is the relation between the VDM definitions and the DDL definitions? It was clear that to describe the whole of both levels separately would involve an insufferable amount of duplication. A compromise was reached which is embodied in the final standard:

- No judgement need be made between the one-world and the two-worlds views.

- Two forms of words for defining the effects of operations are defined: one couched in conceptual terms and one in representational terms. However both are interpreted as having the same meaning: in the two-worlds view, they imply effects on entities of both worlds; in the one-world view, they are different ways of referring to the same entities. As the conceptual form is a great deal shorter and clearer than the representational, it is almost always preferred (except when referring to links, where a convenient naming convention was not found that would avoid confusion between a link and its destination object). For example the meaning of the representational phrase:

  the value of the "contents_confidentiality_label" attribute of the "volume" object X

  is expressed conceptually as:

  the contents confidentiality label of the volume X

- The relation between VDM and DDL is not formally defined (though it could be, e.g. by defining the DDL in terms of VDM invariants on the state); both define both the conceptual and representational worlds (or views of the world).

The typing mechanism of PCTE presented a problem; it has to be defined in order to define DDL, but is itself represented (in a rather complicated way) in the object base. The solution adopted (after many attempts at more elegant solutions) was to define in VDM, as part of the foundation, those aspects of the typing mechanism needed for the definition of DDL, and to redefine the whole typing mechanism in DDL.

4.1.3 Abstract Operations

In contrast with the abstraction of data types and objects described in the last subsection, the abstraction of operations was fairly straightforward. VDM-SL provided a convenient notation for defining the signatures (parameter and result types and names). The description of the effect of the operation was easy once the decision on the conceptual form of words had been taken. A number of common features of operation descriptions were found, which were replaced by common phrases defined elsewhere. The most noticeable example is the treatment of errors detected by operations, which illustrates the notion of the Abstract Specification as an informal version of a formal specification. The definition of the effect of an operation is for the normal case only; the error cases, that would be defined in a VDM specification by error preconditions, are separated out into error specifications: parameterized descriptions of error cases, defined in an Appendix. An implementation is required to detect all error cases, and to distinguish them at least to the granularity defined in the Abstract Specification; the effect of an error case is to leave the state unchanged and to report the error in the appropriate way for the binding language.

Having decided not to distinguish entities from their representations in the description, it was natural not to distinguish them as parameters to operations; so for example a parameter representing a workstation is a reference to an object of type "workstation". It cannot be the object itself, because parameters in VDM are values, i.e. inwards only. VDM does not provide pointers as such; the normal way of giving entities an identity in a VDM specification is to define a map in the state from identifiers to the entities. This was done; but the question remained as to what the identifiers should be. In PCTE+ an object can be referred to by a pathname denoting a sequence of links from another object, or by a "referenced_object" link from the process; in ECMA PCTE these were abstracted into a generalized object identifier called an "object designator", as a VDM type with no properties other than equality and inequality. It was then natural to specialize object designators according to object type, so that a workstation would be represented by a parameter of type "workstation_designator" i.e. an object designator denoting an object of type "workstation". This however opened a gap between the Abstract Specification and the bindings: the Abstract Specification could assume that its parameters were well-typed, whereas the binding operation would have to check and raise an error if necessary. There was another difficulty; in PCTE+ it is possible for a pathname not to denote an object at all. It was decided to abstract all this away from the abstract operations, and to fill the gap by defining as much as possible of the mapping to the binding languages within the Abstract Specification document. Similar considerations arise for other object base entities: attributes, links, and types all have their own form of designators.

4.1.4   Use of English

One of the advantages of writing a formal definition first and then translating it into English would have been that the translation could be done in a controlled way, avoiding those twin banes of careful readers of technical specifications, the use of different terms with the same meaning, and the use of the same term with more than one meaning. An attempt was made to achieve the same effect in writing the Abstract Specification; for instance, in PCTE+ the terms "station", "workstation", "user station", "host", and "host station" are used apparently indiscriminately for the same concept; in ECMA PCTE the term "workstation" is used throughout. The idea of unique technical terms was greatly helped by the normative use of DDL: all DDL names of object, link, and attribute types became *de facto* defined technical terms. The text has been reviewed many times to weed out synonyms and ambiguities, though it is impossible to avoid introducing them when writing in a natural language and undoubtedly some remain.

Another benefit of the pseudo-formal approach is that every term is identified, and so it can be ensured that it is properly defined. The definition of a term in the Abstract Specification is either its defining occurrence in DDL or VDM, or else is marked by being in italics. A simple indexing procedure then ensures that each term is defined exactly once; and rigorous reviewing ensures that the definitions are adequate. An example is the term "replicated set"; it is difficult to discover what this means in PCTE+: is it the set of all master objects or the set of all masters and all copies? Indeed there seems to be some doubt as to whether a master and all its copies are one object or many. It does not matter a great deal which decision is made, provided it is made once and carried through consistently.

4.1.5   Bindings

Although the PCTE Abstract Specification is a pioneering effort in some ways, it is not the only effort to produce a language-independent specification; indeed the fact that there is general agreement on the advantages of doing so was one argument used by the PIMB ASTF. There is a good deal of activity at present in this field, in particular in the Bindings working group ISO/IEC JTC 1/SC22/WG11, and TGEP tried to take full advantage of their work. Two documents in particular were relevant: the Guidelines [DTR10182] and the Common Language-Independent Datatypes [CLID90]. Both of these are drafts but both are in a complete state.

The Guidelines provide an analysis of different binding methods, with a set of guidelines for each. The relevant method was clearly Method 1: provide a completely defined procedural interface; but the existence of Method 5: Binding pre-existing language elements, brought to light the issue of what to do about the binding language input-output facilities. (In the end it was decided to provide PCTE-defined input-output and to leave the effect of using the binding language input-output to be defined by the implementation.) Each Guideline was examined and a response formulated: accepted, accepted with modification, not applicable, or rejected. These will be published in the Rationale. Most of the applicable guidelines were accepted, sometimes with modifications (for example to take account of the fact that ECMA PCTE does not use error numbering, but still needs to keep common and language-specific messages separate; see Guideline 33). One rejected guideline was to provide lists of abbreviations for operation and other names; in fact two rival lists of abbreviations were produced before it was realized that even C does not place a limit on the length of an identifier, provided the first 31 characters are unique, (except for an obsolescent concession to existing compilers for external names). It was ensured that all names would be unique within the first 31 characters and the lists of abbreviations were scrapped. (A binding to Minimal Basic is not expected!)

The second document from WG11 that gave a lot of help was the Common Language-Independent Data Types. This gives a mathematically exact definition of a set of base data types and constructors for defining further types, and solved the problem of defining a satisfactory mapping from the data types defined in the Abstract Specification to those used in the bindings. This is done by a two-stage process: first the Abstract Specification data types (called "PCTE types") are mapped to a selection of CLI data types (called "PCTE standard types"); and then the PCTE standard types are mapped to the binding language. In simple cases like Integer (for attribute values) the first mapping is common to all bindings, and is given in the Abstract Specification; in other cases (such as lists or sequences) both mappings are language-specific. The mappings from designators are gathered together in the same clause, using the same technique of a map to an intermediate set of types, called "references"; these are a mixture of private types and CLI data types, with characterizing operations in the CLID style. The Binding document contains the map from the intermediate types to language types, and the specifications of the characterizing operations.

4.2 Composite object model

4.2.1 Complex objects and composite entities

One input to ECMA PCTE was provided by the German PCTE Initiative (GPI). This was an initiative by a group of German companies, which had produced a raft of proposals for enhancing the modelling capability of PCTE [GPI88a, b]. The German members of TGEP in particular were keen to establish two principles which differed from PCTE+: complex objects and n-ary relationships.

The essence of the GPI complex object model is that every object contains a set (which may be empty) of component objects; thus instead of defining object composition by means of special links, with special operations for manipulating such 'composite entities", as is done in PCTE+, with very few exceptions all operations would act on a composite object as a whole. This was a very attractive point of view for some members of the Task Group, but the ramifications of adopting it and trying to merge it into PCTE+ proved many and varied. In the end most of the detailed issues were deferred, and a compromise was adopted: the PCTE+ model would be retained, and the structure in terms of composition links would be visible at the interface, but the description would be couched primarily in terms of complex objects (renamed "composite objects" to reflect their mixed parentage). This has been carried through to an extent: the fundamental notion of an object is indeed a composite object with a set of component objects, and all operations act on composite objects unless stated otherwise; but the notion of "atomic object" (which can be loosely defined as an object without its components) is introduced at an early stage, and used rather a lot thereafter.

One feature of the GPI complex object model that TGEP wished to retain was the separation of access control between an object and its components. This has been achieved by associating with an object two access control lists (ACLs), the "atomic ACL" governing access to the direct attributes and links of the object, and the "object ACL" governing access to the components of the object. To ensure integrity, a new discretionary access control mode called OWNER has been introduced; it is similar to CONTROL_DISCRETIONARY but applies only to the object ACL, and it governs the ability to change the discretionary control access, and is itself subject to controls based on the composite object structure.

4.2.2 Relationships

The second major thrust of the GPI proposals was for n-ary relationships (i.e. able to associate more than 2 objects) as entities in their own right. Again this is an attractive idea that would enhance the modelling power of PCTE, but again it introduces endless ramifications. In this case, after long and full debate, it was regretfully decided that TGEP just did not have the resources to carry through the necessary investigations, and deferred the issue, retaining the PCTE+ concept of links attached to their source objects. In fact TGEP went further, and stopped pretending that PCTE has a concept of relationship at all; mutually inverse pairs of links are just that. The word "relationship" is retained only in some operation names, for sentimental reasons.

4.2.3   Archiving

A problem from PCTE+ that has been solved in ECMA PCTE is archiving, or the ability to move a number of objects to a volume which is then dismounted. The problem lies not with the archiving, but with the retrieval; unless some accessible trace of the objects is left behind to maintain consistency, then it could prove impossible to restore a proper subset of the objects. The solution is to create an object of type "archive" for each set of archived objects, with a designation link to each archived object, and an "archive directory" with a link to each archive object. The archived objects are inaccessible; this is allowed because designation links do not guarantee referential integrity. Specific operations are provided for archiving and restoring sets of composite objects on particular devices.

4.2.4   Other changes to the object model

A number of other changes to the object model from PCTE+ may be mentioned more briefly.

- Finer access rights. One GPI proposal was for separate access control on attributes. This was seen as rather heavy on implementation, so a simpler solution giving almost the same functionality was adopted: to replace the 3 access modes READ, WRITE, and APPEND of PCTE+ by a set of 10 modes allowing separate control over access to attributes, links, and contents, and separate control of object deletion. A new access mode APPEND_IMPLICIT has been added; it governs the adding of implicit links from an object, giving more control over sharing of component objects between composite objects

- Cardinalities of links. The GPI proposals allow more control than PCTE+ over the cardinalities of relationships (i.e. how many relationships of a particular type an object may enter into with a particular rôle). This is similar to CAIS-A. This has been adopted in ECMA PCTE: precise minimal and maximal cardinalities for link types can be specified, with nonstrict (violable) minimal cardinality.

- Stabilizing links. There are problems with PCTE+'s stability relationships: no special rights are required to set them, all write accesses must be revoked before setting a stability relationship, an object cannot be stabilized forever, and stability always depends on the existence of another object. The ECMA PCTE solution is that a stabilizing link can be created or deleted only if one has the discretionary control right on the destination; a stability link can be created even if the destination has a WRITE right granted. It is possible to create a stabilizing link with the origin and destination being the same. As a consequence, the destination is stabilized for its lifetime, as such a link cannot be removed. However the destination can be deleted by deleting its enclosing object, as the stabilizing link is an internal link and so is deleted implicitly at the same time.

- 4-valued access rights. The 3 values of access rights in PCTE+ are "granted", "denied", and "undefined". As "denied" and "undefined" have the same immediate effect (no access), the GPI proposed to do without denial. However, it was felt that the functionality of explicit denial was needed; and this led to the need for an explicit value "denied" to make it obvious that the functionality is present, so as to convince an assessor when necessary to achieve a desired security rating. In fact, to cope with access control to composite objects a fourth value "partially denied" is also required to cover the cases where access to some components is granted and to others is denied.

- Access right implications removed. PCTE+ defines some implications for granted access rights (e.g. WRITE implies READ), but implications for denied access rights are not defined and it is not clear whether this is intended. Furthermore, no consistent definition of implication for denial could be found. Accordingly, all implications of access rights have been abolished, except that OWNER right on a complex object implies CONTROL_DISCRETIONARY right on its components. The result is that operations are partitioned into disjoint sets according to the access rights they require, giving a simpler interface. Implications, if required for particular reasons, can be provided by tools.

- Object numbers. It is not clear whether all information contained in the "system identifier" (volume number, number of object on volume) and the "object exact identifier" (surrogate) in PCTE+ needs to be visible at the interface. Probably only the number of the volume and the object exact identifier are of interest to the user. Accordingly the predefined system attribute "object_number" has been deleted, and the object exact identifier (renamed just "exact identifier") is used as a key for the links which in PCTE+ use the object number.

- New attribute type Natural. A new attribute value type Natural has been introduced; its values are unsigned integers, and it is used (among other things) for integer key attributes.

4.3   Other changes from PCTE+

Many other small changes have been made from PCTE+. For instance, TGEP felt free to change the names of predefined links and attributes where the PCTE names seemed inapposite. Among the more significant changes are the following.

- Operations have been added for the creation and deletion of workstations; these were implied but not defined in PCTE+.

- Changes to the process model. The most obvious change, presentational in nature, concerned the vexed question of self-referentiality. In PCTE+ the specification of the process model is complicated and confused by the inclusion of both a Process entity and an object of type Process (a natural effect of adding self-referentiality for processes). Therefore the choice was made to specify the process model entirely in terms of objects of type Process in ECMA PCTE.

- Predefined discretionary groups. A number of changes have been made from the discretionary access group structure of PCTE+ issue 3. Specifically, the predefined groups are now represented in the object base; the group WORLD has been renamed ALL_USERS (this is just a change of name); and the inheritance of discretionary group types has been restricted.

- Predefined schema definition sets (SDSs). PCTE+ has four predefined SDSs, one of which ("system") is automatically included in every working schema. ECMA PCTE has the same four predefined SDSs, but some changes have been made to avoid unnecessary importations.

- VOLUME_LIST_OBJECTS. There was some interest in adding non-navigational access to objects to PCTE, or at least to allow a tool presenting non-navigational access (e.g. a query language interpreter) to be efficiently supported. Pending a more complete resolution, a new operation VOLUME_LIST_OBJECTS has been added; this operation returns a list of objects of specified types on the volume (or an error if the volume is offline).

- New kinds of contents have been introduced for accounting logs and for audit files. They can be written to and read from only by using specific operations, and their structure cannot be violated by using standard object contents read and write operations.

5   Future Plans

With the issue of the Abstract Specification and the imminent issue of the C and Ada Bindings and the Rationale, the work of TGEP is entering a new phase. A number of overlapping activities can be seen for TGEP in future: maintenance of the existing standards, longer-term evolution of the standards, and internationalization of the standard (i.e. converting it into an International Standard).

5.1   Maintenance of the Standards

For maintenance of the Standards TGEP is setting up a procedure to cover receiving, considering, and responding to comments received, resolving problems, and publishing corrections. When ready it will be published in the PCTE Newsletter. Meanwhile comments may be sent to the address given at the end of this paper, if possible electronically and in the following format (note the use of paragraph numbering within a clause):

Sender	J.Dawes, ICL, tgep@win.icl.co.uk
Date	91-01-27
Document	ECMA-149
Clause	8.7.2(16)
Title	Misspelling
Comment	In line 4 "Asociated" should be "Associated".

Comments received will be acknowledged and logged, and then passed to TGEP for resolution. Several different possible resolutions are envisaged at present: e.g. acknowledged error to be corrected in a defect list; query answered but no action required; problem acknowledged but outside the scope of the Standard. No doubt others will turn out to be needed in practice. The originator will be informed of the final resolution.

5.2   Evolution of the Standards

During the standardization process, a list was maintained of issues that arose. It currently contains 104 issues, of which 41 have been resolved and will contribute to the Rationale. The remaining 63 were deferred on the grounds that they did not affect the consistency of the specification, and to attempt to resolve them would jeopardize the production of the Standard. These deferred issues are being fed in to the comment system. Many of them will require a good deal of analysis to resolve (which is why they were deferred) and may be more suitably handed over to a different programme.

One relatively independent evolutionary process is the generation of new language bindings. The next candidate is probably C++, which has a certain vogue at present. There appear to be no insuperable problems to providing a C++ binding which makes sensible use of its object-oriented features, though of course that is not the same as providing a fully object-oriented interface to PCTE.

5.3   International Standardization

When the PIMB requested ECMA to standardize PCTE it was in the knowledge that ECMA as a Category A liaison organization of ISO/IEC JTC1 could propose the ECMA standard for processing by the fast-track procedure as a Draft International Standard. The validity of this procedure is based on the fact that ECMA, as a Liaison member, has sufficient understanding and experience of ISO standardization to ensure that ISO requirements have been taken into account during ECMA standardization. For example it is essential that an ISO standard uses an acceptable Formal Description Technique (FDT) and that its relation to other standards is agreed by formal or informal liaison with appropriate working groups.

Some examples of actions taken during PCTE standardization follow:

- The combination of VDM (an accepted FDT) and English in ECMA-149 has been chosen with ISO acceptability in mind.

- Having decided that PCTE is separate from but must be conformant with POSIX, ECMA has had a formal liaison with the ISO/IEC POSIX Working Group (SC22/WG15) since October 1989.

- Section 4.1.5 describes how the work of the ISO/IEC Language Binding Working Group (SC22/WG11) has been used in the Standard.

It has been decided by ECMA TC33 that ECMA-149 will not be submitted to ISO until a language binding has been approved. We expect TC33 to make a decision on ISO submission later in 1991.

References

[ASTF88]   Report to the PCTE Interface Management Board of the Task Force on Abstract Specification, 24th June 1988. (PIMB/ASTF/REP/01, 02, 03.)

[BGMT89]   G. Boudier, F. Gallo, R. Minot, I. Thomas. An Overview of PCTE and PCTE+. ACM SIGPLAN Notices, Vol. 24, No. 2, February 1989.

[CLID90]   ISO/IEC JTC1/SC22/WG11/N190 Common Language-Independent Datatypes, Working Draft #4, 6 September 1990.

[DaDa89]   H.F.Davis and S.J.Dawes. ECMA PCTE: Formalizing an Interface Definition. Ada UK 8th International Conference, September 1989 (Ada User volume 10 Supplement).

[DTR10182] ISO/IEC DTR 10182 Guidelines for Language Bindings (6 February 1990)

[GPI88a]   The German PCTE Initiative. Requirements for the Enhancement of PCTE/OMS, version 2.0, 26 September 1988.

[GPI88b]   Introduction to the Specification of the GPI OMS Data Model, version 1.0, 16 December 1988.

[PCTE+a]   PCTE+, C, Functional Specification, Issue 3, 28 October 1988.

[PCTE+b]   PCTE+, Ada, Functional Specification, Issue 3, 28 October 1988.

[PCTE86]   PCTE, A Basis for a Portable Common Tool Environment, Functional Specifications, Fourth Edition, November 1986.

[PCTE87]   PCTE, A Basis for a Portable Common Tool Environment, Ada, Functional Specification, First Edition, June 1987.

[PCTE89]   IEPG TA13. Introducing PCTE+, April 1989.

[RAT03]   PCTE+/RAT/03 Rationale for the Changes between the PCTE+
             Specifications Issue 3 dated 28 October 1988 and the PCTE
             Specifications Version 1.5 dated 15 November 1988 (Issue 3, 6
             January 1989)

[VIPK88]   VIP Kernel Interface: Final Specification, December 1988.

Acknowledgements

Standardization is a consensual process based on existing definitions. The work
reported in this paper is therefore the achievement of the many past and present
members of ECMA TC33-TGEP and the many individuals who have contributed to
previous PCTE and PCTE+ specifications.

Address for submission of comments

John Dawes,
Convenor, ECMA TC33-TGEP
ICL Secure Systems,
Eskdale Road,
Winnersh,
WOKINGHAM,
Berkshire RG11 5TT,
U.K.

e-mail: tgep@win.icl.co.uk

---

8.   Foundation

8.1   The State

(1)
```
            state PCTE_Installation of

            SYSTEM_TIME              : Time
            OBJECT_BASE             : map Object_designator to Object
            WORKING_SCHEMAS         : set of Working_schema
```

(2)
```
            Object_designator is not yet defined
```

(3)
```
            Working_schema ::
                VISIBLE_TYPES       : set of Type_in_working_schema
                SDS_NAMES           : seq of Name
```

(4)   The system time is the date and time of day at any instant, as given by some system clock. For the format of the time see clause 23.1.1.5.

(5)   The object base is a set of objects identified by object designators (see clause 8.2.1).

(6)   A working schema is associated with a process and defines the rules which determine what properties of the objects are visible (and thus accessible) to the process. It contains types in working schema (see clause 8.5).

(7)   The initial value of the state consists of the following objects:

(8)   -   at least one workstation, at least one device managed by that workstation, at least one volume mounted on that device, and at least one process running on that workstation (see clauses 18.1.2, 11.1.1, and 13.1.5);

(9)   -   the common root and the administrative objects (see clause 9.1.2);

(10)   -   at least one user and at least one user group (see clause 19.1.1);

Example of VDM-SL – The State

<table>
<tr><td colspan="2">

8.2.1   Objects

</td></tr>
<tr><td>(1)</td><td>

```
Object ::
    OBJECT_TYPE                 : Object_type_designator
    DIRECT_ATTRIBUTES           : set of Attribute
    DIRECT_OUTGOING_LINKS       : set of Link
    DIRECT_COMPONENTS           : set of Object
    PREFERRED_LINK_TYPE         : [ Link_type_designator ]
    PREFERRED_LINK_KEY          : [ Key ]
    CONTENTS                    : [ Contents ]
```

</td></tr>
<tr><td>(2)</td><td>

Key = **seq1 of** (String | Natural)

</td></tr>
<tr><td>(3)</td><td>

Contents = Structured_contents | Unstructured_contents

</td></tr>
<tr><td>(4)</td><td>

Structured_contents = Accounting_log_contents | Audit_file_contents

</td></tr>
<tr><td>(5)</td><td>

Unstructured_contents = File_contents | Pipe_contents | Device_contents

</td></tr>
<tr><td>(6)</td><td>

The object type constrains the properties of the object (see clause 8.3.1).

</td></tr>
<tr><td>(7)</td><td>

There is a basic set of direct attributes and direct outgoing links which all objects have; it is defined in clause 9.1.1.

</td></tr>
<tr><td>(8)</td><td>

The preferred link type and preferred link key, if present, are used as defaults in the identification of a direct outgoing link of the object (see clause 8.2.3).

</td></tr>
<tr><td>(9)</td><td>

Every direct component of an object is the destination of a direct outgoing composition link of the object.

</td></tr>
<tr><td>(10)</td><td>

A *primitive object* is an object with an empty set of direct components.

</td></tr>
<tr><td>(11)</td><td>

A *composite object* is an object that is not a primitive object.

</td></tr>
</table>

Example of VDM-SL – Definition of "Object"

9.1.1   The Basic Type "Object"

(1)   **sds** system:

(2)   object:
             with
                 attribute
                     exact_identifier   : (**read**) **non_duplicated string;**
                     volume_identifier   : (**read**) **non_duplicated natural;**
                     replicated_state   : (**read**) **non_duplicated enumeration**
                         (NORMAL, MASTER, COPY) := NORMAL;
                     last_access_time,
                     last_modification_time,
                     last_change_time,
                     last_composite_access_time,
                     last_composite_modification_time,
                     last_composite_change_time
                         : (**read**) **non_duplicated time;**
                     num_incoming_links,
                     num_incoming_composition_links,
                     num_incoming_existence_links,
                     num_incoming_reference_links,
                     num_incoming_stabilising_links,
                     num_outgoing_composition_links,
                     num_outgoing_existence_links
                         : (**read**) **non_duplicated integer;**
                 link
                     predecessor : (**navigate**) **non_duplicated existence**
                         link (predecessor_number: **natural**) **to transitive**
                         stable object **reverse** successor ;
                     successor : **implicit link** (system_key) **to** object **reverse**
                         predecessor;
                     opened_by : (**navigate**) **non_duplicated designation**
                         link (number) **to** process;
                     locked_by : (**navigate**) **non_duplicated designation**
                         link (number) **to** activity_object **reverse** lock
                     with attribute
                         locked_link_name : (**read**) **string;**
                     end locked_by;
             end object;

Example of DDL – Definition of "Object"

13.2.15   PROCESS_UNSET_REFERENCED_OBJECT

(1)
```
PROCESS_UNSET_REFERENCED_OBJECT (
    process          : [ Process_designator ],
    reference_name   : Key
)
```

(2)   If no value is supplied for *process*, *process* designates the calling process.

(3)   PROCESS_UNSET_REFERENCED_OBJECT unsets a referenced object of *process*.

(4)   If there is no "referenced_object" link from *process* with key *reference_name*, the operation has no effect. Otherwise, the link "referenced_object" link from *process* with key *reference_name* is deleted.

Errors

(5)   If *process* is not the calling process:
      ACCESS_ERRORS (*process*, ATOMIC, WRITE_LINKS)

(6)   PROCESS_IS_UNKNOWN (*process*)

(7)   If *process* is not the calling process:
      PROCESS_HAS_NOT_GOT_REQUIRED_STATUS (*process*, READY)

(8)   REFERENCE_NAME_IS_INVALID (*reference_name*)

(9)   REFERENCED_OBJECT_IS_NOT_MUTABLE (*reference_name*)

Example of Abstract Operation Specification

13.2.15   PROCESS_UNSET_REFERENCED_OBJECT

Abstract Specification

(1)
PROCESS_UNSET_REFERENCED_OBJECT (
           process   : [Process_designator],
           reference_name : Key
)

C Language Binding

(2)
```
int Pcte_unset_referenced_object (
    Pcte_object_reference     process,
    Pcte_string               reference_name
)
```

Parameters

(3)
The *process* argument is optional. If not provided it should be specified
as NULL.

Example of C Binding Operation Specification

22

Constructing software engineering environments using the Software BackPlane

Michael Aslett
GEC-Marconi Software Systems, Elstree Way,
Borehamwood, Hertfordshire, WD6 1RX, UK

1 Introduction

The development of large and complex systems necessarily involves a significant level of management and control. When a large software component is present, additional problems arise due to the intangible nature of software and its intrinsic flexibility. Some of the common problems are:

- Failure to build to specification;
- Missed delivery schedules;
- Frequent budget overruns;
- High maintenance costs;
- Marginal reliability.

As we enter the 1990's, this "software crisis" has reached the point where user expectations may exceed developers' ability to produce successful products. On large projects there may be literally thousands of components such as text, diagrams, source code, etc. which need to be controlled. The sheer volume of information swamps paper-based methods, thus tools, in particular computer-based tools, become essential. However current computer aided software engineering (CASE) tools tend to solve only a portion of the system development problem or address a particular part of the lifecycle. Project and configuration managers trying to organise, control and coordinate large projects need tools as well.

Recognising the need for managing the people, data and tools in a system development environment, Atherton Technology have developed the Software BackPlane. The Software BackPlane provides a framework for building, using and maintaining integrated project support environments. Since every software organisation has unique requirements, Software BackPlane is designed to be independent of tools, methodologies, languages and platforms.

1.1   Overview of the Software BackPlane

The Software BackPlane framework serves three main functions:

a. It supports the storage of project data in a repository - Project data includes source code, executable code, documentation, etc. It is clearly one of the most important assets of a software development organisation. Software BackPlane's repository has three major benefits:

- *It maintains data integrity;*

- *Users have distributed access to it;*

- *It is object-oriented* (see section 1.1.1).

b. It supports the integration of tools - With its open architecture, Software BackPlane enables users to incorporate future tools as well as those currently available. The major goal of tool integration is to allow Software BackPlane users to apply the tools they are comfortable with; there is no need to change current working habits. There are three categories of tools for Software BackPlane:

- *The SoftBoard Series* - These tools are companion products to Software BackPlane. They are special tools that extend and enhance the BackPlane.

- *Third party software tools* - A number of tools have already been integrated into Software BackPlane by third party vendors. These include CASE tools for project estimation, analysis and design, productivity tools and various utilities, e.g. Software through Pictures, Interleaf TPS and GECOMO Plus.

- *In-house tools* - Any tools that have been developed in-house can be integrated into the Software BackPlane.

c. It supports the incorporation of work flow controls - With Software BackPlane users can institute and enforce policies and procedures related to software development. This *work flow control* ranges in complexity from simple step procedures to the implementation of sophisticated software methodologies. An example of a simple work flow control is requiring a sign off prior to the release of a software module.

The next two sections describe the basic components of the Software BackPlane and communication in the BackPlane. For a more detailed introduction to the Software BackPlane please refer to [1].

1.1.1   Basic Components of the Software BackPlane

Software BackPlane is an *object-oriented* system. The elements of Software BackPlane are implemented as discrete units (*objects*) of a particular class (*object type*). Each object performs actions after receiving *messages*, where the same message sent to different objects can result in different actions occurring (*polymorphism*). The code that implements the particular action that takes place after an object receives a message is called a *method*. Attributes of objects are represented as *instance variables*.

Class structure is supported by the use of sub-classes. Sub-classes inherit definitions from their parent class and refine existing capabilities. Within the Software BackPlane a class can only have one parent (single rather than multiple inheritance).

Software BackPlane objects are stored in a *database*. Typically a database contains the information for a complete project. The objects contained in a database are *collections* and *components*. Collections are analogous to directories and components to files in conventional operating systems. The main function of a collection is to group together components and subordinate collections. A collection is different from a traditional directory in that it is an individual entity rather than a mere grouping of entities.

The process of creating a new working version of a component or a collection is called *checkout*. Depending on his or her privileges, a user can request to use either the *mainline version* or a *branch version* of the data. The mainline version is the version which is universally agreed upon as the official version. A branched version is a duplicate of the mainline version that is established primarily to avoid alteration of the mainline version.

Every collection or component in the repository has a *version number*. This number is increased by one whenever an element is checked out. The user who checks out the mainline version of an element has the exclusive privilege of changing it. When the user has made the appropriate changes,

he or she can insert the element back into the mainline by performing the
checkin operation. After this new version is checked in, it becomes available
to any other user with the appropriate access privileges. Note also that an
audit history is maintained for each element in the database, recording, for
example, its checkout/checkin history.

All valid users have access to the database via *contexts*. A context is a
view on to the database stemming from a collection or component in the
database hierarchy. The only way to gain access to any portion of a database
is through a context. A context is used to isolate a portion of the database
so that

- only one user can work within its scope at a time and

- no work outside the context will affect the data within the context.

Software BackPlane classifies users in three ways: *user names*, *groups* and
roles. A user name is the name by which a user logs in to the system. A group
is a set of users. Groups generally correspond with departments or teams. A
role is used to define interactions between a class of user and different types
of objects. Roles generally correspond with jobs or tasks. Typically a user
is a member of some groups and is allowed to assume a set of pre-defined
roles, e.g. User Fred is a member of the development group and can assume
the roles designer and reviewer. The roles designer and reviewer will restrict
the operations which Fred can perform on the various types of objects in the
database.

1.1.2   Communication in the Software BackPlane

Project SoftBoard (PSB), a product in the SoftBoard series, is used to structure and formalise communication in the BackPlane. PSB lets users create
action request forms, which are text files that can be associated with project
data in the repository and tracked over time. Action requests contain such
information as the:

- sender,

- receiver,

- description of the requested action,

- deadline,

- severity level,

- status.

If desired, an action request can be set up to create related action requests automatically. PSB comes with a query mechanism that supports the monitoring of action requests over the life of a project. PSB also has an optional closed loop mail facility so that members of a project team can share action request information.

1.2   Customising the Software BackPlane

Software BackPlane's flexibility allows the basic environment to be modified to meet the needs of a software development organisation. This ability is referred to as *environment customisation*. It is based on the following features of the BackPlane:

- **Safeguards for objects in the database can be set up.** This refers to the repository services (context management, versioning and access control) which are part of standard Software BackPlane usage.

- **New types of objects can be created.** If the standard types of objects do not totally cover the needs of an organisation, then new types of objects can be created, based on existing types in the BackPlane.

- **Objects' functionality can be changed.** The standard methods associated with an object can be modified. Also new messages/methods can be defined.

- **Software tools can be incorporated into the BackPlane.** Tools can be integrated so that they are directly accessible from objects in the BackPlane.

- **Work flow control procedures can be defined.** Procedures can be set up to control how users can manipulate objects and/or tools in the BackPlane.

Integration SoftBoard (ISB) is a tool which is used for performing environment customisations. It provides a template-driven programming interface that makes it easy to modify the definition of object types in the BackPlane. In particular it provides:

- a C-based template for integrating tools,
- an edit/compile/test loop and
- a toolbox of utility programs.

It is also possible to customise Software BackPlane by creating programs in shell scripts, C or Software BackPlane's character interface language. A summary of the facilities provided by the Software BackPlane is shown in figure 1.

There now follows an example of how the Software BackPlane can be customised to support the needs of a software development project. Section two describes some of the procedures which must be followed by a project called "project X." Section three describes how these features are implemented in the Software BackPlane. Section four contains some concluding remarks.

2   Project Description

Project X will be managed by a project manager, who will be assisted by two team leaders. Each team leader will control a team of between five and ten software engineers. On the quality assurance side, there will be a quality manager and two quality engineers.

The software will be developed according to the configuration practices recommended by the U.S. government's DOD-STD-2167A standard. Thus the software will consist of Computer Software Configuration Items (CSCIs), Computer Software Components (CSCs) and Computer Software Units (CSUs). The structure that will be enforced is: CSCIs will contain CSCs; CSCs will contain CSUs and CSUs will contain the source code and any associated documentation.

Every CSCI, CSC or CSU will be identified by an issue number. This issue number will comprise of a release number and a version number. The release number refers to a major release of the system; the version number refers to minor updates, e.g. issue 2.6 refers to the sixth version within release two.

Every CSCI will be defined by a build state file. This file will record the issue number of the CSCs contained in a CSCI. Similarly every CSC will be defined by a build state file which will record the issue number of the CSUs contained in a CSC.

Every CSCI, CSC and CSU will have an associated quality status. Initially this status will have no value. When the item is ready for testing the status will be set to registered. When the complete system is ready for system testing the status will be set to chilled. Finally when the system is released the status will be set to bonded.

Once the quality status has been set, the following procedures will be used for authorising changes:

- When the status is set to registered, a member of the quality department has to approve a change request.

- When the status is set to chilled, a team leader has to approve a change request.

- When the status is set to bonded, the project manager has to approve a change request.

The SA/SD design method [2] will be used. This will be supported by an appropriate tool set.

3 Software BackPlane Solution

This section describes how the Software BackPlane can be tailored to support the needs of project X described in the previous section. Firstly new groups and roles are identified. Then new object types are introduced for representing the 2167A requirements. Finally tool integration is discussed. In fact a demonstration system, based on these requirements, has been produced by GEC-Marconi Software Systems with assistance from IBM and Atherton Technology.

3.1 Groups and Roles

From the above description there are two development teams and a quality assurance (QA) department involved in project X. Thus three groups could be represented in the BackPlane - team A, team B and QA. However as no differences are specified between the work done by the two teams, only two groups will be defined - *development* and *QA*.

In order to represent the interactions between the different classes of users and the objects stored in the database, roles need to be defined. From the first paragraph in the description of project X, the following roles have been identified: *manager*, *team_leader*, *engineer*, *QA_manager* and *QA_engineer*.

The groups and roles are created in the BackPlane using the character interface language as follows:

```
create role name:manager
create group name:development
```

3.2 New Object Types

As CSCIs contain CSCs, CSCs contain CSUs and CSUs contain source code and documentation, it is natural to make them all special types of collections.

However as they all have an issue number and a quality status and CSCIs and CSCs each contain build state files the following type hierarchy will be included in the database:

```
Collection
        2167A
                CSCI_CSC
                        CSCI
                        CSC
        CSU
```

All of the new types descend from the collection type. Only objects of type CSCI, CSC and CSU can be created. Thus types 2167A and CSCI_CSC are not instantiable — they are used as place holders for representing common features.

There now follows a detailed description of the 2167A type. Then brief descriptions of the other new object types are given followed by a summary of the properties of these new types.

3.2.1   Type 2167A

As identified above, issue number and quality status are common to CSCIs, CSCs and CSUs. Thus type 2167A will include instance variables (attributes) for representing this information. The issue number will be represented as a string of the form [release.version] where release and version are integers. Validation will be provided to ensure that it is always of this form.

The quality status will be represented as a string which can take the following values:

- registered,
- registered_amending,
- chilled,
- chilled_amending,
- bonded,
- bonded_amending.

The quality status can only be updated when the collection is checked in. The amending values were not specified in the description of project X. They have been introduced to allow for the authorisation of change requests as described below.

When the quality status has not been set, changes can be made by any user, i.e. anyone can checkout (create a new version of) a collection. Once the quality status has been set to registered, chilled or bonded, no-one can checkout the collection. The following procedure will then be used for making changes.

First of all Project SoftBoard will be used to generate an action request which describes the problem. Then this action request will be analysed to identify where the problem is occurring. Once the problem has been identified, authorisation to checkout the various collections involved in the problem will be given as follows:

When a 2167A collection has its quality status set to registered, the status can be updated to registered_amending by any member of the QA group. When a 2167A collection has its quality status set to chilled, the status can be updated to chilled_amending only by a user in the team leader role. When a 2167A collection has its quality status set to bonded, the status can be updated to bonded_amending only by a user in the project manager role. Thus when the quality status has been set to one of the three amending values, anyone can checkout the collection.

The 2167A type will be defined using the template provided by ISB. The instance variables will be defined and new methods created for getting and setting their values. Also the checkin method will be modified as described above.

3.2.2   Other new Object Types

Type CSCI_CSC will modify the checkin method so that a new version of the build state file is created which contains the issue number of the collections attached to the current collection. This functionality will be implemented by modifying the definition of checkin in the ISB template for type CSCI_CSC.

Type CSCI will specify that only collections of type CSC can be attached to collections of type CSCI. This is done using the character interface language as follows:

```
create type name:CSCI, type: CSCI_CSC, mode: yes
setvalue element name:CSCI, type:ELEMENTTYPE, msg:okTypeAttach,
                         value: CSC, mode: entire
```

The first command creates the CSCI type with its parent as CSCI_CSC and because mode is set to yes, the type is instantiable. The second command specifies the type of objects which can be attached to instances of type CSCI.

Note that even though the CSCLCSC type has been created using the ISB
template, it can still be manipulated using the character interface language.

In a similar way type CSC will specify that only collections of type CSU
can be attached to collections of type CSC. Finally type CSU will specify
that only components or standard collections can be attached to collections
of type CSU.

With this type structure, only collections of type CSC can be attached
to a collection of type CSCI and thus the build state file for such a collection
will be of the correct form. Similarly the build state file will be of the correct
form for collections of type CSC.

3.2.3   Summary of the new Object Types

With the new type structure as presented in the previous two sections, users
will be able to create collections of type CSCI, CSC or CSU. On a collection
of type CSU users will be able to:

- set and display the issue number (type 2167A definition),

- set the quality status only in specific circumstances (type 2167A definition),

- display the quality status (type 2167A definition),

- checkout the collection either when the quality status has not been set
  or when it has been set to one of the three amending values (type 2167A
  definition),

- only attach components or standard collections (type CSU definition).

On a collection of type CSCI users will be able to:

- set and display the issue number (type 2167A definition),

- set the quality status only in specific circumstances (type 2167A definition),

- display the quality status (type 2167A definition),

- checkout the collection either when the quality status has not been set
  or when it has been set to one of the three amending values (type 2167A
  definition),

- checkin the collection which will result in a new version of the build state file being created which contains a list of the issue numbers of the CSCs contained in the current collection (type CSCI_CSC definition).

- only attach collections of type CSC (type CSCI definition).

These examples show how inheritance is used to generate the correct functionality for instances of a given type. Also for maintenance purposes, all code is kept is a single place and so can easily be changed with no unexpected side effects.

3.3 Tool Integration

The manager of project X wishes to use TeamWork as the design tool for supporting the SA/SD design method and Interleaf TPS as the documentation tool. Both of these tools have already been integrated into the Software Back-Plane by Atherton Technology. However the project manager also wishes to use a tool to help him produce estimates for the project. He has decided to use GECOMO Plus, a tool from GEC-Marconi Software Systems which supports Boehm's Cocomo model [3].

Full integration of GECOMO Plus into the BackPlane would involve extensive changes to the tool itself. However GECOMO Plus can be integrated in to the BackPlane with no source code changes by *encapsulating* it in a new type. When source code is not available, this is clearly the only form of integration which is possible. However once a tool has been encapsulated, the integration can be easily extended to bring more information about the tool into the BackPlane. Below is a description of an initial encapsulation of GECOMO Plus in the Software BackPlane.

GECOMO Plus has its own database, which consists of a number of data files. Thus a new type, called GECOMO, will be defined which is a specialisation of a collection. The database can then be stored as components attached to a collection. As the database can not be directly modified, these components will not be visible to a user.

Checkout will be modified so that components attached to the collection are exported to the native file system. Similarly checkin will be modified so that the database is imported back into the BackPlane. Thus version control will be added to GECOMO Plus. In order to invoke the tool, the open message will be refined as this is the standard way of invoking tools in the BackPlane.

The GECOMO type will be defined using the template provided by ISB. In order to restrict access to the tool, only the role manager will have access to the methods associated with the GECOMO type. This is done using the character interface language as follows:

```
setvalue element name:GECOMO_*, pattern: yes, type: METHOD,
msgname:access, value: "{USER/*, ROLE/manager, ACCESS/rwedav}
                       {USER/*, ROLE/*, ACCESS/}", mode:entire
```

What this command does is to set the *access* instance variable for all objects of type METHOD whose name starts with "GECOMO_" such that a user in role *manager* has read, write, execute, delete, append and version privileges whereas a user in any other role has no access at all.

From this integration of GECOMO Plus into the BackPlane, three main advantages have resulted: version control, access control and invocation control. Also, now that the database of GECOMO Plus is stored in the Back-Plane, additional information could be extracted from it without invoking the tool.

To summarise, all of the tools used in project X will be available from the Software BackPlane. This means that access control can be enforced for all of the tools. Also enhancements to the integrations can be made at a later stage in the project if required.

4   Conclusions

This paper has identified that in order to support the real needs of a software development project, more facilities are required than stand-alone software development tools. Control and management of the information which is generated during the lifecycle of a project is as important as the final product. Thus some from of integrated project support environment is required which provides a central database that can support both tool integration and work flow control. By considering an example project, this paper has shown that both of these facilities are provided by the Software BackPlane.

References

1. Software BackPlane - Introduction and Concepts. Atherton Technology 1990.

2. Structured development for real-time systems. P.T.Ward, S.J.Mellor. Yourdon Press 1985.

3. Software Engineering Economics. B.Boehm. Prentice-Hall 1981.

Trademark Acknowledgements

- SoftBoard Series, Project SoftBoard and Integration SoftBoard are trademarks of Atherton Technology.

- Software through Pictures is a trademark of Interactive Development Environments Inc.

- TeamWork is a trademark of Cadre Technologies Inc.

- TPS (Technical Publishing Software) is a trademark of Interleaf Inc.

- GECOMO Plus is a trademark of GEC-Marconi Software Systems.

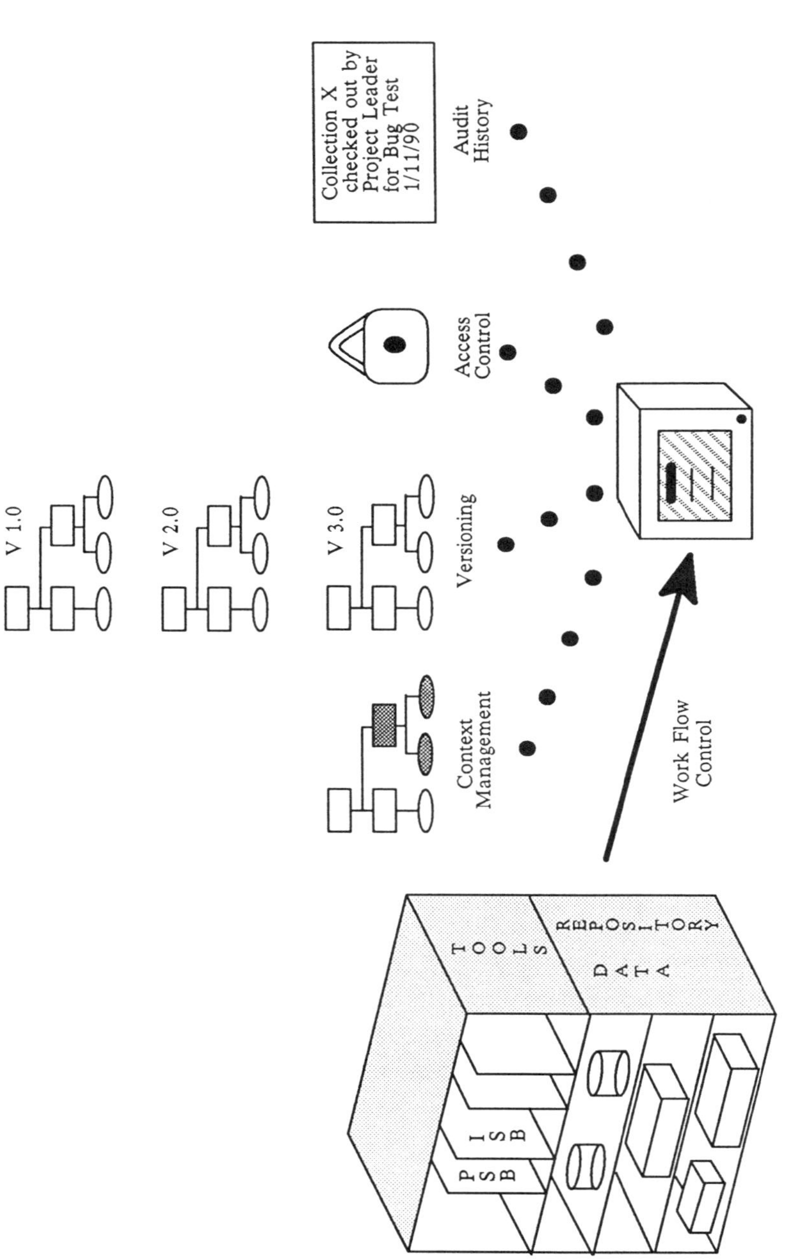

Figure 1: **Software BackPlane**

23

The Software Bus® – its objective: the mutual integration of distributed software engineering tools

Malcolm Verrall
Sema Group plc, Trafalgar House, Richfield Avenue,
Reading, Berkshire, RG1 8QA, UK

"I don't know what you mean by 'glory' ", Alice said.

Humpty Dumpty smiled contemptuously. "Of course you don't till I tell you. I meant 'there's a nice knock down argument for you' ".

"But 'glory' doesn't mean 'a nice knock down argument' ", Alice objected.

"When I use a word," Humpty Dumpty said in a rather scornful tone, "it means just what I choose it to mean – neither more nor less." [1]

1.0 INTRODUCTION

The Eureka Software Factory project, ESF [2], is a large scale project concerned with creating a class of SEEs which support the industrialised production of software. The SEEs of this class are called Factory Support Environments, FSEs; they are distinguished from traditional data-centric SEEs [3] by being communications-oriented. The communication in the FSE takes place between the software engineering tools and their constituent parts by an abstract communications channel called the Software Bus®. The objective of the Software Bus is the integration of these tools and parts with one another.

® Software Bus is a registered trademark of ESF

† Sema Group plc, Trafalgar House, Richfield Avenue, Reading, Berkshire RG1 8QA, UK.
  Tel: +44 734 575900

The novelty of the architecture involved led to difficulties in discerning what the Software Bus was supposed to do to achieve this objective - these details were not just lying around waiting to be picked up; furthermore it was necessary to construct a suitable framework in which to understand them. Thus the significance of this paper in reporting on the results of elaborating the terse statement of objective lies in both the content and the structuring of the elaboration.

Firstly, the paper looks at the views of an FSE and the users of the functionality to be provided by the Software Bus, in order to provide the framework. Then, it populates this framework with notable detailed demands of the users.

Next, the paper describes the needs that the Software Bus has of each Component and the SEE as a whole and the needs that the Software Bus may be misconceived to address, but which it does not. Finally, it dwells on the tensions between the desire to look upon integration in two different ways.

1.1   The problems of finding out what will be needed

The base document for ESF is the Technical Reference Guide [4] which "provides a framework for the set of all possible ESF instances". It says that "ESF has chosen to build the FSE architecture on ... service oriented building blocks [called components[†], and] a communication oriented architecture", with communication "taking place over an abstract channel", and that the Software Bus

- is an abstract communication channel

- hides distribution and heterogeneity aspects

- allows exchange of data with as little structural and conceptual loss as possible

- provides the necessary mechanisms for component integration

- allows components to be added without being accounted for *a priori* to an existing FSE

- allows type inheritance across components

- allows bindings to be established at different times

[†] Throughout this paper the term "component" is used as ESF jargon for a piece of software which is a service oriented building block and which can be attached to the Software Bus. It is never used as a synonym for a part.

The novelty of this communication oriented architecture - as compared to the traditional data centric SEEs [3] - made the elucidation of the needs of potential customers of the Software Bus working in ESF difficult. Typical responses to "what do you want of a Software Bus?" varied from "what is a Software Bus" - meaning the respondee did not know what the problem was - to "do X" - meaning the respondee was not going to let that stop him giving the answer. Interestingly, to the author it seemed that X tended from a branch of computer science to software packages as the respondee tended from industry to academia; which is the opposite way round to what would be expected. Statements about solutions also presented the problem of provoking long arguments over definitions of terms; which is why in the end several neologisms were invented - at least the inventor is in charge of meanings instead of having to debate them; hence the quotation at the front of this paper which also appears in our statement of requirements.[5] Add to this some detailed, heterogeneous demands and there was clearly a need to get organised, if the very high level assertions of the Technical Reference Guide were to be elaborated to a detailed list that could be analysed and designed against.

This was achieved by looking at the views of an FSE in which the Software Bus featured and identifying the types of users of the parts of the FSE which appeared in these views and classifying them into a type hierarchy. A day in the life of each of these users was imagined and thus individual demands generated to start populating the hierarchy. In order to add worth and remove ambiguity from each demand they were recorded in more detail than is reported in this paper, each one attempted to state

- the action of the Software Bus in terms of what the user would like to do in the course of his duties

- qualification of how the action is to be executed

- what things the action produces

- what implications this is felt to have in terms of artifacts or functionality needed from inside or outside the Software Bus

Thus an exemplar existed. Publishing this into the ESF project stimulated the potential customers into expressing the sought demands and gave somewhere to put them in an organised fashion when they arrived.

2.0 VIEWS OF AN FSE

There are two views in which the Software Bus features: the Structural View,
which is for the purpose of making components, and the Physical View, which is for
the purpose of implementing ESF software.

2.1 Structural view

The structural view of an FSE that conforms to the ESF architecture is of a set
of mutually interacting Components, which are the pieces of software that do the
software engineering, joined together by a Software Bus, figure 1.

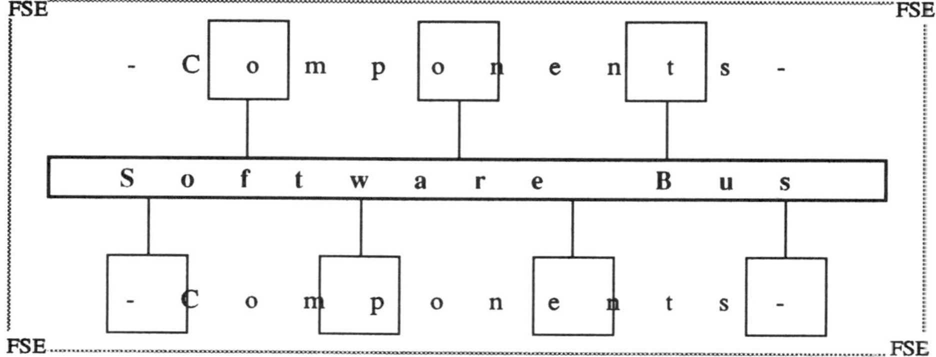

Figure 1: Structural view of an FSE

[In an ESF conformant FSE the components fall into two classes: Service Components, which are the engines and information stores, and User Interaction Components, which provide human beings with access to the SEE; though this classification does not feature in the work of the Software Bus, it helps in understanding
an FSE]. An orthogonal classification of Components [which does feature in the
work of the Software Bus] is arrived at by considering their mutual interactions;
this is described by the client-server model in which one Component makes Requests upon another, and thus at any one moment in time a Component can be acting as a Client or a Server, or indeed both.

The parts of an FSE of concern to the Software Bus are Component, Tool and
Frame. If a piece of software is not conformant with the Software Bus it is an Alien
and has to be fitted with an Adaptor to make it into a Component. A Tool is a col-
laborating set of Components. The architecture of the Software Bus is itself recursive upon the ESF architecture, in that it is made of a set of Components joined together by a Communication Channel; the complete aggregation of these Components and the Communication Channel is called the Frame. For those of you who
are wondering what the difference between the Software Bus and the Frame is, it is
this: there are parts of the Software Bus which support Components or the FSE at

earlier stages of their life cycles, before the FSE is up and running. These parts are not readily visible in these views.

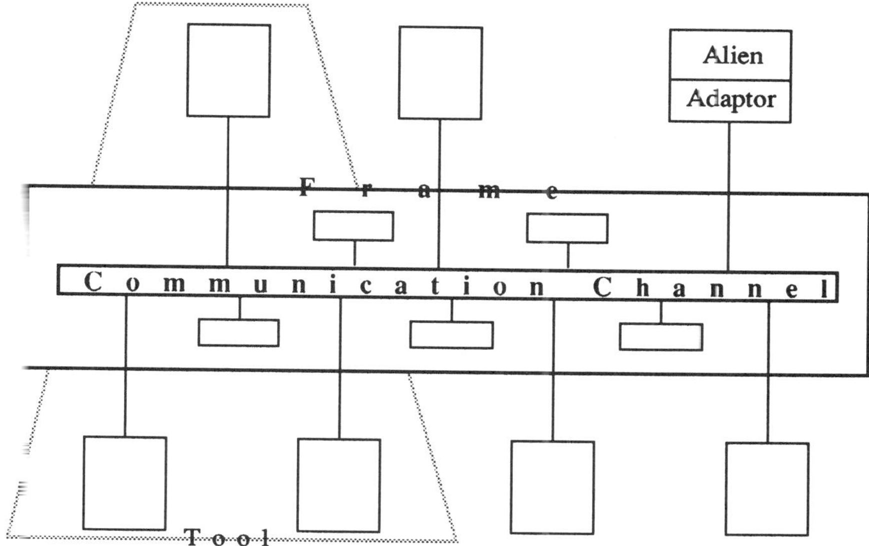

Figure 2: Parts of an FSE

2.2 Physical view of an FSE

The Physical View is less well developed than the Structural View, but does identify the operational software of an ESF as lying on a Platform. The platform is made up of software and hardware Planks from different eras in the software's life cycle. For any one FSE there are several types of plank (e.g. operating system, communication interconnection, programming language), each of which may have several sub-types (e.g. MS/DOS, UNIX™ SVR4, C++, LeLISP), and each of which may have several instances.

To some extent, where the platform stops and operational software begins is subjective; but any two communicating pieces of operational software must share a common platform. In the case of the Software Bus this is where a component touches the communication channel and, if the communication channel is disjoint within a particular FSE, where the parts of it touch one another.

Certain parts of the platform of all of the FSE have not only shape but amount, they are consumable and are called Resources.

™ UNIX is a trademark of AT&T Bell Laboratories

3.0 USERS

Each of the parts - adaptor, client, communication channel, component, frame, FSE, platform, resource, server, and tool - has a User type and we can identify three other types of User as follows.

A part of a Software Factory that is not part of the FSE is the user himself. Thus there is a user called the User Manager, who is concerned both with the management of the surrogates for the users which lie within the FSE and with communication with the real people.

An important resource for a Software Factory is money. Thus there is also a Financial Accountant to manage the surrogates for Money which lie within the FSE.

Finally there is the concept of security which does not manifest itself as a part of the FSE or Software Factory; the corresponding user is the Security Officer.

3.1 Taxonomy

The people who wish to use the Software Bus fall firstly into two classes: those who are concerned with building the parts of an FSE and those who are concerned with managing the whole FSE. This gives the top levels of classification of user types into which the above user types can be slotted to give the following taxonomy

```
Software Bus User
        FSE Part Builder
                Component Builder
                    Client Builder
                    Server Builder
                    Adaptor Builder
                Tool Builder
                Frame Builder
                    Communication Channel Builder
        FSE Manager
                {FSE} Entirety Manager
                Platform Manager
                Resource  Manager
                Frame  Manager
                Component and Tool Manager
                User  Manager
                FSE  Regulator
                    Financial  Accountant
                    Security Officer
```

Figure 3: Taxonomy of Software Bus user classes

Interestingly, the "end-user", the software engineer using the tool, does not appear.

4.0 ELABORATING THE OBJECTIVE: THE POPULATED FRAMEWORK

In order to structure the set of demands on the Software Bus, the set is partitioned by considering the actors in the world of the Software Bus, that is to say, the Users in the above taxonomy. In matching a demand with a User it is important to associate it with whoever makes the demand not with those whom it affects.

In the following discussions some generic classes are not presented - making no demands - and some classes are grouped together - making few individual demands.

4.1 FSE part builder

The needs of the generic builder of any part arise not from technical, but from commercial considerations. They are that his software development expenditure is protected, by making life difficult for the pirate. The software must be associated with a copyright statement and must not be able to execute in a pirated version in the presence of the Software Bus. The Software Bus must also provide a licensing model which allows licences to be given, to be for restricted use including the notion of expiry date, and to report to the giver of the licence on the usage of the software under licence.

4.2 Component builder

There are four main considerations for component builders: how to describe components, requests between client and server, component state and the implementation of the component.

As the Software Bus demands that components be described to it, it must provide a language in which to describe components and must be able to hold and have an understanding of such descriptions. As the descriptions will be used for the integration of tool interactions, they must be more than interface signatures and must contain the conceptual items as manipulated (possibly in the abstract) by the component; this semantic information is, however, for human rather than computer use.

When it comes to requests for service, components may be coded to place or accept these in many combinations of ways - e.g. procedure call, stream i/o, synchronously, polled or interrupted - the Software Bus must cope with a wide repertoire of interaction mechanisms, and this in a fashion that is independent of data volumes. The arguments of the requests must allow a wide repertoire of primitive and constructor data types, including visual layout information and information opaque to the Software Bus; furthermore, the arguments must also be able to be requests themselves. The integrity of temporal sets of requests for service must be supported.

The Software Bus must be able to inform one component about changes of state in another; these states are not all the states represented by the values of the information manipulated by a component, but the level of activity of the component as seen by the Software Bus, including requests for service.

The interface to a component must be able to be coded in the language of the component and not in a special Software Bus language; in those languages which can control bitwise representation, this must be permitted; in those languages which allow strings, linguistic forms of the interface must be permitted.

4.3 Client builder

The considerations of a builder of a component which is to act as a client elaborate upon those of the component builder in general.

The component description language must be able to define those services which a client seeks. All descriptions must be accessible by components as well as people.

Requests for service must be able to exhibit the usual static distribution transparencies:[6] access, location, address, and replication. The Software Bus must allow multicasting, multiplexing and reuse of the invariant part of previous requests. The service must be able to be requested by name, attribute, type of component, or specific component - while taking into account versioning of components. A response must be guaranteed to be made (eventually) and that response must be capable of reporting failure of server or Software Bus during the execution of a request, or expiry of a time limit.

A client must be able to demand that encryption take place.

The Software Bus must supply facilities to test a client's placement of requests.

4.4 Server builder

The considerations of a builder of a component which is to act as a server elaborate upon those of the component builder concerning description, requests and implementation.

The component description language must be able to define those services which a server provides.

Services being supplied must be able to exhibit the usual static distribution transparencies:[6] access, location, address, and replication. The Software Bus must allow both servers which wait for work and those which ask for work. It must allow the response to start emerging before the whole request has arrived and it must multiplex requests onto a server. It must identify the client and user requesting the service.

The Software Bus must supply facilities to test a server's acceptance of requests.

4.5 Adaptor builder

Before looking at the needs of an Adaptor Builder, it pays to ask what makes a piece of software an Alien. The first and most likely reason for an existing (stand alone) software engineering tool is that it has no service interface for interacting with other components. The second is that it does not supply all those services mandated by the Software Bus. A third, but unlikely, reason is that it runs on a platform that is unable to be supported by the Software Bus. One fact that does not make it an Alien is that it runs on a platform on which the Software Bus is not currently implemented, expending the effort to implement the Software Bus will immediately naturalise the software.

A particular class of software that may need to have Adaptors built will be the operating systems of the platforms of the Software Bus. It must be possible to build Adaptors for a sensible selection of services of these.

4.6 Tool builder

The needs of a Tool Builder are these: to achieve pairwise fitting of clients and servers, to bind the appropriate server to a client, to manage the topology of a tool, to express tool management in platform terms.

To achieve pairwise fitting differences have to be overcome in what the client-server pairs are talking about and how they are saying it to each other. Thus the component description language must allow description of the abstraction and the representation of the services separately. Differences in representation can be dealt with by automation, only a human being can understand the correspondences between different abstractions; thus the Software Bus must have a language to express these correspondences and must be able to perform the transformations necessary to take advantage of the correspondences described to it.

When binding clients and servers the most important generalised expression of need is that the Software Bus must cooperate with the Factory Process Engine,[7] which runs the Process Models [8,9] and one of whose tasks is to maintain <user role, tool, information items> tuples describing the contexts in which users work. Bindings must be able to be established and changed at any time from when the tool is first built to when it is running and the clients within it are making requests. The bindings must be able to be affected by the Factory Process Engine or the platform and the values of the requests in transmission can be affected by the work contexts.

Tool topology covers the shape of the tool and the extra nodes of services able to be introduced by the Software Bus. The Software Bus must be able to build and display the structure of tools. It must supply services which provide a query language, exception handling, failure reporting, triggers, and association between components which do not have any type of client-server or "uses" relationship. The events which these services respond to are the requesting of services, state change of components, or platform specific events to which such meaning can be attributed.

The Software Bus must make ready tools, and thereby components, for requesting, in platform specific manner.

4.7 Frame builder

A demand that is commercially driven, is that the Software Bus must permit the inclusion of "small" computers in an FSE. As the Software Bus will have a public interface and thereby Software Bus instances can come from any supplier, the interface to components must be testable as must the interfaces between any parts of which the Software Bus is specified as being made.

The Communication Channel must be able to be built on disjoint platforms.

4.8 FSE entirety, platform, resource and frame managers

An FSE must be able to be brought into existence and identified. It must be able to exist in the same Software Factory as other FSEs, and be able to inter-operate with these and other FSEs.

The Software Bus platform must be able to be (re)configured

The Software Bus must obtain resource loadings and produce resource analyses.

The Software Bus must be able to be brought up and down gracefully and report its current state, current traffic and usage during a user, component or platform session. It must verify that any particular transmission path is clear and have debugging facilities.

4.9 Component and tool manager

A component can be installed in an FSE, be moved around it, have its state changed and be reported on. The same is true, sometimes by implication, for a tool.

When a component is installed it must be made known to the FSE, together with its type and instance description, and be attached to the Software Bus. It can subsequently be replaced or reattached.

A component can migrate in its installed, executable or executing forms; all these must be concealed by the Software Bus.

The Software Bus must be able to start, restart, suspend, resume and shutdown a component; it must be able to abort a request in progress.

The Software Bus must be able to report on components' existence, description, location and state.

These facilities must be available *mutatis mutandis* for tools also.

4.10 User manager

The User Manager wants to manage the surrogates, within the FSE, of the human beings in the Software Factory and to communicate with the human beings.

The Software Bus must allow creation and configuration of users and their roles, and societies thereof. It must relate login sessions to these. It must report on user actions.

It must communicate with users upon occurrence of these events:

- tool, component or resource becoming (un)available

- user query on tool, component or resource availability

- component reset

- component or transaction failure

- user commentary to or from FSE Manager

4.11 Financial accountant and security officer

The Software Bus must provide component usage reports on which to base charging, which may be in advance or in arrears.

The Software Bus must authenticate users and identify users attempting to defeat security. It must grant, revoke and police access rights for users with respect to components.

It must encrypt requests for services as commanded.

5.0 NEEDS AND MISCONCEPTIONS

As well as the set of demands upon the Software Bus there are two sets of needs of interest.

First, the needs that the Software Bus itself has of each component, plank and FSE instance. Most importantly for components, they must use the Software Bus for all interactions whose integrity is to be maintained by the FSE; also they must describe themselves, have claimed and mandatory interfaces, and maintain upward compatibility between versions. Each type of platform plank must allow instanciation and initiation of components and requesting of services; it must supply a communication channel continuum; and, it must be able to report on resource consumption. The FSE as a whole must supply services for logging, load balancing, and notification of users.

Second, there are needs that the Software Bus might be misconceived to address, but which it does not. The Software Bus is not:

- a network operating system: it is not concerned with the management or unification of a multiplicity of CPUs and devices

- an object management system: it does unify components into one global object management system, it does not supply object management systems as platforms for components, it does not concern itself with the objects inside components

- an AI system: it does not seek to understand the conceptual world of each component, thus it cannot match or transform requests unless explicitly told to by a human being

- a high security system: it does not prevent subversion or damage of components via their platforms

- an ESF catalogue: it does not maintain a library of ESF accredited components

- a component development or execution system: it does not provide a component writing language, it is not concerned with the internal structure of a component with regard to the component's platform

6.0 AN INTERESTING TENSION

Throughout, this paper has looked at integration acting between Components, but what about the values and virtues of the data-centric tradition? Indeed, from this tradition there is a desire to look upon integration as acting between Items of information which has led to a tension in the expression of various demands.

An initially attractive resolution would seem to be to generalise over Components and Items and treat them both as abstract data types, ADTs. In this case is a Component to be seen as an ADT, a composite ADT or an ADT management system? The answer is probably a combination of the second and third of these. Putting these difficulties together with the fact that Components and Items are truly different things leads to the conclusion that it is unwise to pursue this tactic.

But the integration of Components and Items cannot be developed separately and be expected to co-exist in the same FSE. Therefore taking Component management as more essential[†] in ESF it must be made to encompass the concept of Item and solve the integration problems thereof - namely identification, location and conversion. These problems are also to be solved for Component integration; thus, what will be necessary will be to ensure that the integration algorithms

- are fine grained enough

- can be programmed in terms of descriptions of Items

Of course this must not jeopardise the Component perspective in doing so; that is, a wide spectrum of policies must be allowed, and on being told which is operable, the Software Bus must adopt the minimum granularity for maximum efficiency.

7.0 CONCLUSION

This paper has presented a survey of the terrain in order that the detailed elaboration of the objective of integrating tools within a distributed SEE are made explicit to the software engineering community.

It is now necessary to describe and understand the universe of discourse of the problem. This is achieved by mapping out a conceptual model which it is hoped will be presented later this year.

8.0 REFERENCES

1. Lewis Carroll, *Through the looking glass and what Alice found there* The People's Edition, Macmillan and Co., 1898.

2. C.Fernstrom, L.Ohlsson *ESF - An approach to Industrial Software Production,* [10]

[†] bearing in mind the etymology of this word

3. M.S.Verrall *SFINX Project - The Componentry Approach to SEE Building,*
    10

4. ESF team *ESF Technical Reference Guide, Version 1.1* EUREKA Software
    Factory, Berlin, May 1989.

5. Software Bus team *ESF Software Bus User Requirements, Version 3.1* EU-
    REKA Software Factory, Berlin, July 1989.

6. ANSA team *ANSA Reference Manual, Release 01.00,* (Part II, Chapter 16)
    Architecture Projects Management Ltd, Cambridge, 1989

7. L. Hubert, G.Perdreau *Software Factory: Using Process Modelling for Inte-
    gration Purposes,* [12]

8. R.Pierce, J.Smith *The ARISE Process Modelling System,* [11]

9. V.Gruhn *Analysis of Software Process Models in the Software Process
    Management Environment MELMAC,* [11]

10. K.H.Bennet, ed. *Software Engineering Environments: Research and Prac-
    tice,* Proceedings of 4th Conference on Software Engineering Environments,
    Durham, April 1989, Ellis Horwood, 1989.

11. F.Long, ed. Proceedings of 5th Conference on Software Engineering Environ-
    ments, Aberystwyth, March 1991, Ellis Horwood, 1991.

12. P.A.Ng et al, eds *Systems Integration '90,* Proceedings of 1st International
    Conference on Systems Integration, Morristown, April 1990, IEEE Compu-
    ter Society Press, Los Alamitos, 1990

24

ANSA: Assumptions, principles, and structure

John P. Warne
ISA Project Core Team, Architecture Projects Management Limited,
Poseidon House, Castle Park, Cambridge, CB3 0RD, UK

1   Introduction

ANSA is an architecture for building distributed systems which can individually or collectively operate as a unified whole so that the fact of distribution can be made completely transparent to application programmers and users. This is an entirely different approach to that which is typically assumed when networking single systems together. It allows full advantage to be taken of the inherent concurrency and separation of distributed systems for the provision of increased performance, decentralisation and reliability, while better masking the disadvantages that arise from communication errors and partial failures. It produces systems that can be managed as coordinated sets of sub-systems appropriate to the enterprise they serve rather than as random combinations of boxes.

2   The Problem Space

Many of today's computer systems are designed to work within
"closed" localised contexts, either within limited physical areas,
or within limited logical boundaries, possibly shared by other
similar systems. When systems are required to cooperate freely
in "open" distributed contexts with other dissimilar systems, both
physical and logical separation can cause major difficulties.

Problems frequently arise from trying to separate and
distribute closed systems in ad hoc ways, instead of applying the
discipline of sound engineering practice to create open distributed
systems founded on a clear understanding of carefully considered
design assumptions, principles, and structuring rules.

The purpose of this paper is to examine the design approach
taken by ANSA in addressing the technical problem space of
building "integrated" open distributed computing systems. It is
recognised from the outset that such systems may inevitably need
to function in environments incorporating heterogeneous
computing elements, and that such elements may be subject to
different administrative authorities.

The paper concentrates on different aspects of the ANSA
computational model (application writers viewpoint) and the
ANSA engineering model (system builders viewpoint).
Throughout the discussion reference is made to the concept of
"service" from two perspectives: (1) as an abstract computational
specification of some set of system/application functions; and (2)
as an engineering entity that animates the same functions and
makes them accessible as a service to other parts of the system.

3   ANSA Design Assumptions

In designing systems to be implemented in a single host
environment, it is commonly the case that a number of
assumptions are made which simplify the modelling of those
systems. In the presence of distribution, however, those features
from which the simplifying assumptions abstract cease to be
negligible, and must be explicitly catered for in the design models.
It is important, therefore, to identify explicitly the assumptions

which are made for non-distributed systems, and to ensure that they are absent from the models for distributed systems.

Among the most important assumptions to be _avoided_ are:

- _Single global name space_: in distributed systems, which may arise from federation of pre-existing systems, context-relative naming schemes are required in order to interpret names unambiguously across different administrative boundaries.

- _Global shared memory_: in distributed systems, global shared memory would form a performance bottle-neck, and so is replaced by multiple, disjoint memories.

- _Global consistency_: in distributed systems, consistency of state and data may converge more slowly than state and data in non-distributed systems.

- _Sequential execution_: in distributed systems, execution may occur in any and all possible orders including sequentially, concurrently, and independently.

- _Total failure_: in distributed systems, the failure of one component can lead to partial failure of other operational components participating in services affected by the failure. Redundancy of components is thus essential to detect and mask failures in order to allow operational components to continue dependably. Moreover, there is a class of partial failure modes which can only be prevented by distributed cooperation; in particular, neither forward nor backward error recovery performed on behalf of a particular failed component may on its own be sufficient.

- _Synchronous interaction_: in distributed systems, both asynchronous and synchronous interactions are necessary in order to reduce communication delay.

- _Locality of interaction_: in distributed systems, interactions may be either local or remote, with consequent implications for communication delay and reliability.

▸ *Fixed location*: in distributed systems, which may have multiple locations, it is possible for components to move during the system lifetime. Advantage may be taken of this to improve performance by co-locating some interacting services, but the processes for finding services must be extended to cater for this.

▸ *Direct binding*: in distributed systems, indirect binding is necessary to cater for the potential remoteness of interactions and the mobility of services.

▸ *Homogeneous environment*: in distributed systems, there can be no guarantee of homogeneity of components and so interacting parties must agree on abstract rather than physical data representations.

Summaries of the design principles observed by ANSA and the way in which they avoid these assumptions are presented below.

4   ANSA Design Principles

It is convenient to discuss the design principles of ANSA in the context of five key issues of distribution: *separation*, *heterogeneity*, *federation*, *concurrency*, and *scaling*.

4.1   Approach to Separation

Physical separation of interacting computational entities brings the need for a general computational model for interworking.

With respect to separation, ANSA observes the following principles:

- *Assume all services are remote, allowing co-location as an optimisation*

- *Require each service to be entirely responsible for transforming its encapsulated data*

- *Perform all interactions with services via instances of interfaces*

- *Allow propagation of interface references as the means of acquiring access to services*

- *Name and report all detected interaction faults and failures*

Part of the solution to separation is to assume from inception that all services are physically or logically remote from each other leaving the possibility of co-location, with the potential for optimisation it yields, as an engineering concern. This view leads to the requirement for each service to encapsulate its data.

Another part of the solution is to ensure that the state and data of each remote service can only be manipulated indirectly via interaction with the interface supported and made available by the service. This approach is similar to the programming view of manipulating data through abstract data types.

This picture mirrors the essential properties of the ANSA computational model in which remote services are shared by propagating interface references between interacting parties. The components between which service interactions occur are formulated as "computational objects", each of which encapsulates data and the service operations for manipulating that data. Consequently, each object, together with its **data**, is wholly contained within a private memory space, which is disjoint to the private memory spaces of other objects.

Specification of what each object does is primarily in terms of the services it provides, and thus the types of its interfaces. Likewise, specification of how an object achieves its required services may be modularised in terms of the services they use. The technique of one service using other services can be applied recursively to yield computational objects of extremely fine granularity.

This object model is synergistic with, but not dependent on, specific object-oriented programming models.

A client-server relationship applies to service interactions. One object (the server) provides one or more services to other objects (the clients). There is prior agreement about service specifications: services conform to particular interface types, and the interactions occur by mutual consent, and at the initiative of the clients. The same object may participate in interactions with many different services of the same or different interface type (concurrently and/or consecutively, as client and/or server, and with many different partners).

In distributed systems the physical separation of services (and their containing objects) is unavoidable, introducing the possibility both of failures occurring during communication and of partial failures of the services. In order to have equivalent failure semantics to non-distributed services, the service interaction model must allow such failures to be reported and processed.

Service interactions therefore require multiple outcomes (each of which may comprise multiple results). In ANSA, this approach has been integrated into a general model for reporting different kinds of outcome. Such outcomes are distinguished by name and are known as *terminations*. Connotation of "failure", as well as which terminations represent failure, is defined as part of the service semantics rather than as part of the interaction model.

4.2   Approach to Heterogeneity

There are variations in the design of different hardware and communications systems which arise for a variety of reasons. Not all systems are designed to be the same, nor is it always desirable that they should be, since there can be benefits in diversity and specialisation. The challenge is to make such diversity work harmoniously and to derive positive benefit from the specialisations it provides.

To provide the flexibility to cope with inevitable variation in distributed systems, ANSA observes the following principles:

- *Assume heterogeneity and identify unnecessary diversity*

- *Abstract away from unnecessary diversity, while still retaining the benefit of specialisations*

- *Request remote services to manipulate their encapsulated data through interface instances*

- *Pass interface references rather than data presentation syntax*

Consideration of *heterogeneity* and the discovery of *unnecessary diversity*, and the impedance that these *phenomena* present to interworking compatibly across different systems, leads to the identification of the root problems: the incompatibility of different operating system interfaces, the incompatibility of different physical (hardware) and logical (software) data representations, and the incompatibility of different communications protocols.

Standards for logical data presentations and communications protocols exist, but these in themselves produce neither sufficient nor complete solutions to the problems of heterogeneous interworking.

These difficulties can be addressed by appealing to the principle of abstraction.

ANSA specifies an integrated platform which can be built onto existing heterogeneous operating system environments to form the basis for compatible interworking across dissimilar technologies. The definition of this platform does not require or force a particular implementation, but does require adherence to conformance on all matters of interaction between distributed services (§7).

This architectural platform supports an object based computational model for simplifying the way in which remote applications are structured and are permitted to interact (§4.1); and an engineering model which specifies the components and structuring rules for building practical realisations of the platform (§5).

Even with this platform in place, there are still other principles that must be observed if successful interworking is to be achieved. Different data representations imply that one system cannot manipulate data directly in another system. Remote information must be represented abstractly. It is important to characterise the services available, without knowing how encapsulated data is to be transformed. The approach of read/modify/write styles using primitive operations, as in stand alone systems, or homogeneous networks, are inappropriate in a heterogeneous distributed system. They result in an attempt to create a global database as a vehicle for transforming a heterogeneous environment into a homogeneous one.

These arguments suggest that it is dangerous to present the application writer with a data encoding scheme such as ASN.1. Use of a presentation syntax for transporting data from one environment to another perpetuates the view of the read/modify/write styles of data access. Moreover, there are further problems. Cooperating applications must still agree on a presentation syntax, and agree on the semantics of the data as information. The ASN.1 approach moves data to the processing, whereas the object based approach moves processing to the data, requesting the responsible service to process and transform the data wherever it happens to be.

This principle of avoiding the mechanistic view of data encoding schemes in the computational model does not of course preclude their practical application in the engineering model. Ultimately, systems have to be built with agreement on the syntax and semantics of data presentations for passing requests, parameters, and results in interactions. A standard such as ASN.1 may well be the choice for specific implementations.

The guiding principles of *performing remote service interactions through interface instances*, and of *propagating interface references to share services* provide a sound basis for dealing with problems of heterogeneity. All useful diversity and specialisations can be defined as service objects and accessed through instances of interfaces.

4.3   Approach to Federation

In large-scale distributed computing systems, the existence of centralised ownership and universal and technical control cannot be assumed. There will inevitably be separate sources of authority (e.g. separate enterprises, autonomous departments, different technical policies, dissimilar technologies, and separate administrations). In such cases, interworking can only be achieved via cooperation in "federal" style, and not by "dictat".

To accommodate federation of separate systems, ANSA observes the following principles:

- *Allow each system to control its own policies and services locally*

- *Allow cooperating systems to negotiate the sharing of services*

- *Require cooperating systems to identify all available services via a context-relative naming scheme*

- *Provide a trading facility through which federated cooperating systems can organise and control the sharing of services*

A local system cannot reliably or effectively control a remote one for all the reasons underpinning the issues of separation and heterogeneity discussed earlier. Furthermore, stand-alone systems are designed to meet individual requirements, and are not deliberately built to assume non-local administrations.

A need for interoperation between individual systems arises when it is realised that some mutual benefit can be most effectively met by federating them. Since the systems were not designed to fit within some agreed overall structure, they must combine forces as cooperating peers, ideally without impairing their individual functionality or performance.

The federation of separate systems directly affects the architectural views of "naming" and "trading".

4.3.1   Naming

Names are the general means of referring to entities within a system. In information systems there are many different entities to be named, and many different ways of naming them. Any large-scale distributed computing system will inevitably encounter such diversity.

ANSA provides a naming model to address this issue:

▸ *Separation of naming domains*

  Separate naming domains are formulated for the different kinds of entities that can be named.

▸ *Separation of naming conventions*

  Different ways of naming entities are distinguished as different naming conventions. For each naming convention there is a defined syntax and semantics. In an ideal world, there might be exactly one naming convention per naming domain; but in the real world there is usually more than one (if only for historical reasons).

▸ *Separation of naming contexts*

There should be considerable freedom in the way in which particular names can be associated with particular entities. Each set of bindings between the entities in a naming domain and the names in a name set is known as a naming context. Different naming contexts arise for reasons of scaling and management for instance. For consistency, each naming context must adhere to a single naming convention. The validity of names is tested with respect to the naming context: the name must be constructed using the naming conventions, and a binding with an entity in the naming domain must be defined.

▸ *Naming networks*

Some of the entities that can be named are themselves naming contexts. Thus, it may be possible to name one naming context from another naming context. The structure that is formed by the manner in which naming contexts can be so linked is called a naming network. ANSA imposes no constraints on the structure or size of the naming network in a particular system and so allows arbitrary administrative structures (hierarchies as well as federations) to be reflected in the naming network.

▸ *Path names*

To name a particular entity in some domain, it may be necessary to refer first to (i.e. name) the naming context in which the name is valid. The name for a particular entity is thus extended by the name of the naming context in which it is known. A path name is such an extended name - it traces a path through the naming network.

▸ *Name transparency*

Each naming context that is named in a path name is logically independent of all other naming contexts in the path name. Therefore, name resolution involves successive logically independent interpreters. For each interpreter, all other elements in the path name are transparent, leaving unresolved names for successor interpreters. Each name interpreter may be modelled (and implemented) as a service object which internalises the naming context and the naming convention concerned.

The above naming model provides an orderly basis for cooperation between disjoint naming domains and contexts which can be separately administered under different authorities. This arrangement is referred to as *federated naming*.

4.3.2   Trading

It was stated earlier that interface references may be obtained by clients in response to interactions with any accessible server; and that this is the basic method by which distributed computations naturally acquire access to different services dynamically. However, it is also important to provide a means by which separate clients and servers can rendezvous for the very first time in order to allow subsequent interaction between them. In ANSA, this process is called *trading*, and is available through a special service provided to clients and servers.

Trading gives access to a graph structure that can be searched by clients via *import* requests and updated by servers via *export* requests, qualified by *typename* and optionally by *property name/values* pairs.

▸ *Typename*

A *typename* denotes the set of permissible interactions that a service instance can engage in. It identifies a set of common service interface instances.

▸ *Property name/value pairs*

A set of *property name/value pairs* is used to help make a choice from a set of interface instances with the same typename.

For example, there may be several Fourier transform services, that all calculate the same transform. The computational cost associated with each service may vary according to the algorithm used. A client of the service will get charged for each transformation. It must then be possible for the client to state how much it is prepared to pay on the basis of a choice of the most suitable Fourier transform service.

▸ *Typed imports and exports*

Servers can export instances of interface types by *typename* and *property name/values* to the trading service to make these instances accessible to clients. An import operation is provided to clients so that they can retrieve references to interface instances of the required type.

The trading service will only search through exports of the required type (and its subtypes) when trying to match on interface type conformance and required service properties.

The trading service of different systems may be structured as a federation of autonomous trading domains and managed by separate administrative authorities.

4.4   Approach to Concurrency

Assumptions made about concurrency and synchronisation mechanisms in single host systems are frequently invalid for distributed systems. This can create difficulties when transporting single host applications to distributed, possibly heterogeneous, environments.

ANSA addresses the problems of distributed concurrency and synchronisation by observing the following principles:

- *Distinguish between the computational and engineering views of concurrency*

- *Require declarative expression of parallel execution and concurrency control in the computational model*

- *Provide programmers with suitable linguistic tools for building distributed applications*

- *Provide engineering tools to map computational specifications to engineering mechanisms*

An application writer generally assumes that his program executes serially; that is, with a concurrency of one. It may be possible for components to execute in parallel, but except where meeting an explicit functional requirement, parallelism is rarely accommodated. Mechanisms to apply parallel processing to assumed serial code, for example *pipelining*, have been adopted in many systems. However, such ingenuity may not be possible with the many processors of a distributed system. Furthermore, if specific serialisation and synchronisation mechanisms are built into an application, the opportunity for exploiting parallelism via distributed processors using different mechanisms will be lost.

Distribution introduces special problems. If a server has many clients, it will inevitably be faced with overlapped requests. If a server does not make provision for concurrency, the delay imposed upon clients will become excessive. Only by designing applications with the greatest scope for parallel execution will optimal scaling characteristics be obtained.

When interacting with a remote service, an application writer may assume two options:

(1)   synchronous service request: *execution continues when the remote activity is complete.*

(2)   asynchronous service request: *execution proceeds in parallel with the remote activity.*

With option (2), and assuming a dependency between the interacting parties, a synchronisation mechanism will be needed to suspend execution of the issuing activity until completion of the remote activity. This type of synchronisation becomes increasingly complex if several remote parallel activities are involved. For example, the issuing activity may desire to wait for the remote activity that finishes soonest - but which one is that? And how are the remaining remote activities subsequently handled?

There are many engineering techniques for the obtainment of concurrency control, but these are too numerous to mention here.

To tackle these issues, ANSA provides a Distributed Processing Language (DPL) which makes a clear distinction between the concurrency expressed in the computation, and that which is realised by engineering mechanism. The application writer is required to indicate declaratively where in a computation parallelism is possible, or where sequencing or synchronisation is required, but without any preconceived ideas about their mechanisation, whether through local or remote resources. The engineering domain is accordingly given proper control over the choice of appropriate implementation strategy. In particular, the decision on whether to take advantage of the parallel options of a computation is controlled at the proper place.

DPL is supported by engineering tools that map abstract computational specifications to appropriate engineering mechanisms.

4.5   Approach to Scaling

Systems will constantly change, grow, and merge. This introduces variations in scale: small to large, slow to fast, specific to general.

In response to these needs, ANSA observes the following principles:

- *Allow for scaling variability by building expansion capability into the architecture*

- *Provide extensible naming and trading facilities*

- *Federate through negotiable, cooperating, remote services*

- *Do not assume global mutable knowledge*

The principles of separation, federation, and heterogeneity enforce the view that it is not possible to assume the existence of a widely distributed global resource pool which can be accessed directly from anywhere. It is simply not realistic to encompass the entire universe of systems for all space and time.

The ANSA view is that scaling differences must be accommodated as needs arise in much the same way as the federation principles described allow naming and trading to expand in ever wider domains and contexts.

Scaling issues are also greatly eased if data is manipulated where it is held, and all requests for its manipulation are permitted only via references to instances of interfaces. Although this requires negotiation of service agreements, it makes no assumptions of global mutable knowledge.

5 Engineering Structure of ANSA Systems

The following presents a sketch of the way in which the principal components of ANSA systems fit together.

Figure 1 shows two ANSA systems. Each system is running several applications (comprising clients and servers), together with a *node manager* (N) and a *trader* (T).

Figure 1: ANSA Systems

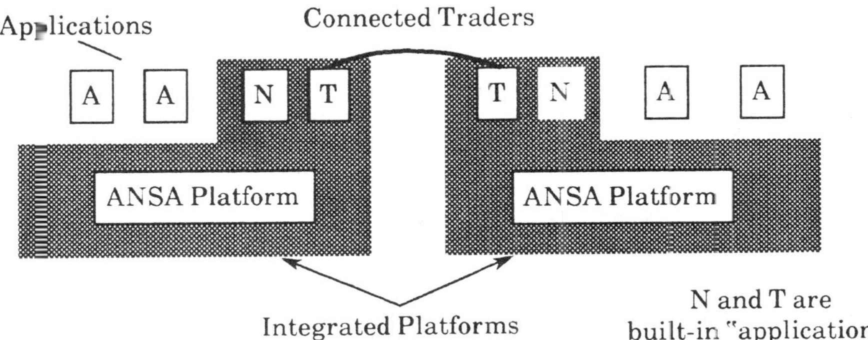

Each trader provides a trading space that can be searched by *type name* and by optional *property values*. Any server can export instances of interface types to the trader in order to make them accessible to clients. Any client can use import operations on the trader to acquire access to required interface instances.

The traders are connected (possibly federated) to permit the sharing of services across the systems. This federal arrangement, together with the distributed integrated platforms, gives the illusion to clients and servers in both systems that they exist in a single homogeneous system.

Each node manager maintains a database of configuration details pertaining to its node in the distributed system. A *node* is the engineering abstraction of a host machine in the system.

As shown in figure 2, a node supports one or more nucleus components (Ns), each of which takes the basic resources of its local host's infrastructure (operating system and hardware) and builds upon it to provide a basic distributed computing environment common to all hosts in the distributed system. The nucleus components are then able to work together, along with the traders and the node managers, to provide an integrated support platform for distributed computing.

Figure 2: Distributed Nucleus Components

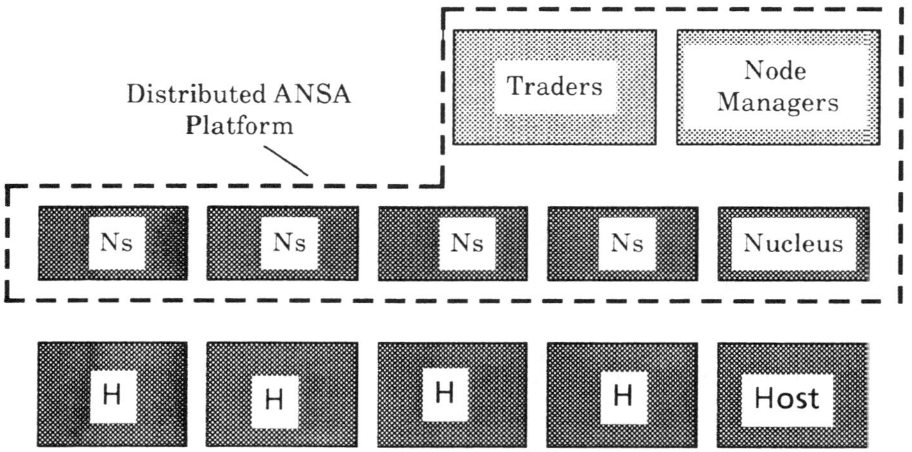

Node managers work in conjunction with a distributed *factory service* (not shown) to instantiate application objects above the platforms. The factory service creates capsules for the containment of instantiated application objects.

Figure 3 reveals the structure of an ANSA *capsule*. Each capsule's address space will be logically partitioned to provide a private memory space for each contained application object. The distributed system will comprise one or many objects per capsule, one or many capsules per node, and many different nodes.

Transparency services are the components that enable the various aspects of distribution to be hidden from application clients and servers (see §6).

Figure 3: An ANSA Capsule

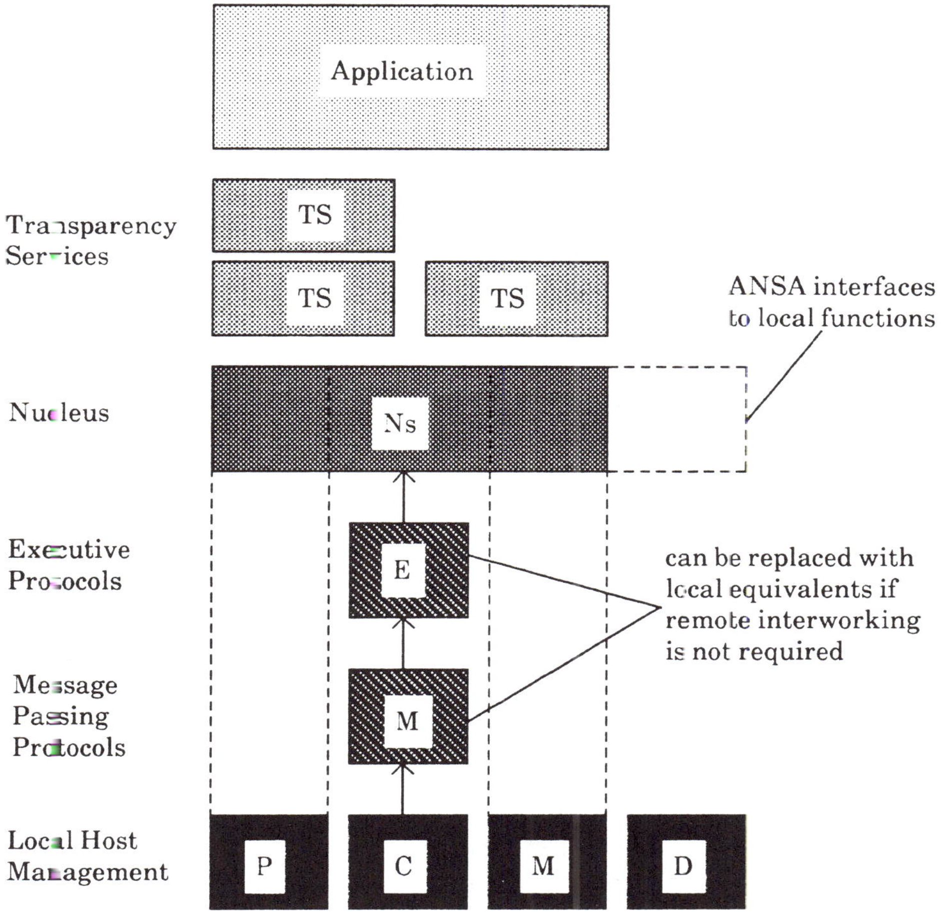

At a level below the nucleus are the components that provide executive (O/S) and message passing protocols. (If interworking between heterogeneous systems is not required, either or both of these can be replaced by local equivalents.) The lowest level contains the physical host's processor (P), communications (C), memory (M), and device (D) management functions.

The ANSA engineering model specifies the mechanisms needed to provide the various kinds of transparency and the protocols for interaction between nucleus components on different node/hosts. Application components are structured according to the ANSA computational model, and the distributed computing aspects of the application are compiled into calls on the interfaces to the appropriate transparency and platform components.

The engineering model can also be taken as a template for the implementation of the nucleus and the transparency components, although this is not mandatory for either application portability across implementations, or for interworking between them. The conformance criteria for portability are the interfaces to the transparency and platform components. Once conformance to the computational model has been established, it is possible to conceive of multiple implementations of the architecture which make different engineering trade-offs (see §7).

Many hosts will provide a range of functions and resources beyond those needed by the platform and may wish to contribute them to the distributed computing environment as potential application components. This can be achieved by extending the nucleus with additional interfaces that map onto the locally available functions. Thus the nucleus acts as an architectural switch, transparently linking application components to both local and remote resources in a uniform way.

6   Transparency Services

The question of whether it is practicable to distribute a computation may depend on many things. Where communication costs are high it may be prudent to minimise the distribution of those parts that are expected to interact heavily. Where parts of a computation are processor intensive, the extra concurrency introduced by distribution may lead to improved performance.

Where replication is used to increase reliability and availability, it is essential that software replicas are located on distinct hardware replicas.

The extent to which an application writer needs to be concerned with the integration of distributed system components can be controlled by the selective application of *transparency services*.

In an application with complete distribution transparency, the application writer has delegated all responsibility for distribution to the underlying support environment. Without such support, the writer must assume full responsibility for all aspects of distribution.

In practice, the application writer may require control over *selected* aspects of distribution. For example, a configuration management application would obviously require control over the location of system components. By allowing the selection of transparency services, each application need only deal with those distributions aspects that are pertinent to the application.

ANSA supports the following transparency services:

▸ *Access transparency* hides the difference between local and remote provision of services. The overriding criterion is to remove the concept of co-located clients and servers. (Local optimisations can be effected by engineering decisions where appropriate.) With this transparency service in place, all invocations are considered to be remote.

▸ *Location transparency* hides the location of servers from the clients that interact with them, and vice versa; thus enabling interacting parties to be located anywhere in the distributed system.

▸ *Migration transparency* hides the effect of servers moving from one location to another while clients are interacting with them.

▸ *Concurrency transparency* hides the existence of concurrent users of servers. If a server is supported by concurrency transparency, then each of its clients is unable to observe any effects due to other clients that make simultaneous use of that service

▸ *Failure transparency* hides the effects of partially completed interactions that fail for what ever reason. This transparency service is built upon mechanisms which

   (a) make interactions *atomic* so that they either complete entirely, or fail with complete removal of partial effect;

   (b) make interactions completely impervious to single point failures in client and server configurations comprising *replicas*

▸ *Replication transparency* hides the difference between replicated and non-replicated clients and servers

The technique for providing any transparency service is based on the single principle of replacing an original service by a new service, which combines the original service with the transparency service, and which permits clients to interact with it as if it were the original service. The clients need not be aware of how these combined services are achieved.

7   Conformance

A *conformance point* is a place where a test can be made of a system component (a platform component or an application object) to see if it meets a set of *conformance criteria*. A *conformance statement* for a component must identify where the conformance point is, and what criteria are satisfied at that point.

In ANSA, all architectural conformance points are described abstractly rather than by reference to concrete data formats and protocols. Thus architectural conformance does not automatically guarantee interworking or portability. Practical interworking and portability guarantees require systematic choice of actual formats and protocols, or the use of translators between alternative formats. These are *system conformance* choices and fall outside of the architecture's rules and recipes.

Note however that conformance to the architecture does not always guarantee compatibility of interworking, as the following example makes clear.

Imagine two airline reservation systems built using the same hardware, protocols and programming languages, conforming to ANSA throughout. The information structures for flight reservations and cancellations are the same. Since both systems serve the same purpose it might be hoped that they will work together. Suppose however they have different ways of treating cancellations. One may have an exchange policy: "make the customer a booking on another airline"; the other a refund policy: "give the customer's money back". When both systems are interconnected, the clash of policies could cause problems to reservation staff as well as to passengers, since the composite system will not exhibit a consistent cancellation policy.

To overcome this class of problem, service specifications must be cross-checked for compatibility on all points of policy between the application components, and between all supporting ANSA components.

The following provides some guidelines on system conformance in the context of the ANSA computational model and the ANSA engineering model.

7.1   Conformance in the ANSA Computational Model

The ANSA computational model is in two parts:

▸ the *interaction model* defines permitted forms of interaction and a type scheme within which potential interactions are to be classified.

▸ the *construction model* defines elements from which the interacting objects may be constructed.

The structure of the model and the organisation of the description of the model are derived from the relationships that exist between computational objects and the relationship between a computational object and its supporting environment. The model establishes conformance requirements that must be satisfied if the pieces of a distributed system are to fit together.

There are two computational conformance points; the
interworking conformance point and the *portability conformance
point.* Figure 4 shows two objects and the positions of the
conformance points with respect to the objects and the
environment that animates them.

Figure 4: Computational Conformance Points

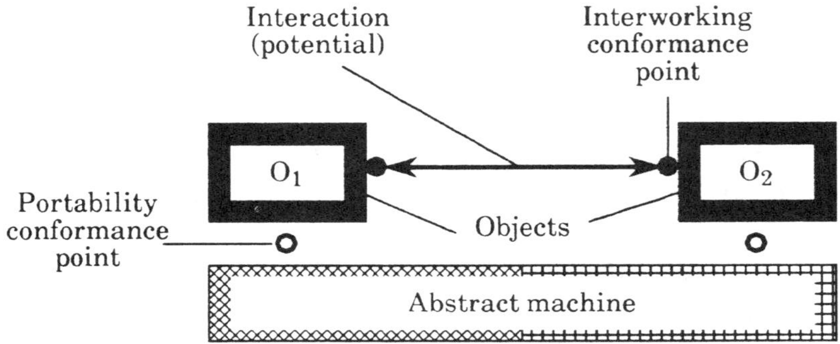

It is possible to conform to the interaction model without
conforming to the construction model. Conforming to the
construction model guarantees conformance to the interaction
model since there are no interaction facilities other than those
corresponding to the interaction model.

7.1.2   Computational Interworking Conformance

At the interworking conformance point there are two kinds of
conformance. The first is conformance to the interaction model.
The second is interface type conformance for potential
interactions.

An *interaction conformance* statement for an object asserts
that all interactions at the conformance point follow the rules of
the interaction part of the ANSA computational model.

Interface type conformance applies to the potential interactions
between objects rather to the objects themselves. An interface
type conformance statement can be made only about a potential
interaction in which the participant objects are interaction
conformant. An interface type conformance statement for a

potential interaction asserts that neither party to the interaction will attempt to interact in a way that the other does not expect.

Objects cannot interact if their models of interaction are different. Interaction conformance is mandatory for an object that is to participate in an ANSA system.

7.1.5   Computational Portability Conformance

The *portability conformance* point is between an object and the abstract machine which animates it.

A *portability conformance* statement for an object asserts that the object is defined in terms of the elements of the ANSA construction model.

A statement of *portability conformance* for an abstract machine asserts that it can animate objects that conform to the ANSA construction model.

Each object must match the animation environment that supports it. The animation environments in a system need not conform to the ANSA construction model. If a system has animation environments based upon more than one model then there will be restrictions upon where each object may be placed which will limit the way in which the system resources can be exploited.

The ANSA construction model has been designed to be well matched to the interaction model and also to permit the development of mechanisms and techniques that allow the resources of a distributed system to be exploited effectively.

7.2   Conformance in the ANSA Engineering Model

Figure 5 shows an engineering structure of an ANSA system that illustrates application objects, transparency services, nucleus components, operating systems, and the underlying communication networks.

7.2.1   Engineering Interworking Conformance

In the engineering viewpoint there is an *interworking conformance* point between interacting engineering objects. Two kinds of conformance statement can be made at this point.

Figure 5: Engineering Conformance Points

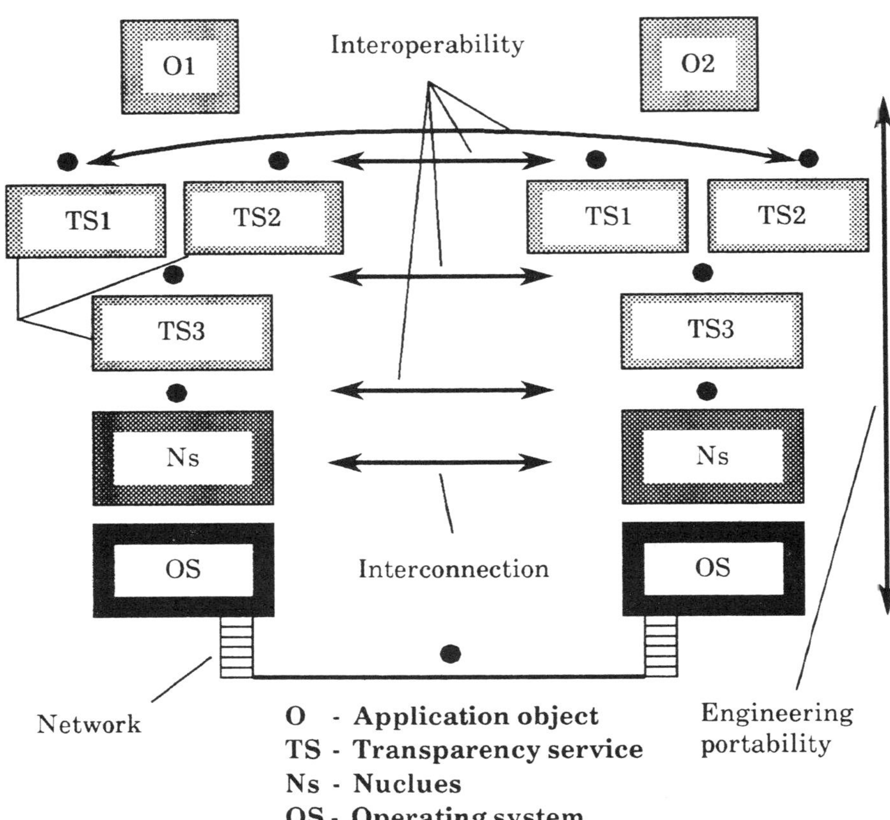

A statement of *interoperability conformance* for an object
asserts that a stated layering of transparency protocols will be
applied above the nucleus-to-nucleus protocol to all interactions
through the conformance points. Interoperability conformance
guarantees that the required transparency can be maintained
with other nodes asserting the same interoperability
conformance. System interoperability conformance can be tested
relative to a specified test service, test interface, and stack of
interconnection protocols.

A statement of *interconnection conformance* for a node asserts
that identified nucleus-to-nucleus communications services will

be used to exchange data and synchronisation messages. Interconnection conformance guarantees remote interaction between nodes. System interconnection conformance can be tested relative to a specified test service, test interface, interconnection protocols and data formats.

7.2.2 Engineering Portability Conformance

In the engineering viewpoint there is an *engineering portability conformance* point between an engineering object, and the transparency services and nucleus upon which it depends.

A statement of *engineering portability conformance* for an object asserts that the procedures and data structures comprising the object conform to the definition of a given engineering object specification, and that the object depends upon a specified selection of particular transparency service interface types.

A statement of *engineering portability conformance* for a node asserts that it provides a nucleus and a given set of transparency services for the execution of engineering objects.

Engineering portability guarantees the ability to exchange engineering objects, including transparency services, with other conforming nodes. Systems conformance at this point asserts that the node will accept one or more concrete representations of objects conforming to the nucleus and the interface types of the transparency services.

Engineering portability conformance can be omitted when exchange of engineering objects between nodes is not a requirement.

8 Summary

This paper has presented a a brief picture of the technical design philosophy of the ANSA architecture from the perspectives of the ANSA computational model and the ANSA engineering model. These two different but complementary viewpoint models do not, however, tell the whole story. ANSA also defines other models with specific focus on enterprise, information, and technology viewpoints. Moreover, many technical issues and/or details have not been discussed, e.g. security, atomic transactions, interface groups, fault management and recovery, concurrency control methods and event ordering techniques, distributed programming language facilities and interface type systems, and system installation management. The architecture covers these aspects, and much more, but the interested reader will need to consult specific ANSA technical reports and manuals. This technical literature is available through Architecture Projects Management Ltd, Cambridge, England.

9   Acknowledgements

The editor would like to take this opportunity of expressing gratitude for all written and verbal contributions to this paper given by technical members of the ISA Project Core Team: John Bull (APM), Jane Dunlop (APM), Andrew Herbert (Chief Architect, APM), Yigal Hoffner (APM), Nicola Howarth (APM), David Iggulden (APM), Rob van der Linden (Research Manager, APM), Erling Lindholm (Ellemtel), Cosmos Nicolaou (APM), Dennis Nyong (CASE), Michael Olsen (HP), Ed Oskiewicz (BT), Dave Otway (GEC Marconi), Owen Rees (APM), Alastair Tocher (STL), John Warne (STL), and Andrew Watson (APM).

Additional thanks are due to John Dobson (Newcastle University) for contributing points of clarification to parts of the text.

Appreciation is also extended to all management, business, sales and secretarial staff of APM for their dedicated support of the ISA/ANSA pursuit, its ideas, and its promotion: Janice Crofton, Mike Eyre (Managing Director), Andrew Herbert (Technical Director), Chris Jones, David Learmonth (STL seconded to APM), Elaine Mills, Garth Shephard (Director), Bill Talbot (Company Chairman), Judy Tillotson (Company Secretary), and Hugh Tonks (Business Manager).

Finally, special thanks must be given to all collaborators and associates of the Esprit ISA project, without whom this opportunity would not have arisen.

10   Background

The Advanced Networked Systems Architecture (ANSA) originated in a project undertaken by BT, DEC, GEC/Marconi,

GPT, HP, ICL, ITL, Olivetti, Plessey, Racal and STC within the UK Alvey Information Technology Programme . As the results of the project became more well known it became apparent that a more formal structure was needed to manage the development and exploitation of the architecture. To this end Architecture Projects Management Ltd (APM) was set up as a company in 1985. APM undertakes work on ANSA on behalf of the sponsors at a central laboratory in Cambridge, England. Much of the work is currently funded via the Commission of the European Communities (CEC) ESPRIT II Programme within a project called ISA - Integrated Systems Architecture - in which many of the sponsors of APM are joined by AEG, CASE, Chorus Systèmes, CTI-Patras, Ericsson Telecom, Televerket, Philips, France Telecom (SEPT), and Siemens. The architecture continues to be known as ANSA, and APM also trades under the name ANSA.

11   Standards

Standards are an essential part of the development of distributed processing systems. This was recognised early in the ANSA phase of the project, and strong efforts have been made to introduce the architecture into standards work. The main activity has centred on the ISO/IEC JTC1 WG7 Open Distributed Processing project where project members are active at the national and international level. In this particular forum the ideas of the ANSA Architecture have been accepted and incorporated into the working draft of a prescriptive model of Open Distributed Processing.

There are two other standards activities where the project is active through the participation its members. The first is ECMA whose technical reports are directed to the ISO ODP work and the second is CCITT whose work on a Distributed Applications Framework has a technical orientation based more on telecommunications but which nevertheless has a strong overlap with the ISO work. This overlap shows itself in a number of project members who contribute to both activities. An agreement has recently been made between ISO and CCITT for joint working which is expected to lead to joint text. Work has also started on specific standards related to the ODP framework, notably Remote

Procedure Call, and on plans to generate new work items, for example, on trading, are emerging as the framework activity matures.

Other relevant standards activities, reflecting on the large scope of the topic, such as document architecture, dictionaries, application programming interfaces, user architectures, database reference models, upper layer architecture, etc are kept under review by the team. Contributions to the ECMA work on Support Environments for ODP, Remote Procedure Call, and Open Systems Architectural Framework are made either directly or by review.

12   References

(a)   The ANSA Reference Manual, Vol. A, B and C, *Architecture Projects Management Ltd., Cambridge*, 1989.

(b)   ANSA: An Engineer's Introduction to the Architecture, *Architecture Projects Management Ltd., Cambridge*, 1989

(c)   ISO/IEC JTC1/SC21/WG7: Topic 4, Doc. N309, *ODP*, October 1990.

(d)   JTC1/SC21/WG7 & CCITT/SG VII, Doc. N314, *ODP*, December 1990.

(e)   JTC1/SC21/WG7 & CCITT/SG VII, Doc. N314, *ODP*, December 1990.

(f)   Bull, J. A., Object Management Group, Object Request Broker, CO.059, *Architecture Projects Management Ltd., Cambridge*, 1991.

(g)   Rees et al., The ANSA Computational Model, RC.205, *Architecture Projects Management Ltd., Cambridge*, 1990.

(h)   Linden, R.v.d., Trading in the Five Projections, RC.101, *Architecture Projects Management Ltd., Cambridge*, 1990.

(i)   Linden, R.v.d., Federated Naming Model, RC.216, *Architecture Projects Management Ltd., Cambridge*, 1990.

25

The CASE Data Interchange Format (CDIF) standards

Mike Imber
Vice-Chair, CDIF Technical Committee, LMBS,
Eveleyn House, 62 Oxford Street, London W1N 9LF, UK

1.   Introduction

This paper describes the technical background to the CDIF (CASE Data Interchange Format) Standards effort, the CDIF architecture, the set of components forming the CDIF standards family and the current status of their development.

2.   Objectives of CDIF

The objective of the CDIF is to provide a set of standards that will enable CASE Tools to interchange information in a standard format. This requires two areas to be defined in a standard. The format of the information exchange must be defined, but this in itself will not enable complete communication; it defines only the 'grammar' of the language, not its meaning. The second area of standardisation is the definition of the semantics of all objects conveyed in the exchange. This is a much more complex task, and significantly more difficult.

The interchange format must be neutral, and method-independent, but able to support the semantics required by many different methods. It must be extensible to enable semantics not covered in the standards to be conveyed.

3.   CDIF Architecture

3.1   Introduction

This section describes the underlying architecture of the CDIF Standards. It covers the separate components of the Architecture and how they fit together to provide the complete interchange definition.

3.2   Four-layer Architecture

CDIF has adopted the by-now common four-layer architecture for repositories and similar applications. The terminology used for the different layers is shown in Figure 1, alongside the ISO IRDS four-layer model [IS 10027 : 1989 : IRDS Framework].

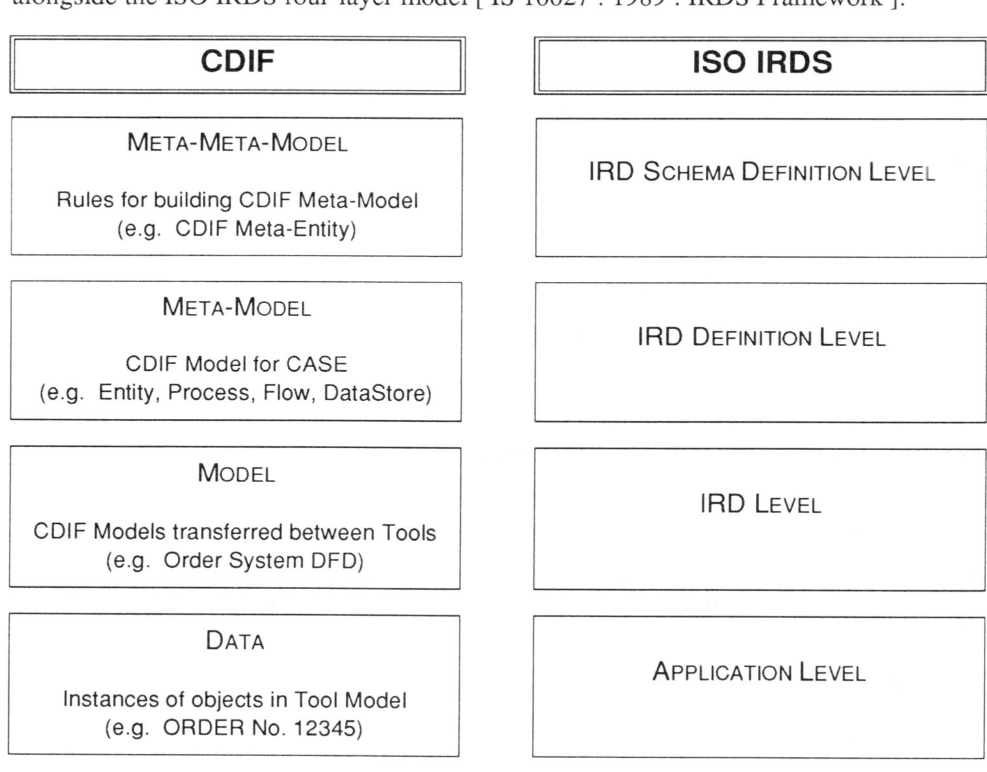

Figure 1 - CDIF 4-layer Framework

Each level of the modelling framework is used to define the level below it. The CASE Tool is used by the developer, analyst or programmer to define a model of the system being developed. This model is itself instantiated into individual occurrences of process and data objects in the final running system, which has been called the Data Level: this level, which is the bottom of the four levels, is not discussed further. The model developed by the user of the Tool is the third level. This information held in the CASE Tool in the models of the systems under development is itself defined in the second level, a Meta-model. This is the formal definition of the semantics of the information to be transferred between the tools. This level has itself to be defined using a fixed notation, which is called the Meta-meta-model and forms the top level.

4.   CDIF Meta-meta-model

4.1   Introduction

The goal of the Meta-meta-model is to provide a tool for the CDIF Technical Committee and those using extensibility to define the semantics of the CASE information that they wish to transfer. It is not intended to be used as a general modelling notation.

The Meta-meta-model is composed of an Entity-Relationship-Attribute (ERA) modelling language and an associated graphical representation of the Meta-meta-model objects. It is defined in terms of its own notations.

4.2   Entities

Entities may be defined, which contain attributes. The Entity must be given an unique name, and the attributes are names locally within the entity. A pre-defined set of data types is provided.

4.3   Relationships

Binary many-to-many relationships are supported. The relationships may themselves have attributes. The concepts of optionality and explicit cardinalities are supported. They are combined into Minimum and Maximum Number of Occurrences for both the Source and the Destination Entity.

Where Relationships are attributed, it is defined that there is a distinct instance of the Relationship for every different combination of Source and Destination Entity Instances. This means that, for example, an attribute on a one-to-many relationship between two entity types could not be used to hold a single value that relates to the single master entity instance, instead of to each detail entity instance. For example, consider a master entity instance *Order* with several detail entity instances *Order-Line*. The attribute *Total-Value* is an attribute of the sum of the order lines belonging to the order, and as such could be considered to be a property of the relationship *Order.Contains.Order-Line*. For this to behave correctly, there would need to be a single instance of the relationship connecting an *Order* to its *Order-Lines*, so that there existed a single instance of the attribute *Total* for each *Order*. If there is an instance of the relationship for each distinct instance of *Order-Line*, then this will not work; there is not a single instance of *Total-Value* for the set of *Order-Lines*, but one each. Therefore the attribute would have to be attached to the entity *Order* itself. The attribute could have been related to the relationship if a mechanism for defining that there should only be a single occurrence of the relationship connecting the master occurrence to all the detail occurrences was provided.

The concept of defining the number of occurrences of relationship instances is alien to most data modellers. In the context of unattributed binary relationships, with which most people are familiar, the problem does not arise, since no attributes can be defined for the relationships. Even where attributed relationships, either binary or n-ary, are used, the issue is left vague, or is based on the physical implementation, which generally would provide multiple instances of the relationship. But in conceptual terms, one should be able to define whichever is required for any situation, since in the example of 'Total', this really is a property of the relationship between the two entities, rather than a property of either entity in isolation.

Despite the above argument, the CDIF Technical Committee took the decision that the flexibility provided by the ability to define the cardinality of relationship instances was not essential to the goals of the meta-meta-modelling, and that the costs of explanation and education outweighed any benefits that such flexibility would provide; in cases where this facility could have been used, the attributes would need to be defined as belonging to the master entity.

4.4   Subtyping

The CDIF Meta-meta-model provides support for the subtyping of entities. Multiple inheritance is allowed. The subtype inherits all the attributes and relationships of the supertype(s). Both concrete and abstract supertypes are permitted; a concrete supertype may be instantiated in a Transfer, whereas an abstract one can never be instantiated. Abstract supertypes may appear at any point in the type hierarchy, and may themselves have concrete supertypes.

Since CDIF is intended to be a transfer definition, not a programming environment, the rules for name clashes on inherited attributes are simple; they are not allowed. The only exception is an object with multiple supertypes which lead back up the hierarchy to a common supertype. In this case, the subtype will 'inherit' the same set of attributes via each of the supertypes; they are treated as only occurring once in the subtype. Any other form of inheritance of two attributes with the same name is illegal, and users of CDIF must not define any such attributes.

4.5   Complex Relationships

Since only binary relationships are supported directly, a mechanism has been provided to record more complex underlying semantics than can be directly expressed. Entities can be classified to indicate that they exist to represent an n-ary relationship or an associative object. This enables tools supporting such concepts to be able to capture the information explicitly.

If this capability were not provided, tools which can capture the rich semantics available with n-ary relationships would lose that richness when using CDIF; with the facilities provided, they have to map the information to binary relationships, but can preserve the fact that this mapping has been made from the richer semantics. This was considered important; CDIF should be able to represent the conceptual models supported by tools, rather that just the implementation of the richer conceptual model forced by constraints of the physical DBMS.

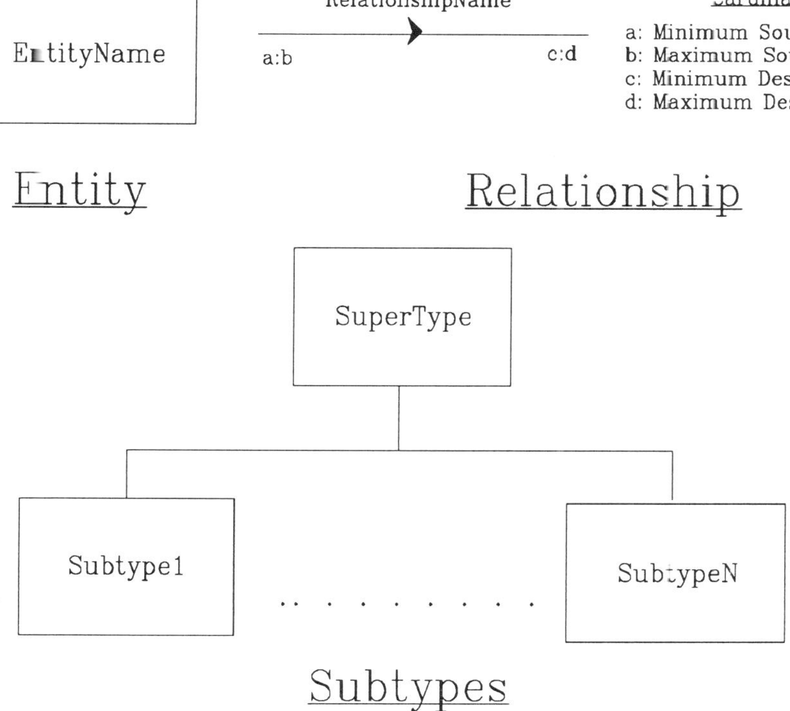

Figure 2 - CDIF Graphical Notation

4.6 Graphical Notation

The notation used is based on existing notations. The components are shown in Figure 2. The direction of the arrowhead on the relationship defines the way in which its name is read, and thereby the source and destination entities; it has no deeper semantic significance.

4.7 Extensibility

Extensibility allows for the definition of new Entities, new Relationships and new Attributes on existing objects. Nothing that is pre-defined can be removed or renamed.

A single object is pre-defined in the CDIF Meta-model called *RootObject* which has a single attribute of *CDIFIdentifier*. This is used as the unique identifier for objects in the transfer. This is discussed further in the section on the Meta-model. This acts as the root object for all other entities; they must all be subtypes of it at some level. This applies both to those defined in the CDIF Standardised Meta-model and to all entities added using extensibility.   No supertypes may be defined for *RootObject* using extensibility.

Extensions to the Meta-model are contained in the CDIF Transfer, defining new Entites, new Relationships and new Attributes. These can then be used within the single Transfer.

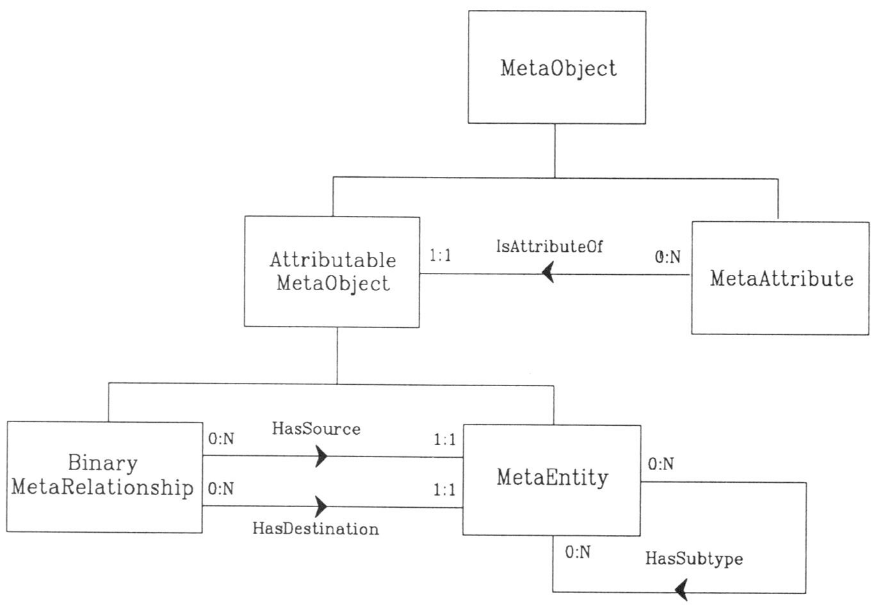

Figure 3 - CDIF Meta-meta-model

5.   Components within the CDIF Architecture

5.1   Separation of CDIF Semantics and CDIF Transfer Format

Once a Meta-meta-model has been defined, the syntax definition of the Transfer Format and the semantic definition can be separated.   The syntax definition must define how anything that can be modelled using the Meta-meta-model should be represented, without the need to have the explicit instances in the resulting meta-model defined.

The syntax will use the Meta-meta-model objects as tokens in the definition, which will be replaced by any instance of these objects in a concrete transfer file. For example, the Meta-meta-model defines that there are Meta-entities, which have an attribute called Name.   The Syntax can therefore refer to a token called <Meta-entity.Name>, and this provides a sufficient definition of all the values this token can take, given a Meta-model containing Meta-entities with names defined.

Quite separately, the semantics are defined in terms of the modelling notation defined in the Meta-meta-model, without any reference to the syntax with which the information will be represented in the actual Transfer File.

This separation makes the job of defining the standards much simpler since the syntax and semantics are effectively decoupled from each other.

5.2   Separation of CASE Semantics and Presentation

CASE Tools present information to the user of the tools in a variety of ways. Diagrammatic notations vary from tool to tool. For example, many different notations have developed for Entity Models.

It was decided that the CDIF Standards should provide a clear and complete separation of the underlying semantics of the information being transferred and the presentation information employed by a tool to present that underlying information to the tool user. This has several advantages. The modelling of the underlying semantics is greatly simplified by the removal of all presentation information. The presentation information can be modelled in a standard manner regardless of the semantics being expressed. There can be multiple sets of presentation information for a single set of underlying semantics.

5.3   Separation of Syntax and Encoding

With the separation of the Syntax from the semantics of the information to be passed, the CDIF Architecture can support the concept of multiple Syntaxes. The CDIF Technical Committee will initially define a single syntax, but it is likely that other syntaxes will be developed in the future, either by the Technical Committee or by other bodies. The CDIF Standards provide a set of rules to which any syntax and encoding must conform to be used as a CDIF-conformant transfer mechanism.

Within any Syntax, it is possible to provide multiple encodings. The syntax is a set of rules dictating the production of a set of terminals from any given instance of the model. For a given syntax and a given model instance the set of terminal tokens is invariant. The encoding is the definition of how the terminal tokens are expressed as actual characters or bytes.

Different encodings are required to achieve different objectives. A 'Clear Text Encoding' is one where none of the information is compressed into a shorthand notation of any form, and is intended to be human-readable. A 'Character Encoding' may express all keywords as numbers to reduce the size of the transfer file, but would keep all information as ASCII characters which can be transmitted down a communications line. A 'Binary Encoding' might compress the information into a more compact form, and be intended for transfer between communication processes within the same computer.

To achieve this, the Syntax takes the definition of the grammar to a level at which it is required to give different encodings freedom over the way detailed components of the Syntax are expressed. In terms of a BNF description of a grammar, the Syntax will treat some tokens as terminals in the definition of the Syntax, and these tokens will be further decomposed in the Encoding to provide the Encoding-specific representation of the object.

The Syntax defines a grammar for a language, and takes the tokens to a certain level of detail, such as <ExtendKeyword> or <Integer>. The encodings would define whether the <ExtendKeyword> was represented by the string 'EXTEND' or the number '15' for compactness, and whether an <Integer> was in 16-bit binary or as a sequence of ASCII digits.

6.   CDIF Meta-model

6.1   Introduction

There is a single Meta-model defined in the CDIF Standards family. For the purposes of
development and clarity, it has been split into two parts; the Semantic Model and the
Presentation Model. The former covers the underlying meaning of the information and
the latter covers the presentation of the information to the user.

The purpose of the CDIF Meta-model is to define a set of objects, attributes and
relationships which cover the information that needs to be transferred between CASE
Tools, with very precise meaning given to all objects.

6.2   Semantic Meta-model

6.2.1   Subject Areas

Within the Semantic Model standard, Subject Areas or partitions are used; these have no
existence outside the document defining the Semantic Model - they form no part of the
Meta-meta-model or the Syntax of the transfer format.   They exist to divide the
Semantic Model into related areas for ease of understanding and explanation.

6.2.2   Current status

There are currently four Subject Areas defined:

- Core
- Data Flow Modelling
- Entity-Relationship Modelling
- Data Inventory

As can be seen from the Subject areas, the CDIF Technical Committee has initially
concentrated on areas related to the Analysis phase in Information Systems
Development. These represent an initial set, not the full scope. The Committee decided
that the time it would take to develop a fuller set would be prohibitive, given the level of
definition required for effective communication to take place. They plan to add new
Subject Areas rapidly once the first release of the Standard has been issued. For new
areas to be developed, the committee also needs access to expertise in the areas covered;
those selected reflect the expertise available to the committee at the current stage of
development and the priorities of those involved.

6.2.3   Core Subject Area

The Core Subject Area concentrates on aspects required for any objects transferred in a
CDIF Transfer. Examples of the things defined here include the concept of Alternate
Names, details of the User who created or updated any object, Constraints on objects and
similar general information. It provides facilities for defining hierarchies of users and
for defining LifeCycles and LifeCycle Phases. It also provides two objects
SemanticObject and *PresentationObject* from which all objects in the Semantic Model

and Presentation Model respectively are subtyped. The Core subject area is shown in Figure 4.

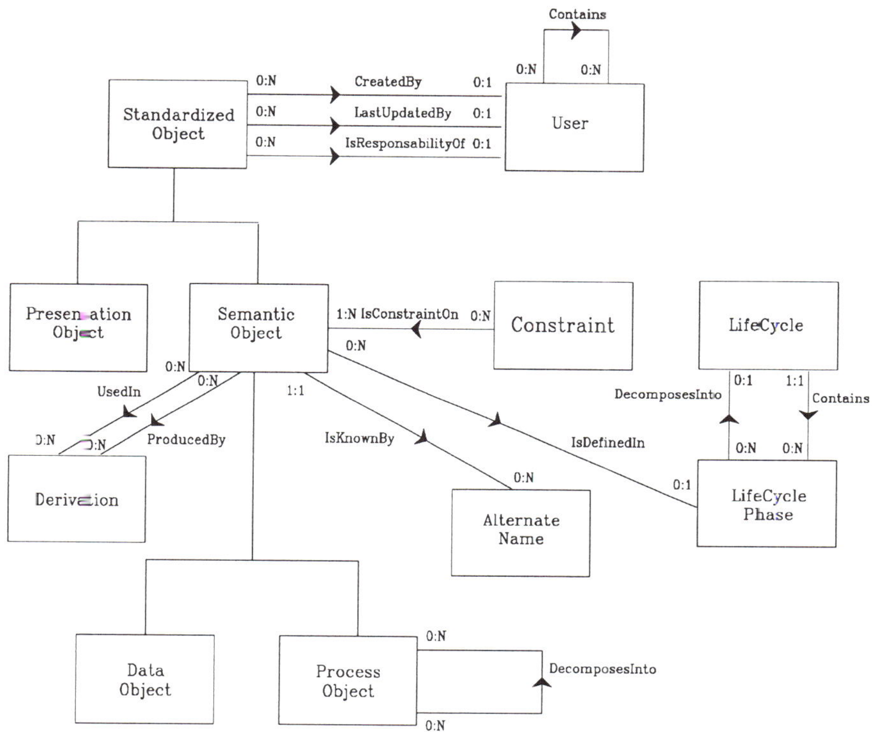

Figure 4 - Core Subject Area

6.2.5   Data Flow Modelling Subject Area

The Data Flow Modelling Subject Area covers the semantics represented by the technique of Data Flow Diagramming. The semantics underlying this notation do not vary much from one method to another. The main differences are the degree of decomposition allowed on different object types. Some methods only allow the processes to be decomposed, others allow the Store, External and Flows to be decomposed as well. This information must be represented in the Semantic Model.

The Data Flow Model subject area is shown in Figure 5. Note that *DFMAttribute* can be related to both *Flow* and *Store* through the inherited relationship *DataObject.Contains.Attribute* which is defined in the Data Inventory subject area.

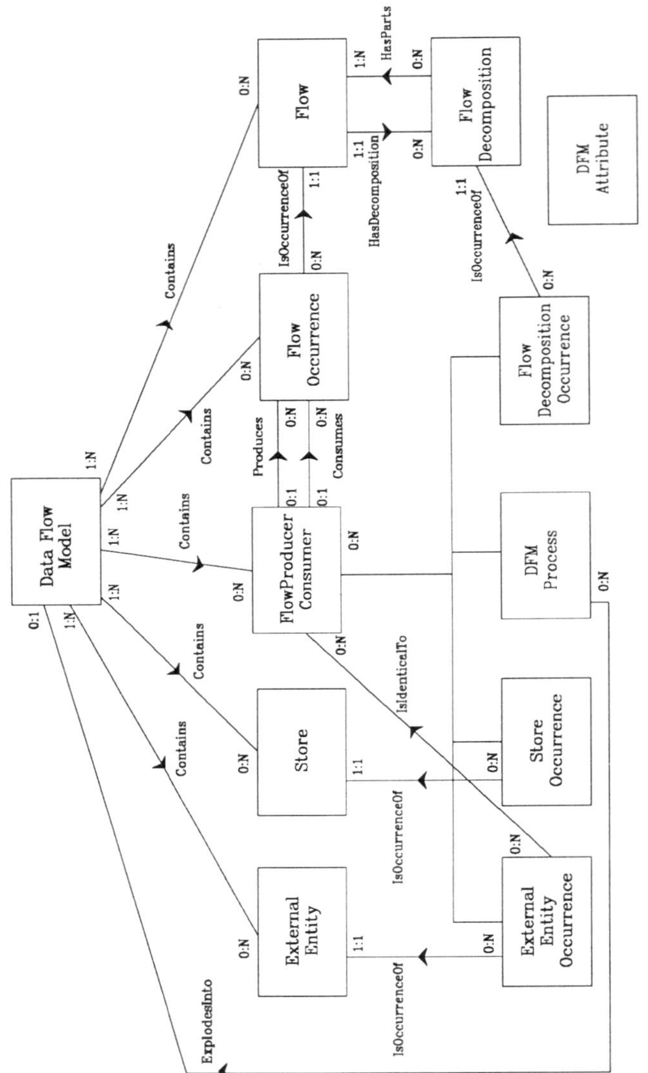

Figure 5 - Data Flow Model Subject Area

6.2.6   Entity-Relationship Modelling Subject Area

The Entity-Relationship Subject Area covers the main forms of Entity-Relationship-Attribute modelling encountered in Information Systems development. It is not intended to cover the Object-oriented approach; this is one area for extension in the near future. It does cover forms of ER modelling ranging from those supporting only binary unattributed relationships to those allowing n-ary attributed relationship. The standard defines how each variation on the technique must represent its information in the CDIF Standardised Meta-model so that a tool using any of the other forms can understand it. This detail covers such aspects as how to hold bidirectional naming of binary relationships, with one name preferred over the other, or with implicit directionality on the names.

The Entity-Relationship Model subject area is shown in Figure 6. Note that *ERAAttribute* can be related to *Entity* through the relationship *DataObject.Contains.Attribute* which it inherits, defined in the Data Inventory subject area.

6.2.7   Data Inventory Subject Area

The Data Inventory Subject Area covers the definitions of attributes of any object containing data from the other subject areas, and the underlying data type definitions, including complex structures and domain definitions.

The Data Inventory subject area is shown in Figures 7 and 8.

6.2.8   Directions

Once the first version of the standards family is out for public comment, work will proceed on the definition of other subject areas. The CDIF Committee decides on the areas to be covered on the advocacy principle; if there is someone willing to drive work in a particular area that the Committee feels is relevant and able to review, it will get done.

The next areas likely to be covered are the definition of Programs and Screens, including windowed dialogues, real-time extensions to Data Flow Modelling, and generalised Process and Functional Decomposition.

The work of standardising new areas of CASE Semantics for the purposes of interchange between tools will go on for a long time; CASE is a vast area, and the requirements are forever changing as methods advance and change. This is a major reason for the architecture that CDIF has developed; the underlying framework and the syntax can all remain stable and unchanged as the semantic definitions develop and extend over time.

Constraints on objects are currently defined using free text. The CDIF Technical Committee is not planning on defining a language for this; work is being done by other committees on this, and will be adopted when an appropriate language is defined.

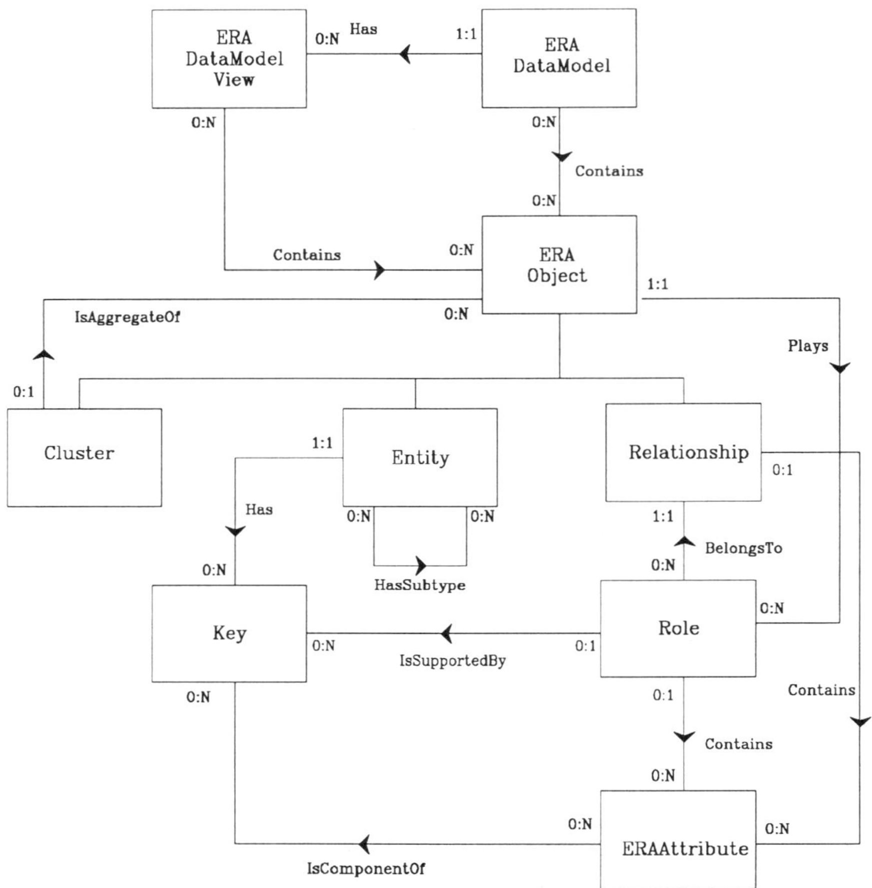

Figure 6 - Entity-Relationship Model Subject Area

6.3   Presentation Meta-model

6.3.1   Introduction

The Presentation Model defines the way information is presented by the tool for the
user. It enables the exporter to define and transfer a type of presentation once, for DFDs
for example, and also pass actual instances of the presentation, in this example several
different DFD pictures all using the defined notation. This approach enables the amount
of information required for each diagram instance to be reduced and also allows
configureable tools to capture most of the information required about a drawing style.

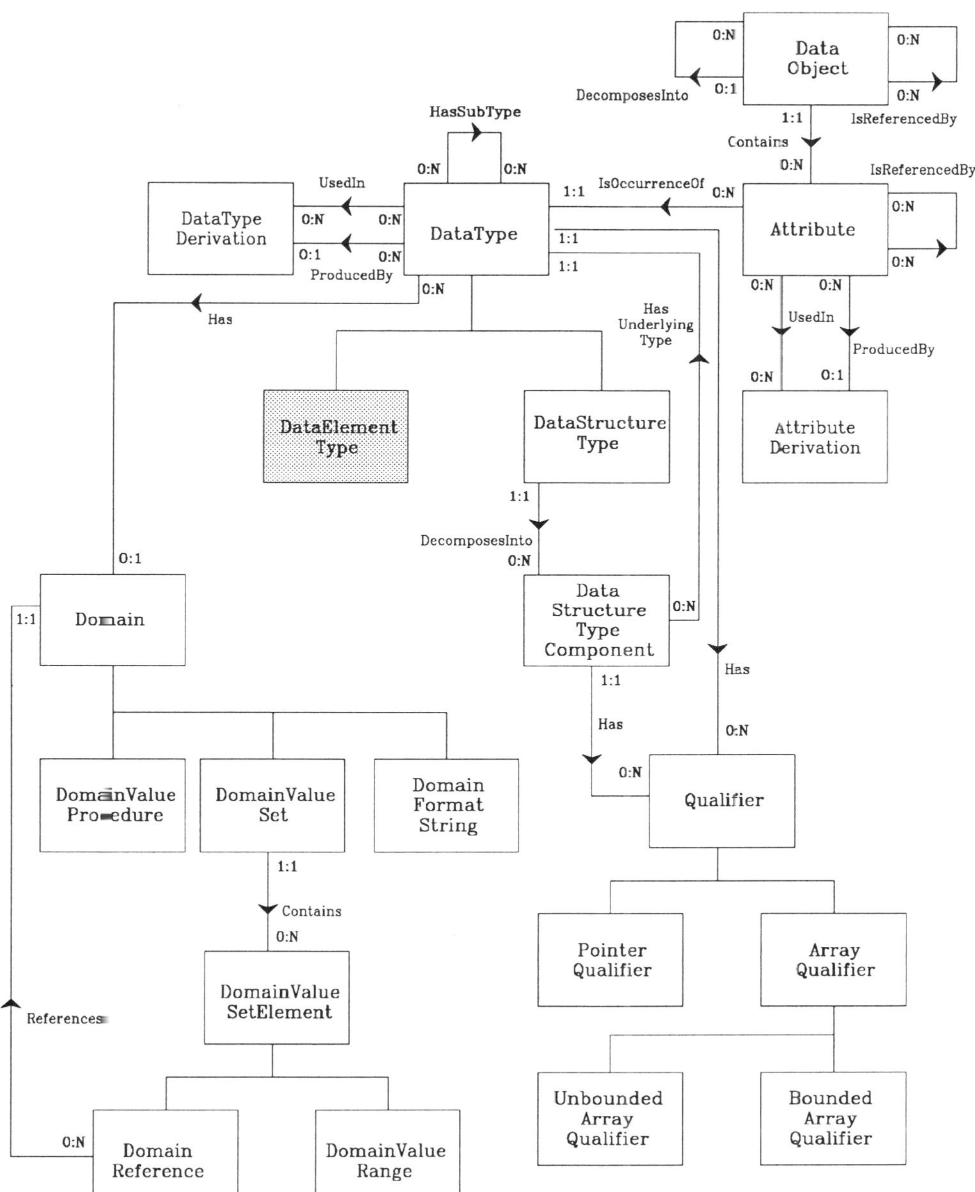

Figure 7 - Data Inventory Subject Area - Main Part

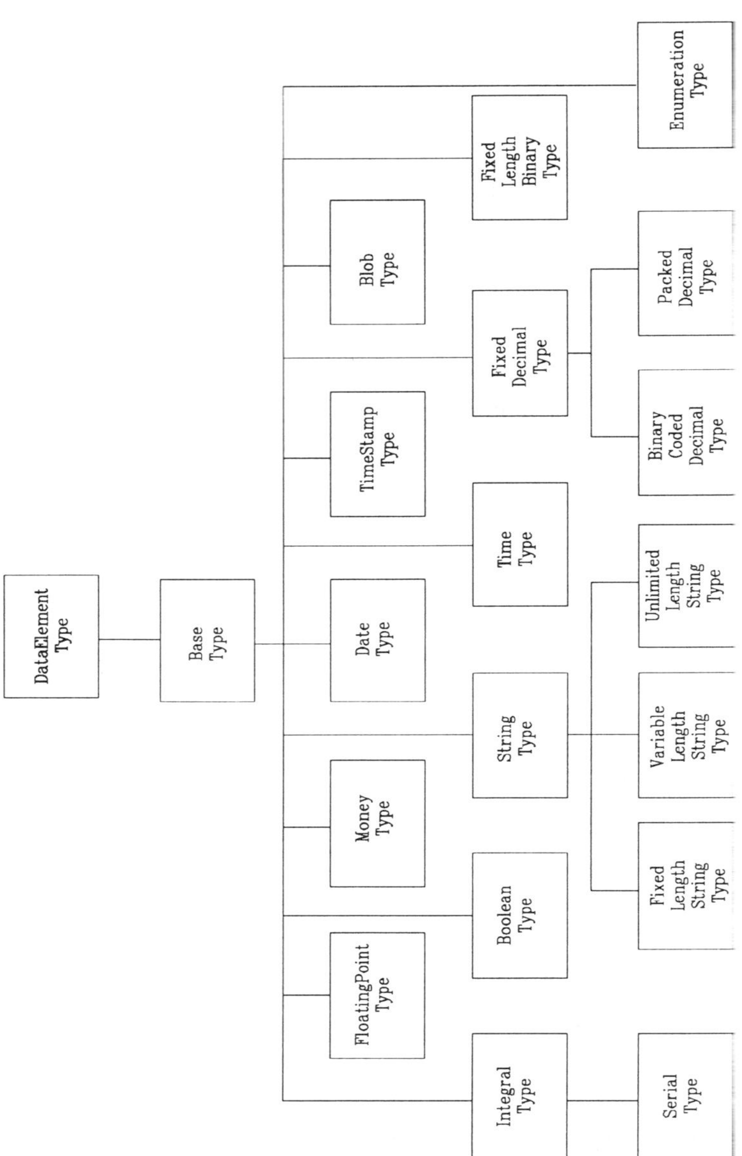

<u>Figure 8 - Data Inventory Subject Area - Data Element Subtypes</u>

6.3.2   Current Status

The only form of presentation that will be supported in the initial version of the CDIF Standardised Meta-model is that of icon-link diagrams, where the diagram is composed of distinct icons which are connected together by links. The majority of diagrams supported by CASE Tools fall into this category.

The Meta-model provides the means for the definition of diagram types, including the icons and links allowed on the diagram. Icons can be complex structures, made up of many components. Rules can be defined for the display of information from the underlying Semantic Meta-Model attached to the defined icons and links; for example an Entity Name can be displayed within the icon defined to represent an Entity. These rules cover the most common cases where the attribute is contained within the object that the icon represents, or one that is related to it through an unambiguous path of named relationships. They can also be used to define the presence or absence of graphical annotation based on underlying attribute values, such as 'Optional' indicators on relationships. Defaults of colour, size, font, orientation etc. can be defined for all drawing structures.

Instances of diagrams are defined through a set of objects mirroring the definition objects, which contain the actual coordinate information for the diagram instance, and a reference to the underlying semantic instance represented by the icon or link. Any of the defaults can be overridden on a per-instance basis, and other information added, such as details not definable using the rules capability provided.

6.3.3   Directions

The Technical Committee will look at other forms of information presentation used within CASE Tools and extend the Presentation Model to cater for them; the next addition likely is the capture and expression of matrices, which are used in many tools.

The rules for the derivation of attribute values from the underlying semantic information may be extended. As with constraints, the CDIF Technical Committee does not intend to develop a new language for this. It is intended that whatever language is adopted for constraint definition will also be capable of being used for attribute derivation rule definition.

7.   CDIF Transfer Format

7.1   Introduction

As was stated earlier, the CDIF architecture provides for multiple syntaxes, each with possible multiple encodings. The transfer formats can be defined in isolation from any Meta-model due to the existence of the Meta-meta-model definition, in terms of which the syntax and encoding rules are defined.

7.2   Transfer Format Definition

All CDIF Syntaxes and Encodings must provide a standard 'envelope' which identifies the contents as a CDIF Transfer, and defines the Syntax and Encoding used in the body of the transfer.

The body consists of three sections: the header, the meta-model definition and the model definitions.

The header defines such things as the identity of the exporting tool, the default character sets and text formats used in the transfer and details of the date and time of the export. There will be a registration scheme for the definition of keywords for use in the header section.

The Meta-model definition defines the complete Meta-model used in the transfer. Reference to the CDIF Standardised Meta-model is made by a single statement, giving the version number of the Meta-model. This may not be omitted if the standardised Meta-model is not used, since it is required to avoid conflict between extensions in one version which are added to the standardised model in a later version.

Any Meta-model extensions are then given in full, with no forward references permitted. If only the standardised Meta-model is used, no extensions are required.

The Model definitions follow, which are the actual instances of the model data to be transferred between the two tools.

7.3   Current Status

The CDIF Technical Committee is initially producing a single syntax - SYNTAX.1, with a single clear-text encoding - ENCODING.1. These conform to the spirit of the EDIF Standard, which was the starting point for the work of the committee. It is a LISP-like language, using round brackets to delimit related grouping of tokens.

7.4   Directions

In the future the CDIF Technical Committee may define other encodings for SYNTAX.1, and also may define other syntaxes, for example an ASN.1-conformant syntax.

8.   CDIF Standards

The CDIF Technical Committee has developed CDIF as a set of three related standards. One covers the underlying architecture or framework and also contains the definition of the Meta-meta-model. The second defines the Transfer Format, giving, in several parts, the general rules for all transfer formats, and the initial CDIF Syntax and Encoding. The final standard gives the CDIF Standardised Meta-model.   The full set, with their EIA numbers are:

EIA-PN2387   CDIF - Framework for Modeling and Extensibility

EIA-PN2329   CDIF - Standardized CASE Interchange Meta-Model
             Part 1: Semantic Model
             Part 2: Presentation Model

EIA-PN2389   CDIF - Transfer Format Definition
             Part 1: General Rules for CDIF Syntaxes and Encoding
             Part 2: CDIF Transfer Format Syntax - SYNTAX.1
             Part 3: CDIF Transfer Format Encoding - ENCODING.1

9.   Use of CDIF

9.1   Exporter

A CDIF Exporter should use CDIF to export as much information as it can, using the predefined Meta-model where possible. It can have no knowledge of the capabilities of the importing tool and should provide all the detail it can to aid the importer.

Where any of the semantics covered by the CDIF Standardised CASE Interchange Meta-model are exported, the standard definitions should be used. The exporter will have to map its internal model of the objects and relationships held by the tools underlying database or file system into the semantics required by the CDIF standard.

Where any diagrammatic information is passed, the exporter should give details of the drawing definitions and the derivation rules of information from the semantics, as well as the details of the drawing instances to be transferred.

The exporter may create and use any extensions to the Meta-model required for it to convey the semantics and presentation information it holds, where this is not covered by the CDIF Standardised CASE Interchange Model.

9.2   Importer

An importer can only use information passed to it in a CDIF Transfer that it is capable of understanding; it may discard other information.

If a tool uses particular icons for certain objects, it should use the positional information provided with each drawing instance, but would ignore all the icon definition information provided by the exporter, since it only supports internal pre-defined icons. It may need to rescale some of the drawing information, or it may choose to only use some aspects of it.

If a tool does not support some attributes of an object, or a particular type of relationship, then there is no way that it can retain such information if it receives it in a transfer; it has little option but to discard it. Where it can hold the information, it may still require a transformation from the CDIF Standardised model to its own internal scheme. An example of this is the different forms of ER modelling. If a tool can only represent binary unattributed relationships, then there are choices open to the developers of the importer when deciding how to process a CDIF Transfer. They may choose to ignore any ER models except those which they can represent, or they may choose to carry out the necessary mapping of n-ary relationships to a set of binary relationships, or many-to-many relationships to a pair of relationships with an associative entity and create the additional entities and relationships as appropriate to be able to capture the information conveyed in a more powerful notation.

9.3   CDIF Facilities

As can be seen from this brief example, there is a considerable scope for the developers of CDIF Importers and Exporters to provide facilities ranging from the basic to the sophisticated, based on the power and configureability of the underlying tools and the complexity of the importers and exporters themselves.

The guiding principle behind the implementation of interfaces should be the minimal loss of information and a view of what a 'reasonable tool user on the Clapham Omnibus' would expect, knowing the facilities of the exporting and importing tool.

Given the different facilities of two tools, there can be no guarantee that if a set of information is exported from Tool A to an empty Tool B, and then back to an empty Tool A, that the second Tool A will have the same information as before the initial export, since detail may have had to be discarded by Tool B when performing its import.

10.   Wider Role of CDIF

The CDIF Standards work potentially has a wider role than just the interchange of information between CASE Tools. There is little work going on elsewhere to define the semantics of CASE information. This work is vital if information is to be held in a common format in Repositories. All the repository standards define is a mechanism for defining Meta-model, pertinent to each organisation. If tools which are tightly-coupled to a repository are going to work together, they must have a common understanding of the data they share. This cannot be done on an ad-hoc basis and be expected to work. The Meta-models that CDIF has developed can easily be mapped into the slightly different Meta-meta-models provided by the different repository environments, and provide a basis for repository content standardisation.

Similarly, the Transfer Format Definition defined by CDIF may have a role in the definition of repository Import/Export Languages.

11.   Current Status

At the time of writing, all the CDIF Standards are in their final internal draft form. It is intended that they be finalised and issued as EIA Interim Standards in mid- 1991, and that in parallel, experiments are carried out to prove the viability of the approach. Interim Standards are valid for a period of one year, after which they must be revised. This period will give the community time to review them in a practical way through prototypes and improve them where required before a full standard is produced.

12.   Summary

The CDIF Standards family provide a mechanism for the interchange of information between CASE Tools. The CASE Standardised Meta-model provides a firm basis for communication between tools, and also has a wider scope than just within tool-to-tool transfer. The CDIF Framework provides a basis for tools to exchange information other than that pre-defined in the Meta-model, thereby increasing the applicability of the standards beyond the current initial scope of the pre-defined Meta-model. The architecture allows for the development of multiple transfer formats, each suited to a particular need, and an initial format is being defined.

The CDIF Standards family meets a real need in the industry for the provision of an interchange mechanism between the large variety of CASE and other development tools in use in the industry today, and a basis for use of the efforts of the Technical Committee in other related areas of standardisation that could benefit from its efforts.

As can be seen from the above descriptions, the scope of the CDIF Standards development is far wider than the narrow area of direct interchange between CASE Tools. It is the wish of the CDIF Technical Committee that their work is used as widely as possible within the standards community to bring the maximum benefit to the industry.

26

ROSE-ADA an instance of the ESF-ROSE system to reuse Ada code

Thierry Moineau
Sema Group, 19 Rue Barbès, F–92126 Montrouge, France

Introduction

Software reusability is a topic of first practical importance and of great practical difficulty, which has been recognized as such for a long time (since the first subroutine libraries). There is however no general approach to this problem: most current systems are specific to the reuse of one kind of software element, mainly reuse of code, and they consider a specific language such as Ada [1] (STARS [DRR83], ASR [Con87]) or Eiffel [Mey87].

The aim of the ESF-ROSE project [2] is to develop an environment (the ESF-ROSE System) supporting reuse of any kind of software elements produced within a Software Development Environment: specifications, designs, and code, but also documentation (e.g. project management plan or user manual). Hence the ESF-ROSE System is a generic system that can be instantiated by the kind of software elements to be reused.

The various approaches to reusability can be classified into two basic groups [BR87]:

---

[1] Ada is a trade mark of the DOD Ada Joint Project Office.

[2] The ESF-ROSE project is a subproject of the Eureka Software Factory project and must not be confused with another project on reusability which is called ROSE [Lub87]

- In the composition approach, building blocks are stored in a library and are combined according to well-defined rules to form more complex systems.
- In the generative approach, the final program is generated from its "specification" written in a Problem Oriented Language [CLP84, Nei84].

The ESF-ROSE project follows the first approach: the ESF-ROSE System is basically meant to manage libraries of software elements. But unlike other library based reuse systems such as RSL [BAB$^+$87] or STARS [DRR83], which concentrate on basic components, the ESF-ROSE System lay a special emphasis on the composition mechanisms and support storage of complex systems. Indeed it is important to support reuse of systems, because a system is not only the union of its constituent parts: the whole is more than the sum of its parts.

Another characteristic of the ESF-ROSE System is its extensibility. This is necessary on the one hand to be able to evolve with the future innovations arising from the research community and on the other hand because total coverage of the reuse process requires a large number of tools that cannot be developed in one step.

Hence the ESF-ROSE System is divided into two parts: the kernel and a set of tools. The kernel, called the **Library System** (LS), supports the basic mechanisms for the storage, the classification and the retrieval of reusable elements. The tools provide more advanced functionalities; they act as an interface between the user and the Library System. The set of tools, called the **Reuse Tool Kit** (RTK), is extensible and it is possible to add new tools provided that they conform to the LS interface.

Defining a new ESF-ROSE instance consists then in defining a composition mechanism adapted to the kind of software elements to be reused, in instantiating the LS by the description of the objects to be reused and in building the tools specific to that instance. Among these tasks the first one is by far the most difficult. Hence the ESF-ROSE project is defining some instances that could be adapted by the final users so as to fit with their own requirements. One of these instances is devoted to reuse of Ada code and is called ROSE-ADA.

The aim of this paper is to present how the various features of ESF-ROSE have been used to build the ROSE-ADA environment supporting reuse of Ada code. For that we will first explain the philosophy of ROSE-ADA (originally presented in [BM91]). We will then show how Ada reusable components can be retrieved and adapted. Finally we will give a short guided tour to ESF-ROSE and ROSE-ADA.

Note that this paper is neither a complete presentation of the ESF-ROSE project (see [MAR90]) nor of ROSE-ADA (see [BM91]).

1   The philosophy of ROSE-ADA

1.1   As-it-is reuse

ROSE-ADA supports reuse of Ada code, following the *as-it-is reuse* paradigm: the aim is to identify possible reuses such that there is no need to modify the reused code. When it is possible, *as-it-is reuse* is especially interesting since the absence of code modifications results in important benefits: there is no need for retesting and redocumenting the reused components. But, the main benefit of *as-it-is* reuse arises during the maintenance phase [LG84, BR87]. One can explain that by the following facts:

- Reusable components are usually of greater quality level than those developed from scratch, because they have been developed more carefully and because they have been tested more extensively (at least because they have been used many times by different people).

- Reusable components maintenance can be performed only once by a central team. Bug corrections and enhancements can then be done and tested very carefully, avoiding waterfall errors. After that the enhanced component can be broadcasted and automatically reinstalled within the various applications that have reused this component.

Such a maintenance factorisation is possible only if each component is associated with a detailed specification and if new versions keep this specification unchanged. Moreover the reuser must only need to know the specification of the code he wants to reuse, and should not need to know anything about implementation details (see [PCW83]).

1.2.   Basic Ada components

The first thing to decide is the granularity of the objects to be reused. These objects must be self-contained, i.e. they must contain all the information needed for their reuse. Such objects are called **Reusable Elements** (RE) in ESF-ROSE. As usual in the Ada framework, Ada components will correspond in ROSE-ADA to sets of Ada packages. As explained above these sets of Ada packages must be associated with a specification. Other information are also needed, like informal description, examples of use, hardware requirements, and so on. Of course, all these information are not mixed together: in ESF-ROSE each RE is split into several partial descriptions, called **views**, which describe different characteristics of the RE. Hence an Ada RE (also called Ada component) consists of, at least a specification view, a code view (a set of Ada packages), an informal description, etc.

The specification of an Ada component is expressed by a rooted directed acyclic graph of Ada package specifications (without the `private` part). The package specification part of the Ada language is used here, because it is obviously well adapted for Ada and because it should be well known by people developing Ada applications. We enrich the Ada language with the concept of generator as defined in [NS88]: roughly speaking generators are the subprograms that generate the possible values of a data type, while non-generators can only yield values which are denotable by a composition of the generators. Moreover we require to specify for each subprogram the exceptions it can raise. A simple example of a component specification for list of colours is given in figure 1 (the distinction between basic and extraneous operations is explained later).

Note that the code view of an Ada RE may contain packages which are not described in the specification. These packages are hidden and are used only for implementation purpose; the reuser should not use the types and the subprograms of these packages (as explained above it should even not be aware of their existence).

1.3   Complex Ada components

We want to reuse also complex components, i.e. sets of components interconnected together with respect to a well-defined composition mechanism. ROSE-ADA uses the plug-socket mechanism [Gog84] [3]. In this approach, each component consists of three parts:
- a **plug** which is the specification of the capabilities exported by the component,
- a **socket** which is the specification of the capabilities imported by the component, and
- a **code**.

The code part of a RE may contain hidden capabilities which are not exported in its plug, and the code is not required to implement all the capabilities described in the plug: some of these capabilities may be imported by the socket.

Two components C (client) and S (server) can be composed together provided that all the capabilities imported by the socket of C are exported by the plug of S (cf. figure 2). This composition results in a new component whose plug is the one of C, whose socket is the one of S and whose code is built by merging the codes of C and S. This composition mechanism can be performed until all the sockets are filled, so as to get a complete software component.

---

[3]In fact ROSE-ADA also uses the genericity/instantiation composition mechanism; we do not discuss this mechanism here because it is already well known.

```
package COLOUR is
    -- <Types >
    type Colour is private ;
    -- <Generators >
    function blue return Colour ;
    function red return Colour ;
    function yellow return Colour ;
    -- <Basic Operations >
    function equal (a_colour1, a_colour2 : Colour) return Boolean ;
end COLOUR ;

with COLOUR;
package LIST is
    -- <Types >
    type List is private ;
    -- <Generators >
    function empty return List ; -- < raise no_more_room >
    procedure add (a_colour : in COLOUR.Colour; a_list : in out List) ;
                -- < raise no_more_room >
    -- <Basic Operations >
    function head (a_list : List) return COLOUR.Colour ; -- < raise empty_list >
    procedure remove_head (a_list : in out List) ; -- < raise empty_list >
    function is_empty (a_list : List) return Boolean ;
    -- <Extraneous Operations >
    function contains (a_list : List; a_colour : COLOUR.Colour) return Boolean ;
    function length (a_list : List) return Natural ;
    -- <Exceptions >
    no_more_room : exception ;
    empty_list : exception ;
end LIST ;
```

Figure 1: Example of Ada specification : LIST

Such a composition mechanism is modeled in ESF-ROSE by means of **complex REs**: a complex RE contains views but also other REs (its sub-REs). For instance the RE corresponding to the CS component of figure 2 will contain the REs corresponding to C and to S.

Usually the various views of a complex RE are built by means of the views of its sub-REs (the plug of CS for instance is exactly the copy of the plug of C). This is expressed in ESF-ROSE by means of inferred views and of inference connections. An **inference connection** builds the content of an **inferred view** (its output view) by means of the content of other views (its input views). Hence there are two kinds of views: the plain views whose content has to be stored, and the inferred views

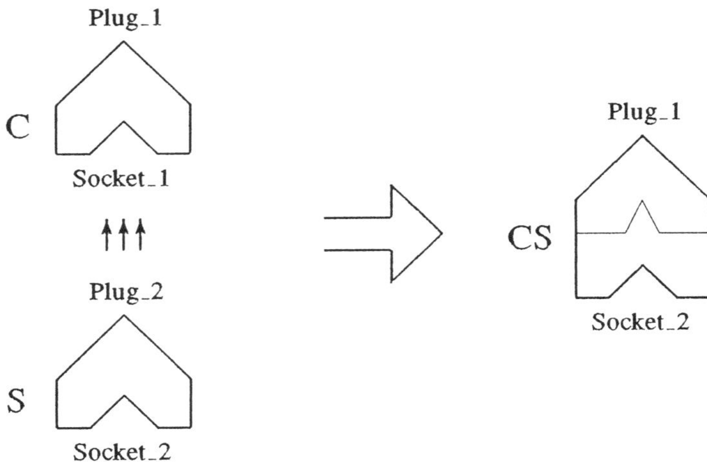

Figure 2: The plug-socket composition mechanism

whose content is inferred and is not necessarily stored.

To implement this inference mechanism, the ESF-ROSE System makes currently use of the Virtual Tree Processor (VTP) of Centaur [BCD+87]: each type of view is described by its grammar in a BNF like notation and each time a new RE is created, its views are parsed according to this grammar and are stored as abstract syntax trees. Each inference connection type is thus associated with a VTP program which extracts subtrees from the input views so as to build the output view.

2 Retrieval and adaptation of Ada Components

As-it-is reuse is difficult to achieve.   Indeed, as cited in [Mey87], a needed component is "neither ever quite the same, nor ever quite another" as an existing reusable component. A common problem is the one of renaming: the reusable component actually corresponds to the needs at a semantical level, but not at a syntactical level (e.g. the subprogram names do not correspond, or a function corresponds to a procedure). But we do not want to change the specifications of other components when we reuse an already existing component. Hence we need a method for adapting a reused component in such a way that the resulting code is actually an implementation of the goal specification, even when the specification of the reused component is not syntactically equivalent to the goal specification.

```
package COLOR is
    -- <Types >
    type Color is private ;
    -- <Generators >
    function blue return Color ;
    function red return Color ;
    function yellow return Color ;
    -- <Operations >
    function equal (a_color1, a_color2 : Color) return Boolean ;
end COLOR ;
```

```
with COLOR;
package COLOR_LIST is
    -- <Types >
    type C_List is private ;
    -- <Generators >
    function nil return C_List ; -- < raise no_more_room >
    function cons (a_color : COLOR.Color; a_list : C_List) return C_List ;
                -- < raise no_more_room >
    -- <Basic Operations >
    function car (a_list : C_List) return COLOR.Color ; -- < raise empty_list >
    function cdr (a_list : C_List) return C_List ; -- < raise empty_list >
    function nilp (a_list : C_List) return Boolean ;
    -- <Extraneous Operations >
    function member (a_color : COLOR.Color; a_list : C_List) return Boolean ;
    -- <Exceptions >
    no_more_room : exception ;
    empty_list : exception ;
end LIST ;
```

Figure 3: Example of Ada reusable component specification : COLOR_LIST

2.1 Implementation by reuse

Suppose that we have to implement the simple specification of list of colours given
in figure 1 (for instance to fill the socket of another Ada component), and suppose
that we have an Ada component C_LIST whose plug is the specification COLOR_
LIST of figure 3 (here `nil`, `cons`, `car`, `cdr`, `nilp` and `member` are the usual
names in the Lisp community for `empty`, `add`, `head`, `remove_head`, `is_empty` and
`contains`).

According to our experience of programmer, we know that we can reuse the
component C_LIST to implement the specification LIST. But the specifications
COLOR_LIST and LIST are not equivalent: the names are not the same and some
functions correspond to procedures. Hence we have to adapt the C_LIST component

before to reuse it. As explained before we do not want to modify the code of C_LIST. Thus we encapsulate the reused code within packages which contain the relevant renamings [4], and we rewrite the package specifications of LIST and of COLOUR as follows (cf. figure 4):

- The LIST package specification imports the COLOUR package (as requested by the goal specification) and imports the COLOR_LIST package (here comes the reuse of COLOR_LIST). It contains a subtype clause to rename C_List into List, and some Ada renaming clauses to rename nil into empty, car into head, etc.

  The LIST package body contains some code to implement the add procedure by means of the cons function, to implement the remove_head procedure by means of the cdr function and to implement the contains function by means of member [5]. This body also contains a skeleton to be filled out in order to provide an implementation for the length function.

- The package specification COLOUR imports the COLOR package. It contains the subtyping and the renaming clauses for Colour, blue, red, yellow and equal. Since all the subprograms of COLOUR are implemented by renaming, there is no need for a COLOUR package body.

Using the plug-socket mechanism, we will build a stub component whose plug is the LIST specification of figure 1, whose socket is the COLOR_LIST specification of figure 3 and and whose code is given in figure 4. We can then plug the C_LIST component into this stub so as to get a new component whose code is a correct implementation of the goal specification LIST.

In the previous example, we can reuse the C_LIST component to implement the LIST specification even if the length function is not defined in COLOR_LIST. Indeed we do not need to know about the detailed implementation of the lists to implement length: we only have to remove the first element of the list and to increment a counter until the list is empty. The subprograms which can be implemented without any knowledge about the internal representation of the data types are called **extraneous** subprograms, the other ones are called **essential** subprograms. Implementing a goal specification by a reusable component is definitely not possible when an essential subprogram of the goal specification cannot be implemented by means of the subprograms exported by the reused component.

---

[4]In this paper renaming means changing the names, but also permuting the order of the arguments and transforming functions into procedures or procedures into functions.

[5]We can also use the **inline** pragma, to avoid a function call and to have better performances.

```ada
with COLOUR , -- as in the goal specification ;
     COLOR_LIST ; -- reuse of COLOR_LIST
package LIST is
    subtype List is COLOR_LIST.C_List ;
    function empty return List
            renames COLOR_LIST.nil ;
    procedure add (a_colour : in COLOUR.Colour; a_list : in out List) ;
    function head (a_list : List) return COLOUR.Colour
            renames COLOR_LIST.car ;
    procedure remove_head (a_list : in out List);
    function is_empty (a_list : List) return Boolean
            renames COLOR_LIST.nilp ;
    function contains (a_list : List; a_colour : COLOUR.Colour) return Boolean ;
    function length (a_list : List) return Natural ;
    no_more_room : exception
            renames COLOR_LIST.no_more_room ;
    empty_list : exception
            renames COLOR_LIST.empty_list ;
end LIST ;

package body LIST is
    procedure add (a_colour : in COLOUR.Colour; a_list : in out List) is
    begin
        a_list := COLOR_LIST.cons (a_colour, a_list);
    end ;
    procedure remove_head (a_list : in out List) is
    begin
        a_list := COLOR_LIST.cdr (a_list);
    end ;
    function contains (a_list : List; a_colour : COLOUR.Colour) return Boolean is
    begin
        return COLOR_LIST.member(a_colour, a_list);
    end ;
    function length (a_list : List) return Natural is
    begin
        null ; -- to be filled
    end ;
end LIST ;
```

Figure 4: Implementation of LIST by reuse of COLOR_LIST

2.2   A retrieval method for Ada Components

Finding the good renaming between a goal specification and a reusable component is a tedious and error prone task. Hence we have decided to build a tool to assist Ada programmers in this task and to guarantee an errorless result (at least with respect to the static semantics of Ada).

The main problem with such a tool is the huge number of potential renamings. For instance there are 12 possible renamings between the COLOUR and the COLOR data types (including the permutations of the arguments of equal). Moreover the number of potential renamings usually increases as an exponential function of the number of subprograms of the specifications. The solution to this problem is to avoid constructing all the possible renamings: the time needed for that would be far too long and the user wouldn't know what to do with such a long list of renamings. To reduce the computation duration, we only compute what we call fragments: a fragment is a part of renaming dealing only with one data type. We then let the user build incrementally the adequate renaming by choosing one fragment per data type. Of course we have to check that the selected fragments are compatible, and we only propose the user the fragments which are compatible with his previous choices.

To avoid dead-end choices (i.e. choosing a fragment which is correct for one data type, but which is incompatible with all the fragments of another data type), we have to propose only fragments that can actually lead to a correct renaming. For that purpose we begin by the so-called *check* phase which verifies that there exists at least one complete renaming between the goal specification and the reused components and which removes the fragments leading to dead-end choices. The good performances of this phase allow to run it as a filter so as to extract from a library all the components which correspond modulo a renaming to a given specification.

As explained above, some subprograms requested in the goal specification may be missing in the reusable components, but can be implemented without knowing the actual implementation of the reused components (the extraneous subprograms of the section 2.1). Hence we ask the user to further split the non generator subprograms of his goal specification between basic and extraneous subprograms, and we search for the renamings that give a value to at least each essential subprogram (an essential subprograms is either a generator aor a basic subprograms).

Hence we say that a type t in a goal specification SP_g is **possibly implementable by reuse of** a component R of specification SP_r modulo a renaming ρ if each essential subprogram of t can be found in SP_r modulo the renaming ρ, and if each type t' occurring in the profiles of these essential subprograms is *possibly implementable by reuse* of R modulo ρ.

In other words, we require to find modulo a renaming all the essential subprograms of the type `t` and moreover to be able to implement by reuse all the types that occur in the profiles of these essential subprograms, and so on until an Ada predefined data type. Indeed the types in the profile of the essential subprograms of a type `t` are needed to implement the type `t`.

As an example, the `List` type in the `LIST` specification is possibly implementable by reuse of the `C_LIST` component modulo the renaming given above, since:

- the essential subprograms of `List` (i.e. `empty`, `add`, `head`, `remove_head` and `is_empty`) can be found in COLOR_LIST, and
- the `Colour` type, which is the only type occurring in the profile of these essential subprograms, is possibly implementable by reuse of C_LIST (since `blue`, `red`, `yellow` and `equal` can be found in C_LIST, and all the other data types in the profiles are predefined).

Clearly the above conditions are neither necessary nor sufficient: a reusable component can be found not *possibly reusable* for a goal specification SP even when reuse is possible and conversely a component can be found *possibly reusable* even if its semantics is completely different form those of SP (for instance a stack management package will usually be *possibly reusable* for implementing queue management). But due to the recursion in the above conditions, the number of junks is not too large. Moreover this method allows us to discover potential reuse we never thought of before, as for instance implementing a tank temperature and pressure controller by reuse of an artificial heart controller [ESF90].

3 The ESF-ROSE System and ROSE-ADA

We will describe hereafter some of the functionalities of the ESF-ROSE System and of the ROSE-ADA tools, by simulating a typical session with ROSE-ADA. For that, we will suppose that we have to implement an Ada program to be executed on a machine M under the operating system O and corresponding of the specification given in figure 1 (the lists of colours).

3.1 Preambule

The ESF-ROSE Library System manages several libraries. This allows to have libraries on a project level, on a department level, on a division level, and so on. This also enables to have libraries specialized to one kind of software element or to one application domain.

Before being allowed to use a library a user have to subscribe to the library; subscription and access rights are given by the library administrator.

3.2   Using the classification schema

Once the user has opened a library, he has to locate REs corresponding to his needs. For that ESF-ROSE proposes a classification system.

A precise description of classification approach in ESF-ROSE can be found in [MAR90]. Shortly, the classification approach in ESF-ROSE is an adaptation of the faceted classification presented in [PF87]: each library is associated with a set of criteria (also called facets), each criterion contains a set of classes organised as a semantic network (i.e. the classes can be connected by links such as *inclusion* cr *see-also* links), each class containing a set of Reusable Elements.

A criterion can be considered as a particular view on a Reusable Element. One can for instance have a *Machine* criterion (resp. an *Operating System* criterion) classifying the REs according to the machine (resp. operating system) on which they can be executed. A class describes a concept of the universe of discourse within the criterion. All the REs of a class share at least one characteristic that other REs do not have.

Using a classification schema consists in opening the appropriate criteria, in navigating within the classes of each criterion by means of the links and in selecting the classes of interest within the various criteria, so as to get the REs that belong to the intersection of these classes. In our example, the user will select the class corresponding to the M machine in the *Machine* criterion and the class corresponding to the O operating system in the *Operating System* criterion; the intersection of these two classes results in the sets of REs executable on machine M under the operating system O.

3.3   Using the ROSE-ADA retrieval tool

Using the classification tool results in a set of candidates. To restrict this set, the user can use the ROSE-ADA filter, which implements the retrieval method described above: it allows to select the REs whose plug correspond to a goal specification modulo an adaptation (to be performed by the adaptation tool below).

The performances of this filter allow to use it on relatively big sets of reusable components: the check phase for the `LIST` and `COLOR_LIST` example above takes less than 0.05 seconds on a SUN3/60, and it take usually less than one second on components having around 50 packages. Hence filtering 200 components will usually takes less than 2 minutes. Of course this tool is not meant to filter big reusable component libraries having millions of components.

3.4 Assessing the retrieved components

Now he user has to choose one RE among those resulting from the previous steps. For that he can consult the various views of the RE (informal description, example of use, etc.). But software reuse can become effective if and only if the reuser can be confident in the piece of software he will reuse. Otherwise the well-known *Not Invented Here Syndrome* will inhibit software reuse. To inforce confidence, the ESF-ROSE System provides quality information and reuse history.

Quality information result from quality procedures depending on the kind of software elements being reused. Each time a new RE is entered in a library, the quality procedures are applied and the results are stored with the RE. A reuser can consult these results to make him sure that the quality level of the RE is in conformance with its needs [6].

The reuse history of a RE is the collection of reuse reports on this RE (i.e. who has reused it, when, in which context, what were the difficulties, what was the gain and so on). Indeed a RE which has been successively reused many times is a RE which gives confidence. There is also a special case of reuse reports called bug reports: they report about a bug found in some reusable element. Bug reports have also a special behavior: when a bug report is received, all the users that have reused this reusable element are immediately alerted, and the reuse of the corresponding RE can be forbidden.

3.5 Adapting the chosen component

Having chosen a reusable component R, the user can reuse it to implement the goal specification. ROSE-ADA assists the user in building the corresponding renaming in an incremental way, as described in section 2.2. This is very useful since the number of possible renamings may be quite big (12 for the COLOUR type). A first window (cf. figure 5) enables the user to choose which type of R will implement a type of the goal specification. After that, he has to build the fragment corresponding to this goal type: he has to choose, for at least each essential subprogram of this type, the subprogram of R which will implement it, and the same for the exceptions raised by these essential subprograms. Whenever the user attempts to rename a type, a subprogram or an exception, he is supplied with all the possible choices which assure a compatibility between all the fragments. In case there is just one possible choice, it is automatically displayed, and the user has only to validate the choice. This is true, for instance, for the LIST type of figure 5. Once the renaming

---

[6]Note that low quality level components can be reused as well, for instance to build a prototype. The key point here is that the reuser can determine the exact quality level of the RE.

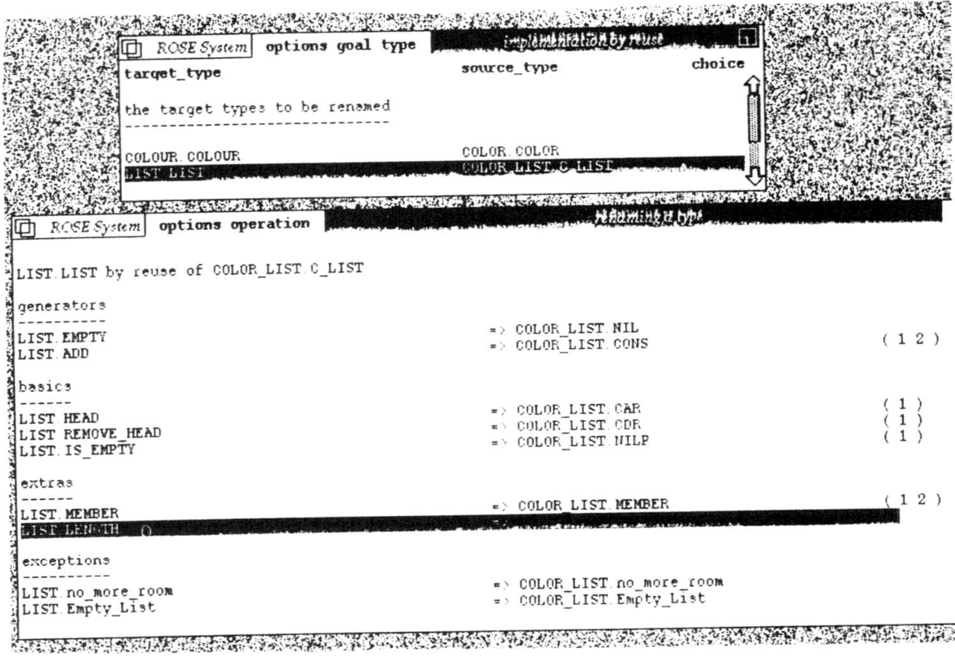

Figure 5: User-interface of ROSE-ADA

is built, the user may ask ROSE-ADA to implement the goal specification by reuse of R. This results in a new complex RE built as explained in section 2.1.

3.6   Extracting the adapted RE

The tools presented above allows the reuser to retrieve, select, compose and adapt REs, so as to build a new RE corresponding to its goal specification. After that the reuser has to extract the relevant information from this RE [7] and to export them toward its Software Development Environment. The actual procedure to extract a RE depends on the Software Development Environment used by the reuser. Hence he has to define this procedure and to store it in his profile.

Each extraction is recorded by the Library System together with the extraction procedure. This allows to automatically re-build and re-export a RE when a new

---

[7]Note that only some views are extracted, since some of the views are of interest only for reuse purpose.

version of one of its constituents is inserted in the library (for instance to correct a bug or to improve the performances).

Conclusion

A mockup of the ROSE-System was completed by the end of 1989. It is implemented using Y3 (an object oriented environment on top of Le_Lisp [*Cal.*86]) and runs on SUN workstations under X11. The first version of the ROSE System is planned for end 1991.

We have presented here how some of the features of the ESF-ROSE System have been used to build a powerful reuse environment for Ada code. Apart from the ROSE-ADA tool, the ESF-ROSE mockup has been instantiated for reuse of HOOD objects. Other instances devoted to reuse of Ada skeletons, of C++ classes and of Man-Machine Interface dialog management fragments are currently developed.

Acknowledgements

A special thank to N. Badaro, V. Dzuba and J.-C. Luchet for their help during the implementation of the mock-up and of ROSE-ADA.

References

[BAB+87] B.A. Burton, R.W. Aragon, S.A. Bailey, K.D. Koehler, and L.A. Mayes. The reusable software library. *IEEE Software*, 1987.

[BCD+87] P. Borras, D. Clement, Th. Despeyroux, J. Incerpi, G. Kahn, B. Lang, and V. Pascual. Centaur the system. Technical Report 777, INRIA, France, 1987.

[BM91]   N. Badaro and Th. Moineau. ROSE-ADA a method and a tool to help reuse of Ada. In *Proc. Ada Europe Conference*, Athene, Greece, 1991.

[BR87]   T. Biggerstaff and Ch. Richter. Reusability framework, assessment and directions. In *Proc. 20th Annual Hawaii Int. Conf. on System Sciences*, 1987.

[Cal.86] J. Chailloux and *al.* LE_LISP de l'INRIA, Version 15.2, Reference Manual. 1986.

[CLP84]   T.T. Cheng, E.D. Lock, and N.S. Prywes. Use of very high level languages and program generation by management professionals. *IEEE Transaction on Software Engineering*, SE-10(5), 1984.

[Con87]   R. Conn. The Ada software repository and software reusability. In *Proc. 5th Annual Joint Conf. on Ada Technology and Washinton Ada Symposium*, 1987.

[DRR83]   L.E. Druffel, S.T. Redwine, and W.E. Riddle. The STARS program : Overview and rationale. *Computer*, Nov. 1983.

[ESF90]   ESF-ROSE Consortium. Scenarii for HOOD reuse : analysis, method and examples. ESF-ROSE internal report, 1990.

[Gog84]   J.A. Goguen. Reusing and interconnecting software components. *IEEE Software*, Feb. 1984.

[LG84]   R.G. Lanergan and C.A. Grasso. Software engineering with reusable design and code. *IEEE Transaction on Software Engineering*, SE-10(5), 1984.

[Lub87]   M. D. Lubars. Wide spectrum support for software reusability. In *Proc. Workshop on Software Reusability and Maintainability*, Oct. 1987.

[MAR90]   Th. Moineau, J. Abardir, and E. Rames. Toward a generic and extensible reuse environment. In P.A.V. Hall, editor, *Proc. SE'90*. Cambridge University Press, July 1990.

[Mey87]   B. Meyer. Reusability : The case for object-oriented design. *IEEE Software*, March 1987.

[Nei84]   J.M. Neighbors. The DRACO approach to constructing software from reusable components. *IEEE Transaction on Software Engineering*, SE-10(5), 1984.

[NS88]   K. Nielsen and K. Shumate. *Designing Large Real-Time Systems with Ada*. McGraw-Hill, New York, NY, 1988.

[PCW83]   D.L. Parnas, P.C. Clements, and D.M. Weiss. Enhancing reusability with information hiding. In *ITT Workshop on Reusability in Programming*, Newport, R.I., 1983.

[PF87]   R. Prieto-Diaz and P. Freeman. Classifying software for reusability. *IEEE Software*, 5(1), Jan. 1987.

List of Addresses

Collected here are the addresses of the members of the programme committee and the authors of the papers. Each group is arranged in alphabetical order. Where the information is to hand, telephone and fax numbers, electronic mail addresses, etc. have been included.

Committee

Professor Keith H. Bennett
Centre of Software Maintenance
School of Engineering
University of Durham
Science Laboratories
Durham
DH1 3LE
UK

Tel. +44 91 374 2632
Email: Keith.Bennett@durham.ac.uk

David Callahan
Commission of the European
     Communities
DG XIII/A/4
Rue de la Loi 200
B-1049 Brussels
Belgium

Tel. +32 2 236 0422
Fax. +32 2 236 1948

Dr Fred W. Long
Department of Computer Science
University College of Wales
Penglais
Aberystwyth
Dyfed
SY23 3BZ
UK

Tel. +44 970 622440
Fax. +44 970 617172
Telex: 35181
Email: fwl@cs.aber.ac.uk

Gavin Oddy
GEC-Marconi Research Centre
West Hanningfield Road
Great Baddow
Chelmsford
Essex
CM2 8HN
UK

Tel. +44 245 73331 Extn. 3251
Fax. +44 245 75244
Telex: 995016 GECRES G
Email: gco@gec-mrc.co.uk

Professor Dr Wilhelm Schäfer
Informatik X
Universitat Dortmund
Postfach 500 500
D-4600 Dortmund 50
Germany

Tel. +49 231 755 2782
Fax. +49 231 755 2047
Email: wilhelm@
     udo.informatik.uni-dortmund.de

Professor Mike D. Tedd
Department of Computer Science
University College of Wales
Penglais
Aberystwyth
Dyfed
SY23 3BZ

Tel. +44 970 622422
Fax. +44 970 617172
Telex: 35181
Email: mdt@cs.aber.ac.uk

Malcolm Verrall
Sema Group plc
Trafalgar House
Richfield Avenue
Reading
Berkshire
RG1 8QA
UK

Tel. +44 734 575900
Fax. -44 734 502590
Telex: 848913

Dr Ray Welland
Computer Science Department
The University
Glasgow
G12 8QQ
UK

Tel. +44 41 339 8855
Fax. +44 41 330 4913
Telex 777070 UNIGLA
Email ray@dcs.glasgow.ac.uk

Aut

erman
Ger hilosophy
Dep Logic
Sect recht
Uni
2
Hei t
358 ls
Th

M tt
G Software Systems
E
B d
V
I

ormatics ApS
rk Aarhus
iedsvej 10
Århus C

rsp@mjolner.dk

n W. Brown
nent of Computer Science
ity of York
ton

DD

Hugh Davis
ICL Secure Systems
Eskdale Road
Winnersh
Wokingham
RG11 5TT
UK

Tel. +44 734 693131 Extn. 6099
Fax. +44 734 693131 Extn. 6004
Telex: 847557
Email: hfd@win.icl.co.uk

John Dawes
ICL Secure Systems
Eskdale Road
Winnersh
Wokingham
RG11 5TT
UK

Tel. +44 734 693131
Fax. +44 734 693131 Extn. 6004
Telex: 847557
Email: sjd@win.icl.co.uk

Dr Jeremy Dick
Centre de Recherche Bull
F3/2G07
Rue Jean Jaurés
78340 Les Clayes-Sous-Bois
France

Tel. +33 1 30 80 69 23
Fax. +33 1 30 80 69 53
Email: Jeremy.Dick@crg.bull.fr

Ted J. Dowling
Ferranti Computer Systems Ltd
Ty Coch Way
Cwmbrân
Gwent
NP44 7XX
UK

Tel. −44 633 871111
Fax. +44 633 873974
Telex 497636

Dr Anthony Earl
Software Environments Group
Hewlett Packard Laboratories
Filton Road
Stoke Gifford
Bristol
BS12 6QZ
UK

Tel. −44 272 799910
Fax. +44 272 790554
Telex 44 92 06
Email: ane@hplb.hpl.hp.com

Christer Fernström
Cap Gemini Innovation
  Research Center
7 Chemin du Vieux Chene
Zirst 38240 Meylan
France

Email: christer@capsogeti.fr

Marcel Franckson
Sema Group SA
16 Rue Barbès
F-92126 Montrouge
France

Mark Gibbons
RT3153 Support Environment Group
G21/23 SSTF Building
British Telecom Research Labs.
Martlesham Heath
Ipswich
IP5 7RE
UK

Tel. +44 473 642056
Email: mgibbons@axion.bt.co.uk

Volker Gruhn
Computer Science
Software Technology
University of Dortmund
Postfach 500 500
D-4600 Dortmund 50
Germany

Email: gruhn@
  udo.informatik.uni-dortmund.de

Matthias Hallmann
Systemhaus GEI
Software Tools
Pascalstraße 14
D-5100 Aachen
Germany

Mike Imber
LMBS
Evelyn House
62 Oxford Street
London
W1N 9LF
UK

Tel. +44 71 636 4213
Fax. +44 71 636 2708

Thorsten Janning
RWTH
Informatik III
Ahornstraße 55
D-5100 Aachen
Germany

Antoinette Kieback
Dornier GmbH
Friedrichshafen
Germany

Jørgen L. Knudsen
Computer Science Department
Aarhus University
Ny Munkegade 116
DK-8000 Århus C
Denmark

Email: jlknudsen@daimi.aau.dk

Wilfried Koch
Technische Universität Berlin
REX-Project Sekr
MA073 Straße des 17
Juni 136
D 1000 Berlin 12
Germany

Email: wilfried@coma.cs.tu-berlin.de

Ron L.C. Koymans
Philips Research Laboratories
P.O. Box 80.000
5600 JA Eindhoven
The Netherlands

Markus Lindqvist
Nokia Telecommunications
P.O. Box 33
SF-02601 Espoo
Finland

Email: lindqvist@tele.nokia.fi

Jérôme Loubersac
Centre de Recherche Bull
F3/2G07
Rue Jean Jaurés
78340 Les Clayes-Sous-Bois
France

Tel. +33 1 30 80 69 23
Fax. +33 1 30 80 69 53
Email: Jeremy.Dick@crg.bull.fr

Ole L. Madsen
Computer Science Department
Aarhus University
Ny Munkegade 116
DK-8000 Århus C
Denmark

Email: olmadsen@daimi.aau.dk

Dr John A. McDermid
Department of Computer Science
University of York
Heslington
York
YO1 5DD
UK

Thierry Moineau
Sema Group SA
16 Rue Barbès
F-92126 Montrouge
France

Email: moineau@semadt.metra.fr

Klaus Nagel
Technische Universität Berlin
REX-Project Sekr
MA0-3 Straße des 17
Juni 136
D 1000 Berlin 12
Germany

Email: klausn@tubprz.prz.tu-berlin.de

Joachim Niemeier
Fraunhofer IAO
Stuttgart
Germany

Claus Nørgaard
Mjølner Informatics ApS
Science Park Aarhus
Gustav Wiedsvej 10
DK-8000 Århus C
Denmark

Email: cn@mjolner.dk

Wolfgang Obst
Technische Universität Berlin
REX-Project Sekr
MA0-3 Straße des 17
Juni 136
D 1000 Berlin 12
Germany

Email: wolfgang@coma.cs.tu-berlin.de

Leon Osterweil
Department of Information and
    Computer Science
University of California at Irvine
Irvine
CA 92717
USA

Ron H. Pierce
IPSYS Software plc
Marlborough Court
Pickford Street
Macclesfield
Cheshire
SK11 6JD
UK

Elmer Sandvad
Mjølner Informatics ApS
Science Park Aarhus
Gustav Wiedsvej 10
DK-8000 Århus C
Denmark

Email: ess@mjolner.dk

Jeremy Smith
IPSYS Software plc
Marlborough Court
Pickford Street
Macclesfield
Cheshire
SK11 6JD
UK

Colin J. Tully
Colin Tully Associates
2 Myrtle Cottages
Park Road
Crowborough
East Sussex
TN6 2QW
UK

Heikki Tuominen
Nokia Telecommunications
P.O. Box 33
SF-02601 Espoo
Finland

Email: htuomine@tele.nokia.fi

Malcolm Verrall
Sema Group plc
Trafalgar House
Richfield Avenue
READING
Berkshire
RG1 8QA
UK

Tel. +44 734 575900
Fax. +44 734 502590
Telex: 848913

John P. Warne
Architecture Projects
    Management Limited
Poseidon House
Castle Park
Cambridge
CB3 0RD
UK

Tom Welsh
Digital Equipment Co Ltd
P.O. Box 110
Reading
RG1 3JJ
UK

Jean-Daniel Zucker
GIE Emeraude
Bull - 58F32
68, Route de Versailles
F-78430 Louveciennes
France

Email: JeanDaniel.Zucker@lv.bull.fr